Oliver and Chapmans'

Data Processing and Information Technology

9th Edition

C S French, BSc.(Hons), M.Sc., Grad.Cert.Ed., AFIMA, FBCS, C. Eng.

Carl French currently works in the financial sector of the computer industry where, in recent years, he has been involved in the design and implementation of a number of large database systems. He was previously employed as a Principal Lecturer in Computer Science at Hertfordshire University following several years' experience of teaching on a wide variety of computer courses.

DP Publications Ltd
Aldine Place
London W12 8AW

1993

Acknowledgements

The authors wish to thank the following:

Institute of Chartered Accountants in England and Wales (ICA)

Chartered Association of Certified Accountants (ACCA)

Institute of Chartered Management Accountants (CIMA)

Association of Accounting Technicians (AAT)

Institute of Company Accountants (IComA)

Institute of Data Processing Management (IDPM)

for permission to reproduce past examination questions.

The authors wish to express their thanks to the following for permission to reproduce photographs of their products (separate acknowledgments are included with each photograph):

Apple Computers UK Ltd, CalComp Ltd, Compaq Computer Ltd, Digital Equipment Corporation (DEC), Feedback Data Ltd, IBM UK Ltd, International Computers Ltd, MICOM-borer Ltd, NCR Ltd., Norsk Data, Philips, Rediffusion Computers Ltd, Sun Microsystems Ltd, and Toshiba.

Copyright © DP Publications Ltd 1993

ISBN 1 85805 027 8

First Edition 1972
Second Edition 1973
Reprinted 1975
Third edition 1975
Reprinted 1976
Fourth edition 1979
Reprinted 1979, 1980
Fifth Edition 1981
Reprinted 1982
Sixth Edition 1983
Reprinted 1984, 1985
Seventh edition 1986
Reprinted 1987, 1988, 1989
Eighth Edition 1990
Ninth Edition 1993

Printed by The Guernsey Press Co. Ltd, Braye Road, Vale, Guernsey

Preface

Introduction

The primary aim of the manual is to provide a simplified approach to the understanding of Data Processing (DP) and Information Technology (IT). It is intended for those with little or no knowledge of the subject.

It covers the Data Processing and Information Technology syllabus requirements of the following professional bodies' examinations.

The Chartered Association of Certified Accountants:
Paper 2.7 'Information Systems in Development and Operations'

The Association of Accounting Technicians:
Paper 6 'Elements of Information Systems'
Paper 11 'Analysis and Design of Information Systems'

The Institute of Cost and Management Accountants:
Paper 7 'Information Technology Management'

It also covers parts of other syllabuses which have a Data Processing or Information Technology requirement. These include The Institute of Data Processing Management, BTEC, The Institute of Chartered Secretaries and Administrators and The Institute of Administrative Management.

Need

All business personnel, management staff and accountants need to have a good knowledge of Data Processing (DP) and Information Technology. In more recent years there have been major developments in Information Technology (IT), i.e. the technologies associated with the creation, manipulation, storage and communication of information, principally computing, telecommunications and electronics. These developments have given rise not only to the rapid evolution of DP techniques but to the greater integration of data processing techniques with other activities in organisations. These developments all create an even greater need for business and management professionals to have a knowledge of DP and its related Information Technology. This need is reflected in the broadening of Data Processing examination syllabi, when they are updated, and in the titles of examinations such as 'Information Technology Management' and 'Business Information Technology'.

A vast number of books have been written on the various aspects of Data Processing and Information Technology. Most of them tend to be of a technical nature, aimed at technically minded people. Others are so brief and introductory as to be of little practical value and very few are suited to study by students of business and accountancy. The need as seen by the authors was for a manual covering all aspects of Data Processing and the relevant aspects of Information Technology written specifically for business and accountancy students.

Approach

The book has been designed for independent study but is well suited for use in conjunction with tuition at colleges, etc. Great efforts have been made to present a simplified and standardised layout.

End of chapter

At the end of chapters is found:

☐ A summary of the chapter.

☐ Points to note. These are used for purposes of emphasis and clarification.

☐ Questions and answers. Their use is explained in Appendix 4.

Appendices

Use has been made of appendices and the student should note carefully the purpose of each one:

Appendix 1 contains answers to questions set at the ends of chapters.

Appendix 2 contains questions *without* answers for use in conjunction with classroom tuition. The questions, taken from recent papers of the ICA, ACA, CIMA, AAT, IComA and IDPM, are grouped according to the Parts of the Manual.

Appendix 3 contains details which have been excluded from the main text in the interests of clarity.

Appendix 4 contains notes on: using the questions and answers; effective study; examination technique.

How to use this book

Students are advised to read the manual chapter by chapter since subsequent work often builds upon topics covered earlier.

The subject matter of DP and IT is spread over many separate areas and it is inevitable that certain questions will remain unanswered as the student proceeds. The pieces should fit together as progress is made through the manual.

Students are advised to view the equipment described in this manual at first hand. Failing this, they should try to get hold of manufacturers' 'glossies'. Many specialist business and computer magazines can also act as a useful source of illustrations and topical articles on current technology.

Suggestions and criticisms

The author would welcome any suggestions or criticisms from students or lecturers and would like to take this opportunity to thank those who responded to the same invitation given in previous editions.

Note to the ninth edition

The text has been extensively revised and brought up to date for this new edition. The revisions include a reorganisation of the contents which reflects the ever growing importance of desktop computing alongside ongoing changes in conventional data processing.

Following the trend set in the previous edition, the text contains significant new material on **workstations, GUIs, applications packages, development methodologies, databases and 4GLs** plus numerous updates and additions throughout. Obsolete material has been removed throughout.

Carl French
1993

Contents

Contents

Introduction

1. This Part introducing the reader to Data Processing (DP) and Information Technology (IT). Many readers will already have some prior knowledge of the subject matter from previous study and because of the widespread use of computers in everyday working life. Whether or not that is the case, readers are recommended to read the whole of the material so that there are no gaps in their understanding of the basic ideas and terms. The material introduced here will be covered in greater detail in later parts of the text.

2. As the reader's study progresses through the text it will involve the following:

   a. Understanding the basic concepts of DP and IT.

   b. Understanding the basic elements which make up the computer systems, which are at the heart of modern DP and IT. The reader is *not* expected to be a computer technologist and the material will only be taken to the depth indicated in the preface to this manual.

   c. Understanding the basic elements of IT systems, also to an appropriate depth.

   d. Gaining knowledge of how management can best use computers and other IT equipment to provide better information and to increase profitability.

   e. Understand problems posed to management by DP and IT and how best to deal with such problems.

1 Introduction to data processing and information technology

Introduction

1.1 This chapter starts by putting Data Processing (DP) and Information Technology (IT) into the general context of 'Information Systems' in organisations. The terminology is defined as it is introduced, as is the case throughout this text. The chapter goes on to provide an overview of the technological aspects of DP and IT.

Information System

1.2 The term 'Information System' is normally used in situations where an organisation is being considered *as a whole* with respect to its information requirements and information utilisation. The **'Information System'** of an organisation is, therefore, the total apparatus for handling information within the organisation in all respects. The advantages of taking such a broad view are highlighted by the following points.

1.3 Broadly speaking, organisations strive to achieve certain goals for the benefit of their owners or clients. These goals may be expressed in terms of objectives such as increasing revenues, increasing profits, avoiding costs, or improving services. Such objectives will need to be met within various financial constraints, and within the limitations of available resources.

1.4 In order to reach its objectives an organisation must be able to plan ahead, and control and co-ordinate its activities. For this it depends on the provision and communication of information. The information is likely to be used most effectively if it is seen as a resource which needs to be exploited to best advantage by the whole organisation and not just by its individual departments. The idea that 'the whole can be more than the sum of its parts' lies behind this information systems view of organisations. Whether or not such a view is taken, the requirements of providing and communicating information remains. These requirements are met, at least in part, by the **'Data Processing Systems'** within the organisation.

Data Processing

1.5 **Data Processing (DP)** is the collection and manipulation of items of data to produce meaningful information. Despite this general definition the term DP is more commonly associated with specialist business tasks of this nature such as sales order processing, purchase ledger processing and payroll processing. For very many years the methods of Data Processing have involved electronic means, principally the computer. Any modern study of Data Processing must therefore look at **Electronic Data Processing (EDP)** in detail. However, EDP must be seen in context as one of a number of important areas of Information Technology (IT).

1.6 The reader needs to be aware of a long established convention in DP to distinguish between 'data' and 'information'.

   a. **'Data'** is the term used to describe basic **facts** about the activities of a business. Examples are: the number of hours worked by any employee on a particular machine; his or her rate of pay; the amount and type of materials consumed in a particular process; the number of tons of finished product produced in a day or week.

   b. **'Information'** is obtained by assembling items of data into a meaningful form, e.g. a payroll, an invoice, a financial statement or an efficiency reports. Information can range from a simple report about routine operations up to a report required by top management to make strategic decisions.

1.7 Other conventions of traditional DP will be explained in Chapter 5.

Information Technology

1.8 **Information Technology (IT)** is the technology which supports activities involving the creation, storage, manipulation and communication of information, together with their related methods, management and application. Therefore, Information Technology may be seen as the broadly based technology needed to support information systems.

1.9   Although EDP is part of IT is not sensible to think of EDP as being in a watertight compartment and, therefore, it is important for the Data Processing student to be aware not only of EDP but of other areas of IT. For that reason this Part not only introduces EDP but places it in its IT context.

1.10 Computers play a major and central role in IT. Within this chapter we will examine the computer itself, the types of computers found, the purposes for which they are used and the basic elements that go to make one. Then we will take a look at other Information Technology used in conjunction with the computer. Finally, we will consider software.

The computer

1.11 A computer is a device that *processes* data to produce further data or information. A more precise definition follows shortly. For now it is also worth noting that the data is normally held within the computer as it is being processed, and is often held much longer than that. Also, the nature of the processing may change according to the data entered. The forms in which data is accepted or produced by the computer vary enormously from simple words or numbers to signals sent from or received by other items of technology. So, when the computer *processes* data it actually performs a number of separate functions as follows.

   a. **Input.** The computer accepts data from outside for processing within.

   b. **Storage.** The computer holds data internally before, during and after processing.

   c. **Processing.** The computer performs operations on the data it holds within.

   d. **Output.** The computer produces data from within for external use.

   A more detailed description of these functions is given later in this chapter.

1.12 The processing operations of a computer are determined by 'programs' stored within the computer. A **program** is a *set of instructions* that is written in the language of the computer. A program is used to make the computer perform a specific task, such as calculating interest to be paid to savings-account holders or producing a payroll. (Note the spelling **program** not **programme**.) The computer is only able to obey a program's instructions if the program has first been stored within the computer. This implies that the computer must be able to input and store programs in addition to data. So, the computer works under the *control* of stored programs. This leads to a more precise definition of a computer.

1.13 **A computer may be defined as a device that works under the control of stored programs, automatically accepting, storing and processing data to produce information that is the result of that processing.**

Hardware and software

1.14 **Hardware** is the name given to *all* the physical devices found in a computer system. Whether looking at a small computer on a desktop or at a large computer in the computer room, where the devices look like large, inert metal cabinets, there is little visible evidence of the phenomenal speeds at which data is being processed within. It is the programs which put life into the hardware.

1.15 **Software** is the general term used to describe *all* the various programs that may be used on a computer system together with their associated documentation.

Hardware examples

1.16 Now for a concrete examples of computer hardware to illustrate the ideas presented so far. Since most readers will have access to small computers it is such a computer which is used as for the example. In fact, the example is based upon what is commonly called a **Personal Computer (PC)**, so called because it is designed for independent use by an individual at home or in the office.

1.17 Figure 1.1 illustrates the features of a typical PC. These features can be related to the functions of a computer listed earlier. A brief description now follows but *please note that this is only an introduction with many points of detail deliberately being left till later.*

a. **Input** is performed primarily by typing data on the keyboard which is very similar to a typewriter keyboard. The mouse can also be used for input but the details will be given later.

b. **Storage** is performed by devices within the computer's cabinet so it is less easy to see what is going on. However, there are several external clues as to the features of this particular PC. For instance, there is a slot in the front of the cabinet into which a 3.5" floppy disk can be inserted. A **floppy disk** comprises a flexible circular disc coated in a magnetic material and held in a thin casing. When the floppy disk is inserted into the **disk drive** via the slot in the computer's cabinet it is rotated on a turntable. Then, in a way very similar to that in which the **heads** in an audio cassette recorder record or play back sound on the tape, **read-write heads** inside the disk drive **write** or **read** data.

Lights on the front of the computer cabinet show that it contains a disk drive for another kind of disk called a **hard disk** because it is rigid, unlike a floppy disk. This hard disk is not removable like the floppy disk but works on the same basic principles as the floppy disk. However, a typical hard disk is able to store much more data than a floppy disk of the same size because of technical differences which will be covered in later chapters.

Also out of view within the computer's cabinet is another form of storage called the **main memory** of the computer. Main memory takes the form of microelectronic **silicon chips** housed on an electronic circuit board. A silicon chips is miniature electronic circuit equivalent to hundreds or thousands of components etched onto a wafer of silicon crystal the size of a fingernail. It is housed in a plastic case just big enough to hold the silicon wafer and its electrical contact pins by means of which it is plugged into the circuit board.

c. **Processing** is carried out my a **microprocessor** which, although it serves a very different function, is very similar in construction to main memory because it is another kind of silicon chip. It is also situated on an electronic circuit board. On many larger computers the processing is carried out by a number of separate chips, instead of a single microprocessor. A computer whose processing is done by a microprocessor is called a **microcomputer**.

d. **Output** takes two alternative forms. Data can either be printed out onto sheets of paper using the **laser printer** or it can be displayed on the **monitor's** screen.

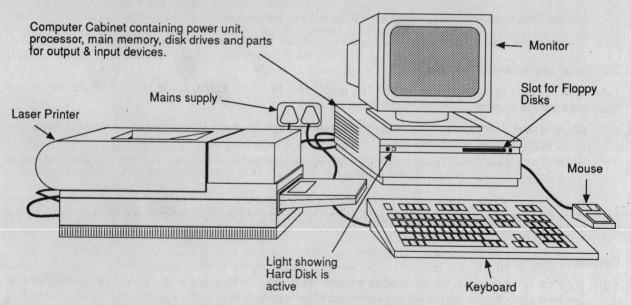

Figure 1.1 An example of a personal computer with laser printer

Computer types

1.18 The PC just described is just one of many types of computer. There are several methods of classifying computers too. The main distinction between digital and analog devices is given next, followed by a classifications by purpose and use. A further classification by age of technology is given later in the chapter.

Basic types of computer

1.19 Digital, Analog and Hybrid.

a. **Digital** computers are so called because they process data that is represented in the form of discrete values (e.g. 0, 1, 2, 3...) by operating on it in steps. Discrete values occur at each step in the operation. Counting on one's fingers is probably the simplest *digital operation* we all know. Digital watches have special, tiny, digital computers within them.

b. **Analog** computers are akin to measuring instruments such as thermometers and voltmeters with pointers on circular dials. They process data in the form of electrical voltages, which are variable like the variable positions of a pointer on a dial. The output from analog computers is often in the form of smooth graphs from which information can be read.

c. **Hybrid** computers, as their name suggests, are computers that have the combined feature of digital and analog computers.

Note. This text is concerned with digital computers, which are by far the most widely used.

Purpose

1.20 Special purpose and general purpose.

a. **Special purpose computers**, as their name suggests, are designed for a particular job only; to solve problems of a restricted nature. Examples are computers designed for use in digital watches, in programmable pocket calculators, in petrol pumps or in weapons guidance systems.

b. **General purpose computers** are designed to solve a wide variety of problems. Within the limitations imposed by their particular design capabilities, they can be adapted to perform particular tasks or solve problems by means of specially written programs. This text is concerned with general purpose digital computers.

Note. This distinction is not as sharp as it first appears because a general purpose computer can temporarily become special purpose through adaptation.

Computer classification by use

1.21 It is possible to provide a very long list under this heading. Here, just a few varied examples are given so as to give an impression of the variety.

a. A **Word Processor** is a *special purpose* computer used in the production of office documents, letters, contracts, etc.

   Note. A general purpose computer can run a word processing program and hence temporarily become special purpose.

b. A **Home Computer** is a low-cost microcomputer of limited capability designed for domestic use with programs that typically are used for such things as computer games or controlling family finances.

c. A **Personal Computer (PC)**, as mentioned earlier, is a microcomputer designed for independent use by an individual at work or in the home mainly for business purposes. Some PCs are portable. Many can be connected to minicomputers and mainframe computers so that the PC user can also gain access to the facilities offered by the larger machine.

d. A **Desktop Computer** is any computer design for use on a desk in an office environment. Therefore, home computers and PCs are types of Desktop computer.

NCR 16-bit Personal Computer Model NCR PC4i.
(Picture courtesy NCR Ltd)

A Personal Computer.
(Picture courtesy of Apple Computer UK Ltd.)

e. **A Workstation** is another kind of desktop computer. Although larger more powerful PCs are sometimes called workstations the term is normally used to imply the presence of advanced features not provided by all PCs. These include inbuilt capabilities for their interconnection and operation in conjunction with other computers, and for them to process pictorial data as well as that presented in the form of text.

f. A **Lap-top** computer is a PC sufficiently small and light for its user comfortably to use it on his or her lap. A typical lap-top computer operates on mains electricity or by rechargeable batteries and is small enough to fit inside a brief case, still leaving room for other items. Lap-tops normally have in built disk drives and flat screens. The latter are commonly Liquid Crystal Displays (LCDs).

The Toshiba 'T1600 Portable Desktop 286' lap-top computer.
(Photograph supplied by courtesy of Toshiba)

g. An **Embedded Computer** is one that is within some other device or system but is not accessed directly. For example, there are embedded computers operating within petrol pumps, watches, cameras, video recorders and many types of domestic and industrial equipment.

Computer classification by size

1.22 Mainframe, minicomputer and microcomputer.

The following classification is in order of decreasing power and size. However, there are no sharp dividing lines in that, for example, a model at the top of a manufacturer's range of minicomputers might well be more powerful than the model at the bottom of a range of mainframes.

a. **Mainframes.** Large general purpose computers with extensive processing, storage and input/output capabilities (see figure 1.2). Conventional large scale Data Processing has traditionally been carried out on these machines. The market for these computers is dominated by IBM.

b. **Minicomputers.** Physically smaller computers compared with mainframes (see figure 1.3). They are used for special purposes or smaller scale general purpose work. Conventional medium scale Data Processing has traditionally been carried out on these machines. Examples are DEC's VAX range, and IBM's AS400 range.

c. **Microcomputers.** These represent a further step in miniaturisation in which the various integrated circuits and elements of a computer are replaced by a single integrated circuit called a 'chip'. Their continuing and rapid technological development have had a major effect on the whole computer industry over the past twenty years or so. Examples are the IBM PS/2 PCs, Apple Macintoshes, and COMPACs.

1.23 As smaller machine become more powerful, and therefore able to do more, there is a steady trend to move work off the larger machines onto smaller ones in order to cut costs. For example, a mainframe may be replaced by a new minicomputer. This is sometimes known as **downsizing**. The use of combination of mainframes, minicomputers and microcomputers with each used for tasks to which it is best suited is sometimes called **rightsizing**.

7

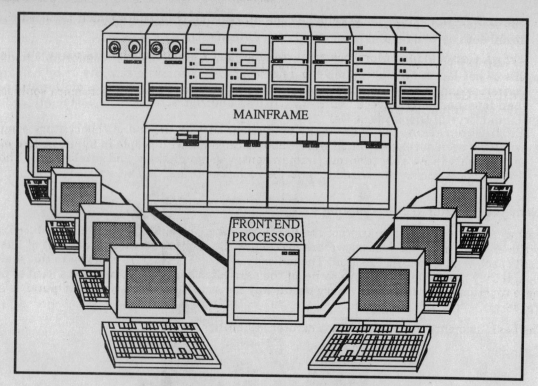

Figure 1.2 A mainframe computer

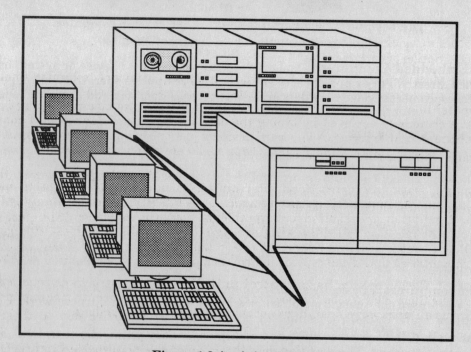

Figure 1.3 A minicomputer

Computer generations

1.24 The first *electronic* computers were produced in the 1940s. Since then a series of radical break-throughs in electronics has occurred. With each major breakthrough the computers based upon the older form of electronics have been replaced by a new '**generation**' of computers based upon the newer form of electronics. These 'generations' are classified as follows:

    a. **First Generation.** Early computers using electronic valves. (circa 1940s).

b. **Second Generation.** More reliable computers using transistors which replaced the first generation (circa 1950s).

c. **Third Generation.** More powerful, reliable and compact computers using simple integrated circuits (circa 1960s and early 1970s).

d. **Fourth Generation.** The computers in use today, and which contain more sophisticated micro-electronic devices.

e. **Fifth Generation.** There are many predictions that by the end of this century computers will have been developed which will be able to converse with people in a human-like manner and which will be able to mimic human senses, manual skills and intelligence. The term 'Fifth Generation' is often used to describe such computers.

Basic elements (functions) of a computer

1.25 Now we resume the examination of the hardware functions of the computer introduced earlier in the chapter. In what follows we are looking at the computer in terms of a set of basic elements each with a specific function. The majority of digital computers conform to this view even though they may differ greatly in terms of the particular hardware components used to provide these functions. It is therefore a very useful way for us to deal with what a computer is in general terms.

1.26 The basic elements that make up a computer system are as follows:

a. Input.

b. Storage.

c. Control.

d. Processing.

e. Output.

1.27 A brief description of each element.

a. **Input.** Most computers cannot accept data in forms customary to human communication such as speech or hand-written documents. It is necessary, therefore, to present data to the computer in a way that provides easy conversion into its own electronic pulse-based forms. This is commonly achieved by typing the data into keyboard devices that convert it into **machine-sensible** forms. A keyboard device is just one of many kinds of **input device**. In some cases machine-readable documents or media are produced as part of the input process. Data finally enters **Storage.**

b. **Storage.** Data and instructions enter **main storage**, and are held until needed to be worked on. The **instructions** dictate action to be taken on the **data.** Results of action will be held until they are required for output. Main storage is supplemented by less costly **auxiliary storage**, also called **backing storage** (e.g. hard disks for mass storage purposes). Backing storage serves an important role in holding **'maintained data'**, i.e. data held by the computer so that it can provide information to the user when required to do so.

c. **Control.** Each computer has a **control unit** that fetches instructions from main storage, *interprets* them, and issues the necessary *signals* to the components making up the system. It directs all **hardware** operations necessary in obeying instructions.

d. **Processing.** Instructions are obeyed and the necessary arithmetic operations, etc, are carried out on the data. The part that does this is called the **Arithmetic-Logical Unit (ALU).** In addition to arithmetic it also performs so-called 'logical' operations. These operations take place at incredibly high speeds, e.g. 10 million numbers may be totalled in one second.

e. **Output.** Results are taken from main storage and fed to an **output device.** This may be a printer, in which case the information is automatically converted to a *printed form* called **hard copy**, or alternatively data may be displayed on a monitor screen similar to that used in a television set.

1.28 The elements are shown in figure 1.4, which shows what is often referred to as 'the Logical Structure' of the computer. Notice particularly the following points:

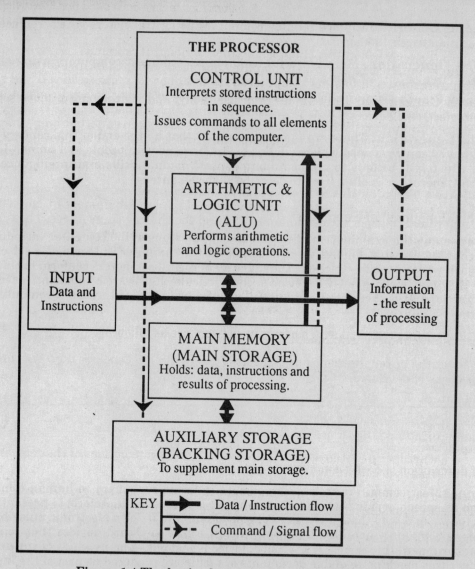

Figure 1.4 The basic elements of a computer system

a. Data normally flows from input devices or backing storage into *main storage* and from main storage to output devices or backing storage.

b. The processor performs operations on data from main storage and returns the results of processing to main storage.

c. In some cases, which will be discussed in later chapters, data flows directly between the processor and input or output devices rather than as described in (a).

d. The Arithmetic-Logical Unit (ALU) and control unit *combine* to form the **processor.** (It needs to be stressed that when referring to 'units' here we are only talking of distinct functions not separate hardware components.) The processor is sometimes also called the **central processor (CP)** or **central processing unit (CPU).** However, the term CPU is also sometimes taken to mean not only the ALU and control unit but main storage too. To avoid possible confusion the term CPU is not used in this text.

e. There are two types of flow shown in figure 1.4. Some lines carry data or instructions but other lines carry commands or signals.

f. Data held on backing storage may be input to main memory during processing, used and brought up to date using newly input data, and then returned to backing storage.

Computer networks

1.29 The PC described earlier in this chapter, in order to illustrate common examples of hardware, was not interconnected to any other compute equipment other than its own printer. Without any such interconnection to other computers it is described as a '**stand alone**' machine. There are clearly economies and efficiencies to be gained by allowing several computers to share hardware such as printers. There are also clear benefits from being able to transfer and share data between computers. When multiple computers are interconnected on a shared link by which they can communicate with each other, the arrangement is called a **computer network**. There are many different types of computer network. Details will be given in later chapters. For now we will consider just one general type of network the Local Area Network (LAN).

1.30 A **Local Area Network (LAN)** is computer network used on a single site within an organisation. The purpose of the LAN is to *connect* a variety of pieces of equipment by means of a shared link in order to allow their intercommunication and the sharing of resources. The physical form of the LAN is lengths of special cable interconnected to one another and to the computers by means of special plugs, adapters and electronic control units. For example, a set of PCs may each be connected to a LAN. Some of the PCs may be given a specific task to do. One may have a printer connected to it and perform the task of printing for all the PCs in the LAN. It will be called the LAN's '**print server**'. Another PC may provide shared access to some backing storage. It will be called the LAN's '**file server**'.

Other information technology equipment

1.31 If we look at the purely technological aspects of information technology then the three most important areas of development are:

a. Computers.

b. Electronics.

c. Communications.

However, we are merely interested in the ways in which combinations of these technologies can be used to satisfy various kinds of information need.

1.32 **Many different kinds of data** are handled by information technology, e.g. text, voice and picture. The established technologies, each able to handle one or more kinds of data, such as telephone, telex, TV and computers, have been developed in recent years so that their functions can be integrated and they may be combined together into single IT systems. Thus in any one IT system we may find:

a. Information in these forms:

   i)   Text (e.g. financial reports, contracts and letters).

   ii) Picture (e.g. printed diagram or video display).

   iii) Voice (e.g. recorded message or synthesised sound).

b. Various means of transmitting the data, for example:

   i)   private telephone exchanges handling voice and data.

   ii) public data communication services.

   iii) conventional or optical fibre cable transmission on private or public circuits.

   iv) satellite communication.

We will now consider common forms of hardware in more detail. The uses of hardware will be covered in later chapters.

Semi-conductor processors and memories

1.33 Although the computer carries out a number of different functions, from a hardware viewpoint the basic electronic components of a modern computer are all very similar. Many of the main components are of a similar shape and size too. This similarity arises from common manufacturing processes.

1.34 Complex circuits such as those found in the ALU, control unit or main storage are manufactured on single minutely sliced wafers of silicon crystal. Such devices are called **'silicon chips'** or **'semi-conductor devices'** (see figure 1.5). Individual components can be as narrow as 0.0000015 inches.

1.35 **Microprocessors.** A microprocessor is an entire small computer processor (usually excluding main memory) manufactured on a single chip. Computers built around such devices are called **'microcomputers'**, or more correctly **'microcomputer-based systems'**.

1.36 The first production microprocessor was produced in 1972 by the Intel corporation. It was the model 4004 and its chip contained about 2,300 transistors. Transistors operate as electronic switches each having two states (ON or OFF). Over the intervening years the technology for constructing microprocessors has been improved so that the microcomputers of today are much more powerful than minicomputers were in 1972. An example of a typical microprocessor used in PCs is the Intel 386. It has a chip some half inch square set in a protective case with connectors on its sides. The chip itself contains 275,000 transistors! Many early models of PC used the Intel 8086 microprocessor which contained about 29,000 transistors. That was followed by the Intel 286 which had about 130,000 transistors. The trend continues with the Intel 486 having about 1,200,000 transistors and the Intel 'Pontium' having an even greater number of transistors. Another major chip manufacturer, Motorola, has brought out a series of processors which have also progressed in a manner comparable to the Intel chips. These are the M68000, M68030 and M68040 processor chips also used on some PCs notably the Apple Macintosh range of computers.

1.37 Most microprocessors do not contain main storage, which is normally produced on separate silicon chips.

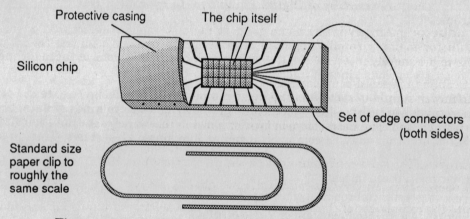

Figure 1.5 A computer component containing a silicon chip

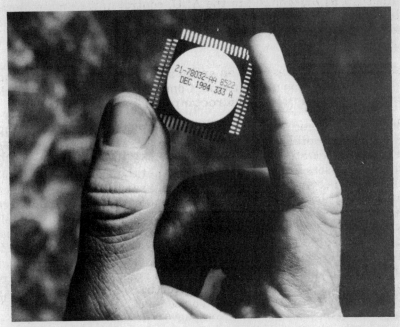

**The 78032 VLSI Chip – the heart of a Microvax II, one of Digital
Equipment's VAX range of computers.
The following are trademarks of Digital Equipment Corporation: VAX, MicroVAX.
(Picture courtesy of Digital Equipment Corporation (DEC))**

1.38 **Semi-conductor memory** is the name given to main storage manufactured on silicon chips. Semi-conductor memory rapidly replaced a former main storage medium, called *'core store'*, during the mid-seventies.

1.39 The most common types of semi-conductor memory are **'volatile'**, which means that all data is lost if the power supply is removed. The most common type of volatile memory is called **RAM** (Random Access Memory). Most computers normally contain a small proportion of **non-volatile** memory too. The most common type of non-volatile memory is called **ROM** (Read Only Memory).

1.40 **Main features.** The semi-conductor devices within the computer have the following features:

a. Their operation is *wholly electronic*, and consequently they are very fast and reliable.

b. Despite the complexity of these devices, modern manufacturing methods have enabled them to be produced at costs that represent only minor portions of the total costs of whole computer systems, e.g. in a microcomputer costing £1000, the microprocessor may only constitute £100 of the total cost or even much less.

c. These devices are *highly miniaturised*. This feature may be exploited in order to provide computer hardware that can be accommodated comfortably in the office, home, petrol pumps, washing machines, cars, etc.

Data storage

1.41 Some specific aspects of data storage have just been discussed under the heading of semi-conductor processors and memories, but now we turn our attention to *general hardware aspects of data storage* applicable to both main storage and backing storage.

1.42 There are several different common types of hardware used for data storage. This variety stems from the fact that there are a number of physical characteristics that must be considered in deciding the appropriateness of a particular device in a given situation.

1.43 Data storage devices will be discussed under these headings:

a. Storage capacity.

b. Access facilities.

    c. Size.

    d. Robustness.

    e. Relative costs.

Storage capacity

1.44 Storage capacities may be expressed and compared in terms of the number of **'characters'** (letters or numeric digits) stored. For example, *main storage* of a small computer may be expressed in terms of tens or hundreds of thousands of characters whereas *backing storage* of a larger computer may be expressed in terms of tens or hundreds of millions of characters.

Access facilities

1.45 Broadly speaking, the two main factors are:

    a. Mode of access.

    b. Speed of access.

1.46 For the time being an everyday example will provide a basic distinction between mode of access and speed of access. You may 'access' data (i.e. get facts) from this book in two modes:

    a. **serially**, by reading through from the first page to the last, or

    b. **directly** by using the index to go straight to the data you need.

1.47 The first alternative is more efficient if you require most or all of the facts, but the latter is faster if you only want a few facts. If you require to have the *immediate recall* of facts, then you may need to use your own memory, instead of this book, as your 'data storage medium'.

1.48 These ideas will be related to particular items of hardware later.

Size

1.49 Despite major strides in miniaturisation (the components within modern chips are more densely packed than the cells of the human brain, although they do not have the same intelligence as brains), some backing storage devices and media remain undesirably bulky. Most backing storage devices have some electromechanical parts, which contribute to their bulk. When data is to be stored for long periods with minimal access the most compact backing storage media are favoured because of the value of saving space.

1.50 Compared with normal paper-based data storage, as in the form of rows of filing cabinets, computer storage methods are all incredibly more compact.

Robustness

1.51 Compared with paper-based storage, computer data storage may appear to be less robust. Such a view is based upon the fact that most computer storage media need handling with care and may only be used in carefully controlled environments. In practical terms this is seldom a serious problem for commercial applications, since the 'office environment' is one which is suitable for most computer hardware. In industrial environments, such as on the factory floor, environmental problems are less easy to solve.

Relative costs

1.52 There are sharp differences in costs between the various types of computer storage. Awareness of the various alternatives allows the most economical alternative to be selected in a given situation. Conversely, if the storage requirements have not been properly specified, an unduly expensive alternative may be selected unnecessarily. In general semiconductor storage is more expensive than storage on magnetic media.

Backing storage

1.53 The main backing storage media in use today are:

    a. Magnetic Disk (hard or floppy).

    b. Magnetic Tape (reel-to-reel, cassette or cartridge).

    c. Optical Disk.

These media will be described in detail in later chapters.

1.54 **Magnetic Disks** are flat rotating circular plates coated with magnetic material. Some magnetic disks are rigid and called **hard disks,** others are *flexible* and are called **floppy disks** or **diskettes.** Hard disks are more expensive but are faster, more reliable and bigger.

1.55 Disks provide direct data access whereas Tapes provide serial data access.

1.56 **Magnetic Tapes** are similar in principle to the tapes used domestically for audio or video recording. Tape, being a serial medium, is mainly used as a **'back-up'** or archiving medium. Tape is sometimes also used as an input medium because data on other media may be converted onto magnetic tape prior to input in order to give faster input.

1.57 **Magnetic media problems.** The common forms of backing storage media in use today are similar in principle to the medium of the domestic tape of cassette recorders. Consequently they are susceptible to stray magnetic fields and to dust.

1.58 There are some advantages associated with these features of magnetic media. For example, whereas confidential data on paper may prove difficult to dispose of, magnetic media are not directly readable by humans and may be wiped clear magnetically.

1.59 **Optical Disks** are currently less common than magnetic disks but are growing in popularity. Some are physically the same as Compact Disks (CDs) used in home audio systems. Other optical disks look similar to CDs but work on different principle. They have the advantage of being less susceptible to damage than magnetic media, but many, including the normal CD, have the disadvantage of recording permanently, unlike magnetic media which can be overwritten.

Data entry

1.60 There are problems associated with entering data into computers because humans communicate less quickly than computers and in a different way, i.e. by speech, writing, etc. A computer's internal communication is electronic.

1.61 The basic problems are overcome by using devices that can encode our data into a form that is usable by the computer.

1.62 Modern methods of data entry fall into three broad categories:

    a. Keyboard entry.

    b. Document reading.

    c. Data capture.

1.63 **Keyboard entry.** The keyboard was introduced earlier (1.9) where it was shown being used with a PC. Data typed on the keyboard is displayed on the monitor screen. In the case of a PC there is just one user so the keyboard and monitor are connected directly to the computer. This arrangement is not satisfactory for large computers with many users. Instead separate keyboard input devices are used.

1.64 One typical keyboard input device is the **VDU** (Visual Display Unit). See Figure 1.6. The **VDU** is really two devices in one; one for input, one for output. Data is fed in via a keyboard, which is like a typewriter keyboard, and is both passed into the computer and displayed on the screen. The VDU can also receive and display messages from the computer.

Screen display

Cable to the computer

Mains power supply

Keyboard

Figure 1.6. A VDU (Visual Display Unit).

1.65 The main way of using a VDU is to connect it directly to the computer. This is known as **on-line** data entry. Any device used for on-line data entry in this manner is called a **terminal**.

1.66 There are many different types of VDU (details later). Although VDUs look rather like PCs they do not have the same processing capabilities. For this reason they are sometimes called **dumb terminals**.

1.67 In the past it was also common to use VDUs in conjunction with some other special purpose data entry system in order to prepare data on a fast and reliable input medium, the most popular modern example of this, still in use, is the key-to-floppy-disk or **key-to-diskette** system. These are microcomputer-based systems that take in data from the VDU and store it on floppy disks. At some later stage the floppy disks are used for input to the main computer. However, such systems are in rapid decline because the same job can be carried out by a normal PC. This use of a PC is another example of a general purpose computer being able to carry out a special purpose task.

1.68 In a key-to-floppy-disk system, or its PC based equivalent, the data can be *checked and corrected* as it is being input and no non-reusable medium is being wasted.

1.69 **Terminal emulation.** Most personal computers, and many home computers, can mimic VDUs by means of special '**terminal emulation**' programs. Under the control of the terminal emulation program, the personal computer's keyboard acts as a VDU keyboard and its screen acts as a VDU screen. Of course, the personal computer must be fitted with a suitable connector and cabling to the main computer. This is yet another example of a general purpose computer acting as a special purpose computer by means of specialist software. VDUs can cost nearly as much as a small micro-computer so it has become quite common for some organisations to spend the extra money needed to buy PCs plus emulation software instead of buying VDUs.

1.70 **Document reading.** The idea behind document reading is to get a machine to read source documents (i.e. the documents on which the data is originally recorded). This avoids the problems associated with transcription and verification of data when using keyboard devices. The data is recorded on the documents using special marks or characters, and is read by optical or magnetic reading techniques. Details will be given later.

1.71 **Data Capture.** This heading covers a wide variety of methods, all of which try to combine data creation with data entry, i.e. the data is 'captured' at source in a machine-sensible form. For example, prerecorded, or preprinted data on some suitable medium attached to goods may be read or collected as the goods are sold. This application is known as **PoS** (Point of Sale) data capture. Further details of this and other data capture methods will be given later.

Output

1.72 At the present time much information produced by computers is output in the form of printed paper documents, reports, etc. Many computer systems are used for 'on-line' information retrieval and this means that considerable volumes of data are also merely displayed on screens instead of being produced in printed form.

1.73 In both these cases the information is expressed in terms of characters (letters and numerical digits), but gradually more and more information is being provided in the form of **images** (i.e. pictures or diagrams, possibly combined with text). Such uses are already very common for such activities as producing original copies for reprinting in the form of reports, newsletters, text-books and newspapers. Indeed, the author of this edition of this text has prepared the entire book using a PC (a Macintosh).

1.74 Quite apart from a number of valuable innovations over many years, the development of output devices has been largely concerned with trying to find ways of improving the speeds, costs and reliability of printers. Print quality and quietness have been additional aims for some printer applications.

1.75 The three main types of printer currently in use are:

    a. character printers.

    b. line printers.

    c. laser printers.

1.76 **Character printers** are low-speed printers that mimic the action of typewriters by printing *one character at a time*. The better character printers can produce output of sufficient quality to be used for business letters. Others may produce **NLQ ('Near Letter Quality')** output.

1.77 **Line printers.** The majority of high-speed printers *print whole lines at a time* (or appear to) and are consequently called *line printers*. Line printers usually have a considerable work load on mini or mainframe computers used for DP.

1.78 **Laser printers.** The first laser printers, which appeared on the market in the late 1970s, were very expensive ultra-high-speed devices intended to compete with the fasted line printers. The use of such printers is now well established. During the 1980s, economical small-size lower-speed laser printers became available and were rapidly adopted for uses where high-quality output is important. They have displaced character printers in many situations. The spelling 'Lazers' is sometimes used.

Software

1.79 In the preceding paragraphs the emphasis was on hardware. We will now look at the general classification of the software applicable to all machines.

1.80 **Types of Software.** The two main classes are as follows.

    a. **Applications software.** This is software that is designed to be put to specific practical use. This broad classification may be further sub-divided into:

        i. **Specialist applications software,** that is, programs, with associated documentation, designed specifically to carry out particular tasks, for example, solving sets of mathematical equations or controlling a company's stock of goods.

        ii. **Applications packages**, that is, suites of programs, with associated documentation, used for a particular type of problem. Many packages are designed in such a way that they can be used for a variety of similar problems. For example, payroll packages are sometimes produced in forms that enable them to be set up and used by different companies each having slightly different ways in which they need to produce their payroll. The most abundant selection of packages is available on personal computers, with the more popular packages selling in tens of thousands of copies or even hundreds of thousands of copies.

    b. **Systems software.** These are programs, with associated documentation, that control the way the computer operates or provide facilities that extend the general capabilities of the system. Within the set of systems software for a given computer there is usually a program, or suite of programs, called the **operating system**. The operating system controls the performance of the computer by doing a variety of jobs to ensure the proper, orderly and efficient use of hardware by applications programs. Most applications programs can only work when used in conjunction with the operating system. Other systems software may extend the capabilities of the operating system further, for example, by providing programs that can monitor how efficiently the hardware is being utilised by the software.

Software's flexibility

1.81 As stated previously, **software** is the term used to describe programs and associated documentation. Compared with hardware, the software used on a given computer is relatively easy to change and it is that capability which gives computers their flexibility of purpose.

1.82 The point is demonstrated well by the home computer used for playing games. Instead of buying a new machine each time a new game is wanted, as would be necessary if the game was solely hardware (i.e. wholly built into electronic components), all that is needed is for a new program to be 'loaded' into the machine each time a different game is needed. Better still, it is relatively easy to chop and change between games at will. This kind of flexibility is soon taken for granted, but it is in sharp contrast to most other items of everyday technology that have far less flexibility of purpose. It is this ability readily to change the computer's function which originally lead to the term **'soft** ware' being used. Additional flexibility is also provided by software because not only is it relatively easy to change from one program to another but also individual programs can be changed, although such changes cannot necessarily be carried out by the computer user.

Software as a product

1.83 When software is purchased for use on a particular computer the purchaser obtains a copy of the programs plus a number of items of documentation. Remember that the term software means *programs plus their associated documentation*. Software is normally purchased directly or indirectly from either a computer manufacturer or a **'software house'**. A software house is a company that specialises in producing software and related services.

1.84 The purchaser of software usually pays for some or all of the following:

   a. **A licence.** Sometimes the purchaser pays outright for all rights associated with using the software but usually that is not the case. Instead, the purchaser pays a licence fee, which gives the right to use the software on a particular computer or a specified number of computers on a particular site. Alternatively, a **site licence** may be paid for which entitles the purchaser to use the software on any computer at a particular place. Sometimes the licence specifies the number of users that may use the software at any one time, and, in the case of a single-user licence, may require that the user's name be registered. Using software in breach of licence agreements is a serious offence for which the user may be sued for damages or subjected to criminal prosecution. Companies are normally very careful to observe licence agreements, but many cases of **pirated software** (i.e. illegally copied software) have been reported in recent years.

   b. **An installation guide.** This guide may be part of a single documentation manual in simple cases or a completely separate manual in the case of larger suites of software. Normally, the guide starts by providing information about what hardware is needed to enable the programs to run satisfactorily. It then goes on to describe the procedures to be followed in order to set up the software so that it can be used satisfactorily and efficiently on a particular kind of computer. According to the complexities of the software involved this may involve some work being carried out by a computer specialist.

   c. **The installation of the software.** A purchaser may not have the necessary expertise to set up the software, or may find it too time consuming or troublesome to carry out. In such cases the purchaser may be able to pay an additional fee to have the software installed.

   d. **Maintenance and updates.** It is unfortunately not uncommon for programs to be supplied which may be faulty in some way. Sometimes these faults, called **bugs**, do not come to light until some time after the software has been delivered and put to use. A good supplier will make every effort to correct bugs as and when they are discovered and will provide a new corrected version of the program containing the necessary **'bug fixes'**. The correction of bugs, i.e. maintenance, is often combined with enhancements to the software, to make it better in some way. Enhancement normally involves increased 'functionality' (i.e. making it do more things) or improvements to performance (e.g. making it work faster). Licensed purchasers may get some of these changes provided free of charge, perhaps during the first year of use. Subsequently the purchaser may be able to pay an annual fee for maintenance and updates.

e. **A support contract.** A purchaser experiencing problems with software, not necessarily caused by bugs, will want to be able to turn to the supplier for help. If a high level of assistance is required it may be available as an additional service subject to a separate contract. Some 'mission critical' software in large corporations may be under 24-hour support contracts. The user can call for help on-site at anytime of the day or night. Obviously such support contracts are not the norm. However, it is very common for businesses to have support contracts that provide telephone assistance during the working day on what is often called a 'hot line'.

f. **User guides.** A user guide is usually a manual provided for an end-user to enable him or her to learn how to use the software. Such guides usually use suitable examples to take the user through the stages of carrying out various tasks with the software.

g. **A reference manual.** A reference manual is normally intended to be used by a user who already knows how to use the software but who needs to be reminded about a particular point or who wants to obtain more detailed information about a particular feature. Reference manuals normally have topics organised in alphabetical order.

h. **A quick reference guide.** These are single sheets or cards, small enough to fit into a pocket, which the user may keep handy for help with common tasks carried out with the software. For example, a quick reference guide for a Command Interpreter might list the commands alphabetically in key words order showing how they should be typed.

i. **Training.** In addition to providing user guides the software supplier may provide training courses on how to use the software. Sometimes some initial training is provided free as part of the initial purchase. Although training is often quite costly it may pay for itself if the software user becomes proficient much more quickly as a result.

j. **Membership of a user group.** A user group is a club for individuals or organisations who use a particular hardware or software product. The club is often run and partly sponsored by the supplier. Members of user groups may have meetings or receive newsletters which enable them to find out more about the product and how to use it.

1.85 It should be clear to the reader from what has just be stated that there is a lot more to producing a software product than merely producing the programs themselves. Even so, the programming is still a key task in the production of a software product. In later chapters a considerable amount of space is devoted to many of the basic methods, tools and languages used in programming. Always remember that, in addition to the production of a well-finished and reliable program with the right functionality, there are numerous other tasks to be done. These include considerable work by such people as those who produce all the documentation (manuals, guides, etc), the **'technical authors'**.

Applications packages

1.86 Applications packages are suites of programs, with associated documentation, used for a particular type of problem or variety of similar problems. Software packages are sold as complete products and in this respect differ from most user applications programs, which are normally produced by an organisation for internal use to perform specific tasks.

1.87 Applications packages may be classified as either:

a. Application Specific or

b. Generalised.

1.88 An application specific package is aimed at providing all the facilities required for a particular class of application problem such as payroll or stock control. A generalised applications package is one that provides a completely general set of facilities that are of use in dealing with similar types of task which arise in a wide variety of *different* applications problems. Well known packages of this type such as **spreadsheet** packages and **word processing** packages will be examined in detail in later chapters. First, consider applications packages that are applications specific.

Packages for specific applications

1.89 Many users have the same type of problem to deal with by means of a computer, and thus manufacturers and specialist software writers have written standard programs to solve these problems and sell them to the many users who want them. Examples are stock control, sales invoicing, network analysis and payroll.

1.90 Applications packages are of major importance to small computer-system users who do not have the necessary resources or expertise to produce their own software.

1.91 **Advantages of packages.**

    a. The main advantage is the saving of programming effort and expense on the part of the user. Development costs are effectively shared between the purchasers.

    b. The user gets a well-tried and tested program, which he or she is able to use with confidence.

    c. Relatively quick implementation results from the use of packages.

1.92 **Disadvantages of packages.**

    a. The purchaser does not have direct control over the package in the same way as would be the case if the software was produced in-house.

    b. The package will have been produced to meet general needs and may therefore not be ideal for a particular customer.

1.93 **Practical considerations.**

    a. Many users' systems will differ in some detailed area, especially if there is a relationship between applications, as there is, for example, between labour cost analysis and payroll.

    b. A solution would be for the users to modify their system to suit the package, but this has its problems.

    c. Some users may decide arbitrarily to design a system to suit the package.

    d. Some software houses build packages on the modular principle and thus are able to combine the various modules to suit a particular user's requirement.

    e. The question of cost must not be ignored and will be reflected in the service provided by the supplier of the package.

    f. A number of trade associations, etc, have sponsored the writing of packages for particular industries. The Motor Manufacturers Association has set up packages for its dealers.

    g. Thorough research should be made into the reliability of the package and the particular software house offering it for sale. It is a good idea to ask current users of the package about their experience.

    h. A program maintenance agreement should be sought where changes to the package are likely, e.g. a payroll package could be affected by government legislation.

1.94 **How the package is supplied.** A package normally consists of:

    a. A program (or suite of programs) actually written onto a suitable medium, e.g. magnetic tape, or floppy disk.

    b. Documentation, which specifies:

        i. How to set up the package.

        ii. How to use the package.

        iii. Necessary technical details.

1.95 Any software that the user buys is likely to be supplied in similar form to that just described. Suppliers tend to provide no more than the necessary technical detail in order to protect their trade secrets.

Overview of manual

1.96 Following this introductory chapter the subject matter of DP and IT is covered in a step by step, manner taking the reader through each topic that needs to be covered.

The topics include:

a. the equipment used to create, process, store and communicate data;

b. the methods needed to exploit the equipment effectively;

c. the role of specialists such as systems analysts and programmers and the tools and techniques they use in designing and implementing systems;

d. the identification, with the aid of examples, of what makes an appropriate application for computerisation and the use of IT;

e. the management of DP and its related IT.

1.97 It must be stressed that many questions will come to the reader's mind while progressing with these studies, many of which will not be answered until the studies are completed.

Much thought has gone into the layout and sequence of chapters. The reader would be well advised to study them in the order presented.

Summary

1.98 a. 'Data' are the basic facts about the activities of a business.

b. 'Information' is data assembled into a useful form.

c. Most computers used for DP are general-purpose digital computers.

d. Computers may be classified as:
   i. Digital or analog.
   ii. Special purpose or general purpose.
   iii. Mainframe, minicomputer or microcomputer.
   iv. 1st, 2nd, 3rd or 4th generation.

e. The basic elements (functions) of a computer system are:
   i. Input.
   ii. Storage.
   iii. Control.
   iv. Processing.
   v. Output.

f. The main technologies of Information Technology are:
   i. Computers.
   ii. Electronics.
   iii. Communications.

g. IT systems create, store, manipulate and communicate data in a variety of forms in order to satisfy information needs.

h. The chapter has provided specific coverage of computer hardware under these headings:
   i. The Silicon Chip.
   ii. Data Storage.
   iii. Backing Storage.
   iv. Data Entry.
   v. Data Transmission and Networks.
   vi. Output.

i. Two main classes of software are **applications software** and **systems software**.

j. The operating system controls the way in which all other software uses the hardware.

k Software was considered as a product to highlight the various requirements of the software user.

l. Application packages are suites of programs, with associated documentation, used for a particular type of problem or variety of similar problems and normally sold as complete products.

m. Applications packages may be broadly classified as

    i. Application specific, e.g. a stock-control package, or

    ii. Generalised, e.g. a spreadsheet.

Points to note

1.99 a. Strictly speaking, the term 'Data Processing' means any data processing operation, regardless of the method used. To many people, however, it is virtually synonymous with computer processing, e.g. a company advertising for a DP Manager wants someone to run its computer installation, not its office.

b. The end product of data processing is information irrespective of the data processing facilities used to produce that information. Throughout any study of data processing, therefore, the reader needs to be constantly aware of the necessity for good presentation of information.

d. No matter how good the data processing systems within an organisation are, if the other aspects of the organisation's information system are poor, the information produced may be under-utilised to the detriment of the organisation.

e. Computers are able to perform repetitive tasks accurately on large volumes of data with the minimum of manual intervention. By exploiting these abilities to process and maintain data, to provide required information, EDP has gained a considerable advantage over conventional DP methods.

f. The computers used for DP today are mostly fourth-generation general-purpose digital computers, which may be mainframes, minicomputers or microcomputers.

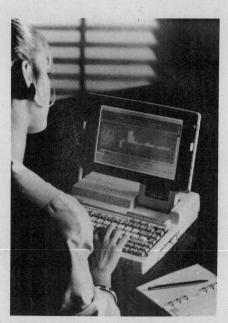

A Toshiba 'T1600 Portable Desktop 286' computer.
Photograph supplied by courtesy of Toshiba.

g. The terms 'Central Processing Unit (CPU)' and 'Central Processor' are sometimes used instead of 'Processor'. Beware of these terms, however, because they have in the past also been used to refer to the processor plus main memory. Their use in this text has been avoided as far as possible because of this possible ambiguity.

h. The various technologies associated with IT are often said to be converging technologies because they are being developed so that their functions may be integrated.

i. Within this text, the interest in hardware is primarily directed at those features which determine its uses and limitations, rather than at how it works.

j. The hardware devices used for input, output and auxiliary storage are called **peripheral devices.**

k. Another name for a floppy disk is **diskette**.

l. A complete software product is not just programs but programs with their associated documentation.

Questions

1. Distinguish between 'data' and 'information'.

2. Define 'Data Processing'.

3. What is a Personal Computer?

4. Describe the flow of data and commands in a computer system.

5. Define what a computer is.

6. a. What is meant by the term 'semiconductor device'?

    b. Give three features of semiconductor devices.

7. List ten things that the purchaser of software might require as part of the purchase.

8. What is an applications package?

Desktop computing

1. Computers designed for use on a desk in an office are called **desktop computers**. A PC is probably the most common example of a desktop computer. It is the common everyday use of desktop computers by non computer specialists which makes them a suitable subject for discussion at this stage. In the next Part we embarking on the more specialised details of conventional DP, which is still more oriented towards minicomputers and mainframes.

2. Chapter 2 describes the features of modern desktop computers with an emphasis on the more advanced types called **'workstations'**. Chapter 2 also examines the ways in which such a computer can be used simply and intuitively by means of what is called a **'Graphical User Interface' (GUI)**.

3. In chapter 3 the emphasis is switched to software commonly used on desktop computers. Spreadsheets are of widespread importance and are examined in detail in this chapter.

4. Chapter 4 provides contrasting examples to the spreadsheet by examining software used in the preparation of documents.

2 Workstations and GUIs

Introduction

2.1 This chapter starts by examining features of desktop computers so as to build up an understanding of what constitutes a workstation. Having established the features and facilities of a workstation the chapter goes on to introduce and describe the basic features of a Graphical User Interface (GUI).

Desktop computers

2.2 The most common type of desktop computer is the Personal Computer (PC) which, as was stated in the previous chapter, is a microcomputer designed for independent use by an individual at work or in the home mainly for business purposes (see figure 2.2). The details of a typical PC are given below together with an explanation of the terms used.

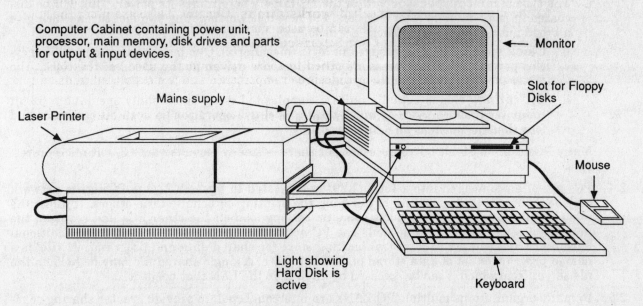

Computer Cabinet containing power unit, processor, main memory, disk drives and parts for output & input devices.

Monitor

Slot for Floppy Disks

Mains supply

Laser Printer

Mouse

Light showing Hard Disk is active

Keyboard

Figure 2.1 A personal computer with laser printer

2.3 **Features of a typical PC**

a. The **keyboard** resembles the QWERTY typewriter keyboard, but it has several additional keys, which are used to control and edit the display. It usually has special **function keys** (labelled F1, F2, F3...) which are used to get the computer to perform special operations. Many keyboards also have a **numeric keypad** to simplify the entry of purely numerical data.

b. Characters are displayed on the monochrome or colour **monitor** screen in a manner that resembles printed text. A typical full screen display is 24 rows by 80 columns (i.e. 1920 characters). Those with graphics capabilities (details later) are also able to display images such as pictures and diagrams. The character display can normally be generated in two different modes:

   i.. **Scrolling mode** in which lines appear at the bottom and move up the screen rather like credits on a movie screen.

   ii. **Paging mode** in which one complete screen-full is replace by another, rather like a slide projector display.

c. **Cursor controls.** A cursor is a small character-size symbol displayed on the screen, which can be moved about the screen both vertically and horizontally by means of special keys on the keyboard. During data input, the display may resemble a blank form. In this case data may be entered by first moving the cursor to a space on the 'form' and then typing in the data. Further keys may allow the data to be edited or corrected.

d. **Local printer.** A printer is often directly connected to a PC. Common types of such 'local printers' are the dot matrix printers, desktop laser printers and inkjet printers. These will be described in later chapters.

e. An **internal hard disk** (1.54) is normally fitted into the PC cabinet. This is used to store data and programs. The capacity of the disk may typically range from 20 to 400 Mbytes.

   Note. One **byte** of storage can hold a character (a letter or numeric digit). So one Megabyte (1 Mbyte) is roughly the equivalent of one million characters.

f. An **internal floppy disk** drive for removable floppy disks is also normally fitted. This is mostly used to store data and programs being transferred to or from the PC. A single 3.5" floppy disk may have a capacity of approximately 1 Mbyte.

h. The **main memory (main storage)** is typically 1 to 16 Mbytes.

i. The type of **microprocessor** within the PC largely determines its power. This will be discussed in more detail in later chapters. For now it is worth noting two measures which give a broad indication of power. These are as follows.

   i. **Clock speed.** This is measured in MHz (megahertz). One megahertz is one million cycles per second. The processor's operations are driven at the speed of the clock. The faster the clock the faster the processor.

   ii. **Bit-rating.** This is actually quite a complicated issue but broadly speaking a 32-bit computer handles twice as much data in a single operation as a 16-bit computer and four times as much as an 8-bit computer.

Many PCs contain 16-bit microprocessor but there is steady move towards 32-bit microprocessors.

2.4 PCs are often connected into a LAN (1.29) as indicated in figure 2.2. One PC in the network may be dedicated to the purpose of handling the printing on behalf of the others. It fulfils the role of a '**print server**'. This takes some processing load off the other PCs and saves on the number of separate printers needed. The PC acting as the '**file server**' will have additional hard disks and will act as a central backing store for shared data and programs. A '**file**' is a named program or set of data stored on backing store. A single shared file may be held on the file server from which it can be accessed by any PC on the LAN that needs it.

2.5 In many organisations multiple PC LANs are interconnected, to provide greater sharing of resources, by means of connections called '**bridges**'. Other types of computers may be connected to these networks too, including minicomputers and mainframes.

2.6 Now that we have examined the features of PCs and PC networks we are ready to move on to examining the definition of a workstation.

Workstations

2.7 A typical workstation looks similar to a PC because it is a desktop computer with screen and keyboard attached. However, it is more advanced than a typical PC in a number of respects as will be seen from the following list of essential features.

a. It is larger and more powerful than a typical PC. For example, many popular workstations use 32-bit microprocessors whereas PCs are typically 16-bit microcomputers. Some larger workstations have multiple processors.

b. It is fully connected into a computer network as another computer on the network in its own right.

c. It has high-resolution graphics on bit-mapped screens as a standard feature. (Details shortly.)

d. It has a **multitasking** operating system which means that it is able to run multiple applications at the same time. This is a feature not found in most PCs.

2.8 **Uses.** Workstations are normally used by professionals for particular kinds of work such as Finance (dealer rooms), Science and Research, and Computer Aided Design. They are also very popular for programming.

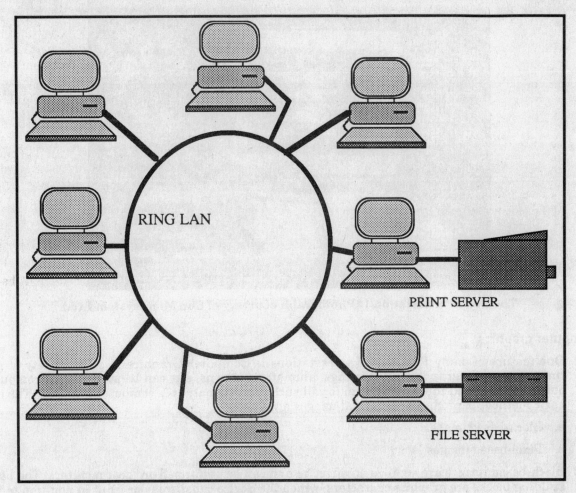

Figure 2.2. A PC LAN

2.9 **Examples** of workstations are the Digital VAXSTATIONs and the SUN SPARCstations.

2.10 **PCs as workstations.** Most workstations are purpose built to provide the essential features listed above. It may be possible for a powerful PC to meet these requirements. The requirements may be met as follows.

a. Higher powered processors such as the higher speed Intel 486 or Motorola M68040 will be desirable. Supplementary **co-processors** will also be preferable. **Maths co-processors** can take computational loads of the main processor and **graphics co-processors** can take load of the main processor in the construction and maintenance of images.

b. The PC will normally be fitted with an extra circuit board able to control and operate a high speed network port.

c. Suitable **Graphics cards** will be fitted to provide graphics capabilities of sufficiently high standard. Details later.

d. A **multi-tasking** capability must be available through suitable software. The operating systems **PC-DOS** and **MS-DOS** found on the majority of IBM compatible PCs are *not* capable of multi-tasking. Only one application program can be run at a time. A form of multi-tasking is available through Microsoft Windows 3 which may be run under these operating systems. Alternatively, operating systems such as OS/2, SCO Unix and Microsoft Windows/NT may be run on the same hardware and do provide full multi-tasking. On the Apple

Macintosh multi-tasking is only available under version 7 of Apple's MacOS operating system or under A/UX, Apple's version of Unix.

The Sun SPARCstation 1 (Photograph courtesy of Sun Microsystem Ltd.)

Computer graphics

2.11 One feature of many PCs and all workstations is Computer Graphics. A wide variety of pictures, diagrams, graphs, line drawings, animated cartoons, etc, can be produced on computer output devices and the general term for all such forms of output is computer graphics. The two basic methods of producing graphical images are:

a. Block-based images.

b. Pixel-based images.

2.12 Block-based images are simple and effective and can be performed on most monitors. The basic building blocks are graphics characters, which the device can display or print in addition to the ordinary alphabetic and numeric characters (see figure 2.3a). The graphics characters available vary from device to device. One standard and very simple form of block-based image is that used on the British TV Ceefax and Oracle services.

2.13 Pixel-based images are of a higher quality than block-based images and are used on **workstations and PCs fitted with 'Graphics Video Adapters'**. The image is built up from an appropriate combination of dots. To achieve this the whole screen is organised into rows and columns of individual 'dot' positions called pixels. On a black and white screen each pixel can simply either be **on** (white) or **off** (black) (see figure 2.3b). On a colour screen each pixel may comprise a cluster of red, green and blue primary-coloured dots which can be on and off in different combinations. Computer memory works in on-off units called **bits (Binary digits)**. Combinations of bits can therefore be used to hold representations of the images displayed.

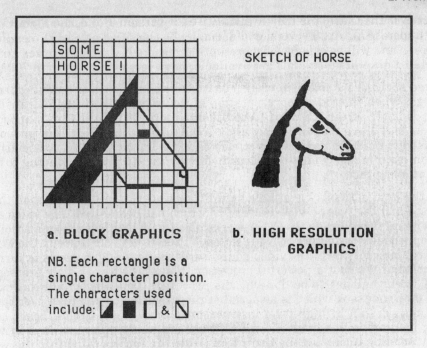

Figure 2.3a Examples of computer graphics images

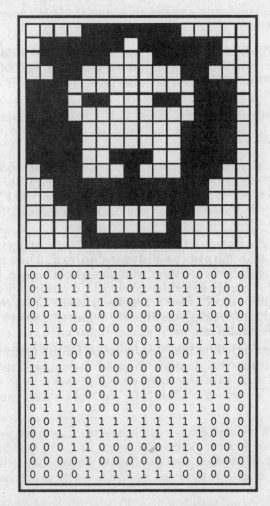

Figure 2.3b A simple graphical image coded in binary to be 'bit-mapped'

2.14 The more pixels there are, the more detail can be represented, i.e. the higher the resolution. A screen with more than 30,000 pixels will normally be classified as a **high-resolution graphics (HRG)** screen and will be capable of representing reasonably smooth curves and accurate drawings. Specialist graphics terminals are available, however, with more than 700,000 pixels.

2.15 As indicated above the memory in the PC or workstation is used to hold a coded representation of the image. When the coded representation of the image in memory is translated into an image on the monitor screen it is said to be **bit-mapped**. To hold the bit-mapped image a PC or workstation may have memory separately available dedicated to this purpose. The area of memory used to hold the data is sometimes called a **frame buffer**. Alternatively, in a PC or workstation main memory may be set aside for storing data corresponding to the pixels being displayed on the screen.

2.16 Normally the kind of display available on a PC or workstation depend upon the quality of the monitor used and the type of '**video adapter**' which has been fitted. The video adapter is a special circuit board fitted inside the PC or workstation with an external connection to the monitor. The bit-mapped memory on the board is called '**Video RAM**'. Software in the PC or workstation sends control instructions to the video adapter informing it which pixels to turn on and off and in which colours. Without a powerful processor this can be a very slow process because of the amount of work that has to be done by the processor. One way of alleviating this is to fit a **graphics co-processor** which is a specialist processor which can take over the pixel-level operations and is driven by high level instruction to draw lines, circles, boxes etc. Graphics co-processing is common in workstations but there are many different ways in which it may be achieved depending upon how the extra processors are incorporated into the workstation's design.

2.17 **Examples** of video adapters found on IBM PCs, and those PC operating to the same standard, known as '**IBM compatibles**' are as follows.

    a. **Colour Graphics Adapter (CGA).** This was the original adapter provided and is now obsolete. It supported 4 colours at a time, chosen from 16, and had a resolution of 640 x 200 pixels. Characters were generated in 8 x 8 pixel grids. It is mentioned here for completeness and to show how the technology has progressed.

    b. **Enhanced Graphics Adapter (EGG).** This low grade adapter supports 16 colours at a time, chosen from 64, and had a resolution of 640 x 350 pixels. Characters are generated in 8 x 14 pixel grids.

    c. **Video Graphics Array (VGA).** This adapter is in widespread use. It supports either 320 200 pixels in 256 colours or 640 x 480 pixels in 16 colours. Characters are generated in 9 16 pixel grids. As a comparison, a grid of 640 x 480 pixels in either 16 or 256 colours is common on video adapters and monitors used on the Apple Macintosh II.

2.18 **Mice, trackerballs and joysticks.** These devices have a variety of uses complementary to the keyboard and are of particular value when used in conjunction with graphical displays. In simple cases they can be used to move the cursor about the screen.

    a. **Mice.** As the mouse is moved about the desktop the cursor moves about the screen. A button on top of the mouse can be pressed when the desired position is reached. The motion of the mouse is sensed by a rolling ball, which is mounted in the underside of the mouse and in contact with the desktop.(Figure 2.4)

    b. **Trackerballs.** A trackerball is really a variation on the mouse (figure 2.5). The ball is on the top side of the trackerball, rather than on the underside as in a mouse. The ball is moved by passing the palm of the hand over it. Trackerballs are intended for use where desktop space is limited or not available, for example, when using a lap-top computer away from a desk.

    c. **Joysticks.** A joystick is an alternative to a mouse. They have proved more popular for computer games than they have for serious applications. The joystick can be moved left, right, up or down to move the cursor and also has a button used like that on the mouse. The movements of the joystick are detected by cause electrical contacts to be made. (Figure 2.6 page 32.)

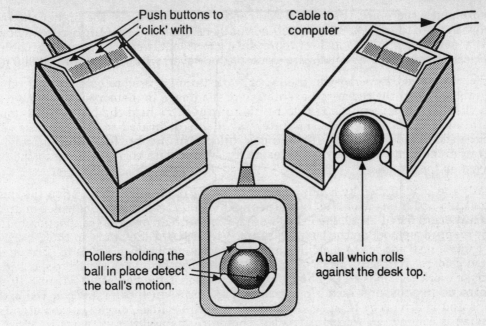

Push buttons to 'click' with

Cable to computer

Rollers holding the ball in place detect the ball's motion.

A ball which rolls against the desk top.

Figure 2.4. The operation of a mouse.

Figure 2.5. Trackerballs – hand-held (above) and desktop model.

2.19 Many graphics workstations provide software that allows pictures to be created by the use of devices such as **mice.** For example, by holding down the button on the mouse while moving the mouse across the desk top a line may be drawn across the screen. The graphics facilities can also be used to allow the user of the device to operate it in simpler and more visually interesting ways.

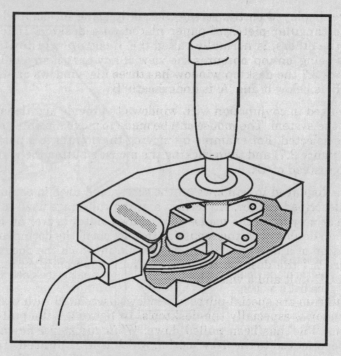

Figure 2.6 A Joystick

Windowing systems

2.20 **A window** is a rectangular area on a display screen in which text or graphical images may be displayed. Several windows may be displayed on a screen at the same time. Most workstations and some PCs use software that handles all screen displays by means of windows. These windowing systems normally have a number of common features:

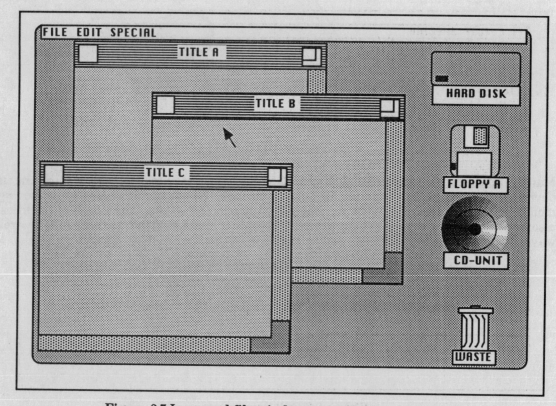

Figure 2.7 Icons and file windows on a 'desktop' window

a. **Windows** are displayed on the screen, normally using bit-mapped graphics, in a manner resembling rectangular pieces of paper placed on a desktop. Indeed, one large window, 'beneath' all the others, is normally called the '**desktop window**' (figure 2.7). A window designated as being 'on-top' obscures the view of any part of any window beneath it. For example, in figure 2.7 the desktop window has three file windows on it. The window with title 'C' is on top. 'B' is below it and 'A' is underneath 'B'.

b. **Mice** may be used in conjunction with windows to provide additional means for the user to interact with the system. The mouse can be made to move a pointer on the screen to an item which is to be selected. For example by moving the pointer to a position above the window with title 'B' (figure 2.7) and then clicking the mouse's button the window 'B' will be made to appear on top instead of 'C'.

c. **Icons** may be displayed in windows on the screen and used in conjunction with a mouse in the manner described earlier. An icon is a graphical image used to represent an object or function. A user may move the mouse so that the pointer is over an icon representing a document and then double click the mouse button to 'open' the document. The document opens with the creation of a new window on the screen in which the document's contents may be seen. In figure 2.7 the desktop window has four icons on it representing: a hard disk, a floppy disk, a CD-unit and a waste bin.

d. **Pull-down menus** are special-purpose windows associated with text headings displayed at the top of windows, especially the desktop's. In figure 2.8 the pull-down menu under the screen heading 'File' has been pulled down. *While the mouse key has been held down* the pointer has been moved to the 'New' option which is **highlighted**. To select the highlighted operation the user merely releases the mouse button. Had the floppy disk icon previously been selected this might result in a window being displayed on the desktop showing documents on the disk. When looking at a document in an open window, there may be a heading at the screen top called 'EDIT'. If the mouse is moved above the word 'EDIT' and then pressed a small window appears beneath it, *while the mouse key is held down*. Again, this **pull-down menu** will list a set of options available to the user (e.g. FIND or CHANGE). If the user moves the mouse over an option and then lets go of the mouse button then the computer will carry out the selected action.

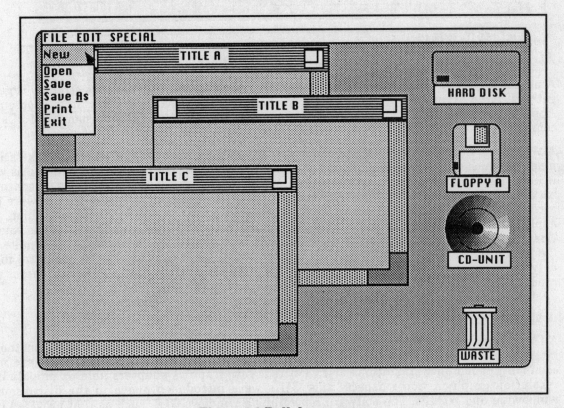

Figure 2.8 Pull-down menus

e. **Pop-up windows.** In figure 2.9 there is an example of a **pop-up menu** which has been displayed because the user has selected the 'SAVE' option on a pull-down menu for a file which already exists. In this case the user is presented with three choices any one of which can be selected by clicking upon the appropriate box by means of the mouse controlled pointer. Once the selection has been made the pop-up window will disappear.

2.21 This combination of features is sometimes known as a **WIMP** interface (Windows Icons Mice and Pull-down menus).

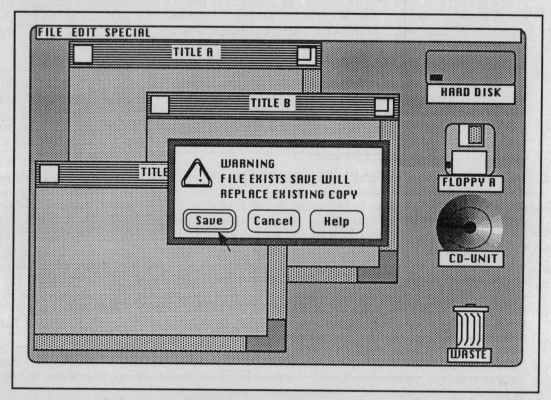

Figure 2.9 Pop-up windows

2.22 A number of windowing systems are in common use today and the reader is strongly urged to get first-hand experience of using one. Two possible alternatives are the system used on the Apple Macintosh or the Microsoft Windows 3 package, which is available on some IBM PCs and compatibles.

2.23 **X-windows.** Rather more advanced windowing capabilities are available on most workstations, many of which conform to a standard known as **X-windows**. The X-window system uses what is known as a **client-server architecture**, which basically means that there is a separation between the application software that is using the windowing facilities and the software that actually manages and controls the screen, keyboard and mouse in the intended fashion. The application is the **client** and the software managing the windowing environment is the **server**. The client and server programs may either both be executed in the workstation or, alternatively, the server may run in the workstation while the client runs on another computer in the network. The X-window system provides a standard means by which the client and server may communicate with each other irrespective of their locations.

Graphical user interface (GUI)

2.24 A **Graphical User Interface** (GUI, commonly pronounced 'guey' like 'gluey') is any method of interaction between a user and a computer based upon a graphical display. GUIs are most commonly found on workstations or PCs fitted with graphics adapters able to support high resolution graphics. Some aspects of a GUIs were introduced above in the discussion of windowing and WIMPs. The software controlling a windows GUI, such as that provided by a WIMP interface, is called a **Windows Manager** or **Windows Management System**.

2.25 The very nature of the subject matter means that there are limits to what can be learned by the reader merely reading the contents. Therefore, the reader is urged to gain some first-hand practical experience of using GUIs. Suitable systems on which to gain GUI experience include: an Apple Macintosh, an IBM compatible PC running Microsoft Windows 3 or a Unix workstation running OSF/MOTIF or Open Look. In addition, the system needs to have a variety of graphically oriented applications packages installed.

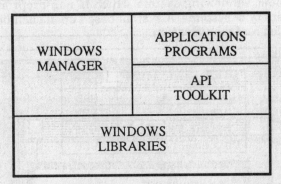

Figure 2.10 The organisation of GUI software

The organisation of GUI software

2.26 Before examining the features of GUI software here is a brief description of how the various software items fit together.

2.27 Fig 2.10 is a simplified representation of how software is organised in a general purpose windows-based GUI system.

    a. At the lowest level there are the **windows libraries**. These consist of sets of standard operation which can be used by the higher level software to interact with the GUI. For example, there may be a standard operation for drawing a line between any two specified points on the display screen, or there may be an operation to check the status of a mouse button. These standard low level operations are sometimes call **intrinsic functions**. Graphical objects created, manipulated, and removed by these standard operations are called **widgets**.

    b. In most GUI systems the windows libraries are not used directly. Instead, a **toolkit** is provided which enables the GUI to be constructed from a set of standard widgets all conforming to a coherent and consistent style. This toolkit provides what is called an **Applications Program Interface (API)**. Programmers writing specialist applications programs or applications packages to be used in conjunction with the GUI do not themselves have to write instructions to manipulate the widgets or other components of the GUI interface, such a the keyboard or mouse. Instead, all they do is get their programs to use the toolkit. Their programs are said to **call toolkit functions**.

    c. As indicated in figure 2.10 each application program can call directly upon the toolkit to manipulate its own widgets. However, there is a need for some overall control of these activities so that, for example, one application does not interfere with the widgets in a window belonging to a separate application currently using the same display screen. This controlling and coordinating task is carried out by the **windows manager**.

OSF/Motif ...... Open Look	Windows 3	Presentation Manager	Finder and Toolkit
X-WINDOWS	MS-DOS	OS/2	MacOS
Various Operating Systems			

Figure 2.11 Diverse GUI software configurations

2.28 Figure 2.11 shows how the simplified arrangement of Fig 2.10 may be set up in practice. Each box on the top layer of figure 2.11 represents a well established GUI comprising a windows manager with its associated API toolkit. The next layer down is the layer which provides the windows libraries. The GUIs on the right of figure 2.11 are proprietary, each belonging to a particular manufacturer: (Windows 3 on MS-DOS – Microsoft; Presentation Manager on OS/2 – IBM; Finder with toolkit on MacOS – Apple Computers). The GUIs on the left side are used by a number of different manufacturers and utilise the X-windows system which was introduced in 2.23 with reference to its client-server architecture. The X-windows system provides a standard, system independent windowing system which is non-proprietary and therefore open to widespread use on a variety of systems. A system based upon such non-proprietary standard facilities is sometime called an **Open System**.

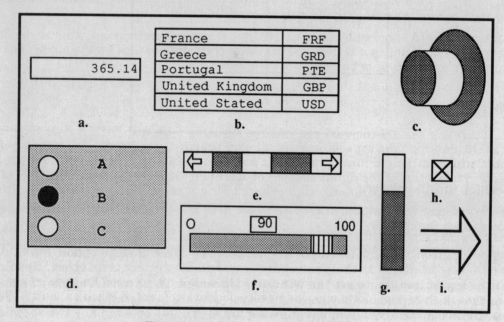

Figure 2.12 Some common widgets

GUI widgets

2.29 As was indicated above, when a GUI interface is used the various displays tend to be constructed from a series of common components called **widgets**. Widgets are created, operated upon and removed, by the applications software through the API toolkit. The widgets used for document processing or graphics tend to be specialised and specific to the application. Such widgets are normally constructed from simpler standard ones. However, general purpose applications tend to be built from a small set of standard widgets. For example, commercial application may require screens which resemble menus and forms. Figure 2.12 shows a variety of widgets commonly used to construct GUI interfaces. A brief description of each widgets referenced in figure 2.12 is given below.

a. A simple **box field** is one of the simplest widgets. It can be used to display text or numbers or it can be used for data entry. It may be possible to tab to such a field in addition to using the mouse to select it.

b. A **table field** is normally used for multiple items of text and numbers. The example shows names of countries and their associated international standard currency code. In some cases a table field acts as a window onto a larger number of rows of data. Some scrolling mechanism is then required.

c. A **button** is commonly used as a simple mechanism for turning options on or off by means of a simple click selection on a mouse button.

d. A **radio field** is normally used to allow the user to choose between a limited number of fixed options.

e. A **scroll bar** provides a means of scrolling up and down or left to right within a document. Scroll bars may also be used with table fields.

f. A **slider bar** is similar in appearance to a scroll bar and is sometimes used in much the same way but it is more like a volume control. The reading in the box shows the current setting. Slider bars may also be used to select from one of a range of numbered pages in a document, whereas within each page the scrolling may be performed using a scroll bar.

g. A **bar field** is normally used as a means of graphically representing a reading. Perhaps the most common use of bar fields is one in which several are put together side by side to form a statistical bar chart.

h. A **toggle field** is normally used to turn options on or off and to show their current status. A blank toggle field box usually indicates that the option is not selected and a cross in the toggle field box indicates that the item is selected.

i. An **arrow field** is normally used as a means of navigation from one window display to the next or previous one in a series. The user uses the mouse to click on the arrow. The arrow is in effect a special type of button.

Using WIMPs

2.30 **Mice.** There are several common conventions for using mice with WIMP style GUI interfaces such as the desktop. The conventions are all very similar but vary with the number of buttons on the mouse and the graphical style of the windows and icons. It is easier to switch from one convention to another if the different types of operation are recognised. For the sake of simplicity in what follows the operations will be described in terms of the actions taken with a mouse having a single button.

2.31 **Types of mouse operation.** Here is a brief description. More detailed examples follow shortly.

a. **Select an item.** The mouse can be used to select an object or menu option. For example, the mouse may be moved so that the pointer on the desktop points at an object. By **clicking** on the mouse button the object can be selected. If an icon is selected its appearance normally changes in some way, for example to white on black instead of black on white. This operation normally involves a single click on the mouse button.

b. **Open an item.** The mouse can be used to **open** a selected icon. For example, the mouse may be pointing at a selected icon for a document. To see the what is inside the document, ie to 'open' it, the mouse button is given a rapid double click.

c. **Show an item's details.** The mouse can be used to show details of an item such as an icon or menu. For example, the mouse may be pointing at a selected item such as a menu name. To see what is on the menu the mouse button is pressed and held down.

d. **Dragging an item.** Items can be moved by means of the mouse. For example, by holding down the mouse button on a selected item, instead of merely clicking the button, and then moving the mouse, the item is moved along with the pointer.

2.32 **Launching an application.** Icons on the desktop are often associated with a particular applications program. For example, documents only to be used with a particular word processing program will all have icons of the same design. When the first such icon is opened to reveal a window displaying the documents contents the Window Management System actually starts the execution of application software. This is know as launching the application.

2.33 In figure 2.13 the mouse has been used to move the pointer above the document 'TITLE A'. If the mouse button is clicked to select the document then the document is brought to the top as is shown in figure 2.14. The documents on the desktop are **open** for use. If the little box in the top left hand corner of a document is selected (i.e. clicked on) the document can be closed (see figure 2.15). As each document is **closed** an icon representing it replaces it on the desktop. In figure 2.16 the situation is shown as it would be after selecting the close box for all three documents shown in figure 2.6). When a document is closed and replaced on the desktop by its icon it has been 'iconized'.

2.34 To restore a document to the open state its icon can first be selected by a single click. It will become highlighted as 'TITLE A' is in figure 2.17. Then it can be opened by double clicking on the mouse button. Alternatively, having selected the item, the **open** option can be selected on the pull-down FILE menu as is shown in figure 2.17. The mouse is first moved above the word 'FILE' at which point the mouse button is held down thus causing the pull-down menu to appear. As the pointer is moved down the menu by means of the mouse, with the button held down all the time, each option is highlighted as the pointer moves over it. For example, in figure 2.17 the option 'Open' is highlighted. By releasing the mouse button when at this point the open operation is selected.

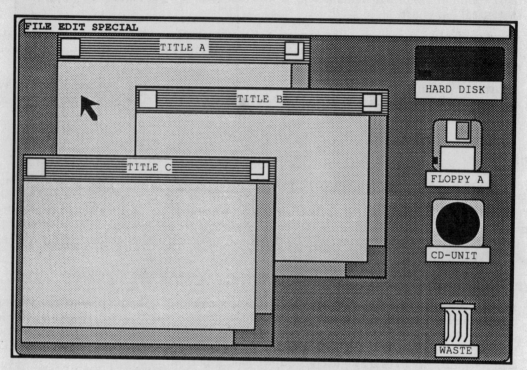

Figure 2.13 A desktop with a WIMP interface

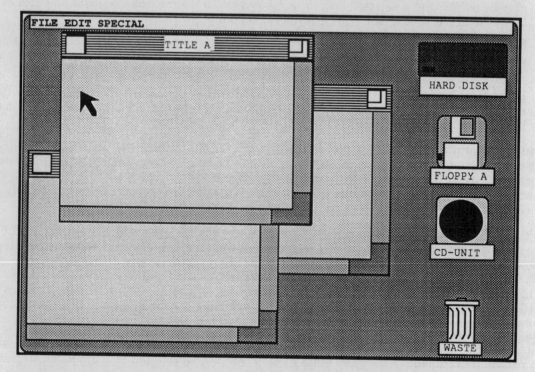

Figure 2.14 A selected window 'title A' brought to the top by a mouse click

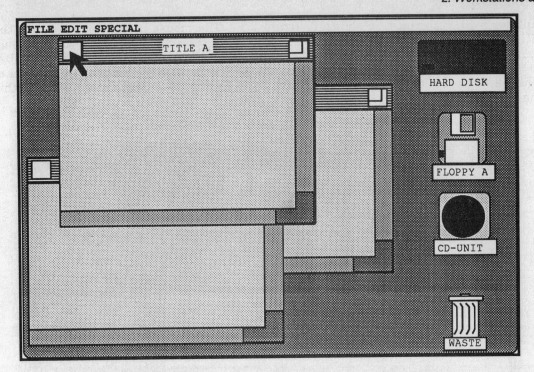

Figure 2.15 The window is closed by clicking the box at the arrow

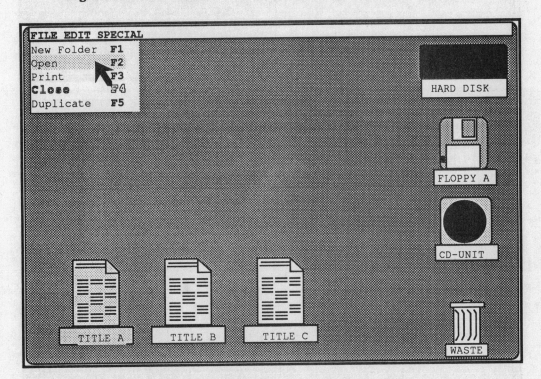

Figure 2.16. The documents have been closed and iconized

2.35 There are some further point to note about the pull-down menu in figure 2.17.

    a. The menu names 'FILE', 'EDIT' and 'SPECIAL' are displayed on what is called the **menu bar**. If a window has a menu bar it normally appears immediately below the **title bar** containing the window's name at the top of the window.

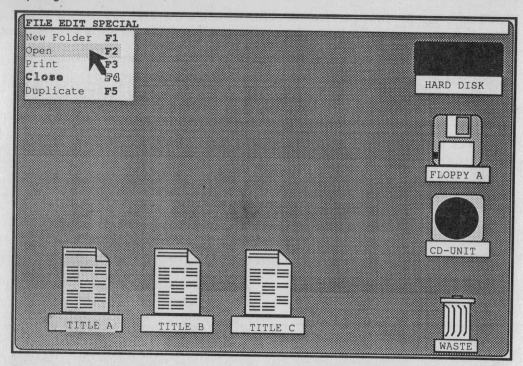

Figure 2.17. A pull-down menu being used to open the selected icon

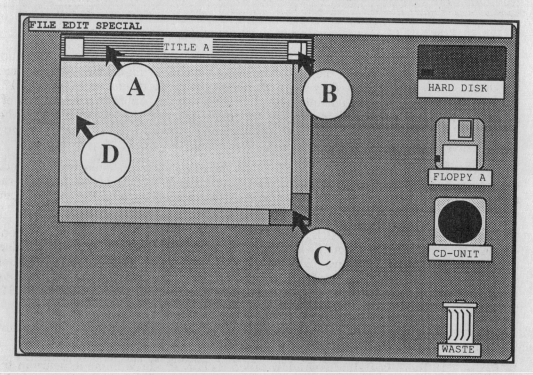

Figure 2.18 Feature of a basic window

b. Beside each option name is the name of a keyboard function key which can be used *instead*. For example, 'F2' is the function key for 'Open'. In general, there may be a combination of keys to use instead of a function key. Some WIMP systems allow for the use of alphabetic characters rather than function keys. Normally, the appropriate letters are underlined where they appear as options in the pull-down menu. For example, the 'O' in 'Open' might be underlined. Such alternatives to using the mouse are called **quick keys**. They are popular with more experienced users because they provide short cuts. This is an example of how a GUI can allow for different levels of expertise in the users. The novice may use the mouse and pull-down menu all the time whereas the expert may use the quick key short cuts.

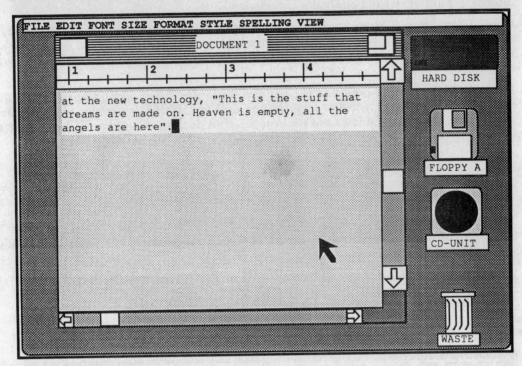

Figure 2.19 A word processor document open on the desktop

c. Sometimes an option appearing on a menu may not be selected because it is not valid in the particular situation. For example, the 'close' option is only available for an 'open' document. This fact is normally indicated by some simple means on the menu, as in figure 2.17 where the word 'close' is shown in outline instead of normal print. Another popular way of representing this is to show the letters of the option word in grey instead of black. If the document 'TITLE A' had not been selected, as shown in figure 2.17, then only the menu option 'New Folder' would have been available.

d. In figure 2.17 the first option on the file menu is 'New Folder'. A folder is one aspect of the desktop metaphor. Just as on a real desktop there may be folders containing several documents, so on the GUI desktop there can be an icon representing a folder which if opened reveals a display of the icons of the documents it contains.

e. The menu headers such as 'FILE', 'EDIT' and 'SPECIAL' may vary depending upon which window is currently selected and what the window contains. For example, when a document is open and selected as in figure 2.19. the 'EDIT' options may depend on the kind of document. For example, if the document is a word processor document there may be lots of options whereas the option for the desktop might be limited to 'CUT', 'COPY', 'PASTE' and 'CLEAR'.

2.36 Within a given Windows Management System the windows all have a set of basic features and facilities. Typical examples are given below.

a. In figure 2.18 there is a simple window called 'TITLE A' whose name appears in the **title bar** (label 'A'). If the window is iconized the icon has the same name as the window. If a document is stored in a file the document's window name is usually the same as the file name.

b. At the left end of the title bar there is normally a box which can be clicked on to close the window (figure 2.18). If there is a menu bar below the title bar that sometimes has a box at its left end with a number of standard options on it similar to those shown under 'FILE' in figure 2.17

  c. Label 'B' in figure 2.18 points to box at the right end of the title bar. Boxes in this position are often used to change the size of the window. In the simplest case a click on the box will alternately either expand or shrink the window.

  d. Label 'C' in figure 2.18 points to another facility to **resize** a window. When this symbol is dragged the top right corner of the document stays where it is but the document becomes wider, narrower, longer or shorter depending upon the direction in which the symbol is dragged.

  e. Label 'D' in figure 2.18 points to the window contents. These depend upon the type of window. For example, the window forming the desktop itself is merely a plain surface upon which icons or other windows are superimposed. A document window will normally contain text (figure 2.19).

Summary

2.37 a. Workstations are desktop computers with advanced capabilities.

  b. Applications packages benefit considerably from the use of GUIs.

  c. The GUI software is organised in layers including components such as windows libraries, API toolkits and windows managers.

  d. Widgets are the basic graphical objects from which GUIs are constructed.

  e. The WIMP interface provides a very successful and popular GUI.

Points to note

2.38 a. A **desktop** computer is, as the name suggests, any computer that can be used on a desk or table. The three common types of desktop computers are Home Computers, Personal Computers and Workstations.

  b. When using graphical displays heavy demands can be made on the memory used to store images if the image is of high resolution or uses many colours. If the video RAM memory is of fixed size there is a trade off between the level of resolution and the number of colours which can be displayed.

  c. A GUI has particular advantage over the traditional **character based interface** notably the following.

    i. **Graphical symbols** are more easily recognised and memorised than text.

    ii. **Direct manipulation**, for example by pointing and clicking on graphical objects with a mouse, reduces learning time for users and gives them a greater feeling of control.

  d. There is no substitute for first-hand experience of GUIs. The reader is urged to gain such experience and to be ready to describe the use of GUI based applications packages in examinations.

Questions

1. What is the difference between 'scrolling' and 'paging'?

2. Explain the meaning of the expression 'high-resolution bit-mapped graphics display'.

3. What features would you expect a workstation to have?

4. What is the meaning of the term 'multi-tasking'?

5. Explain the terms:

  a. Widget

  b. API

  c. Quick key

3 Spreadsheets

Introduction

3.1 Spreadsheets are popular examples of a **generalised software package**. They are general-purpose tools which can be used for tasks which arise in a variety of different applications involving calculations on rows and columns of numbers.

3.2 Included in the many tasks to which spreadsheets may be applied are: analysing statistics; creating business plans; creating business budgets; estimating business cost, calculating profits or losses; sales forecasting and financial analysis.

3.3 One of the earliest spreadsheet packages was the software package called 'Visicalc' produced by Visicorp Inc. for use on microcomputers. Newer, more advanced versions have since been produced by Visicorp and its competitors. Two very popular spreadsheet packages in widespread use today are LOTUS 1-2-3 and Microsoft's EXCEL. Indeed spreadsheet packages are some of the most widely sold items of software.

3.4 This chapter is illustrated by examples from a windows based version of Microsoft's EXCEL so that the reader has practical examples of a real product. The particular version shown works on an Apple Macintosh. However, the features being described are general in nature. Therefore, the practical details can readily be applied to other spreadsheet packages.

	A	B	C	D	E
1		CUSTOMER	F Bloggs	ESTIMATE	
2					
3	MATERIALS	UNIT COST	QUANTITY	TOTAL COST	
4					
5	White Gloss (Small)	2.00	0	0.00	
6	White Gloss (Large)	3.50	2	7.00	
7	Coloured Gloss (Small)	2.50	3	7.50	
8	Coloured Gloss (Large)	4.00	1	4.00	
9	White Emulsion (Large)	2.50	0	0.00	
10	White Emulsion (Large)	4.50	1	4.50	
11	Coloured Emulsion (Small)	3.00	0	0.00	
12	Coloured Emulsion (Large)	5.50	3	16.50	
13	Cleaning Materials	3.00	1	3.00	
14					
15	ALL MATERIALS			42.50	
16					
17					

Figure 3.1 A simple spreadsheet

General features

3.5 Figure 3.1 shows a complete computer display being used for a spreadsheet package. Some of the general GUI windows features should be familiar from the descriptions given in chapter 2. For example, the **menu bar** along the top has a number of menu choices on display. A window with the name, 'Worksheet1', on its **title bar** occupies much of the screen and has **slide bars** on its right side and bottom edge. Within this window is a spreadsheet. Across the top of the screen below the menu bar is what is called a **tool bar.** It containing a set of buttons with **icons** on them which are used to perform special operations (details later). Below the tool bar is a **'formula bar'**. This is a feature specific to spreadsheet packages and will be described shortly.

3.6 The spreadsheet in the window in Figure 3.1 show some estimates relating to a painting and decorating job. The **spreadsheet** comprises a grid of numbered rows and lettered columns.

Each grid position is called a **cell** and can contain text, numerical values or dates. It is possible to define formulae by which values in some cells can be calculated from values in other cells. When using the spreadsheet package on the computer the user sees only part of the spreadsheet in the window. The formula bar displays details about the status of one cell currently being edited. The method of presenting this information varies from on package to another. A cell is selected for editing by moving the cursor about the screen until it is at that cell's position. This may be done by cursor keys or by means of a mouse. In figure 3.1 cell B1 is selected as is indicated at the left end of the formula bar. Cell B1 contains the text value 'CUSTOMER', also displayed on the formula bar where it may be edited by the user typing any changes. The cross and tick buttons on the menu bar may be used respectively to cancel or confirm an edit. In Figure 3.2 Cell B6 contains a numerical value which is currently being edited.

File Edit Formula Format Data Options Macro Window

B6 | 3.5

Worksheet1

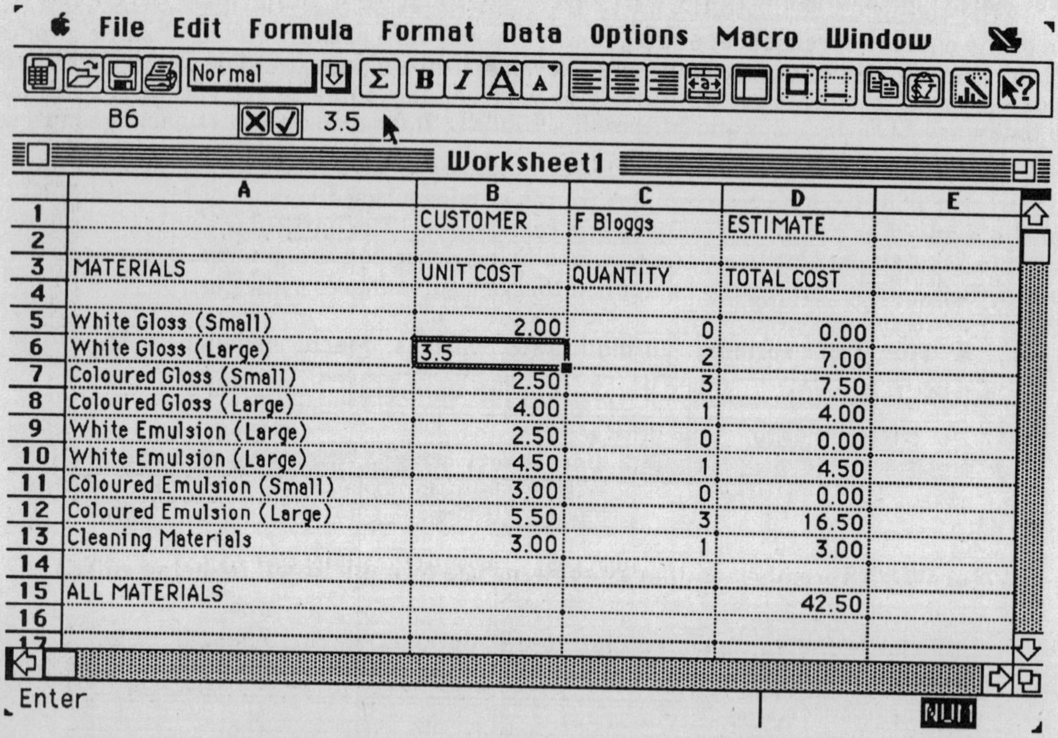

	A	B	C	D	E
1		CUSTOMER	F Bloggs	ESTIMATE	
2					
3	MATERIALS	UNIT COST	QUANTITY	TOTAL COST	
4					
5	White Gloss (Small)	2.00	0	0.00	
6	White Gloss (Large)	3.5	2	7.00	
7	Coloured Gloss (Small)	2.50	3	7.50	
8	Coloured Gloss (Large)	4.00	1	4.00	
9	White Emulsion (Large)	2.50	0	0.00	
10	White Emulsion (Large)	4.50	1	4.50	
11	Coloured Emulsion (Small)	3.00	0	0.00	
12	Coloured Emulsion (Large)	5.50	3	16.50	
13	Cleaning Materials	3.00	1	3.00	
14					
15	ALL MATERIALS			42.50	
16					
17					

Enter

Figure 3.2. A spreadsheet display showing the numerical value in cell B6 being edited.

3.7 Numerical values can either be entered directly, by moving the cursor to the cell position, **OR** they may be calculated from other values. For example, values in columns B and C have been entered directly, but values in column D are calculated by multiplying unit-costs by quantities. Formulae are typed in the same way as values. The formula for cell D6 is '=B6 * C6' (see figure 3.3). The spreadsheet program automatically recognises a formula from the initial '=' sign as it is typed in by the user on the formula bar. It recognises formulae by initial '+' and '-' signs too. The symbols for add, subtract, multiply and divide are respectively '+', '-', '*', and '/'. The formula for cell D7 will be like the formula for D6 except that the row number will be different. To save the laborious task of typing in the formula again a facility is provided for copying formulae from one cell to another and making the necessary adjustments on the way. So to get the formula into cell D6 the user may use the 'Edit' menu on the menu bar to copy the formula in D5 and then paste automatically adjusted version of it into cells D6, D7, D 8, D9, D10, D11, D12 and D13. As the formulae are entered in each cell the cell values are automatically calculated.

3.8 Mathematical functions may also be used in formulae. In figure 3.4 the total of the number in column D rows 5 to 13 is specified by a formula in cell D15 by means of a 'SUM' function in which a range of cells in a row or column can be specified and added up. The expression 'SUM(D5:D13)' means add all cell in column D from row 5 to row 13 inclusive. This is clearly much more convenient than writing a formula such as '= D6 + D7 + D8 + D9 + D10 + D11 + D12 + D13'. Many other functions are available too for a number of different purposes in these areas:

a. General Mathematics.

b. Statistics.

c. Trigonometry.

d. Logic.

e. Text manipulation.

f. Logic.

g. Finance.

h. Dates.

These are in addition to basic operations such as '+', '−', '*', '/', '>', '<', '<=', '< =', '< >', and '&'. The last one performs string concatenation (i.e. joins two text values together).

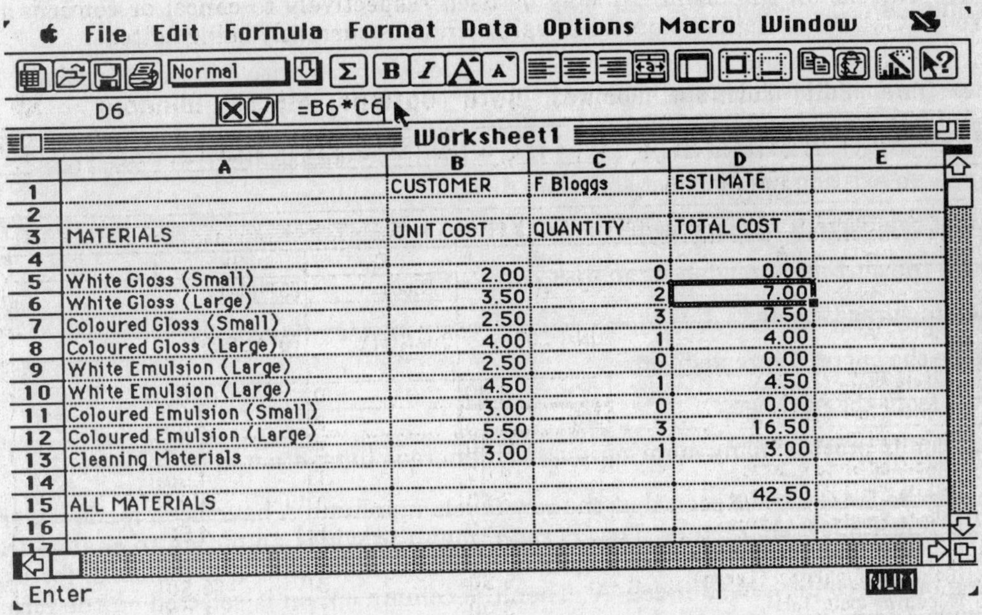

Figure 3.3 A spreadsheet display showing the formula in cell D6 being edited

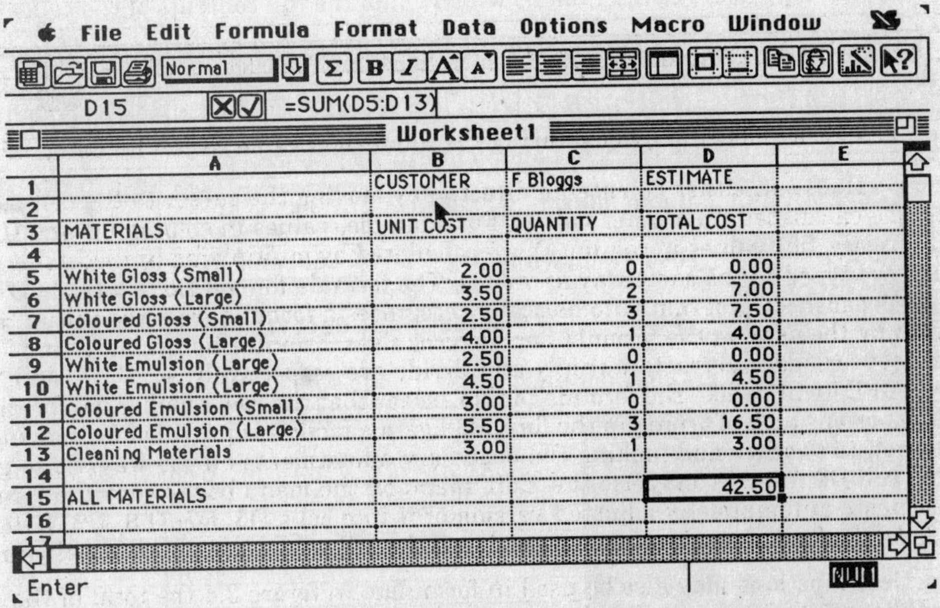

Figure 3.4 A spreadsheet display showing the formula in cell D15 being edited

3.9 Having done the basic calculation the user can then carry out enquiries of the **'what if?'** variety such as 'what if I mark up the material costs by 10%' Various kinds of data manipulation are possible:

a. Inserting, deleting or copying rows and columns.

b. Changing the spreadsheet layout or the precision of displayed numerical values.

c. Printing the spreadsheet or saving a copy on disk for future use.

d. Performing comprehensive computation using mathematical functions and formulae.

3.10 With these functions the spreadsheet can be used for a wide variety of problems: job costing or production estimation; balance sheets and statements; simple forecasting; asset depreciation. Now for more examples of the spreadsheet package.

Further examples

3.11 Each **pull-down menu** on the menu bar provides the user with a series of options. For example, the file menu provides the means to:

a. create a new spreadsheet,

b. open an existing spreadsheet stored on disk,

c. print the current spreadsheet,

d. save the current spreadsheet on disk,

e. delete spreadsheets,

f. close the current spreadsheet,

g. quit from the package.

Other menus provide many more options, to numerous to mention in detail here.

3.12 From Figure 3.4 it can be seen that the row labels in column A have been made wider than the default width of 10 characters. The 'Format' menu provides an option to change the column width in this way. The user first selects the column by means of the mouse, for example by clicking on the column header cell 'A'. Then the column option is selected on the format menu. In Figure 3.5 the user has typed in the new column width of 24 and is ready to click on 'OK' for it to be applied. Incidentally, if the column width is left at 10 then longer text can be typed into the cell but the cell will act as a scrollable window into the full contents of the cell.

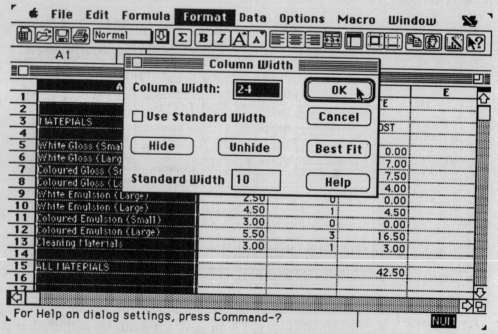

Figure 3.5 Adjusting the width of column A from the FORMAT menu

3.13 The FORMAT menu has a number of other options. It can be seen from the figures described so far that the format of the numerical values in columns B and D are to two decimal places whereas those in column C are formatted as whole numbers. A format can be applied to a single cell, a range of cells or a whole columns. In figure 3.6 the cell D15 is having its format set.

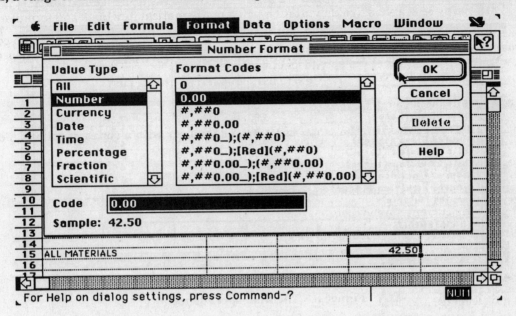

Figure 3.6 Adjusting a numerical cell format from the FORMAT menu

3.14 In Figure 3.7 a further FORMAT menu option is being used to put lines around the border of the cells on row 15. The user merely points and clicks on the options required by means of the mouse. The result is more easy to see in figure 3.8.

3.15 Also in Figure 3.8 it can be seen that the text in rows 1, 2 and 3 and in column A has been altered to appear in bold type. This is achieved by first highlighting the cells by means of the mouse and then clicking on the 'B' symbol on the tool bar. The 'I' symbol on the tool bar is used to produce italic style text.

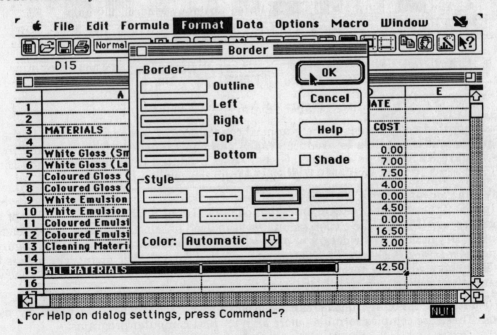

Figure 3.7 Placing borders around cell

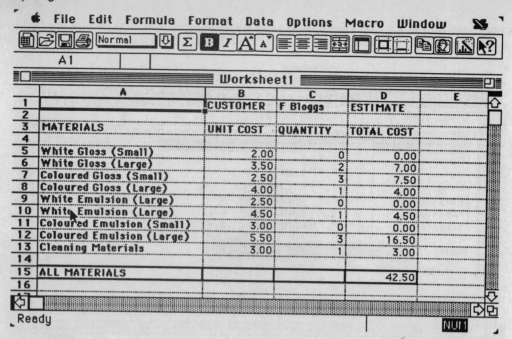

Figure 3.8 The final spreadsheet

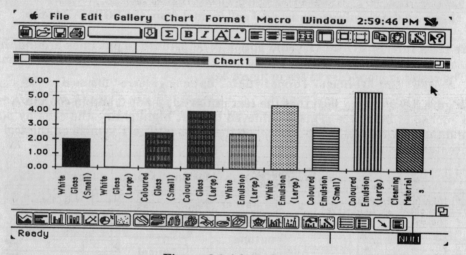

Figure 3.9 A bar chart

3.16 Now we come to two examples of the graphical capabilities of spreadsheets. Within the spreadsheet package it is possible to produce graphs and charts directly from the data on spreadsheets. Figure 3.9 shows an example of a bar chart produced from columns A and B of worksheet1 and Fig 3.10 shows a pie chart produced from the same data.

3.17 By way of a contrast Figure 3.11 shows a different spreadsheet containing simple revenue figures. In row 2 the columns contain dates, which may also be displayed in a number of alternative formats, e.g. '1/2/93'. The option menu has been used to select an area of the spreadsheet to be printed. Discussions of the details of precisely how to do this are not merited. In figure 3.12 a print preview screen is shown. This option was selected from the file menu. The idea is to allow the user to check what the spreadsheet will look like before printing it. Figure 3.13 shows a further example of a chart, which is based upon this spreadsheet.

3.18 Further more complex arithmetic can be performed by spreadsheet packages by means of **macros**. These are complex formulae more akin to short computer programs.

3.19 There are still more features present in many modern spreadsheet packages, including means of connecting spreadsheets to databases and linking data across multiple spreadsheets and with text in word processors. However, the methods are somewhat specialised and product specific.

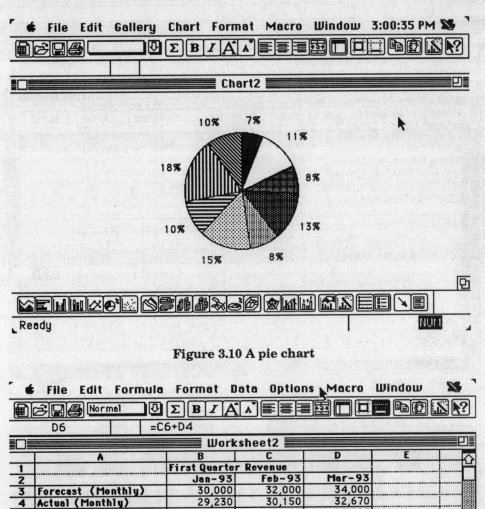

Figure 3.10 A pie chart

	A	B	C	D	E
1		First Quarter Revenue			
2		Jan-93	Feb-93	Mar-93	
3	Forecast (Monthly)	30,000	32,000	34,000	
4	Actual (Monthly)	29,230	30,150	32,670	
5	Forecast (Cumulative)	30,000	62,000	96,000	
6	Actual (Cumulative)	29,230	59,380	92,050	

Figure 3.11 Another simple spreadsheet.

3.20 This concludes the discussion of spreadsheets. The reader is urged to seek first hand experience of spreadsheet packages.

Summary

3.21 A **spreadsheet** comprises a grid of numbered rows and lettered columns intersecting in cells. A cell can contain either text or numerical values.

3.22 **Spreadsheet packages** provide a wide range of facilities for creating and manipulating formatted tables and charts of values.

Points to note

3.23 A typical spreadsheet can contain a large numbers of cells e.g. 8192 rows (numbered 1,2,3...) and 256 columns (labelled A,B,C...AA,AB,AC...).

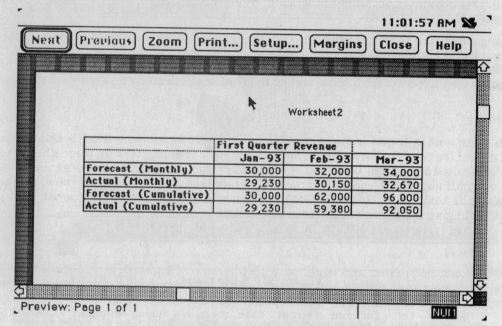

Figure 3.12 A print preview

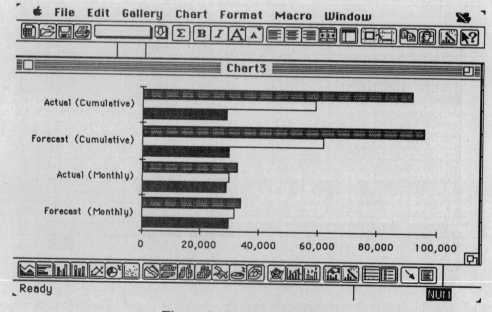

Figure 3.13. Another chart.

Question

Explain this statement. 'Spreadsheets are very valuable for carrying out 'what if' calculations'.

4 Document processing

Introduction

4.1 Computers are very widely used for the creation, manipulation and storage of documents but there is enormous variation in the methods used and in the levels of sophistication. This chapter surveys computer document processing from the most basic forms to the more complex and specialised.

4.2 When considering software used for a particular kind of application it is always important to judge it by its appropriateness for its purpose and by whether the benefits justify the costs. This applies to document processing software where the simpler and less costly software is aimed at purposes very different from those served by more sophisticated and expensive software.

Document files

4.3 Each document is stored in the computer individually *by name* in what is called a **file**. Many document files take the form of a formatted sequence of characters. In their simplest form such files are called **text files** because they consist of printable characters organised into lines of text. A small number of 'control characters' signify tabs, page breaks and the divisions between lines. If the text file is output the control characters cause the output device (e.g. printer or monitor) to give the document the required format.

Editors

4.4 Text files can be created and modified with the aid of a special program called an **editor** (or more precisely a **text editor**). Many documents not requiring anything but a very basic page layout are prepared in this way. This applies to most computer programs.

4.5 The most basic types of editor provide means of editing text files on a line by line basis with each line being identified by a line number. These **'line editors'** are rather outdated and do not merit further discussion.

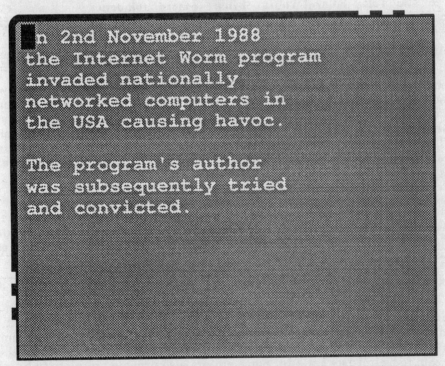

Figure 4.1 Top left corner of a screen display when using a simple text editor

4.6 Modern text editors normally display the file's text on the screen. There are numerous text editors in use today and they are often associated with particular operating systems. For example, the editor 'Vi' is commonly found on computers using an operating system called 'Unix'. However, the functions provided are broadly the same.

4.7 The common functions of text editors are illustrated by the following example based upon a text file with the name 'mydoc.txt'. The '.txt' at the end of the file name follows a common practice of indicating the type of file by means of a suffix following a '.'. Here 'txt' is a common abbreviation for 'text'.

4.8 Text editors can be used both to create new and to edit existing files. When an existing text file is edited the editor 'reads' the characters from the file and displays them on the screen. The editor may also display the cursor in the top left hand corner as shown in figure 4.1 on the previous page.

4.9 The cursor can be moved around the document by means of the four cursor keys (figure 4.2). So, for example, if the 'down' cursor key is depressed three times followed by four depressions of the 'right' cursor key the cursor will end up as shown in figure 4.3.

4.10 The text file will normally hold far more characters than can fit onto one screen display. A typical screen is 80 characters wide and may only display about 24 lines of text (slightly less than half of a printed page). The document size is not limited to this size. As more lines of text are typed, the earlier lines move off the top of the screen. Although they have disappeared from view they are still retained within the computer's memory.

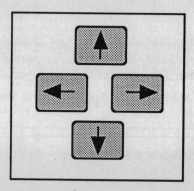

Figure 4.2 The four cursor keys

4.11 The screen thus acts like a **window** on the text, which can be moved up or down by means of the **cursor keys**. For example, if the cursor is at the bottom of the screen then a further depression of the 'down' cursor key will cause the next line of text to appear at the bottom of the screen, with all other lines being moved up one position causing the top line to no longer be displayed. The text file is like text on a scroll, only a small part of which can be seen at any one time through the window (see figure 4.4). The scroll is rolled up or down by moving the cursor, a process referred to as **scrolling**.

4.12 As characters are typed across the screen there comes a point when a new line is required. A typist has to decide if the word about to be typed will fit on to that line. In some editors this is catered for automatically because the editor counts the number of spaces remaining and forces the word onto a new line if necessary. This feature is called **word wrap**. The carriage return key is thus used only to force a blank line.

4.13 If a word has been typed incorrectly it is quite easy to move the cursor to the offending word and correct the mistake. This particular process is also referred to as **editing**.

4.14 New characters, words or several lines can also be inserted into existing text. The cursor is moved to the appropriate point and the new characters typed. They will automatically be inserted into the text with the following text being moved along to accommodate the changes. The editor is said to be in **insert mode**. Some editors also provide an **overstrike mode** in which the typed text replaces that previously displayed.

4.15 Most editors also incorporate '**cut and paste**' facilities whereby a section of text can be selected and moved to a different part of the document. A variation on this is to *copy* the selected section of text, without removing it from its original position.

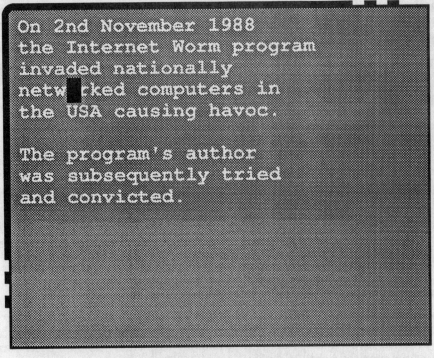

On 2nd November 1988
the Internet Worm program
invaded nationally
netw rked computers in
the USA causing havoc.

The program's author
was subsequently tried
and convicted.

Figure 4.3 The display from figure 4.1 with the cursor moved

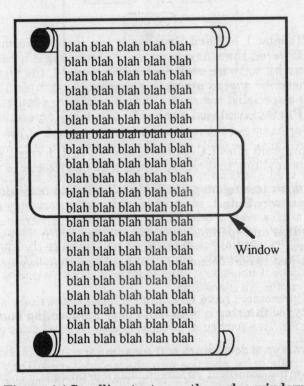

blah blah blah blah blah
blah blah blah blah blah
blah blah blah blah blah
blah blah blah blah blah
blah blah blah blah blah
blah blah blah blah blah
blah blah blah blah blah
blah blah blah blah blah
blah blah blah blah blah
blah blah blah blah blah
blah blah blah blah blah
blah blah blah blah blah
blah blah blah blah blah
blah blah blah blah blah
blah blah blah blah blah
blah blah blah blah blah
blah blah blah blah blah
blah blah blah blah blah
blah blah blah blah blah
blah blah blah blah blah

Window

Figure 4.4 Scrolling text seen through a window

Such operations often require the use of special function keys. The selection is normally made by first 'marking' a start position and then moving the cursor to the end position. A typical set of operations would be as follows.

a. **Key F1.** This is pressed at the current cursor position to mark the start of a selection. Normally the text will be **highlighted** in some way, for example by displaying it underlined, as the cursor is moved to the end position.

b. **Key F2.** This is pressed at the current cursor position to 'CUT' the marked highlighted text.

c. **Key F3.** This is pressed at the current cursor position to 'COPY' the marked highlighted text.

d. **Key F4.** This is pressed at the current cursor position to 'PASTE' the text which was previously cut or copied.

4.16 The editor may provide other function on highlighted text. For example, it might be possible to save the highlighted text in a separate new text file. Another example would be changing the highlighted text from lowercase (small letters) to upper case (capitals) or visa versa.

4.17 A **'search and replace'** facility is another frequently provided feature. It allows the user to replace a single word or phrase wherever it occurs in the document with another word or phrase. A report containing several references to 'Mr. Smith', for example, could be changed quite easily to refer to 'Mr. Reginald Smith'. Again, function keys are often used for such functions. For example, on pressing the 'F5' key the user might be prompted by the question 'FIND ?'. On typing 'Mr. Smith' a second prompt 'REPLACE BY ?' might appear to which the user might respond 'Mr. Reginald Smith'. The editor might provide further prompts to determine whether or not every occurrence of 'Mr. Smith' was to be replaced or just the first one.

4.18 Many more features may be provided by a text editors but the aim here has merely been to make the reader aware of the basic functions of a text editor. It is expected that readers will also gain practical experience of using a particular text editor as part their courses so further discussion is not merited here.

Word processing

4.19 As was mention in Chapter 1, a **Word Processor** is a specialist computer used for the production of documents. However, these days most word processing is actually carried out using specialist **word processing** software on ordinary PCs. Indeed, the term **word processor** is increasingly used to describe a word processing program or complete word processing software package rather than a specialist computer. Examples of very popular word processing software packages are **WordPerfect** produced by the WordPerfect Corporation and **Word** produced by Microsoft.

4.20 A word processing program allows the user to create, edit, format, store and print text documents. A document is anything that can be typed: a memo, a letter, a report or a book.

4.21 At face value a word processing program is very similar to text editor because the two have many functions in common. In fact, some advanced text editors may reasonably be called word processing programs. However, a typical word processing program has far more capabilities than a normal text editor and operates on document files which have a far more complex format than normal text files. To qualify for the title **word processing program** the software must provide facilities not just to edit documents but to define their layout and to enable them to be printed.

4.22 In most offices word processors have virtually replaced typewriters as the means of producing documents. Compared with using a typewriter, word processing has a number of advantages which include:

a. The ability to store typed documents in the computer.

b. The ability to view the document on screen before printing.

c. The ability to correct mistakes.

d. The ability to insert or delete words, sentences or paragraphs.

e.   The ability to move sections of text to another part of the document.

f.   The ability to store documents on backing store for later recall.

g.   The ability to incorporate other text without having to retype it. For example, a standard form or letter can be re-used again and again.

h.   The ability to change the layout of the document.

i.   The ability to print the document many times.

4.23   Many professional writers (journalists, authors, novelists etc.) also use word processing packages.

4.24   Most word processing programs work in a similar way to text editors although they commonly display more useful information on the screen for the benefit of the user. For example, it is common for the word processor to display a **status line** at the bottom of the screen giving details of the documents name and the current page and line numbers. Often, a printed plastic overlay for the keyboard, called a '**template**', is provided too. The template is used to label the function keys with their word processing operations.

4.25   Many packages claim to provide '**WYSIWYG**' or 'what you see is what you get'. This means that the representation of the document on screen is very close to how it will appear when printed. Assuming that a printer is connected to the computer, the document can be printed out at any time as often as is required.

A word processing program allows the user to create, edit, format, store and print text documents. A text document is anything that can be typed: a memo, a letter, a report or a book.

a. Left-justified

A word processing program allows the user to create, edit, format, store and print text documents. A text document is anything that can be typed: a memo, a letter, a report or a book.

b. Right-justified

A word processing program allows the user to create, edit, format, store and print text documents. A text document is anything that can be typed: a memo, a letter, a report or a book.

c. Fully justified

Figure 4.5 Examples of text justification

4.26   The document is viewed on screen before printing and changes to the layout or format of the document can also be made. Controls over the format of the document include:

a.   setting and changing the page size;

b.   setting and changing page header and footer text;

c.   setting and changing the width of the left-hand or right-hand margins for particular paragraphs;

d.   setting and changing the page numbering style and position;

e.   setting and changing the style and size of printed characters (e.g. bold, italic, normal size or subscript size).

4.27 Another common formatting technique is **text justification** which means the alignment of text against a margin. **Left justification** means alignment against the left margin, **right justification** means alignment against the right margin and **full justification** means both left and right justification (see figure 4.5). For full justification, extra spaces are inserted by the program into lines of text to ensure a straight right hand edge to the document. Another example is the centring of text. Adjusting these formatting parameters is often achieved by means of special function keys on the computer keyboard.

4.28 When a document has been completed it can be saved for long term storage onto backing store as a file. The file normally has a format much more complex than that of a text file and is usually only directly usable by the word processing program which created it. The same document can be loaded back into the word processing program at a later time without it needing to be retyped. Further corrections or amendments can then be made.

4.29 This facility also allows other files to be merged into a new document. For example, a file containing a document of a current price list can be added to a letter to be sent out to a potential client. Only the letter needs to be typed. The technique of building up a document from standard paragraphs, such as clauses in a contract, is known as **boilerplating**.

4.30 Within a word processing software package there may be a number of ancillary programs which can be used in conjunction with word processed documents to enhance the standard facilities. One such facility is the process known as **mail-merge**. In this it is possible to produce a standard letter into which the name and address (and other details) of a number of clients in turn are merged and a series of individual letters printed. Each recipient of the letter receives an original print.

4.31 **Spell checkers.** Many word processing packages now include spell checking facilities. The spell check program comes with its own dictionary of from 20,000 to 100,000 words and is able to scan through the document and report wherever a word is found which does not exist in its dictionary. The user is then able to correct the word or leave it as it was originally spelt. Unless they have facilities for adding new words to the dictionary spell checkers have difficulty recognising people's names and postcodes as correct 'words'.

4.32 Some spell checking programs can be left to search through a document and mark every doubtful word for later checking by the user (useful for very long documents) rather than provide interactive facilities. Others can check against their dictionary of words so quickly that they can provide immediate feedback to the user as each word is typed in.

4.33 Many spell checkers provide the user with a list of alternative words which are similar in spelling or sound to the doubtful word. Some also allow the user to create and maintain their own dictionary of words, which is very useful if the user constantly refers to specialised or 'jargon' words in a particular subject area (e.g. chemical compounds).

4.34 It should be pointed out that spell checking programs cannot guarantee that every spelling mistake will be detected in a document. The words 'there' and 'their', for example, are correctly spelt only if used in the correct context. The words 'fore examples' are both correctly spelt in themselves, but are incorrect if 'for example' was intended. Another common mistake in documents is double-typing of the the same word, as in this sentence. Programs aimed at detecting these types of mistakes are often referred to as **grammar checkers** or **style checkers**.

4.35 Style checkers also help to identify unnecessary words or wordy phrases which appear in the document. To help eliminate repetition, these programs can check to see if particular patterns of words appear again and again in the document, and they can also indicate if sentences seem too long.

4.36 Yet another useful facility is a **thesaurus**. This is a program which allows the user to choose an alternative word to a selected word. A thesaurus is basically a dictionary of synonyms (similar words) and antonyms (dissimilar words), and the user points to a particular word and is presented with a list of alternatives.

4.37 Many text documents also need to include tables and charts, and some word processing packages incorporate limited graphics capability to allow lines and borders to be drawn around such tables. There is often a need to bring data into a document which has been produced on another application package such as a spreadsheet, for example a table of numbers, and many word processing packages allow for this 'importing' of data files from other packages including the importing of document produced by other word processors. An **export** facility is also often provided whereby the document is saved as a simple text file or in the file format used by another word processor.

4.38 More advanced word processors allow for many different fonts to be used in the printed document. The size of each printed character in these fonts can also be changed.

4.39 If the word processing software is sufficiently advanced in its control over page layout, printed fonts, diagrams and typography in general it may be said to perform **computerised typesetting**. The use of such computerised typesetting software on small computers such as PCs and Workstation has given rise to the term **Desktop Publishing (DTP)**. However, there is more to DTP than merely using advanced word processing software and, indeed, some forms of DTP do not used word processors for text preparation.

Times Roman 9pt

Times Roman 10pt

Times Roman 12pt

Times Roman 14pt

Times Roman 18pt

Times Roman 24pt

Times Roman 9pt

Times Roman 10pt

Times Roman 12pt

Times Roman 14pt

Times Roman 18pt

Times Roman 24pt

Times Roman 9pt

Times Roman 10pt

Times Roman 12pt

Times Roman 14pt

Times Roman 18pt

Times Roman 24pt

Figure 4.6 The Times Roman type family

Desktop publishing (DTP)

4.40 A **Desktop Publishing System** is a desktop computer with the necessary hardware and software to enable the user to carry out computerised typesetting. Typically, a DTP system will be able to handled document layouts involving not only printed text but diagrams and images too. For this reason the monitor screens used in DTP system are normally **bit-mapped** with the grid of **pixels** on the screen being used to represent both images and text characters. The binary codes corresponding to what is on the screen are stored in the computers memory from where they can be *mapped* onto the screen. Printed output also requires the use of devices which can print text and images. A **laser printer** is a common choice.

4.41 We will examine various key areas of DTP in turn starting with the details of type families and leading through to general aspects of page layouts.

4.42 Figure 4.6 shows an example of a popular **type family** called Time Roman. Although there is considerable variation within the examples there is clearly some basic similarity too. Within the type family shown in figure 4.6 there are three **typefaces**. Each typeface is a different **style** of the same type family. At the top is a **plain** typeface. In the middle is a **bold** typeface. At the bottom is an **italic** typeface. Each typeface comes in a number of sizes. A typeface in a specified size is called a **font**. The size is commonly expressed in terms of **points** normally abbreviated to **pt.** (details later). So, '**Times Roman bold 12pt** is a description of a **font** belonging to the **typeface Times Roman bold** which in turn belongs to the **type family Times Roman**.

4.43 In figure 4.7 two further popular typefaces are shown. They are both in the same style but belong to different type families. By way of contrast figure 4.8 shows a series of different styles in the Times Roman type family.

Helvitica 9pt

Helvetica 10pt

Helvetica 12pt

Helvetica 14pt

Helvetica 18pt

Helvetica 24pt

Courier 9pt

Courier 10pt

Courier 12pt

Courier 14pt

Courier 18pt

Courier 24pt

Figure 4.7 Helvetica Plain and Courier Plain type faces

4.44 **Serifs** are the ornate extra strokes which put decorations on individual characters in a font. Characters in the Times Roman type family have serifs whereas the characters in Helvetica do not. Helvetica is therefore said to be a **sans serif** type family (sans meaning *without*). Plain typefaces with serifs tend to create a more serious impression but, more importantly, they are the most readable for large volumes of type. Research has shown that reading speed and accuracy is much higher when such fonts are used which is why most books and newspapers use type families with serifs. San serif typefaces are clearer and are most commonly used for headlines and titles. Also, san serif typefaces photocopy more clearly than typefaces with serifs and are therefore often used for documents such as news sheets or technical papers which may need to be photocopied for a small circulation.

A series of type family styles:

(i)   Plain

(ii)   **Bold**

(iii) *Italic*

(iv)   Underline

(v)   Superscript

(vi)   Subscript

(vii) SMALL CAPITALS

(viii) Outline

and

(ix)   Shadow

Figure 4.8 Type styles

4.45 **Points** were briefly mentioned earlier as a unit with which font sizes are commonly expressed. A point is $1/72$ of one inch. Twelve points make one **pica**. In other words **a pica is one sixth of one inch and a point is one twelfth of one pica**. Such small units are clearly useful in describing something so small as a text characters. Another such small unit, whose size depend upon a fonts size, is the **Em** which is the size of an imaginary square just containing the letter 'm' in a given font. It can be used to measure or estimate the amount of printed type on a line or page.

4.46 **Ligatures** are characters formed from the combination of two character symbols. Two common examples are 'fi' and 'fl'. Originally, the term referred to the strokes combining or binding the two letters together. Ligatures are not only elegant they are another feature which contribute to making a typeface more readable even though the reader is not normally consciously aware of their presence.

4.47 **Kerning** is yet another feature which can make printed text more readable but it a feature of how particular characters are spaced apart rather than of the characters themselves. For example, if kerning is applied to the word 'To' the letter 'o' is set under the end of the 'T'.

4.48 The particular adjustments made to spacing by kerning are quite separate from the normal spaces given between characters. Typewriters and many computer printers use fonts which take equal horizontal space for all characters. These fonts are said to be **monospaced** since there is only one spacing used. All fonts in the **Courier** type family (figure 4.7) are monospaced. Monospaced fonts have the advantage of simplicity and make vertical tabulations easier, especially with columns of numbers, but they are far less easy to read in volume.

4.49 For volumes of text **proportionally spaced** typefaces are superior to monospaced typefaces (i.e. *non* proportionally spaced). In a typeface with proportional spacing the horizontal space allowed for each character depends upon its shape. So, for example, 'o' is allowed more space than 'i'. It is far more complicated to make text fully justified when a proportionally spaced typeface is used. This is one of the many complexities which a DTP system must handle and with which many word processors can not deal.

4.50 **Leading**, pronounced *'ledding'* from the days when lead metal was use in typesetting, is the name given to the vertical space allowed between successive lines of type. **Leading** is also sometimes called the **baseline skip**. The size of the leading is another measurement which affect how readable a text may be and which may adjustable in a DTP system but fixed in a normal word processor.

4.51 DTP systems normally give considerable control over the way the printed page may be formatted. Normally the basic layout, comprising **header**, **body** and **footer** (figure 4.9) can be specified in terms of size position and format. Additionally, the body may be subdivided into a number of **frames** each of which contains a separate portion of the page such as a column of picture. Controls over headers and footers may include the positioning and style of such things as, page numbers, page headers (e.g. italic left justified on even page and right justified on odd), dates and footnotes.

4.52 Most DTP systems provide means of handling diagrams and pictures but the facilities vary considerably. There are basic features such enclosing text in boxes or forming simple figures from boxes circles and lines. More advanced features allow for the inclusion of whole diagrams and pictures as in the case of the DTP system used to produce this book.

4.53 Before a document is output to the printer the user will normally wish to have an indication of what it will look like. In the case of a WYSIWYG system (4.25) this is simple, although the screen display never looks exactly like the printed output. If WYSIWYG is not use a preview option is normally available which creates and displays a close approximation to what the final document will look like. This becomes particularly important in typesetting systems which use special symbol codes to define the way the text is to be typeset. For example, a high quality typesetting system called TeX was produced by Donald Knuth with particular features for defining complex mathematical formulae. In the special version of TeX called LaTeX formulae are defined using standard symbols in a normal text file. The text file is processed by a program to produce a typeset version of the document which can be previewed on the screen or printed.

4.54 The screen display of the WYSIWYG page or preview page normally represents font characters, diagrams and pictures as bit-mapped images. In figure 4.10 an enlarged representation of a bit-mapped letter 'A' is shown to the left. Clearly, a different bit-mapped representation is needed for each font size since, for example, merely scaling up a small font size will result in a jagged image. Scaling down a large font size to a small one typically result in distortion. An alternative approach to this problem is to define each character in the typeface in terms of a series of dots which can be joined up to form an image as is shown to the left in figure 4.10. The principle is basically the same as that used in children's dot-to-dot puzzle books, although done in a more mathematically precise way. The character definition is more complex than one based upon a bit-map but has the advantage of being **scalable**. That is to say the same definition can be used for each font size. The best bit pattern can be generated for each size as and when required.

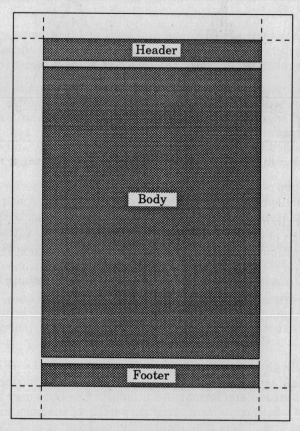

Figure 4.9 Page layout

4.55 The representations just described can also be used as the basis for printed output. The more basic printers capable of printing characters, diagrams and pictures are only able to use bit-mapped representations. The more advanced models are able to interpret instructions defining **scaled image representations** and generate the 'best' bit-mapped representation internally. However, the quality of the image is ultimately limited by the **resolution** of the printer which is normally expressed in terms of the number of **dots per inch (dpi)** that the printer can produce. The higher resolution, ie the higher the number of dpi, the better the image quality can be. A typical laser printer can print 300–400 dpi making a total of 90,000–160,000 dots per square inch. Higher resolutions of about 1,200 dpi are achieved with photo typesetting machines such as **linotronics**. The term **Near Photographic Quality (NPQ)** is sometimes used to describe them although the term NPQ more commonly applies to colour printers of similar resolution.

4.56 The instructions that define scaled image representations of characters to a printer, mentioned previously, are part of what is normally called a **Page Description Language (PDL)**. A PDL is essentially a set of standard instruction for drawing shapes. The shapes may be the scalable characters in a typeface, scalable geometric figures or fixed size bit patterns. Printers able to process DPLs contain small microcomputers dedicated to that task. The printer receives the PDL instructions and then generate the bit-mapped image of each page in its own memory before printing it out. In the case of a complex figure this can take several seconds, or even minutes in extreme cases. Complex images can also only be formed and printed if the printer's computer has enough memory.

4.57 By far the most common PDL is one called **PostScript** which was devised by the Adobe Corporation for Apple's Laser printer but is now widely used with many different makes of computer. The term **PostScript Printer** merely means that the printer is able to interpret PostScript instructions.

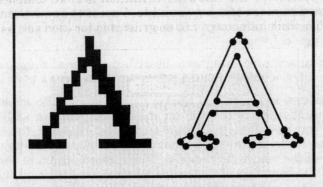

Figure 4.10 A bit-mapped character and its scaled character representation

Document processing using GUIs

4.58 Figure 4.11 shows a simplified representation of a desktop upon which a selected document is being edited by means of a word processor. Note that the menu bar has a series of headings associated with the functions of a word processor. Only one document is open, but in general there is no reason why several documents should not be open at the same time. The selected one will appear on top. If the user select a menu options or types something the actions will be applied to the selected window.

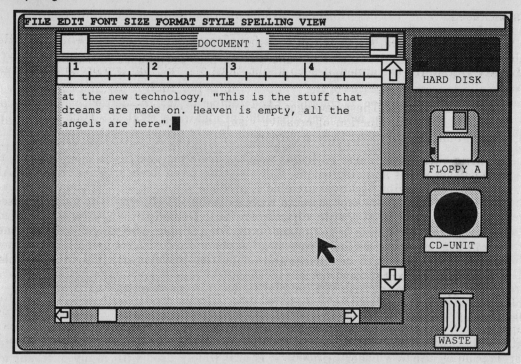

Figure 4.11 A word processor document open on the desktop

4.59 The cut and paste options on the EDIT menu can not only be used within a single document they can also be used to move text between one document and another. Also the user can be editing one document while referring to another. It is these kinds of WIMP features which help users and improve productivity.

4.60 Many aspects of document processing were described earlier so they need not be repeated here. However, there are a few windows related points which deserve a mention.

4.61 **Cursors and pointers.** In figure 4.11 the cursor appears on the screen at the end of the text. This is displayed in addition to the pointer used in conjunction with the mouse. The cursor moves in the same way as it does in a normal situations. However, the cursor can also be moved to a different places in the document by means of the mouse. The pointer is merely moved to the new location and the mouse clicked once. The cursor appears at the new position. To move the pointer beyond the boundary of the visible window so as to scroll the document use is made of the **scroll bar** on the right side of the window. To scroll up the document the top arrow on the scroll bar is selected by means of the mouse. The document scrolls while the mouse button is held down or until the top of the document is reached. Similarly, scrolling down is achieved by performing the same action on the bottom arrow. Alternatively, the rectangular box in the middle of the scroll bar can be dragged up, or down. Its position down the scroll bar signifies the position of the window in the whole document.

4.62 Portions of text can be *selected* for such purposes as cutting, copying and spelling checking. This is done by using the mouse to drag the pointer across the area of text while holding the mouse button down. As the mouse pointer is dragged across the text the selected text becomes highlighted. When the button is released the selected text is left highlighted. Highlighted text normally appears as white on black instead of black on white. A further single click on the mouse, to reposition the cursor, de-selects the text.

4.63 Graphical features can be used to good effect to aid the appearance of the word processor. For example, a ruler can be displayed across the top of the document window so that the user can see the document's width and tab marks. Also, full use can be made of fonts so that the appearance of the document is a close approximation to WYSIWYG. However, the most significant additional facility of the GUI interface for document preparation is the use of graphics packages to produce illustrations for inclusion into documents.

Graphics packages

4.64 As has just be indicated, GUIs can provide benefits even when dealing with text. However, GUIs come into their own when it comes to applications which are inherently visual. **Graphics software packages** are aimed at such applications and fall into two broad categories as follows.

a. **Painting Packages.** These packages are aimed at meeting the needs of artist and graphics designers in the production of creative visual designs. They produce good quality bit-mapped images in black and white or colour.

b. **Drawing Packages.** These packages tend to have a more technical orientation with strict controls over scales and dimensions, although they often have 'arty' features too. Although most modern drawing packages are able to produce output in bit-mapped form they tend to stored images in a more sophisticated ways as **scalable objects**. The principle used is the same as that used for **scalable characters** as described earlier. That is, an object is defined in terms of template of points and lines. For example, a rectangle is defined merely by the relative position of its four corners rather than as a fixed rectangular block of bits. This not only makes it possible to enlarge and reduce the size of objects individually it also make more economic use of storage space.

4.65 In practice the distinction between painting packages and drawing packages is far from clear cut. There are also some packages which are essentially hybrids of the two, such as Aldus Superpaint 3, which within the same package provides both bit-mapped paint facilities and object based draw facilities. Nevertheless, the distinction is a useful one when it comes to indicating the primary use at which the package is targeted.

4.66 Painting packages vary greatly but the more common features can be explained by reference to a simple example. Figure 4.12 on the following page shows a snapshot of a window taken from an Apple Macintosh running an application called 'MacPaint' produced by Claris Ltd. MacPaint is a common and inexpensive package which was one of the very first to be sold and become popular. Most paint packages in use today, even the most sophisticated ones, show the influence of MacPaint. It therefore serves as a useful basic example.

4.67 The features of the example in figure 4.12 are listed below.

a. The main window below the title bar displays part of the complete picture. There are no scroll bars in this package, which is unusual. Instead, the picture is moved beneath the window by means of a 'hand' whose symbol appears on the panel to the left of the picture window.

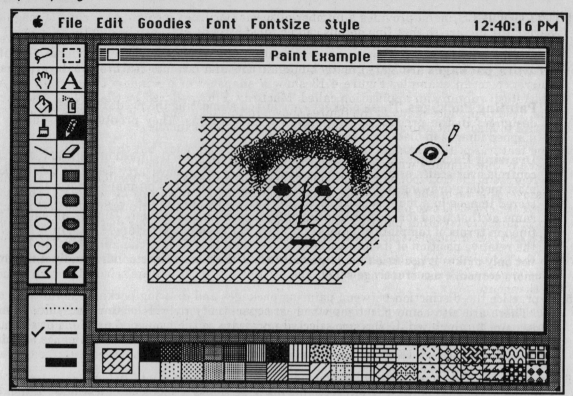

Figure 4.12 A window on a painting document.

b. The panel provides a series of tools which can be used by the user to 'paint' a picture. Currently the **pencil** is selected. Its symbol is highlighted on the panel and it also appears on the picture window just above and to the right of an eye which it has been used to sketch. The mouse controls the pencil on the screen. A line is drawn if the mouse button is held down as the mouse is moved. Other tools on the panel include a brush, a spray can, a paint pot and an eraser. The pain brush was used to paint the eyes on the faces and the spray can was used to paint the hair.

c. Some panel tools are used for drawing lines and shapes as indicated by their symbols. The panel shown bottom left determines line width. The mouse is used to select the required width which is then marked by a tick. One option is a thin dotted line. Lines and shapes are drawn by first selecting them on the main panel and then clicking the position of their start and end points. The remains of a rectangle is visible in the picture. Its top left and bottom corners have been removed by the eraser tool. When the rectangle was drawn the top left corner position was selected by a click on the mouse button. The pointer was then moved to the bottom right corner position which was selected by a second click. Once the rectangle was drawn a pattern was selected from the bottom palette. The selection is still visible in a rectangle at the left end of the palette. That pattern was used to fill the rectangle by clicking the paint pot within the rectangle.

d. The letter 'A' on the panel signifies a tool for producing text on the picture, which is useful for putting labels on diagrams and other illustrations. When this tool is selected the required position for the start of text is selected on the picture by means of the mouse. The keyboard can then be used to type in the required words. Note that there are menu options available for controlling the text style etc.

e. There are two tools at the top of the panel, a lasso and a rectangle, for selecting parts of the picture in order to cut or copy. The lasso is used for irregular shapes.

f. The 'GOODIES' menu provides a number of special facilities including a means of magnifying part of the picture so that fine details can be filled pixel by pixel by clicking them on or off with the pencil.

4.68 **Drawing packages** also vary greatly but again the more common features can be explained by reference to an example. Figure 4.13 show a snapshot of a window taken from an Apple Macintosh running an application called 'MacDraw Pro' produced by Claris Ltd. The package was used to produce many of the figures shown in this text. Since it is a drawing package alternative to MacPaint it provides an appropriate contrasting example.

4.69 The features of the example in figure 4.13 are discussed below but the most obvious point to make is that in many ways it is similar to MacPaint. For example the same symbol 'A' is used to represent the text tool on the left side panel. A new user already familiar with MacPaint will discover that he or she will be able to use many features of MacDraw immediately. This has obvious benefit. The two packages are said to have the same **look and feel**. Readers having the opportunity to try other painting and drawing packages will probably discover that some of the look and feel of these examples will be present in them, although probably to a lesser degree.

4.70 In the picture an irregular shape is part drawn. The little squares on its corners are only displayed because it is currently selected. The position of the corners are selected in turn by means of the mouse.

4.71 The different shapes shown in the picture are separate objects which can be individually moved about and manipulated. Object are selected my means of the mouse. Via options on the menus all manner of operations can be performed upon a selected object. For example, the object may be re-shaped, rotated, filled with a pattern, moved above or below another, enlarged, reduced, cut and pasted and so on.

4.72 A scaled grid is visible on the picture. This hints at the more technical orientation of the drawing package. In this kind of package it is possible to produce drawings to scale and to align objects accurately to a ruled grid or with one another.

4.73 Drawing packages can normally be used to produce very large drawing, covering many pages. The pages can be printed out separately, on a desktop laser printer say, and then pasted up onto one large sheet. However, to gain the full benefit from such a facility the computer needs to be connected to a high quality graphics plotters (details later).

Summary

4.74 a. Documents in the form of text files may be created and modified by text editors.

b. Documents used in word processing typically have more complex forms than text files because of the more advanced document features and are specific to the word processor being used.

c. Typical word processing programs provides more facilities than typical text editors. In particular, they provides more controls over the layout and printing of documents with regard to such things as page size, text justification and page headers or footers.

d. A DTP system uses specialist software and hardware on a desktop computer to perform computerised typesetting. Some advanced word processing packages may be used for DTP but a variety of specialist programs are frequently used too.

e. When documents contain text and images bit-mapping techniques are commonly used and the quality produced depends upon the resolution available and the techniques employed to generate the images.

f. Applications packages used to prepare documents such as word processors benefit considerably from the use of GUIs but GUIs are specially suited to painting and drawing packages.

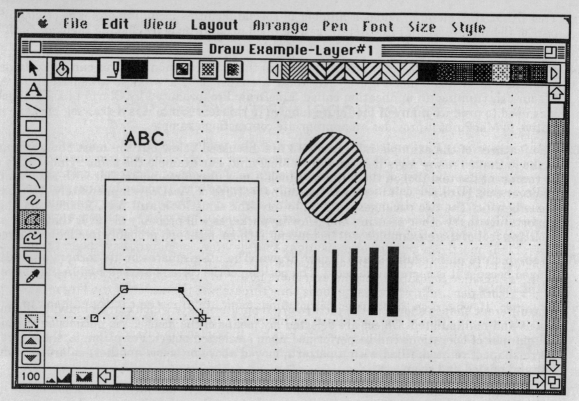

Figure 4.13 A window on a drawing document.

Points to note

4.75 a. The term **word processor** is often used as a *very broad classification* of any program which can be used to created and edit documents.

  b. It is not normally possible to interchange documents in different formats between different document processing programs unless special import or export facilities are provided. Even simple text files come in a variety of formats.

  c. Many word processors are able to export versions of documents as simple text files but most of the document formatting information is lost in the process.

  d. PostScript printers are able to print out simple text documents as well as the more complex ones required for DTP. When printing simple text documents a PostScript Laser printer may print 8–10 documents per minute but the same printer may take several minutes to print a single page if complicated typesetting features have been used.

Questions

1. What are the typical similarities and differences between a text editor and a word processing program?

2. Explain the terms **type family**, **typeface** and **font**.

3. What features of a PostScript printer make it suitable for use with a DTP system?

Conventional Data Processing

In the previous Part on 'Desktop Computing' the reader was familiarised with the use of computers in the office by non computer specialists. This widespread and increasingly familiar use of computers, although very important, is not central to Data Processing (DP). DP continues to be mainly concerned with primary business operations which require the processing of data to provide information. For convenience we will call this 'Conventional DP'. In larger organisations many such conventional DP operations continue to be carried out on mainframe computers and minicomputers. It is mostly in smaller organisations that desktop computers have been established as the main vehicle for conventional DP. Nevertheless, this pattern is changing as smaller computers become ever more powerful and are therefore able to support more demanding processing loads thus threatening the status of the larger machines. However, these changes do not fundamentally alter the continued need to perform conventional DP operations within all organisations. It is the basic principles and practices of conventional DP which are introduced in Chapter 5.

5 Basic DP principles and practices

Introduction

5.1 An **'Information System'** is a complete apparatus for handling all aspects of information within an organisation. It includes everything from the completely human-orientated aspects of information to the technologically orientated aspects. As we have seen, desktop computing can be effective at providing local computer facilities to IT users particularly with regard to document creation and analysis tasks involving spreadsheets. However, the major centralised components of an information system are the data processing systems within it. It is these that provide much of the information that is needed throughout an organisation. Each data processing (DP) system may be designed to fulfil one particular function. Increasingly, however, the DP systems are produced so as to operate as a complete, integrated set of inter-related sub-systems. The more advanced DP systems of this kind are sometimes called 'Information Systems', although they clearly do not deal with all aspects of information and therefore the term is not totally merited.

5.2 Within this chapter the emphasis will be on the practicalities of information systems, this effectively means that the material is focused upon the basic features of DP. Common factors determining the methods of data processing are introduced. The stages of data processing are explained and illustrated. A useful representation of a data processing system is also explained and illustrated. Then the concepts of transactions and batching are introduced.

5.3 **Data processing** (DP) is the term for the process of producing meaningful information by collecting all items of data together and performing operations on them to extract the required information from them. The methods of data processing vary from those that are almost entirely manual to those that rely on the use of large electronic computers. In practice most data processing nowadays will involve the use of some electronic aids such as calculators or small computers, which increase in sophistication year by year.

5.4 At one time electromechanical devices were widely used for DP but the advent of versatile microcomputers hastened their demise.

5.5 Note that prior to the introduction of mechanical, and later electronic, methods of processing large volumes of data, the term 'data processing' was rarely used. The use of computers is so widespread that the term is almost invariably associated in people's minds with Electronic Data Processing (EDP).

Examples of information and data

5.6 The following examples (common to almost all businesses) are explained in relation to the information required and the data needed to obtain that information. The examples have been deliberately selected because they are those with which the reader can (hopefully) readily identify and use as a yardstick throughout his or her studies.

a. **Payroll.** Large and small companies have to pay their employees and the information needs are, at least, the payslip (to show the employee how much he or she has earned and the reasons for deductions, etc), a company record of the payslip details (payroll) and analysis for accounting purposes (total tax deducted, etc). If the employees are paid in cash (as opposed to cheque or direct credit to their bank accounts), then a coin analysis may be needed for the bank. For management control purposes, analysis of labour hours into various categories such as idle time, sickness and absence can be produced. The 'data' from which the information is derived is likely to have come from some form of time records, e.g. time sheets, and recorded details of employees, e.g. tax codes.

b. **Invoice.** Companies selling goods on credit produce an invoice setting out the details of the sale. These include the customer's name and address, the customer's order number, the date of the sale, and the quantity, price, description and value of the goods sold. This invoice (information) is needed to record the customer's indebtedness. The customer order details and seller's details of goods provide the 'data' from which it is compiled.

c. **Statement of Account.** Following on from the invoice example, a summary of all the invoices and payments made by the customer in a month, in the form of a 'statement', is produced and sent to the customer to show the amount still owing. The Statement of Account is the 'Information' coming from invoices and cash receipts (data).

Factors determining the methods of data processing

5.7 Common factors determining the methods of data processing can be explained under the following headings:

    a. Size and type of business.

    b. Timing aspects.

    c. Link between applications.

Size and type of business

5.8 With each of the examples given, the method of producing the information will largely depend on the size and type of business. In a very small company a single person may be able to have the time to produce all the information required, but as the volume of business increases, more people and aids, in the form of calculators and small computers, may be employed. Large volumes of data and information will require the use of large computers.

5.9 In some companies the payroll will be a matter of simply paying a member of staff the same amount each month, whilst in others a complex payment by results system will have to be coped with. Similarly, invoicing may be simply a matter of virtually copying from the customer's order, or it may require complex discount calculations. Simple situations indicate the need for fewer people and aids to produce the information and complex situations indicate the need for more people and aids.

Timing aspects

5.10 Some information requirements are less time critical than others. For example, the Payroll and Statements may only be produced once a month, whereas the invoices may be produced (in certain companies) virtually all the time, i.e. as a customer collects the goods. The timing requirements for information will have considerable bearing on the methods and equipment needed to provide it.

Link between applications

5.11 Where data is needed for more than one information requirement, a different method of processing it may be suggested. For example, an item sold may not only need to be used in the production of the invoice but also be needed to amend the recorded stock position. A manual system would require separate operations to satisfy the requirements, whereas a computer system would include the automatic use of data in both applications. This ability of computer systems to perform a variety of processing operations on a single 'pool' of data contrasts sharply with manual systems. In manual systems the data being used by one individual becomes inaccessible to another individual.

DP stages

5.12 Whatever method, or combination of methods, is used it will be seen that data will pass through the same **basic stages** in the processing cycle. An example is given of the production of a payroll that is simplified for the purpose of illustration but which none the less brings out the salient points.

5.13 Payroll example.

Stage

    i. Details of hours worked by each employee (**data**) is recorded on a time sheet (**source document**). All time sheets are forwarded to the wages office. The source documents will be sorted into the sequence required by the payroll.

    ii. The data is then checked for correctness and validity and some form of copying (**transcription**) onto another document (e.g. summary sheet) may take place. The source documents are then temporarily stored.

iii. The source documents now accumulated for the complete pay period (probably a week in our example) are used for the next stage, which is the actual calculation process.

iv. Details of gross pay, tax, insurance and net pay are arrived at. Reference is made to data held in tax tables, in tables of rates of pay and in employee records. The latter must be brought up to date, e.g. Pay to Date details.

v. Individual pay slips, a summarised payroll and coin analysis are produced (**information**).

5.14 Each of these stages is identified by a name, viz:

i. **Origination** – of data.

ii. **Preparation** – getting the data ready.

iii. **Input** – the act of passing the data to the processing stage.

iv. **Processing** – all that is necessary to arrive at the net pay, etc, and to keep data up to date (e.g. data in employee records).

v. **Output** – the production of the end product. (See figure 5.5.)

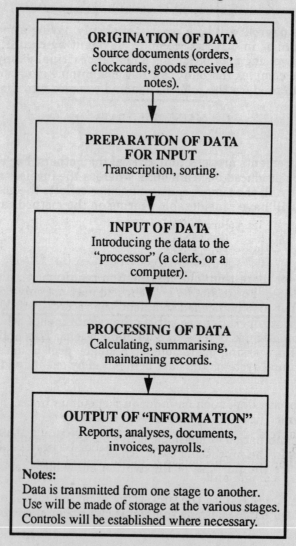

ORIGINATION OF DATA
Source documents (orders, clockcards, goods received notes).

↓

PREPARATION OF DATA FOR INPUT
Transcription, sorting.

↓

INPUT OF DATA
Introducing the data to the "processor" (a clerk, or a computer).

↓

PROCESSING OF DATA
Calculating, summarising, maintaining records.

↓

OUTPUT OF "INFORMATION"
Reports, analyses, documents, invoices, payrolls.

Notes:
Data is transmitted from one stage to another.
Use will be made of storage at the various stages.
Controls will be established where necessary.

Figure 5.1 Data processing stages

Note

a. How data is transmitted from stage to stage.

b. The use made of temporary storage after preparation.

c. The reference to stored data (tax tables, rates of pay and employee records) during the processing stage.

d. Controls will be part of the whole procedure, e.g. checking time sheets.

DP model

5.15 Having seen a general view of the data processing stages (figure 5.1), we now turn to a general view of the data processing system. In essence **all** DP systems consist of the four basic interrelated elements illustrated in figure 5.2. This *representation* may be referred to as a 'model' of the data processing system. It may also be called a 'logical model' to emphasise the fact that it is not representing physical features.

5.16 This concept of a 'model' goes rather deeper and is more useful than this simple illustration suggests. For example, the data within the DP system may be viewed as part of the DP model, in that it *represents* or reflects the state of affairs, e.g. the current balance represents the state of a customer's account.

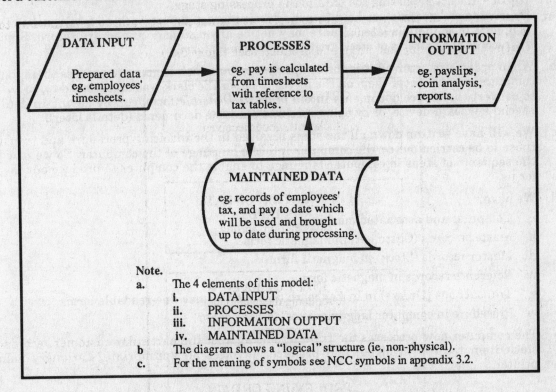

Figure 5.2 The Logical Model of a Data Processing System

Transactions and batches

5.17 The units of data for processing, such as individual customer orders or individual time sheets, are called **transactions**. Incidentally, the act of processing such a unit of data is also called a transaction, but the context should make it clear which meaning is intended. According to the determining factors (5.7 – 5.11), transactions may either be processed singly or in **batches**. A batch is merely a number of transactions (e.g. in the form of source documents) accumulated together and *processed* as a single unit.

5.18 Batching introduces a time-lag into the processing cycle but also introduces some useful controls, e.g. checking that a batch contains the required number of documents helps to detect and correct document loss.

Electronic data processing (EDP)

5.19 Some form of electronic computer-based data processing system is to be found in almost all except the smallest company. Thus it is necessary to concentrate our effort into gaining an understanding of what lies behind such systems. Where manual methods of DP are still in use, they frequently form part of an Electronic Data Processing (EDP) system and involve the use of simple electronic aids such as calculators. The basic principles of DP and EDP are essentially the same. The computer is merely substituted for manual aids or human labour. The same DP activities take place, but instead a computers is used to produce the results (the invoices or payroll, etc). Notice that the computer will not take over all of the steps in a given procedure, e.g. the data may first be collected or recorded by conventional methods.

5.20 In practice, the computerisation of a data processing system entails more than just the automation of parts of the existing system by means of computers. Analysis of an organisation's information requirements may show that the requirements will be better served by a newly designed and implemented system with the virtues of both the manual and computerised elements.

5.21 What is involved in an EDP system? In order to answer this questions imagine a simple invoicing application.

   a. The customers' records are held in a *magnetic* storage device such as a 'magnetic disk' or 'magnetic tape' (details later). There may not be any *visible* documentary record. Similarly the records of our items of stock are held in magnetic form.

   b. When orders are received it is the *computer system* which is going to process them, but the computer cannot accept them on the pieces of paper the clerk was accustomed to, so we have to convert the source documents into a *machine-sensible* form, e.g. by keying in data at a special keyboard device, or by using machine-readable documents (details later).

   c. We will have written down all the steps involved in the invoicing procedure and translated those to be carried out by the computer into the language of the computer. So we now have the sequence of steps in computer language to enable the computer to produce our invoices for us.

   d. We have:

      i. Computer and associated machinery.

      ii. Master records (Customer) in magnetic form.

      iii. Master records (Stock) in magnetic form.

      iv. Reference records in magnetic form.

      v. Transactions (Orders) in by keyboard device or by machine-readable forms.

      vi. Procedure in computer language.

   e. The computer now processes the transactions against the particular customer records and stock item records involved, and produces invoices on appropriate stationery using a printer.

Current EDP practice

5.22 Until the late 1970s the vast majority of EDP activities within most organisations were almost invariably concentrated in specialist DP departments. This was largely a consequence of the cost of computer systems and their specialist staff, and the need to achieve economies of scale. However, conventional DP activities on a small scale, which did not require expensive computer equipment, were often distributed within the various departments of the organisation.

5.23 In the early 1980s it became increasingly common to find departments within organisations which had their own small computer-based business computer systems operating quite autonomously of the data processing department. These small computers were often used for a variety of tasks not all of which might be classified as data processing. In addition, the use of other forms of computerised equipment has become widespread, particularly in the areas of office automation and telecommunications. **Desktop computing** grew in importance. In response to these changes many organisations replaced their data processing departments with what are sometimes called '**Information Centres**'. An information centre normally contains within it all the traditional functions of a DP department but, in addition, it also has responsibility for a wide range of other information systems services, including the provision and support of small computer systems within the various departments of the organisation.

5.24 The new technology has been able to establish itself because technological innovations have reduced costs to a point where it can compete with manual methods. The key feature of the new technology is its ability to deal with **information** in one form or another. The trend has been towards using ways of interconnecting the various types of equipment so as to integrate their functions and manage them more effectively. Thus we see modern EDP taking place not only in specialist DP departments but also being integrated more into the activities of other departments.

5.25 In the 1990s technological improvements have reached the point at which the more powerful PCs can challenge the traditional role of minicomputers in terms of performance for a given price and, similarly, minicomputers can challenge the role of mainframes. This, and pressures on organisations to reduce their computing costs, has given rise to an activity known as '**downsizing**'. Downsizing occurs if computer facilities are transferred from mainframes to a minicomputers, or from a minicomputers to microcomputers. As part of this process the strong central controls are removed and the computer facilities become more closely tied to particular business activities. There are clearly two sides to this process. On the positive side are the savings in costs and the greater availability to business users. On the negative side is the loss of useful coherent controls and the potential to needlessly replicate effort and resources. A variant on downsizing is **rightsizing** which merely means using a combination of computers of all types and sizes with each doing what it does best.

Overview of the rest of the book

5.26 Following the parts on 'Desktop Computing' and 'Conventional Data Processing' the succeeding chapters will concentrate on Electronic Data Processing (EDP) because of its overall importance. Because Electronic Data Processing relies upon Information Technology and through it can be integrated with other functions within an organisation, the IT relevant to EDP is covered too. All this is done step by step, taking the reader through each topic that needs to be covered.

The topics include:

a. the equipment used to create, process, store and communicate data.

b. the methods needed to exploit the equipment effectively.

c. the role of specialists such as systems analysts and programmers and the tools and techniques they use in designing and implementing systems.

d. the identification, with the aid of examples, of what makes an appropriate application for EDP.

e. the management of DP and its related IT.

Summary

5.27 a. 'Data' are the basic facts about the activities of a business.

b. 'Information' is data assembled into a useful form.

c. Data processing stages are: origination, preparation, input, processing and output.

d. A number of factors determine the methods of data processing.

e. A DP system may be represented as a 'logical model'.

f. Data may be processed singly or in batches.

g. EDP methods of data processing substitute a computer for more manual or semi-manual methods, although the system is usually redesigned in order to make maximum use of the computer.

h. Records are not in a visible form. They are in a magnetic form.

i. Procedures are translated into a machine-sensible form to be 'obeyed' by the computer.

Points to note

5.28 a. The data processing stages are sometimes referred to collectively as the data processing 'cycle', because of the way the stages are repeated.

b. The data processing stages and the concept of batching are common to all methods of DP, i.e. whether manual, mechanical, or electronic.

c. The terms 'procedure' and 'system' tend to be used synonymously, e.g. payroll 'procedure', or payroll 'system'.

d. Strictly speaking, the term 'Data Processing' means any data processing operation, regardless of the method used. To many people, however, it is virtually synonymous with computer processing, e.g. a company advertising for a DP Manager wants someone to run its computer installation, not its office.

e. The end product of data processing is information irrespective of the data processing facilities (e.g. accounting machine or computer) used to produce that information. Throughout any study of data processing, therefore, you need to be constantly aware of the necessity for good presentation of information.

f. No matter how good the data processing systems within an organisation are, if the other aspects of the organisation's information system are poor, the information produced may be under-utilised to the detriment of the organisation.

g. A common activity in the creation of a EDP system is **Systems Analysis.** Before the hardware for an EDP system can be purchased or the programs written the requirements of the system have to be investigated, the facts gathered and analysed, and the design specified. This activity is called SYSTEMS ANALYSIS (or SYSTEMS ANALYSIS AND DESIGN (SAD)).

h. In some organisations the replacement of the DP department by an **'information centre'** has gone one stage further with the introduction of an **IT department** responsible for everything from telephones to large computers.

i. It has become established practice within computer-related fields to use the term 'data' as singular rather than plural (e.g. 'The data is...').

j. **Downsizing** and **rightsizing** are of growing importance in changing the face of DP in the 1990s.

Questions

1. Define 'Data Processing'.

2. Outline possible advantages and disadvantages in batching some documents for processing.

Computer storage

1. This Part of the text builds on the introductory material covered in earlier chapters to give a detailed account of storage. The emphasis in the following two chapters is on the features of the hardware used for storage rather than on methods of using the hardware. The latter is covered later in the text.

2. **Main Storage** is described in chapter 6. Main Storage holds data and programs currently in use.

3. **Backing Storage Devices** are described in chapter 7. They are used to provide mass storage of data and programs.

6 Main storage

Introduction

6.1 Main storage plays a vital role in the operation of the central processor. It is wholly electronic and in close proximity to the rest of the processor, therefore any data within main memory is almost instantly accessible to the processor. For this reason main memory is also called Immediate Access Storage **(IAS)** , but is also called **internal storage** or **main memory.**

General features

6.2 a. Its operation is wholly electronic, and consequently very fast and reliable. In the most modern computers the electronic memory circuits are also highly miniaturised.

b. Data is almost instantly accessible from main memory because of its electronic operation and close proximity to the processor. For example, an item of data may be retrieved from main storage in much less than one millionth of one second. This is the reason why main storage is sometimes called **immediate access storage.**

c. Data *must* be transferred to main storage before it can be processed by the processor. High access speeds then contribute to fast processing.

Function and use

6.3 Main storage holds the program instructions and the data being processed. It will also store the intermediate results of processing awaiting transfer to the output devices.

6.4 Ideally, main storage would be used to store all data requiring processing, in order to achieve maximum processing speeds. A number of practical considerations prevent this from happening. Main storage is also relatively expensive, although its price has come down dramatically in recent years as the manufacturing methods have improved. So, the practical solution is to limit the size of main storage and supplement it with less expensive backing storage. Thus restrictions on size, coupled with the need to hold data in main storage for processing, results in main storage being *used* as a short-term memory. Nevertheless, the significant fall in real costs means that the size of main storage in modern computers is typically bigger than those of just ten years ago by a factor of tens or even hundreds!

6.5 It stores:

a. Instructions waiting to be obeyed,

b. Instructions currently being obeyed,

c. Data awaiting processing,

d. Data currently being processed,

e. Data awaiting output.

Physical features

6.6 Main storage in modern computers is constructed from semiconductor memory chips (3.21). The features of the basic types of semiconductor memory are covered here.

6.7 The most common type of semiconductor memory is called **RAM** (**R**andom **A**ccess **M**emory). RAM is *volatile* , i.e. data is lost when the power supply is removed. A non-volatile alternative to RAM is **ROM** (**R**ead **O**nly **M**emory), in which all contents are permanently set during manufacture.

6.8 a. **ROM** usually forms a small proportion of main storage, and is used to store vital data and programs which need to be held within main storage *at all times*.

b. **RAM** usually forms the major proportion of main storage, and is used to store data and programs *temporarily* during those times when they are needed in main memory. It is constantly being re-used for different data items or programs as required.

Representation of data

6.9 Inside the computer, data is represented electronically by storage cells which are either charged or discharged, i.e. in one of two possible states. In RAM the cells may be charged and discharged at will, and can thus be re-used to store different data items. In ROM the cells are *permanently* set to one state or the other.

The binary system

6.10 As has just been indicated computer storage is based upon the two-state concept (e.g. charged *or* discharged), and use is made of a numbering system which has TWO as its base, the BINARY system. Remember this is a digital computer.

6.11 **Binary representation of numbers.** The basic points which you need to be aware of are detailed here.

    a. *All* numbering systems are based on *two* concepts:

        i. Absolute value.

        ii. Positional value.

    b. The decimal system has absolute values   0 to 9

    c. The binary system has absolute values   0 to 1

Example 1 The number 26 in *decimal* is made up thus:

Positional values	10^3 (1000)	10^2 (100)	10^1 (10)	10^0 (1)		10^1	10^0
Digit 6 in position 10^0				6	$= 6 \times 10^0 =$		6
Digit 2 in position 10^1			2		$= 2 \times 10^1 =$	2	0
					$= $ **Decimal** $=$	**2**	**6**

Example 2 The number 26 in *binary* is made up thus:

Positional values	2^4 (16)	2^3 (8)	2^2 (4)	2^1 (2)	2^0 (1)		2^4	2^3	2^2	2^1	2^0
Digit 0 in position 2^0					0	$= 0 \times 2^0 =$					0
Digit 1 in position 2^1				1		$= 1 \times 2^1 =$				1	0
Digit 0 in position 2^2			0			$= 0 \times 2^2 =$			0	0	0
Digit 1 in position 2^3		1				$= 1 \times 2^3 =$		1	0	0	0
Digit 1 in position 2^4	1					$= 1 \times 2^4 =$	1	0	0	0	0
						$=$ **Binary** $=$	**1**	**1**	**0**	**1**	**0**

Notes:

    a. The 1's and 0's making up a binary number are referred to as **B**inary Dig*its* or BITS. Thus the number 26 is composed of 5 BITS.

    b. Inside the computer's storage a '1' would be represented by an electronic 'cell" in a chip being in an electrically charged state (or ON) and a '0' by an electronic 'cell' in a chip being in an electrically discharged state.

6.12 **Binary Codes.** Most computers nowadays use a derivation of the 'pure' binary notation just described, in what may be called 'binary coded' representations of data. These methods use a *fixed* number of binary digits (bits), in fact the basis for most systems is the use of just 4 binary positional values only. Each *decimal digit* may be represented by four bits (see Figure 6.1 on the following page).

Decimal value	Binary (pure)	Binary Coded Decimal (assuming a 6-bit code)		
0	0000			001010
1	0001			000001
2	0010			000010
3	0011			000011
4	0100			000100
5	0101			000101
6	0110			000110
7	0111			000111
8	1000			001000
9	1001			001001
10	1010		000001	001010
11	1011		000001	000001
22	10110		000010	000010
26	11010		000010	000110
34	100010		000011	000100
47	101111		000100	000111
90	1011010		001001	001010
631	1001110111	000110	000011	000001

Figure 6.1. Selected examples of decimal, binary and binary-coded decimal.

6.13 In order to accommodate 26 letters, and a number of 'special' characters (i.e. full stops, commas, etc) further bits are added to make a total of 6, 7 or 8 bits according to the coding system used.

6.14 The three most commonly used codes are:

a. **ASCII** (American Standard Code for Information Interchange).

A set of 128 characters is represented by this code. Most of the characters are used for normal printing purposes (see Figure 6.2), but a few characters are not printable and are used to control the hardware used in printing characters or transmitting them, e.g. the Delete character at the end of the table. The code shown in Figure 6.2 is actually the British version of the printable characters because the '£' character has been substituted for the '#' character which is present in the standard American version, this is normal for British data processing applications.

b. **BCD (Binary Coded Decimal)** – a 6-bit code (see Figure 6.3a). This code is by far the least common of the three listed here.

c. **EBCDIC (Extended Binary Coded Decimal Interchange Code)** – an 8-bit code (sometimes called 8-bit ASCII) (see Figure 6.3b). This code is very widely used on large computers, especially by IBM.

Alternative storage designs

6.15 Since bits need to be grouped together in order to represent numbers or characters, main storage is organised that way. Each group of bits is a separate entity called a **'location in main storage'** or just 'storage location' and can be addressed by the control unit.

6.16 To understand the principles of how data is placed into main storage we will imagine it to be arranged like a set of boxes, and deal with the physical details of main storage afterwards. The boxes are numbered from zero upwards so that each box can be identified and located. What is usually called a **storage location** corresponds to one of our boxes, and the **'location address'** corresponds to the number of the box.

e.g.

Location 0	Location 1	Location 2	Location 3	
				etc....

Binary code	Decimal value	Character	Binary code	Decimal value	Character	Binary code	Decimal value	Character	Binary code	Decimal value	Character
0010 0000	32	space	0011 1000	56	8	0101 0000	80	P	0110 1000	104	h
0010 0001	33	!	0011 1001	57	9	0101 0001	81	Q	0110 1001	105	i
0010 0010	34	"	0011 1010	58	:	0101 0010	82	R	0110 1010	106	j
0010 0011	35	#	0011 1011	59	;	0101 0011	83	S	0110 1011	107	k
0010 0100	36	$	0011 1100	60	<	0101 0100	84	T	0110 1100	108	l
0010 0101	37	%	0011 1101	61	=	0101 0101	85	U	0110 1101	109	m
0010 0110	38	&	0011 1110	62	>	0101 0110	86	V	0110 1110	110	n
0010 0111	39	'	0011 1111	63	?	0101 0111	87	W	0110 1111	111	o
0010 1000	40	(	0100 0000	64	@	0101 1000	88	X	0111 0000	112	p
0010 1001	41	)	0100 0001	65	A	0101 1001	89	Y	0111 0001	113	q
0010 1010	42	*	0100 0010	66	B	0101 1010	90	Z	0111 0010	114	r
0010 1011	43	+	0100 0011	67	C	0101 1011	91	[	0111 0011	115	s
0010 1100	44	,	0100 0100	68	D	0101 1100	92	\	0111 0100	116	t
0010 1101	45	-	0100 0101	69	E	0101 1101	93	]	0111 0101	117	u
0010 1110	46	.	0100 0110	70	F	0101 1110	94	^	0111 0110	118	v
0010 1111	47	/	0100 0111	71	G	0101 1111	95	_	0111 0111	119	w
0011 0000	48	0	0100 1000	72	H	0110 0000	96	`	0111 1000	120	x
0011 0001	49	1	0100 1001	73	I	0110 0001	97	a	0111 1001	121	y
0011 0010	50	2	0100 1010	74	J	0110 0010	98	b	0111 1010	122	z
0011 0011	51	3	0100 1011	75	K	0110 0011	99	c	0111 1011	123	{
0011 0100	52	4	0100 1100	76	L	0110 0100	100	d	0111 1100	124	|
0011 0101	53	5	0100 1101	77	M	0110 0101	101	e	0111 1101	125	}
0011 0110	54	6	0100 1110	78	N	0110 0110	102	f	0111 1110	126	~
0011 0111	55	7	0100 1111	79	O	0110 0111	103	g	0111 1111	127	del

NOTE: The binary codes corresponding to the decimal values 0 to 31 are used as 'control characters', i.e. they are used to control the transmitting device rather than to represent data. (Details later)

Figure 6.2 The ASCII character set

Alpha character	Binary code	Alpha character	Binary code	Alpha character	Binary code
A	11 0001	J	10 0001	–	–
B	11 0010	K	10 0010	S	01 0010
C	11 0011	L	10 0011	T	01 0011
D	11 0100	M	10 0100	U	01 0100
E	11 0101	N	10 0101	V	01 0101
F	11 0110	O	10 0110	W	01 0110
G	11 0111	P	10 0111	X	01 0111
H	11 1000	Q	10 1000	Y	01 1000
I	11 1001	R	10 1001	Z	01 1001

a. Representation of characters in BCD

Alpha character	Binary code	Alpha character	Binary code	Alpha character	Binary code
A	1100 0001	J	1101 0001	–	–
B	1100 0010	K	1101 0010	S	1110 0010
C	1100 0011	L	1101 0011	T	1110 0011
D	1100 0100	M	1101 0100	U	1110 0100
E	1100 0101	N	1101 0101	V	1110 0101
F	1100 0110	O	1101 0110	W	1110 0110
G	1100 0111	P	1101 0111	X	1110 0111
H	1100 1000	Q	1101 1000	Y	1110 1000
I	1100 1001	R	1101 1001	Z	1110 1001

b. Representation of characters in EBCDIC

Figure 6.3 BCD and EBCDIC CODES

32-BIT MACHINE					16-BIT MACHINE				8-BIT MACHINE		
LOCATION ADDRESS	CONTENTS				LOCATION ADDRESS	CONTENTS			LOCATION ADDRESS	CONTENTS	
10	D	C	B	A	10	B	A		10	A	
11	H	G	F	E	11	D	C		11	B	
12					12	F	E		12	C	
13					13	H	G		13	D	
14					14				14	E	
15					15				15	F	
16					16				16	G	
17					17				17	H	
18					18				18		

Figure 6.4 Alternative storage designs

Once data is stored in a location in main storage it remains there until it is replaced by other data. Data placed into the same location will destroy what was there previously (rather like the latest recording you make on a tape recorder will destroy the previous one). Accessing and fetching data from main storage is really a copying action which does not result in the data being deleted from main storage (just as playing a tape recorder does not erase the tape).

6.17 There are numerous ways in which this is done in practice, but the basic ideas should be covered in sufficient detail by the following examples:

a. In the smaller microcomputers bits are grouped together 8 at a time, i.e. in semi-conductor memory the storage cells in RAM or ROM are constructed using groups of 8 cells. Every storage location has its own unique address called its **location address** and can be addressed independently in this way. A single storage location is large enough to hold one ASCII character, one BCD character, one EBCDIC character or two BCD numeric values. Microcomputers using this method of storage are often referred to as 8-bit microcomputers (see Figure 6.4).

b. On larger microcomputers and smaller minicomputers a common size for a memory location is 16 bits and computers with memory locations of this size are called 16-bit computers. A single storage location on a 16-bit computer will be able to hold two characters (e.g. ASCII or EBCDIC), but will normally ' *pack* ' characters two to a location for that reason (see Figure 6.4). Such computers usually have facilities for accessing the right half and left half of each word separately in order to handle individual characters.

c. 32-bit storage locations are found on the more advanced microcomputers, many minicomputers and smaller mainframe computers. Such computers normally have a variety of ways of accessing all or part of each memory location.

6.18 Any group of bits treated as a separate unit of data by the control unit is called a **word**. A word is normally a single storage location or some small number of storage locations. Words may be subdivided into **bytes**, which normally correspond to the size of a character. For this reason a 'byte' is often taken to be 8 bits.

6.19 **Performance.** Computers with longer storage locations are normally faster than those with shorter storage locations because it takes fewer operations to transfer data between main storage and the processor. For example, a 32-bit computer can transfer four 8-bit characters in a single operation,whereas an 8-bit computer will require the equivalent of four such operations and could therefore take roughly four times as long. This gain in speed is only properly realised if the processor is also built to handle 32 bits at a time too. Data is transferred via physical connections called **buses** corresponding in 'width' to the number of bits transferred in a single operation. Therefore, the **bus sizes** involved give an indication of performance. For example, a 32-bit computer having an internal bus of 32 bits but a memory bus of only 16 bits, will typically be using 16-bit memory designed for a 16-bit computer and, therefore, may not be much faster than a 16-bit computer of similar manufacture. There are other factors involved in performance, however, of which the two other most significant are:

a. **Manufacturing technology.** Main storage manufactured to operate on a mainframe will typically be much faster than memory manufactured to operate on a microcomputer, even though both may have the same location size, 32 bits say.

b. **Clock speed.** The speed with which a processor transfers data to and from main storage is tied to the rate at which the processor can carry out operations. For many computers, and practically all microcomputers, this rate is itself directly related to the rate at which the processor receives pulses from a special digital clock built into the computer. A processor running with a clock speed of 20 MHz (20 MegaHertz, i.e. 20 million cycles per second), will be approximately twice as fast one of comparable design running at 10 MHz.

6.20 **Parity check.** We have been referring to storage as consisting of, for example, 8, 16 or 32 bit groups. In fact each one of these groups will have *another* bit added to it, so that *physically* the main storage will consist of groups of 7, 17 and 33 bits. This additional bit is called a Parity Bit. A parity bit is automatically added to the 8, 16 or 32 bits to make the total *number* of bits an odd or even number (some machines have 'even parity' others have 'odd parity'). Whenever the character byte, etc, is moved within the computer, a check is automatically made on the *number* of bits at the receiving end. This is to ensure no bit is 'lost' in transmission. Thus in odd parity machines (i.e. the total number of bits (including parity bit) in every character adds up to an odd number), if an even number of bits were counted on the receiving end, it indicates that the machine is malfunctioning. See Figure 6.5 which has adopted the 'odd' parity system.

Note. Small computers do not always incorporate parity checking systems, which can bring their reliability into question in some situations.

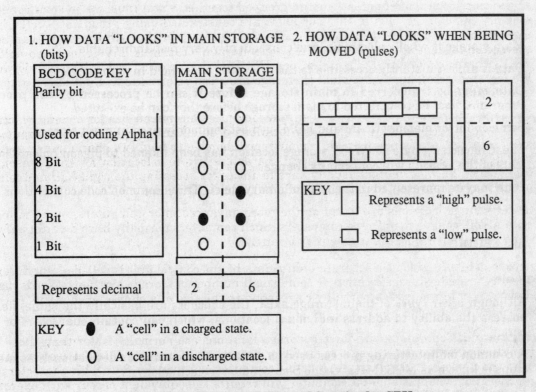

Figure 6.5 Representation of data in the CPU

6.21 **How main storage operates.** Once data is *read* into storage from an input unit it remains there (i.e. the particular cells are charged or discharged) until it is replaced by other data. Data read into the same locations will destroy what was there previously (rather like the latest recording you make on your tape recorder will destroy the previous one). As internal storage is limited and only used for holding data currently worked on, the *contents* of the storage locations will be continually changing. Storage locations can in some ways be regarded as pigeon holes in a mail room. Each pigeon hole (storage location) is addressable and will contain different data depending on what was last put in.

Access time

6.22 Each item of data stored in main storage, whether stored as characters, bytes or words, is accessible to the control unit on a completely random basis. The speed with which this access is made is so fast as to be called immediate, i.e. accessible in less than one millionth of one second.

Storage capacity

6.23 Storage sizes are sometimes expressed in terms of 'K' (K = 2^{10} = 1024), e.g. a typical 8-bit microcomputer may have a main storage capacity of 32K bytes. Larger capacities are sometimes expressed in terms of megabytes (mega for a million).

Cache memory

6.24 In recent years it has become common practice to use memory chips with extra high access speed to supplement those in main memory. The chips tend to be too expensive to use for the whole of main memory. These memory chips are used to provide a 'cache', which is a temporary holding area for data that is currently subject to repeated access. The processor can access this data more quickly and there is therefore an overall speed improvement. The cache effectively sits between main storage and the processor acting as a holding area through which all data and instructions pass. Old data in the cache is overwritten by new because the cache has limited capacity. To make best use of the cache an appropriate strategy must be adopted to decide what data to overwrite. Common methods are the LFU (Least Frequently Used) and LRU (Least Recently Used) rules for determining which data items to overwrite.

Summary

6.25 a. Main storage is wholly electronic, and consequently very fast and reliable.

b. Data is almost instantly accessible to the processor when held in main storage.

c. Data *must* be transferred to main storage before it can be processed by the processor. Programs *must* be transferred to main storage before they can be executed.

d. Semiconductor memory (RAM and ROM) is most commonly used in main storage.

e. The 'Character', 'Byte' or 'Word' storage location has been likened to pigeon holes. The *contents* of the location will continually change.

f. Data may be represented in the form of binary codes. Three common code conventions are:
   i. BCD
   ii. ASCII
   iii. EBCDIC

Points to note

6.26 a. Although other *types* of main storage exist, the concepts are basically the same, i.e. they possess the ability to address individual locations, which can contain characters or numbers.

b. A common manufacturing process used to produce semiconductor devices such as memory chips is known as MOS (Metal Oxide Semiconductor) technology.

c. Pure binary number representations (Figure 6.1) associated with a word of 32 bits would have as many leading 0's as were required to make up the number of bits to 32.

d. You may see main storage size described in terms of K (K = 2^{10} = 1024). For example, 32K words = 32 x 1024 words = 32,768 words. 1000K is normally written M (for Mega). For example 20M bytes means 20,000K bytes. 1,000,000K is normally written G (for Giga).

e. The use of Cache Memory is growing in importance. Since it sits between the processor and main memory it means that the organisation of the computer is slightly different from the arrangement shown in Figure 3.1.

Questions

1. Explain the following terms as they relate to the representation of data in a computer.

   a. bit

   b. byte

   c. binary coded decimal

   d. word. *(ACA)*

2. Explain the basic difference between an 16-bit computer and a 32-bit computer with particular reference to any factors which might affect performance.

7 Backing storage

Introduction

7.1 Ideally, all data for processing should be stored in main storage so that all internal operations can be carried out at maximum speed. As it is, main storage is relatively expensive and is therefore only used for storing the necessary instructions and the data currently being operated on. **Backing storage is provided** for the mass storage of programs and data files, i.e. those programs and data files not currently being operated on but which will be transferred to the main storage when required.

7.2 Although data in the form of files held on backing storage is not immediately accessible, as it would be if held in main storage, it is nevertheless within the computer system. It can therefore serve an important purpose as part of a pool of maintained and accessible data.

7.3 There are many media for backing storage. The main devices and media, which will be described here, are:

a. Magnetic disk unit – magnetic disk.

b. Magnetic diskette unit – magnetic diskette (floppy disk).

c. Optical disk unit – optical disk.

d. Magnetic tape unit – magnetic tape.

e. Magnetic tape cartridges and cassettes.

f. Solid state storage devices.

g. Mass storage devices and media.

Exchangeable magnetic disk unit and magnetic disk pack

7.4 Features of an exchangeable disk unit

a. The disk **unit** is the device in which the disk **pack is placed**. The disk pack is placed into the unit and connects with the drive mechanism. Packs vary in size both in terms of the number of 'platters' and in terms of the diameter of the platters. The photograph shows a pack with eleven 10 inch platters which is more likely to be found on a minicomputer or mainframe. Disk packs with single platters are sometimes called disk **cartridges**. Disk cartridges tend to have platters of 5 inch diameter or less. Disk cartridges are mostly used on microcomputers but are also used on some minicomputers. In what follows assume that what is said of a disk pack also applies to a disk cartridge unless otherwise stated.

An exchangeable disk pack removed from from its protective cover

84

b. Once the pack (or cartridge) is loaded into the unit the read-write mechanism located inside the unit positions itself over the first track of each surface. The mechanism consists of a number of arms at the ends of which there is a read-write head for each surface. All arms are fixed together and all move together as one when accessing a surface on the disk page. See figure 7.1 opposite.

c. The disk when loaded is driven at a high number of revolutions (several thousand) per minute and access can only be made to its surfaces when the disk revolves.

7.5 Features of an exchangeable disk pack

a. Disks are of a size and shape similar to a long-playing record although some have smaller diameters of approximately 5 inches or 3 inches.

b. The surfaces of each disk are of magnetisable material(except the outer-most surfaces of a pack which may be purely protective). Thus there are 10 recording surfaces in a 6-disk pack and 20 in an 11-disk pack. For a disk cartridge constructed from a single platter both surfaces may be recorded upon (figure 7.2 on the following page).

c. Each surface is divided into a number of *concentric* tracks (typically 200) and organised into cylinders with each track being divided into sectors (figure 7.3 on the following page).

d. The disks within a pack are inseparable, i.e. the pack, of 6 or 11 disks, is always used as a single unit.

e. Storage capacities of disks are commonly expressed in terms of the number of bytes of data they can hold. For practical purposes one can take a byte to be 8 bits or the size of one character. The latest models of disk pack can store many hundreds of Megabytes of data (i.e. hundreds of millions of characters). Indeed, it is now common to have disks with capacities in excess of 1 *Gigabyte* (one thousand millions bytes).

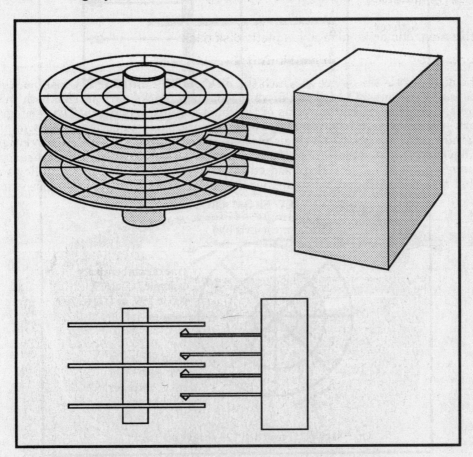

Figure 7.1 Magnetic disk with read-write heads

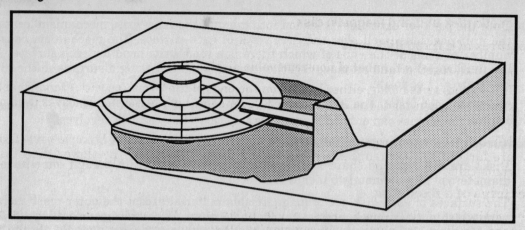

Figure 7.2 A Single double-sided magnetic disk

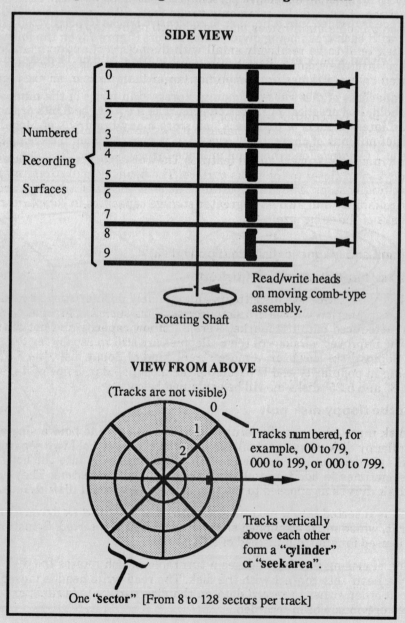

SIDE VIEW

Numbered

Recording

Surfaces

0
1
2
3
4
5
6
7
8
9

Read/write heads
on moving comb-type
assembly.

Rotating Shaft

VIEW FROM ABOVE

(Tracks are not visible)

0
1
2

Tracks numbered, for
example, 00 to 79,
000 to 199, or 000 to 799.

Tracks vertically
above each other
form a "cylinder"
or "seek area".

One "sector" [From 8 to 128 sectors per track]

Figure 7.3 Magnetic disk tracks, cylinders and sectors

Fixed magnetic disk unit and magnetic disk

7.6 Features of a fixed disk unit

a. The unit houses a number of non-removable disks.

b. It has read-write heads, either located on the ends of the 'arms' (as with exchangeable disks) or serving each track. The latter is the case for some high-performance drives used on mainframes.

c. It has a motor that rotates the drive at a high constant rate, but because some fixed disks are larger than exchangeable disks the rotational speed may be slower than that of exchangeable disk units.

7.7 Features of a fixed disk

7.8 The majority of fixed-head disks in use today are 'Winchester' disks (details shortly). Winchester disks are particularly common as a backing storage medium for small computer systems. Indeed, many more expensive personal computers have Winchester disks built into the casing. Capacities of such disks commonly range from 20 megabytes to 200 megabytes. The fixed disks used on some mainframes may have much higher capacities however.

7.9 Winchester disk tend to be relatively small with diameters of approximately 3, 5 or 8 inches with a trend toward the smaller sizes becoming the more common. The older technology fixed-head disks used on mainframes are sometimes larger than disks in an exchangeable disk pack. In other respects they are the same.

7.10 **Winchester disks.** 'Winchester' technology disks were developed by IBM some years ago in order to overcome some problems associated with established disk technology. They are now made by many different manufacturers.Winchester disks are fixed disks in hermetically sealed disk units and have robust mechanical features.They have toughened surfaces, and read-write heads that move even closer to the disks surface. The heads actually 'land' on the disk's surface when the disk finally stops! They can operate in adverse environments that are dusty or humid, have greater reliability and also have greater storage capacities in comparison with the earlier technology disks of the same size.

Magnetic diskette unit and magnetic diskette (floppy disk)

7.11 Floppy disk unit and floppy disk (diskette)

The floppy disk, also called the diskette, is an extremely popular storage medium, particularly when used in conjunction with microcomputer systems such as personal computers. The first floppy disks introduced onto the market were 8", of low capacity and not always very reliable. Although a few improved versions of the 8" floppies are still in use, by far the more popular size is the 5.25" floppy disk. However, a more recent kind of floppy disk, the 3.5" *microfloppy*,has rapidly gaining in popularity and is becoming the most popular. Some of its features are different from the 8" and 5.25" disks as will be explained below.

7.12 Features of the floppy disk unit

a. Floppy disk units are normally **'single-drive'** units able to hold a single disk. Some free-standing floppy disk units are dual-drive units,i.e. able to hold two separate floppy disks at a time. Single-drive units are often incorporated physically into the body of personal computers, sometimes in addition to hard disks such as Winchesters. They are then called **internal disk drives** as opposed to the free-standing **external disk drives.**

b. Each disk is inserted into a narrow slot in the front of the disk drive. The slot has a small flap over it, which must be clipped shut once the disk is inserted. Sometimes a push button or lever is used for shutting instead of a flap.

c. The action of closing the flap engages a turntable, which rotates the disk and also brings a 'read-write head' into contact with the disk. The read-write head is moved to and fro across the disk in order either to record data on the disk surface (a 'write'), or to 'read' back data which has previously been recorded.

d. A typical floppy disk rotates at about 360 rpm compared with a hard disk which rotates about ten times faster.

7.13 Features of the floppy disk.

a. A pliable disk permanently sealed within a rigid, smoothly lined, protective plastic envelope (see figure 7.5).

b. Data is stored on tracks.

c. The common sizes are 8", 5.25" and 3.25".

d. Storage capacities range from 60,000 bytes to 1.25 million bytes. The latter capacities are achieved using 'high density' recording, which is even more dense than that achieved with normal double-sided double-density disks shown in figure 7.5.

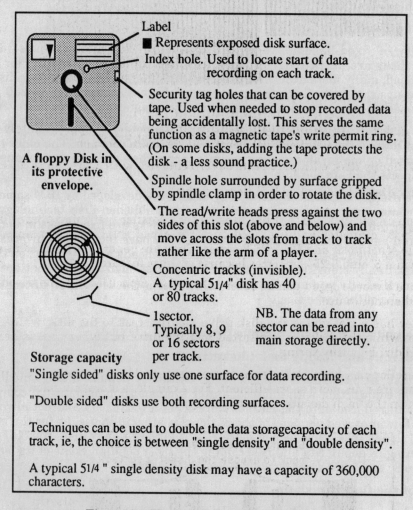

Label
■ Represents exposed disk surface.

Index hole. Used to locate start of data recording on each track.

Security tag holes that can be covered by tape. Used when needed to stop recorded data being accidentally lost. This serves the same function as a magnetic tape's write permit ring. (On some disks, adding the tape protects the disk - a less sound practice.)

A floppy Disk in its protective envelope.

Spindle hole surrounded by surface gripped by spindle clamp in order to rotate the disk.

The read/write heads press against the two sides of this slot (above and below) and move across the slots from track to track rather like the arm of a player.

Concentric tracks (invisible). A typical 5¼" disk has 40 or 80 tracks.

1 sector.
Typically 8, 9 or 16 sectors per track.

NB. The data from any sector can be read into main storage directly.

Storage capacity

"Single sided" disks only use one surface for data recording.

"Double sided" disks use both recording surfaces.

Techniques can be used to double the data storagecapacity of each track, ie, the choice is between "single density" and "double density".

A typical 5¼ " single density disk may have a capacity of 360,000 characters.

Figure 7.4 Floppy disk (diskette) details

Figure 7.5 8" floppy disk with part of its cover removed, with 5.25" floppy disk by its side

7.14 **Microfloppy disks**. (Also called 3.5" floppy disks.)

One variation on the diskette that has become very popular is the microfloppy disk. These disks are normally 3" diameter and are used on a variety of small microcomputer-based systems, e.g.the Apple Macintosh and IBM PS/2 series. They are generally regarded as an improvement over the normal 8" and 5.25" diskettes because of these features:

a. They have a more rugged plastic cover, which keeps the whole disk surface covered and protected when not in use.

b. The cover has a slot giving the disk drive heads access to the disk, which is automatically slid open while the diskette is inserted into the drive but other wise is held closed against dust and dirt by a tiny spring.

c. The microfloppies have storage capacities comparable with those of their larger counterparts and are thus more space efficient. For example, a storage capacity of 1.4 Megabytes is common on the 'high density' disks of this type.

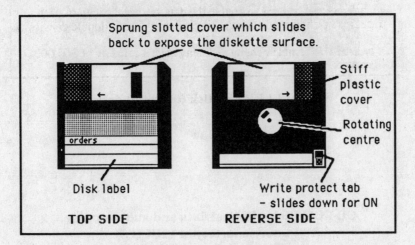

Fig 7.6 3.5" microfloppy disk

7.15 It is quite probable that the microfloppy diskette will supersede the 5.25" just as the 5.25" has superseded the 8" floppy disk.

7.16 Although floppy disks are sometimes used as a primary medium for backing storage on small microcomputer systems they are mainly used for other purposes, such as:

a. A medium on which to supply software for use on microcomputers.

b. A medium on which to collect or input data, for subsequent transfer and input to another system, possibly at a remote site.

c. As a **back-up** medium for small hard disks. For example, the contents of a 20 megabyte Winchester disk could be copied onto about 20 floppy disks so that if the Winchester disk becomes unusable for any reason its contents can still be recovered.

Note. This is directly comparable to the way in which magnetic tape may be used to back-up hard disks on larger systems.

7.17 There are two variants on the floppy disk which have been introduced in recent years and have gained some degree of success. These are as follows.

a. **Bernoulli boxes.** A Bernoulli box is essentially a 'souped-up' floppy drive in which a 8" or 5.25" disk housed in a cartridge is rotated at much higher speed than is normal for a floppy disk thus making the disk more stiff and stable and thus more like a hard disk. Capacities of 40–90 megabytes are possible at very competitive prices.

b. **Megafloppy drives.** These are really effectively a very much more technologically advanced form of the conventional 3.5" floppy disk drive. Capacities of 5–20 megabytes are possible and the speed of access is significantly faster than for a conventional floppy disk.

7.18 There are three basic types of optical disk but all of them use lasers to write or read data. All three provide a means of storing very large volumes of data.

CD-ROM Disks. Optical data and audio storage.
(Picture courtesy of PHILIPS)

7.19 **CD-ROM (Compact Disk Read-only Memory).**

a. **Features of the CD-ROM unit.** These devices work on exactly the same principle as that used for the domestic audio compact disk (CD), which has become so popular in recent years as a replacement for the vinyl LP record. Indeed, some units are manufacture for dual use both for playing audio CDs and accessing data CDs. This is not so surprising since CDs actually record sound in digital form. The devices are *only able to read back prerecorded sound or data by* using a laser at lower intensity and detecting the pattern of light reflected from its beam by the surface of the disk as the CD rotates on a turntable (figure 7.7).

b. **Features of the CD.**The CDs are constructed in the same way as an audio CDs. A CD may hold about 55 megabytes of data. Access speeds tend to be slower than for magnetic disks.

c. **Jukebox options.** Some CD units are incorporated into what is called a '**jukebox**'. The name '**jukebox**' is borrowed from the audio device used in pubs and clubs. A jukebox is able to load one of a number of individual CDs into the disk unit under the control of suitable software. The facility greatly extends the volume of data which can be automatically accessed on-line.

d. **Uses.** CDs are of use in providing reference works, catalogs, directories, encyclopaedias, software, font descriptions, graphical images and sounds.

7.20 **WORM (Write Once Read Many).**

a. **Features of the WORM unit.** The device is similar in appearance to a fixed device magnetic disk unit, but data is written into the disk by burning a permanent pattern into the surface of the disk by means of a high-precision laser beam. A similar method may be used in the manufacture of a CD. The reading of data is conducted in the same way as that used for a CD. That is, data is read back by using the laser at lower intensity and detecting the pattern of light reflected from its beam by the surface of the disk as it rotates on a turntable. The WORM disks are exchangeable.

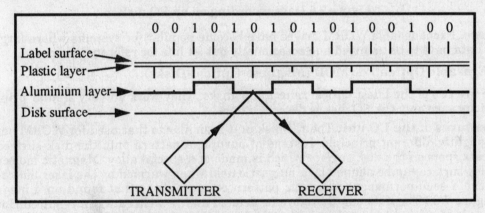

Figure 7.7 Read data from a CD

b. **Features of the WORM disk.**A typical disk looks like a CD and has a surface of 40,000 tracks each divided into 25 sectors and a total capacity of a staggering one Gigabyte (i.e. 1,000 million bytes). (CDs have a lower capacity than this because of their mass produced nature.) The WORM disks are less prone to data loss than magnetic disks but are non-reusable at present. It is for this reason these optical disks are referred to as '**WORM**' storage. WORM stands for 'Write Once Read Many times'. As for CDs, access speeds tend to be slower than for magnetic disks.

c. **Variants.**WORM drives are also available with capacities of 13.5 Gigabytes and better transfer rates. When fitted with a jukebox unit of 6 disks they can provide access to 27 Gigabytes, with cartridge exchange times of approx. 2.5 seconds.

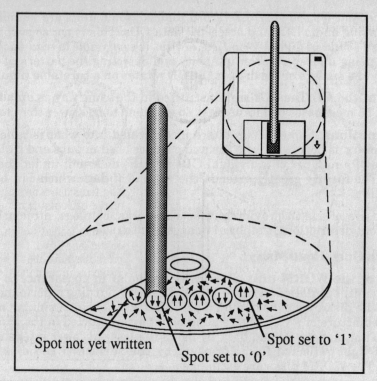

Spot not yet written

Spot set to '0'

Spot set to '1'

Figure 7.8 Data recording on an EO disk

d. **Uses.** Exchangeable WORM drives have become popular for systems where large amounts of data have to be archived and occasionally put on-line for reference purposes.

7.21 EO (Erasable Optical) or MOD (Magneto-Optical-Disks).

These are two of the latest optical *re-writable* disks. They work on very similar principles. For simplicity sake only the EO disk is described here.

a. **Features of the EO unit.**The EO disk unit is similar to that used for WORM but works on a slightly different principle. Instead of burning a pattern onto the disk surface the laser heats spots on the disk surface which is made of a special alloy. Magnetic molecules in the alloy surface can be aligned by a magnetic field when warmed by the laser but cool again to leave a semi-permanent magnetic pattern comparable to that found on a magnetic disk. (figure 7.8.) The data can therefore be deleted and re-written when required.However, the speeds of writing and reading are much slower than those of a WORM drive.

b. **Features of the EO disk.**Again the disk is similar in appearance and size to a CD but enclosed in a casing which looks like that used for a 3.5" floppy disk. The capacity of a typical EO disk is about 650 megabytes.

Magnetic tape unit and magnetic tape

7.22 The main magnetic tape medium is ½" tape which traditionally has come in reel-to-reel form. However, cartridge forms have become popular alternatives because they are easier to use. Magnetic cartridges come in a number of shapes and sizes and vary in the mechanism by which they operate. A lesser alternative to the magnetic tape cartridge is the magnetic tape cassettes which also comes in a variety of forms. In order to bring out the basic principles more clearly the following description deals with ½" **'reel-to-reel'** versions. Special features of tape cassettes and cartridges are covered later.

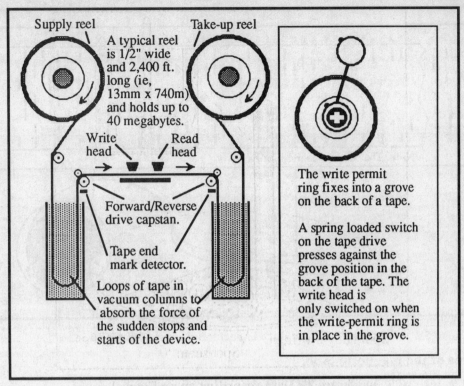

Supply reel   Take-up reel

A typical reel is 1/2" wide and 2,400 ft. long (ie, 13mm x 740m) and holds up to 40 megabytes.

Write head   Read head

Forward/Reverse drive capstan.

Tape end mark detector.

Loops of tape in vacuum columns to absorb the force of the sudden stops and starts of the device.

The write permit ring fixes into a grove on the back of a tape.

A spring loaded switch on the tape drive presses against the grove position in the back of the tape. The write head is only switched on when the write-permit ring is in place in the grove.

Figure 7.9 Main features of a Magnetic Tape Unit

7.23 Features of the tape unit

a. It holds the magnetic tape reel and also a second reel for 'taking up' the tape (similar in concept to a tape recorder) (see figure 7.9).

b. It has a **'read hcad'** for 'reading'the information stored on the tape, i.e. for transferring data from the tape into main storage, and it has a separate **'write head'**, for recording the information. Usually an individual tape is mounted onto the tape drive either to be read from or to be written to.

c. The tape moves past the read head at up to 200 inches per second (ips). Typical speeds are 30, 45, 75 and 125 ips. When the tape is travelling at these speeds data can be read from them at rates between 100,000 and 200,000 bytes per second or even higher!

d. The tape can be accelerated to maximum speed or decelerated from maximum speed to a halt in approximately 5-15 ms, while the tape travels about $^1/_4$" to $^3/_8$" of one inch.

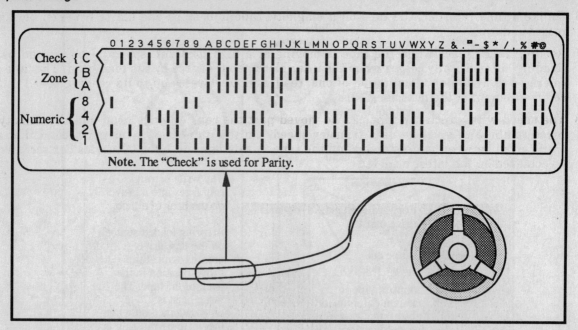

Figure 7.10 How data is recorded on magnetic tape

7.24 Features of the magnetic tape.

a. It is $\frac{1}{2}$ inch wide and 300, 600, 1200, 2400 or 3600 feet long.

b. It has a plastic base, coated with magnetisable material on one side.

c. Data is stored in tracks. There are 7 or 9 tracks (depending upon the tape unit), which run the length of the tape. The data is coded so that one byte (character) is recorded across the 7 or 9 tracks (see figure 7.10, which illustrates 7-track tape).

d. An aluminium strip, called a **'load point marker'**, marks the physical beginning of the tape for recording purposes (the first 20 ft. or so is not used, apart from threading into the unit). Similarly the physical end of the tape is marked with an 'end of reel marker' (the last 20ft. or so is not used for recording).

e. The recording **density can vary between** 200–6,250 bytes to the inch. Common forms are 800 bpi NRZI, 1,600 bpi PE and the newer 6,250 PE. **'bpi'** stands for bits per inch but is effectively bytes per inch because each byte is recorded across the width of the tape. 'NRZI' stands for Non-Return Zero Inverting and 'PE' stands for Phase Encoding. Both are more sophisticated than the simple coding conventions for 0's and 1's explained in 2.14.

f. The tape is reusable, i.e. can be overwritten (as can tape used with tape recorders) – 20,000–50,000 passes are possible.

g. The same tape can be used both for input and output. For security purposes a special device called a **'write permit'** ring must be attached to a tape reel when writing onto the tape is required. Without the write permit ring the tape cannot be written on to when on the tape unit and the information on the tape is therefore protected against accidental deletion while being read.

h. It has a storage capacity of up to 40 million bytes per reel when recorded at 1,600 bpi depending upon the size of the reel.

7.25 Manner of recording.
Data is recorded (written) in blocks as the tape moves past the 'write' head at a constant rate. After a block has been written, the tape slows down and stops. On being instructed to write again, the tape accelerates up to the speed required for writing and another block is written onto the tape. No writing takes place during the acceleration and deceleration time and this therefore leaves a gap between each block of data on the tape. This Inter **Block Gap (IBG)** measures some $\frac{3}{4}''$.

7.26 Unlike a tape recorder, the tape on a magnetic tape unit stops and starts between blocks of recorded data.

7.27 Reading takes place when the tape is moving at a high,*constant*, speed past the read head. Reading automatically ceases when the inter-block gap is sensed by the read head. The tape decelerates to a stop on termination of one 'read' and accelerates up to its reading speed at the commencement of the next 'read'.

7.28 The speed with which the tape can be moved past the read or write head and the density of bytes combine to give the data transfer speed, i.e. the number of bytes per second that are transferred between main storage and the tape. A rate of up to 1,250,000 bytes per second can be achieved on the latest models.

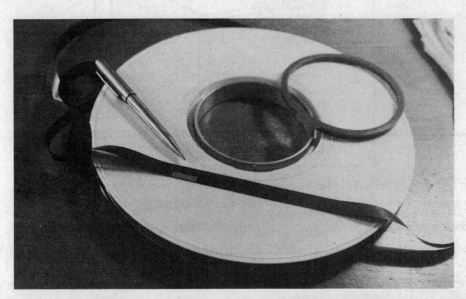

Magnetic tape tape (reverse side) with a write permit ring visible and removed from the back of the tape. The pen tip is pointing to the 'Load point marker' at the start of the tape.

7.29 The theoretical storage capacity (i.e. length x maximum density) is not achievable in practice because of the inter-block gaps that are required, each taking up about $^3/_4''$. Thus the practical capacity can be as little as 20 million bytes on a tape with a theoretical capacity of 40 million bytes. The size of blocks can have a significant effect on the practical capacity. The bigger the blocks, and therefore the fewer the gaps, the more data is stored.

Magnetic tape cartridges and cassettes

7.30 **Cartridges and Cassettes come** in a number of different forms. They operate on the same principles as $^1/_2''$ reel-to-reel tape. Indeed, many cartridges are designed mainly to overcome the bother of loading and unloading tapes. The cartridge just pops in a slot which is clearly simpler than threaded tape onto a reel. Apart from convenience, a tape cartridge also gives greater protection against dust and dirt and thereby makes the tape more trouble free. The more basic cartridges and cassettes are exactly the same as, or very similar to, the tapes and cartridges used for home audio.However, tape cartridges specially designed for computer use are of more advanced construction. Several computer manufacturers use their own particular designs.For example, DEC have a series of $^1/_2''$ tape cartridges.

7.31 A variety of forms of tape cartridge have established themselves as backup media in recent years. The *primary purpose of* these tape cartridges is to provide an effective way to copy the contents of disks to guard against data loss. Data loss can occur for a number of reasons ranging from simple human error in deleting data by mistake to a mechanical failure such as a **'disk crash'** in which the read-write heads smash into the disk's surface. If data is backed up from a disk onto a tape cartridge on a regular basis, perhaps daily, then when a data loss occurs the backup copy can be read back again onto a replacement disk. Tape cartridges are also used as a means of distributing large volumes of software or data from one computer to another.

7.32 **¹/₂" cartridges.** A typical ¹/₂" tape cartridge contains 600 feet of tape and holds from 60 Megabytes to 600 Megabytes depending on the recording density. Longer,high capacity models can record up to 2.5 Gigabytes. When a typical unit is operating at full speed data may be read or written at a rate of about 2.5 Megabytes per second. Large volume backups can be carried out using multi-hopper cartridge stacker units (figure 7.11). The cartridges are automatically loaded and unloaded one at a time so that very large volumes of data can be backed-up unattended (i.e. without the need for an operator).

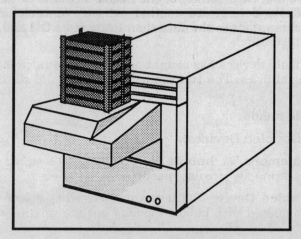

Figure 7.11 A multi-hopper magnetic tape cartridge stacker unit

7.33 **¹/₄" cartridges.** A typical ¹/₄" tape cartridge (figure 7.12) contains 1,000 feet of tape and holds from 250 Megabytes.

Figure 7.12 A ¹/₄" magnetic tape cartridge

7.34 **8mm cartridges.** 8mm tape cartridge have a more compact and modern design than the cartridges mentioned above. A single compact 8mm cartridge may store up to 10 Gigabytes in some cases.

7.35 **¹/₈" cassette.** The more basic cassettes are generally slower than tape cartridges and store up to 340,000 bytes at 800 bytes to the inch on a 280-foot tape.

7.36 **Digital Audio Tape (DAT).** DAT tapes are produced in the form of 4mm cassettes (Non DAT 4mm cassettes are also in use). The DAT tape was first devised as a digital tape alternative to the CD for domestic music systems. DATs have so far had more success as a means of computer storage. DAT tape units use rotating read-write heads similar to those used in domestic video recorders. The heads are placed at a slight angle to the tape and are made to spin in the opposite direction to the moving tape. The high relative speed of the heads and tape mean that reliable high density recording can be attained.This **'helical scan'** method is similar to that used

96

in 8mm video camcorders and, as a result, the 4mm DAT tapes look like small scale versions of the 8mm camcorder cassettes. A standard DAT tape has a capacity of 1.3 Gigabytes.

Solid state storage devices

7.37 Other forms of storage have been developed which are called solid state (i.e. no moving parts). The (comparative) slowness of current disks and tapes is caused by the physical movement of the recording surface and (with disks) of the heads. There is no such physical movement in solid-state devices.These devices are another category of semi-conductor memory but give somewhat slower access speeds to the data than RAM and ROM and are therefore not suitable for main storage.

7.38 None of these solid state devices has caught on to any degree, probably because they are not competitive in terms of price. The two common types of solid state storage devices used for backing storage are:

a. **Magnetic bubble memory.**

b. **CCDs (Charge Coupled Devices).**

7.39 **Magnetic Bubble Memory.** In **'bubble memories'** data is stored as tiny magnetic domains (the bubbles) which continually circulate past read-write heads.

7.40 **CCDs (Charge Coupled Devices).** These are produced by a form of MOS technology. They are relatively fast compared with bubble memory but are volatile whereas bubble memory is not.

7.41 In the current state of development, solid-state storage is halfway between established memory systems and backing storage. It provides access to data that is faster than conventional backing storage devices but slower than memory. On the other hand, it has a capacity higher than memory but lower than backing storage. Disk technology continues to improve at such a pace that solid state devices have not yet made a breakthrough.

Mass storage devices and media

7.42 Some large corporations and government agencies have a need for vast data storage capacities. This need can be met by mass storage devices. These devices are 'automated libraries' of disk and tape cartridges, rather like the jukeboxes mentioned earlier. The total capacity of such a system tends to be expressed in terms of Gigabytes (thousands of millions of bytes). Further detail is not merited.

SCSI Interfaces

7.43 SCSI stands for 'Small Computer Systems Interface' and is normally pronounced 'scuzzy'. SCSI is a standard for high speed communication between devices to which peripheral connections may be built. SCSI has become widely adopted in recent years. As its name suggests, the SCSI interface is aimed at small computer systems where there is often a need to connect several different types of external storage devices and other peripherals. A SCSI 'host adaptor' circuit board in the computer is connected to a single plug-in socket on the computer's cabinet into which a chain of **'SCSI devices'** can be connected with each also fitted with an adaptor circuit board. Each device has two sockets to enable it to be chained to the next by a cable. At one end of the chain is the computer, and at the other end is a **'terminator'**. (No cracks about 'I'll be back'!) (Figure 7.13 overleaf.)

7.44 Data is transferred at high speed between the devices which makes SCSI suitable for connecting disk devices to a computer. A transfer rate of 1–5 Megabytes per second is not uncommon and devices built to the new SCSI-2 standard can transfers data at about 10 Megabytes per second.

Physical storage consideration

7.45 'Volume' is a general term for any individual physical storage medium that can be written to or read from. Examples include: a fixed hard disk, a disk pack, a floppy disk, a CD-ROM, a disk cartridge or a tape cartridge.

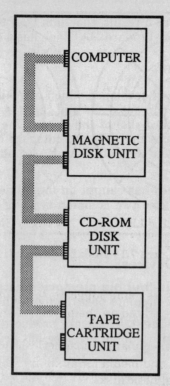

Figure 7.13 An example of a chain of SCSI devices

7.46 **Initialisation.** Before a disk volumes may be recorded upon it normally has to be initialised which involves writing zeros to every day byte on every track. A special program is normally supplied for this purpose. Clearly, the re-initialisation of a disk effectively eliminates all trace of any existing data.

7.47 **Formatting.** In addition to initialisation the disk has to be formatted which means that a regular pattern of blank sectors is written onto the tracks. In the case of floppy disks the 'formatting' program normally combines formatting with initialisation. On magnetic tapes the format is defined when the tape is mounted on the drive. Blocks of data are then formatted as they are written to the tape. The format determines the effective storage capacity of the volume. For example, a double sided floppy disk with 80 tracks per side and 9 sectors per track with each sector containing 512 data bytes will have a storage capacity of 720 Kbytes (i.e. 9 x 80 x 2 x 512 bytes.) Formats depend upon the manufacturer and operating system used. If data is to be transferred from one computer to another not only must the volume be physically interchangeable between drives the volume format must be compatible too.

7.48 **Fragmentation.** As data is stored on a newly formatted disk the data is written to unused contiguous sectors (i.e. those sectors which follow one another). If data is erased then the deleted sectors may leave 'holes' of free space among used sectors. Over time, after many inserts and deletes, these free sectors may be scattered across the disk so that there may be very little contiguous free space. This phenomenon is called 'disk fragmentation'. If a file, such as a document file say, is written to the disk the read-write heads will have to move about as they access the fragmented free space. This slows down the writing process and will also slow down any subsequent reads. Therefore, performance suffers. When this happens it may be possible to use a special disk **defragmenter program** to re-organise the data on the disk so as to eliminate the fragmentation. (Figure 7.14.)

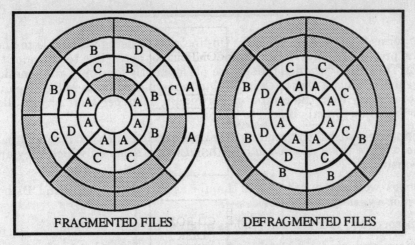

FRAGMENTED FILES   DEFRAGMENTED FILES

Figure 7.14 Disk fragmentation

Summary

7.49 a. Auxiliary storage is used, as its name suggests, to supplement main storage.

   b. The descriptions have concentrated on the physical features rather than uses, which will be discussed later in the text.

   c. The main auxiliary storage media are in magnetic form.

   d. The main hardware devices and media for auxiliary storage are:

   i. Magnetic disk unit – magnetic disk.

   ii. Magnetic diskette unit – magnetic diskette (floppy disk).

   iii. Optical disk unit – optical disk.

   iv. Magnetic tape unit – magnetic tape.

   v. Magnetic tape cartridges and cassettes.

   vi. Solid state storage devices.

   vii. Mass storage devices and media.

   e. The comparative performance of backing storage media and devices is shown in figure 7.15.

Devices and media	Typical access time	Typical storage capacities	Typical transfer rates (bps)	Type of storage (SAS or DAS)	Where used as primary medium
1. Floppy disk (diskette)	260 ms	180 Kbytes to 1.25 Mbytes	24,000 to 50,000	DAS	Small microcomputer-based systems, otherwise as a backup medium for hard disk
2. Magnetic disk	20 to 60 ms	60 Mbytes to 5 Gbytes	312,000 to 2,000,000	DAS	Minicomputers and main-frames
3. Optical disks	100 ms	55 Mbytes to 10 Gbytes	200,000	DAS	Minicomputers and main-frames for archiving or on-line backup
4. Magnetic tape (reel-to-reel)	Search required	40 to 160 Mbytes	160,000 to 1,250,000	SAS	Minicomputers and main-frames mostly as a backup medium for disk
5. Magnetic tape cartridge	Search required	50 Mbytes to 10 Gbytes	160,000 bps to 2.6 Mbps	SAS	Microcomputers and mini-computers
6. Magnetic tape cassette	Search required	Up to 145,000 bytes	10 to 33,000	SAS	Small microcomputer systems

bps = bytes per second; SAS = Serial Access Storage; DAS = Direct Access Storage

Figure 7.15 Comparative performance of backing storage media and devices

Points to notice

7.50 a. Note the terms 'on-line' and 'off-line'. 'On-line' means being accessible to and under the control of the processor.Conversely, 'off-line' means not accessible to or under the control of the processor.Thus,*fixed magnetic* disks are permanently 'on-line'; a magnetic tape reel or an exchangeable magnetic disk pack is 'on-line' when placed in its respective units, but 'off-line' when stored away from the computer, terminals, *wherever their* physic allocation, are said to be 'on-line'when directly linked to the processor.

b. On exchangeable disks, the read-write heads serving each surface will be positioned over the same *relative track on each surface because* the arms on which they are fixed move simultaneously.

c. The 'jukebox' was introduced in this chapter as an option used with CDs but jukeboxes are available for a variety of disk devices.

d. The term 'cartridge' is ambiguous unless prefixed by 'tape' or 'disk'.

e. The devices and media have been separated for ease of explanation. It should be noted,however, that in the case of the fixed disk the media are permanently fixed to the device, and therefore they cannot be separated.

f. Backing storage is also called auxiliary **storage.**

g. Input, output and storage devices are referred to collectively as peripheral devices.

h. Disk packs normally have several platters and are top-loading whereas disk cartridges are side-loading with just one or two platters.

i. Simplified versions of magnetic tape cartridge units used solely for back-up are sometimes known as '**streamers**'.

Computer input and output

1. This Part of the text gives detailed coverage of computer input and output. It builds on the introductory material covered in earlier chapters but also introduces some new material.

2. One of the most common ways of using a computer for general purposes is for an end-user to have an on-line connection to the computer via a device such as a **terminal.** The use of the computer is said to be **interactive**. The situation for the user of a home computer or personal computer is essentially the same, with the screen and keyboard performing a similar function to that provided by a device such as a **VDU**. There are a variety of different devices that provide this kind of facility to input and output data. Chapter 8 looks at them in detail.

3. Terminals are not particularly suitable for outputting large volumes of data nor do they provide permanent copies. All data has to be entered via the keyboard and the forms in which data can be output have their limits too. Therefore, a number of other methods of data input and output are needed. Chapter 9 describes a number of special devices and media for output. They are used to receive data from the processor and to produce the data in a humanly sensible form (or in a machine-sensible form for later re-input).

4. Chapter 10 deals with the problems of how best to get data into the computer. It describes the methods and media that can be used to overcome these problems. The chapter also examines the choices that have to be made when deciding what is the best way to carry out input and output in particular situations.

8 Terminals

Introduction

8.1 In chapter 2 the reader was introduced to 'interactive on-line computing" in the form of PCs and workstations. With such desktop computers the user interacts with the computer via a keyboard, and monitor screen directly connected to the computer. This is not normally the case when it comes to minicomputers or mainframes. Instead the user make use of a device called a terminal to interact with the computer. In most case there are many users connected to the same computer via terminals either directly or via computer networks. The terminal often has a keyboard and screen, which makes it look rather like a PC, but its capabilities fall far short of those of the PC. This chapter describes the features of terminals and explains how they are used.

8.2 Most terminals are '**keyboard devices**', which merely means that their primary means of entering data to the computer is via a keyboard. As is the case for PCs and workstations, the keyboards resemble the QWERTY typewriter keyboard, but usually have several additional keys, which are used for other purposes depending upon the type of device.

Terminal types

8.3 By far the most common form of **terminal** is the **VDU** (Visual Display Unit) which was introduced in chapter 1. Most terminals have a keyboard for input and a display screen or printer to show both what is typed in and what is output by the computer. Terminals which have a printer instead of a screen are called **terminal typewriters**. They are now rather outdated and rare, so the name '**terminal**' is now normally synonymous with **VDU** and is often used instead. However, care need to be taken over this because there are also many kinds of specialist devices for entering data into the computer or displaying it on special screens and these are sometimes called terminals too. There are many different types of VDU terminals in use today. Only the more common features and variants will be described.

The VDU terminal

8.4 **Features of the VDU Terminal.**

A number of these features are very similar to or even the same as those found on PCs or workstations.

a. It is a dual-purpose device with a keyboard for data input and a cathode ray tube screen for output. The latter is similar to a TV screen. The screen is normally housed along with the device's electronic components in a cabinet similar to that used for a PC's monitor.

b. The keyboard resembles the QWERTY typewriter keyboard, but usually has several additional keys, which are used to control and edit the display.

c. Characters are displayed on the screen in a manner that resembles printed text. A typical full screen display is 24 rows by 80 columns (i.e. 1920 characters).

d. The display can normally be generated in two different modes:
   i. **Scrolling mode** in which lines appear at the bottom and move up the screen rather like credits on a movie screen.
   ii. **Paging mode** in which one complete screen-full is replace by another, rather like a slide projector display.

e. Most VDUs have features that allow particular parts of the display to be highlighted or contrasted, e.g.
   i. Inverse (Reverse) video, i.e. black on white instead of white on black.
   ii. Blinking displays.
   iii. Two levels of brightness.
   iv. Colour - on the more expensive models.

f. **Cursor controls.** A cursor is a small character-size symbol displayed on the screen, which can be moved about the screen both vertically and horizontally by means of special keys on the keyboard. During data input, the display may resemble a blank form. In this case data may be entered by first moving the cursor to a space on the 'form' and then typing in the data. Further keys may allow the data to be edited or corrected.

g. **Inbuilt microprocessors.** The numerous internal functions of almost all modern VDUs are controlled by inbuilt microprocessors. The more expensive models are often called **intelligent terminals.** These more advanced devices are sometimes capable of limited amounts of processing.

An IBM 3277 model 2 Information Display Station and Light Pen.
(Picture courtesy of IBM)

8.5 **How it works.** When a key is pressed on the keyboard the character's code is generated and transmitted to the computer along the lead connecting the terminal to the computer. Normally the character code received by the computer is immediately 'echoed' back out to the terminal by the computer. When a character code is received by the terminal it is interpreted by the control circuitry and the appropriate character symbol is displayed on the screen, or printed depending upon the type of terminal.

8.6 The more basic VDU models can only input and display characters and are therefore called a **character terminal.** The superior alternative is a **graphics terminal** which is able to handle computer graphics. It works in a similar way to a PC fitted with a graphics card but does not have the general processing capabilities of a PC.

8.7 Variations on the VDU

a. **Graphics terminals.** As was just indicated, some VDUs have high quality displays that can be used for line drawings, draughtsmen's drawings, etc. These more advanced models are not limited to displaying characters but can handle screen sized images too. There are many kinds of graphics terminal.

b. **X-terminals.** These are graphics terminals which provide special facilities for using the **X-windows** system.

c. **Light pens.** A light pen is a special pen used in conjunction with a graphics VDU. The VDU can detect the location of light shining on the screen by means of special hardware and software. This is a design aid that simplifies input of details of positions on the screen.

d. **Touch terminals.** An alternative to the light pen. The VDU can detect when a point on the screen is touched.

e. **Voice Data Entry (VDE).** Additional circuitry plus a microphone is added to the VDU. The unit can be switched to 'learn' a number of words, typically less than 200, which it achieves by recording a 'sound pattern' for each word typed in. When the unit is switched to input it displays and inputs any word that it recognises. These units are particularly suitable for people wishing to use a few words again in situations where their hands are not free to use a keyboard, e.g. people in laboratories, invalids, etc.

Figure 8.1 Simple VDU graphics output

Consoles

8.8 A **console** is a terminal that is being used for communication between the *operator* (i.e. the person responsible for operating the computer) and the programs that are controlling the computer. For a small single-user computer the special controlling program is often called the monitor and the console operator types one-line monitor commands. More typically, on larger multi-user computers the operator types commands that are acted upon by a program called a **command language interpreter**. At one time terminal typewriter were preferred to VDUs for use as consoles on minicomputers and mainframes because of the permanent printed record which they produced. However, today this requirement is achieved by programming the computer to keep a text file 'log' copy of all input and output carried out on the console.

8.9 Control messages are keyed in by the operator (e.g. the next task required) and acted upon by the program. Messages can also be output by the monitor or command language interpreter for action by the operator (e.g. indicating that a 'run' has finished or that a new tape needs to be placed onto a tape drive). Note that the input in this case consists of operating messages for controlling the system.

8.10 **Note** that if an end-user is able to use a terminal to carry out operator functions the terminal is said to be able to be able to perform console functions.

Personal computers used as terminals

8.11 There are many situations in which people who use terminals connected to minicomputers or mainframes also use Personal Computers (PCs). To save on the cost of hardware, and on desk-top space, they may use their PC as a terminal instead of having a separate terminal. For this to be possible the PC must be fitted with the correct hardware and use **terminal emulation** software.

8.12 **PC features**. The PC's hardware must have suitable features that may require the fitting of some extras. There must be a suitable socket on the outside of the PC to which a terminal lead can be connected. Although this sounds a simple requirement there are a number of things that have to be set up correctly for such an arrangement to work. Usually, small computers such as PCs have a number of sockets fitted to them each of which has been designed to be connected to a particular type of peripheral device. These external points of connection are called ports. A **'communications port'** normally has the properties needed for connecting the PC to a terminal lead. It is helpful to be familiar with some of the issues involved.

a. **Interfaces.** A special piece of circuitry is fitted inside the computer and sits between the computer and the port. Its purpose is to provide a compatible connection between the two. Such a device is called an **interface**.

b. Interfaces are either **serial** or **parallel**. A serial interface sends or receives the bits comprising each character code one at a time, whereas a parallel interface sends the set of bits for each character all at once. As a consequence, more socket pins are used in parallel ports. A very common standard serial interface is the **RS232C**. A SCSI port is an example of a parallel port.

c. Most ports are **bidirectional**, i.e. they can send and receive data. Some printer ports can only send data and can therefore not be used with a terminal connection.

d. The sending and receiving of signals at a port is usually governed by a set of rules known as **protocols**. For example, the **X-on X-off** protocol involves sending the ASCII code 19, which means 'stop transmission' and the ASCII code 17, which means 'start transmission'. This facility may be available to the terminal user by typing the control key plus 'S' for X-off (ASCII 19) and the control key plus 'Q' for X-on (ASCII 17).

e. The speed with which data can be transmitted through the port can usually be varied. Such speeds are often expressed as **baud rates** (details later). Common settings are 330, 1200, 2400, 4800 and 9600. Divide these figures by 10 to get a *rough* approximation of the corresponding speeds in characters per second.

8.13 **Terminal emulation**. By themselves the hardware connections are useless without a suitable program running in the PC to make the PC behave like a VDU. Such a program is called a **terminal emulator**. Many different terminal emulators are on sale as standard 'packages'. A typical terminal emulator has the following features:

a. The emulator normally provides a set-up facility, which enables the user to choose the appropriate characteristics and settings needed. For example, the baud rate may be selected. Also, the emulator may present the user with a choice of standard VDU types. Very common options are VT100 and VT220, which are the model numbers of two popular VDUs manufactured by Digital and since copied by various other manufacturers.

b. The PC's keyboard is made to behave just like a VDU keyboard even to the extent of making special 'function keys' behave in the same way if the emulation is a good one.

c. The screen behaves and looks just like the VDU screen. In a good emulation even special graphics symbols will display the same way.

d. In addition to making the PC behave like a VDU many terminal emulation packages also provide a **file-transfer** facility, i.e. a means by which data and programs may be copied directly between a disk in the PC and the disks on the main computer to which the PC is connected as a terminal.

Note. Although this discussion has been about the use of PCs as terminals it is possible to use some home computers as terminals too and in much the same way as PCs.

Summary

8.14 The following topics have been covered.

   a. Terminals in general
   b. VDU terminals
   c. PC used as terminals by means of terminal emulators.

Points to note

8.15 a. VDU terminals are widely used in conjunction with minicomputers and mainframes.

Question

What is the practical difference between a terminal and a terminal emulator?

9 Output devices

Introduction

9.1 The following devices and media will be described:

a. Printers – Single sheet or continuous stationery.

b. Microform recorder – Microfilm or Microfiche.

c. Graph Plotters – Single sheet or continuous stationery.

d. Actuators.

e. Others.

Printers

9.2 A basic classification of printers is:

a. **Character printers** which print one character at a time. The most common example is the **dot matrix printer**.

b. **Line printers** which print whole lines at a time.

c. **Page printers** (also called **image printers**) which print whole pages at a time. The most common example is the **laser printer**.

9.3 **Print Speeds** tend to be expressed in terms of **cps** (characters per second), **lpm** (lines per minute) or **ppm** (pages per minute). Printers may be classified as

a. **Low speed** (10 cps to approx. 300 lpm) – usually character printers.

b. **High speed** (Typically 300 lpm – 3000 lpm) – usually line printers or page printers.

9.4 Basic methods of producing print.

a. **Impact or non-impact printing.** Impact printers *hit* inked ribbons against paper whereas non-impact printers use other methods of printer, e.g. thermal or electrostatic. Most impact printers are noisy.

b. **Shaped character or dot-matrix printing.** The difference is explained in figure 9.1. A dot matrix can also be used to produce a whole picture or **image** (9.2c) similar in principle, but superior in quality, to the minute pattern of dots in a newspaper picture.

Low-speed printers

9.5 **Dot matrix impact character printers.** These are the most popular and widely used low-speed printers. They are often loosely referred to as '**dot matrix printers**'.

9.6 **Features**

a. As with all character printers the device mimics the action of a typewriter by printing single characters at a time in lines across the stationery. The print is produced by a small '**print head**' that moves to and fro across the page stopping momentarily in each character position to strike a print ribbon against the stationery with an array of wires.

b. According to the number of wires in the print head, the character matrix may be 7×5, 7×7, 9×7, 9×9 or even 24×24. The more dots the better the image.

c. Line widths are typically 80, 120, 132, or 160 characters across.

d. Speeds are typically from 30 cps to 200 cps.

e. Multiple print copies may be produced by the use of carboned paper (e.g. 4–6 copies using **NCR** (No Carbon Required) paper).

f. Some higher quality versions have:

    i.   Inbuilt alternative character sets.

    ii. Very good print quality. The term **NLQ** (Near Letter Quality) is sometimes used to describe them.

    iii. Features for producing graphs, pictures, and even colour by means of multiple-print ribbons.

g. Small versions of these printers are often used in conjunction with computerised tills in shops and service stations, especially for dealing with purchases by credit card.

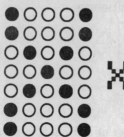

Dot Matrix Characters

Each character is produced by printing the appropriate dot combination.

5 × 7 dot matrix

Shaped Characters

Each character is produced by use of the whole character symbol as on an ordinary typewriter.

Figure 9.1 Shaped and Dot Matrix Character

9.7 Daisywheel printers. This is another popular type of low-speed printer that is favoured when high print quality is demanded.

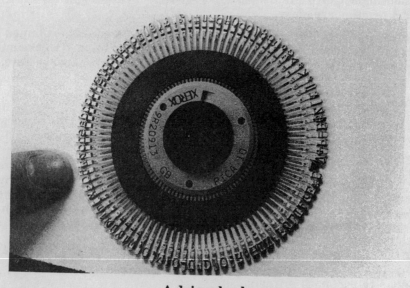

A daisywheel

9.8 Features

a. An impact shaped-character printer.

b. These printers are fitted with *exchangeable* print heads called **daisywheels** (see Figure 9.2 opposite). To print each character the wheel is rotated and the appropriate spoke is struck against an inked ribbon.

c. Speeds are typically 45 cps.

d. They are similar to dot matrix printers in terms of page size and multiple-copy printing.

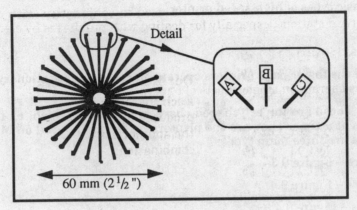

Figure 9.2 Daisywheel details

**The LNO3 desk-top laser printer from Digital Equipment Corporation
(Picture courtesy of Digital Equipment Corporation (DEC))**

9.9 **Inkjet printers.** The original models of these printers were character matrix printers and had only limited success. In recent years improved designs have resulted in very successful page printers which have been competing favourably with daisywheel printers.

9.10 **Features**

a. These are non-impact page printers.

b. They operate by firing very tiny ink droplets onto the paper by using an 'electrostatic field'. By this means a medium quality bit-mapped image can be produced at a resolution of about 300dpi.

c. They are very quiet but of low speed (4ppm).

d. Some models print colour images, by means of multiple print heads each firing droplets of a different colour.

9.11 Other low-speed printers. There are many other low-speed printers too numerous to mention. One worth a mention is the **Thermal printer** which is a non-impact character matrix printer which prints onto special paper using a heated print head. It is very quiet and this gives it a big advantage for some applications.

High-speed printers

9.12 There are two basic types of high-speed printer:

a. Line Printers.

b. Page Printers.

Line printer and the faster page printers operate on continuous stationery but most of the less fast page printers operate on single sheets of paper.

9.13 Line printers. These are impact shaped-character printers which, as their names suggest, print whole lines at a time. They are the printers traditionally used on Mainframes and mini-computers. There are three main types:

a. Drum printers – Figure 9.3.

b. Chain printers – Figure 9.4.

c. Band printers – Figure 9.4.

9.14 It will suffice to indicate how *b* and *c* work. A principle of operation typical of the faster models is that of a moving chain, with the links being engraved character-printing slugs, moving at a high constant speed past printing positions. The band printer has an embossed steel loop instead of a chain. Magnetically controlled hammers force *the paper* against the appropriate print slugs. Typically, there are 120 printing positions to a 'line'. Speeds of up to 50 lines per second *can* be achieved although, as yet, 20 (approx.) per second is a more typical speed. Using continuous stationery with interleaved carbons, up to 7 copies can be obtained (see figure 9.4).

The bands in a band printer may be exchanged quite readily to provide a variety of character sets.

9.15 Page printers. These printers print an 'image' of a whole page at a time. The image may consist of conventional print, diagrams, pictures, or a combination of these, thus making pre-printed stationery unnecessary.

9.16 According to technical features given emphasis in particular designs, these printers are also known as **laser printers**, **optical printers** or **xerographic printers**.

9.17 An electronically controlled laser beam marks out an electrostatic image on the rotating surface of a photo conductive drum. Ink toner is attracted onto the electrostatic pattern on the surface of the drum. The toner is then transferred onto the stationery as the stationery comes into contact with the drum.

9.18 A typical **high-speed laser printer** will print 146 pages per minute. When printed at a normal 6 lines per inch vertically, this represents a speed of 10,500 lpm, but with smaller spacing, speeds up to 30,000 lines per minute may be achieved on some models. These printers are very large and noisy.

9.19 A typical **desktop laser printer** is suitable for use in an office environment and looks very similar to a photocopier. It has paper trays rather like those used in a photocopier too. Speeds are normally no more than ten pages per minute, but the quality of output is very high indeed (400–1200dpi), being much better than that produced by a daisywheel printer. Since it is a page printer the laser printer can print a combination of text and diagrams or pictures and is therefore very useful for producing reports, manuals and other small publications. These printers are therefore often used in conjunction with word processors and more advanced document creation systems, such as those provided on the Apple Macintosh, for what is often called **desktop publishing**.

9.20 Many desktop laser printers are fitted with **Postscript interpreters**. As was mentioned in chapter 5, postscript is a '**page description language**'. Programs written in postscript are used to describe the way in which text and diagrams are to appear on a printed page. If a

Postscript program is output from a computer to a laser printer the printer's postscript interpreter can follow the program's instruction to construct a page of printed output.

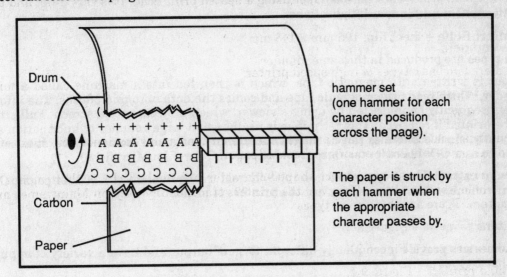

Figure 9.3 A drum printer

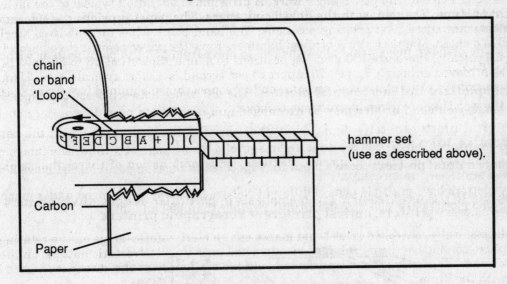

Figure 9.4 A chain or band printer

Print quality

9.21 Comparing print quality. A *rough* comparison of print quality may be obtained from Figure 9.5. It should be noted that the diagram is a copy of a copy and that *some* matrix printers rival daisywheels in print quality.

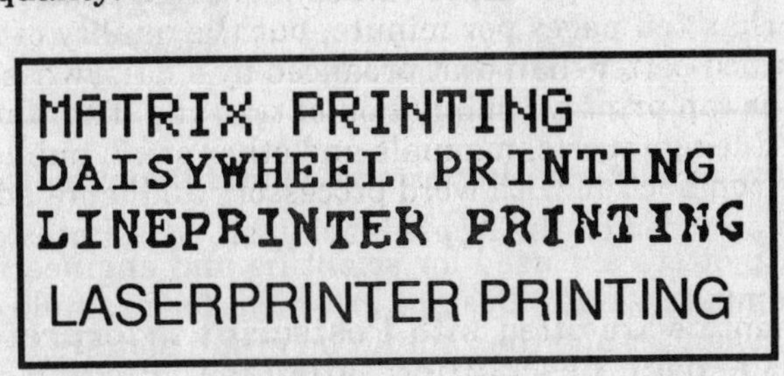

Figure 9.5 A comparison of print quality

Microform recorders and microforms

9.22 **Microforms** are photographically reduced documents on film. There are two types:

    a. **Microfilm** – 16 mm roll film.

    b. **Microfiche** – sheet film 105 mm x 148 mm.

    Both types are produced in the same manner.

9.23 Output is written onto magnetic tape, which is then fed into a machine called a microform recorder, which reads the magnetic tape and copies the data onto microforms. The information can subsequently be inspected by using a viewer, which projects onto a screen. Full-size copies can be printed if required. This technique is useful when large volumes of information are used internally, since economies can be made in stationery costs and storage space. It is usually referred to as a **COM** (Computer Output on Microform/Microfilm/Microfiche).

9.24 **Storage capacities.** A typical 16 mm roll will hold the equivalent of 3,000 A4 pages. *One* typical microfiche will hold the equivalent of about 98 A4 pages.

Graph plotters

9.25 These devices provide a completely different form of output and have a variety of applications. Two basic types are:

    a. **Flatbed type.** The pen moves up, down, across or side to side.

    b. **Drum type.** The pen moves up, down and across. The paper provides the sideways movement.

    Note. The up/down movements allow the pen to move from point to point with or without making a line.

9.26 **Digital plotters and incremental plotters.** The difference between these two types of plotter is in the way they are given instructions to move:

    a. **Digital plotters** receive digital input that specifies the position to which the pen should move, i.e. like a map reference.

    b. **Incremental plotters** receive input that specifies changes in position, e.g. move 2 mm left.

9.27 Many plotters have multiple pens of different colours that may be changed under machine control. Some plotters use 'electrostatic' printing rather than pen and ink.

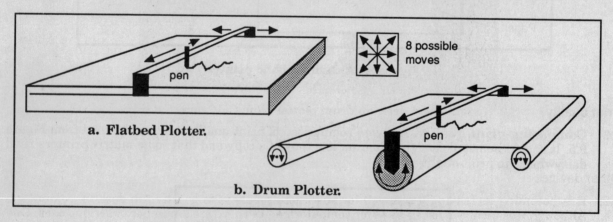

Figure 9.6 Flatbed plotter (above) and Drum plotter

9.28 **Applications.** Graph plotters are used for scientific and engineering purposes. One special application is CAD (Computer Aided Design) in which, for example, machine or architectural designs are created by computer and then output on graph plotters.

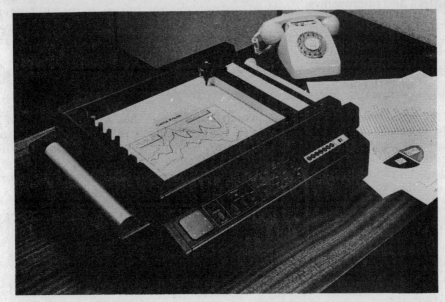

a. **A desktop, A3-size flatbed, 8-pen plotter from CalComp designed for plotting business and scientific graphs and charts on paper or on clear acetate for projection.**
(Photograph with caption by courtesy of CalComp Ltd)

b. A high-speed desktop drum plotter from CalComp that uses
A4-size continuous fan-folded paper or clear film.
(Photograph with caption by courtesy of CalComp Ltd)

Other devices

9.29 It is becoming increasingly common for small loudspeakers to be fitted in desktop computers. Although this facility is often used for computer games there are a number of serious uses. One general use is as a means of providing messages to the user, the simplest form of which is a warning 'bleep' sound when something is wrong. However, loudspeakers really come into their own when used in conjunction with digitised sound. For example, by means of special software a desktop computer may be turned into a sound synthesizer unit which can be hooked up to a audio system.

9.30 Most other output devices are limited in use in specific applications. One notable exception is synthesized speech output.

9.31 Speech output. In principle, spoken output should be an extremely useful medium. Unfortunately the devices currently available produce unnatural sounds and are limited to a few specialist applications. The situation is likely to improve over the next few years.

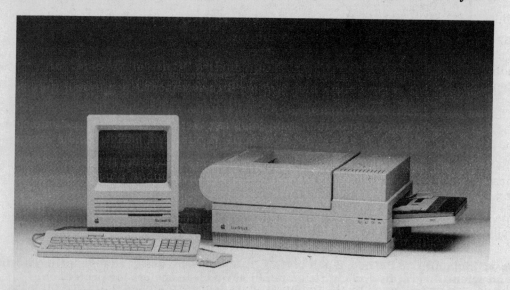

An Apple Macintosh SE with an Apple LaserWriter II laser printer
(Courtesy of Apple Computers UK Ltd)

Summary

9.32 The *features* of the *main* hardware units and media for the output of data from the computer have been covered. They are:

a. Printers – Single sheet or continuous stationery.

b. Microform recorder – Microfilm or Microfiche.

c. Graph Plotters – Single sheet or continuous stationery.

d. Actuators.

e. Others.

Points to note

9.33 a. Line printers can print in *Optical Character Recognition* form, i.e. allowing later re-input without further transcription.

b. Some matrix printers can be used to produce bar-coded strips, e.g. for use as stock labels.

Questions

1. Why do you think a desktop laser printer is a popular choice of printer to use with a workstation?

2. What printers are suitable for producing business letters?

10 Data capture and data entry

Introduction

10.1 These days the majority of computer end-users input data to the computer via keyboards on PCs, workstations or terminals. However, for many medium and large scale commercial and industrial applications involving large volumes of data the use of keyboards is not practical or economical. Instead, specialist methods, devices and media are used and these are the subject of this chapter. The chapter begins by examining the problems of data entry. It goes on to consider the stages involved and the alternatives available. It then examines the factors that influence the choice of methods, devices and media for data input. Finally, the chapter examines the overall controls that are needed over data as it is entered into the computer for processing.

10.2 The selection of the best method of data entry is often the biggest single problem faced by those designing commercial or industrial computer systems, because of the high costs involved and numerous practical consideration.

10.3 The best methods of data entry may still not give satisfactory facilities if the necessary controls over their use are not in place.

Problems of data entry

10.4 The data to be processed by the computer must be presented in a **machine-sensible** form (i.e. the language of the particular input device). Therein lies the basic problem since much data *originates* in a form that is *far* from machine sensible. Thus a painful error-prone process of transcription must be undergone before the data is suitable for input to the computer.

10.5 The process of data collection involves getting the original data to the 'processing centre', transcribing it, sometimes converting it from one medium to another, and finally getting it into the computer. This process involves a great many people, machines and much expense.

10.6 A number of advances have been made in recent years towards automating the data collection process so as to bypass or reduce the problems. This chapter considers a variety of methods, including many that are of primary importance in commercial computing. Specialist methods used for industrial computer applications will be covered in later chapters.

10.78 Data can originate in many forms, but the computer can only accept it in a machine-sensible8 form. The process involved in getting the data from its point of origin to the computer in a form suitable for processing is called **Data Collection**.

10.8 Before dealing with the individual stages of data collection it should be noted that data collection *starts* at the source of the raw data and *ends* when valid data is within the computer in a form ready for processing.

10.9 Many of the problems of data entry can be avoided if the data can be obtained in a computer-sensible form at the point of origin. This is known as **data capture**. This chapter will describe several methods of data capture. The capture of data does not necessarily mean its immediate input to the computer. The captured data may be stored in some intermediate form for later entry into the main computer in the required form. If data is input directly into the computer at its point of origin the data entry is said to be on-line. If, in addition, the method of direct input is a terminal or workstation the method of input is known as **Direct Data Entry (DDE).** The term **Data Entry** used in the chapter title usually means not only the process of physical input by a device but also any methods directly associated with the input.

Stages in data collection

10.10 The process of data collection may involve any number of the following stages according to the methods used.

  a. Data creation, e.g. on clerically prepared source documents.

  b. Transmission of data.

  c. Data preparation. i.e. transcription and verification.

  d. Possible conversion from one medium (e.g. diskette) to another (e.g. magnetic tape).

e. Input of data to the computer for validation.

f. Sorting.

g. Control – all stages must be controlled.

10.11 Not all data will go through every stage and the sequence could vary in some applications. Even today, a high proportion of input data starts life in the form of a manually scribed or typewritten document and has to go through all the stages. However, efforts have been made to reduce the number of stages. Progress has been made in preparing the source document itself in a machine-sensible form so that it may be used as input to the computer without the need for transcription. In practice, the method and medium adopted will depend on factors such as cost, type of application, etc. This will be discussed further in a later chapter.

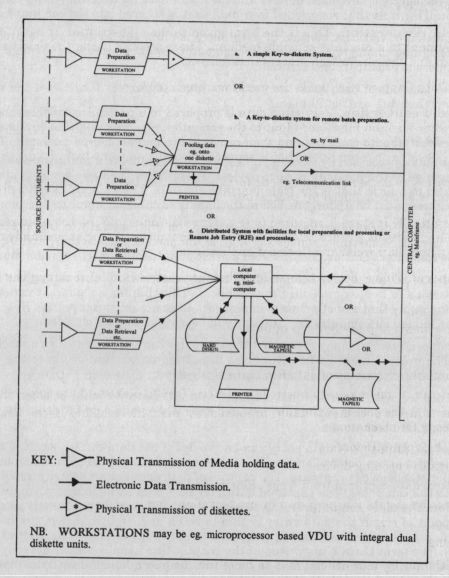

Figure 10.1 Some typical data entry systems

Stages explained

10.12 a. **Data creation.** There are two basic alternatives, the first of which is the traditional method:

　　i. **Source documents.** A great deal of data still originate in the form of clerically prepared source documents.

   ii. **Data capture.** Data is produced in a machine-sensible form at source and is read directly by a suitable device, e.g. a bar code reader (details later).

  b. **Data transmission**. This can mean different things according to the method and medium of data collection adopted.

   i. If the computer is located at a central point, the documents will be physically 'transmitted', i.e. by the post office or a courier to the central point, (e.g. posting batches of source documents).

   ii. It is also possible for data to be transmitted by means of telephone lines to the central computer, in which case no source documents would be involved in the transmission process, (e.g. transmitting data captured at source). A variant on this method is the use of FAXes.

  c. **Data preparation.** This is the term given to the transcription of data from the source document to a machine-sensible medium. There are two parts; the original transcription itself and the verification process that follows.

Note. Data Capture eliminates the need for transcription.

  d. **Media conversion.** Very often data is prepared in a particular medium and converted to another medium for faster input to the computer, e.g. data might be prepared on diskette, or captured onto cassette, and then converted to magnetic tape for input. The conversion will be done on a computer that is separate from the one for which the data is intended.

  e. **Input.** The data, now in magnetic form, is subjected to validity checks by a computer program before being used for processing.

  f. **Sorting.** This stage is required to re-arrange the data into the sequence required for processing. (This is a practical necessity for efficient processing of sequentially organised data in many commercial and financial applications.)

  g. **Control.** This is not a *stage* as such, because control is applied throughout the *whole* collection.

Data-collection media and methods in outline

10.13 The alternatives are as follows.

  a. On-line transmission of data from source, e.g. Direct Data Entry (DDE).

  b. Source document keyed directly into diskette (key-to-diskette) from some documents.

  c. The source document itself prepared in machine-sensible form using Character Recognition techniques.

  d. Data Capture Devices.

  e. Portable encoding devices.

  f. Source data captured from 'Tags', Plastic Badges or strips.

  g. Creation of data for input as a by-product of another operation.

On-line systems

10.14 The ultimate in data collection is to have the computer linked directly to the source of the data. If this is *not* feasible then the next best thing is to 'capture' the data as near as possible to its source and feed it to the computer with little delay.

10.15 Such methods may involve the use of data transmission equipment if the point of origination is remote from the computer. The computer is linked to the terminal point (the source of data or nearby) by a telecommunication line and data is transmitted over the line to the computer system.

10.16 Data enters the terminal either by keying in via a keyboard or by a device such as one that can directly read source documents (details later).

10.17 On-line methods obviate the need for physical transportation of source documents to the processing point. There is also less delay in producing processed information, especially if the data link provides for two-way transmission of data (i.e. from terminal to computer and computer to terminal).

10.18 Such systems can involve large capital outlay on the necessary equipment, which is usually justified in terms of speed of access to the computer's data and quicker feed-back of information.

10.19 On-line systems are the only practical choice for some applications. One example is the computer that controls a machine or factory process. It must receive input directly from source in order to be able to respond at a moment's notice.

10.20 If Direct Data Entry (DDE) is used then data is keyed in to a VDU or workstation by the operator. It is checked, displayed on the screen and then entered for processing.

10.21 A DDE station can also be used to interrogate the computer's stored data so that data can be checked for validity at the time of input. For example, if a customer's order is being entered, it is possible to check details of the customer's account and the availability of stocks.

10.22 Some specialised on-line systems are used by the general public. Probably the most common examples are the 'hole in the wall' machines, more correctly called **on-line cash service tills**, which are provided by many banks and building societies for cash dispensing and other services outside normal office hours.

Key-to-diskette

10.23 Key-to-diskette systems are a popular alternative to on-line systems in some organisations where data is generated at a number of different places.

Note. The key-to-diskette methods need not necessarily involve the use of special hardware. In many cases the same facility is provided by means of PCs running special programs. In what follows the features of specialist equipment are described.

10.24 The simplest key-to-diskette system is a stand-alone specialist 'workstation' consisting of a high-quality VDU with inbuilt dual diskette units and microprocessor (figure 10.1a).

10.25 The workstation operates under the control of its own programs, which format the screen like a document, verify and validate input data, and transfer the data onto diskette. Programs for dealing with different source documents may be held on diskette and loaded by the workstation user when required.

10.26 The workstations are compact, robust, reliable, portable and operate autonomously. They therefore enable distributed data entry (close to the source of the data) together with a simple means of transferring data to a central computer.

10.27 Larger systems often include local printers to provide **hard copy** (i.e. on paper) of the disk output (e.g. for audit trail purposes, and electronic data transmission facilities) (figure 10.1b). The largest systems normally form part of a distributed data-processing system in which workstations are multi-purpose devices and facilities for data storage and transmission are varied and flexible, e.g. a workstation may act as an interactive terminal to the main computer, or large volumes of data on diskette may be converted to magnetic tape for faster bulk input (figure 10.1c).

Character recognition

10.28 The methods described so far have been concerned with turning data into a machine-sensible form as a prerequisite to input. By using Optical Character Recognition (**OCR**) and Magnetic Ink Character Recognition

(MICR) techniques, the source documents *themselves* are prepared in a machine-sensible form and thus *eliminate* the transcription stage. Notice, however, that such characters can *also* be recognised by the human eye (see figure 10.2 and 10.5).

We will first examine the devices used.

Figure 10.2 Specimen characters from two common OCR character sets

Document readers

10.29 Optical readers and documents. There are two basic methods of optical document reading:

a. **Optical Character Recognition (OCR).**

b. **Optical Mark Recognition (OMR).**

These two methods are often used in conjunction with one another, and have much in common. Their common and distinguishing features are covered in the next few paragraphs.

10.30 Features of an optical reader.

a. It has a document-feed hopper and several stackers, including a stacker for 'rejected' documents (Fig 10.3).

b. Reading of documents prepared in optical characters or marks is accomplished as follows:

    i. **Characters.** A scanning device recognises each character by the amount of reflected light (i.e. OCR) (see fig. 10.2). The method of recognition, although essentially an electronic one, is similar in principle to matching photographic pictures with their negatives by holding the negative in front of the picture. The best match lets through the least light.

    ii. **Marks.** A mark in a particular position on the document will trigger off a response. It is the *position* of the mark that is converted to a value by the reader (i.e. OMR) (see fig. 10.4). The method involves directing thin beams of light onto the paper surface which are reflected into a light detector, unless the beam is absorbed by a dark pencil mark, i.e. a mark is recognised by the reduction of reflected light.

Note. An older method of mark reading called **mark sensing** involved pencil marks conducting between two contacts and completing a circuit.

c. Documents may be read at up to 10,000 A4 documents per hour.

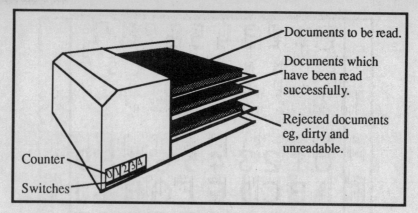

Figure 10.3 A document reader

Number to be coded										
3	0	1	2	3	4	5	6	7	8	9
5	0	1	2	3	4	5	6	7	8	9
1	0	1	2	3	4	5	6	7	8	9

Figure 10.4 A marked document ready for OMR

10.31 Features of a document.

a. Documents are printed in a stylised form (by printers, etc, fitted with a special type-face) that can be recognised by a machine. The stylised print is also recognisable to the human eye. Printing must be on specified areas on the document.

b. Some documents incorporate optical marks. Predetermined positions on the document are given values. A mark is made in a specific position using a pencil and is read by the reader.

c. Good-quality printing and paper are vital.

d. Documents require to be undamaged for accurate reading.

e. Sizes of documents, and scanning area, may be limited.

10.32 Magnetic ink reader and documents. The method of reading these documents is known as Magnetic Ink Character Recognition (MICR).

10.33 Features of magnetic ink readers.

a. Documents are passed through a strong magnetic field, causing the iron oxide in the ink encoded characters to become magnetised. Documents are then passed under a read head, where a current flows at a strength according to the size of the magnetised area (i.e. characters are recognised by a magnetic pattern).

b. Documents can be read at up to 2,400 per minute.

10.34 Features of documents

a. The quality of printing needs to be very high.

b. The characters are printed in a highly distinctive type style using ink containing particles of iron oxide, which gives the required magnetic property, (see figure 10.5). Examine a bank cheque for a further example.

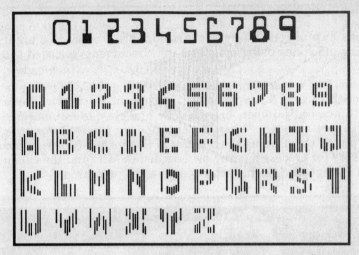

**Figure 10.5 Specimen characters from two common MICR character sets
(upper set: E13B lower set: CMC7)**

Optical character recognition (OCR)

10.35 a. **Technique explained**.

    i. Alphabetic and numeric characters are created in a particular type style, which can be 'read' by special machines. The characters look so nearly like 'normal' print that they can *also* be read by humans.

    ii. Characters are *created* by a variety of machines (e.g. line printers, typewriters, cash registers, etc) fitted with the special type face.

    iii. The special optical character-reading machines *can* be linked to a computer, in which case the data is read from the document into the processor.

  b. Applications. OCR is used extensively in connection with billing, e.g. gas and electricity bills and insurance premium renewals. In these applications the bills are prepared in OC by the computer, then sent out to the customers, who return them with payment cheques. The documents re-enter the computer system (via the OC reader) as evidence of payment. This is an example of the 'turnaround' technique. Notice that no transcription is required.

  c. OCR/keyboard devices. These permit a combination of OCR reading with manual keying. Printed data (e.g. account numbers) is read by OCR; hand-written data (e.g. amounts) is keyed by the operator. This method is used in credit card systems.

Optical mark reading (OMR)

10.36 a. **Technique explained.** Mark reading is discussed here because it is often used in conjunction with OCR, although it must be pointed out that it is a technique in *itself*. Positions on a document are given certain values. These positions when 'marked' with a pencil are interpreted by a machine. Notice it is the 'position' that the machine interprets and that has a predetermined value.

  b. **Application.** Meter reader documents are a good example of the use of OMR in conjunction with OCR. The computer prints out the document for each customer (containing name, address, *last* reading, etc,) in OC. The meter reader records the current reading in the form of 'marks' on the same document. The document re-enters the computer system (via a reader that reads OC *and* OM) and is processed (i.e. results in a bill being sent to the customer). Note that this is another example of a '**turnaround document**'.

Magnetic ink character recognition (MICR)

10.37 a. **Techniques explained.** Numeric characters are created in a highly stylised type by special encoding machines using magnetic ink. Documents encoded thus are 'read' by special machines.

b. **Application.** One major application is in banking (look at a cheque book), although some local authorities use it for payment of rates by instalments. Cheques are encoded at the bottom with account number, branch code and cheque number *before* being given to the customer (i.e. pre-encoded). When the cheques are received *from* the customers the bottom line is completed by encoding the *amount* of the cheque (i.e. post-encoded). Thus all the details necessary for processing are now encoded in MIC and the cheque enters the computer system via a magnetic ink character reader to be processed.

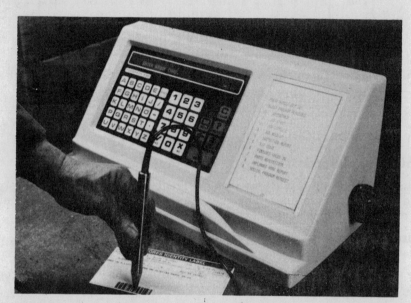

Feedback model 490 Multi-function Industrial Terminal with Slot Bar Code Reader and Feedback 479 Wand Attachment.
(Picture courtesy Feedback Data Ltd)

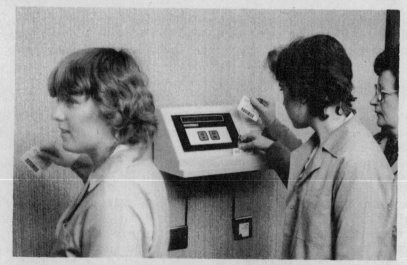

Feedback 496 Time/Event Reporting and Enquiry Terminal.
(Picture courtesy Feedback Data Ltd)

Data capture devices

10.38 These devices are mostly special-purpose devices intended for use in particular applications. Common, special and typical examples are described in the next few paragraphs.

10.39 **Direct Input Devices.**

    a. Special sensing devices may be able to detect events as they happen and pass the appropriate data directly to the computer. For example:

        i. On an automated production line, products or components can be 'counted' as they pass specific points. Errors can stop the production line.

        ii. At a supermarket checkout a **laser scanner** may read coded marks on food packets as the packets pass by on the conveyer. This data is used by the computerised till to generate a till receipt and maintain records of stock levels (details later).

        iii. In a computer-controlled chemical works, food factory or brewery industrial instruments connected to the computer can read temperatures and pressures in vats.

    b. Voice data entry (VDE) devices. Data can be spoken into these devices. Currently they are limited to a few applications in which a small vocabulary is involved.

10.40 **Features**

The specific feature of these devices tends to depend upon the application for which they are used. However, the data captured by the device must ultimately be represented in some binary form in order to be processed by a *digital* computer. For some devices, the input may merely be a single bit representation that corresponds to some instrument, such as a pressure switch, being on or off.

10.41 **Data loggers/recorders.** These devices record and store data at source. The data is input to the computer at some later stage.

10.42 **Features**

    a. The device usually contains its own microprocessor and data storage device/medium or radio transmitter.

    b. *Magnetic tape cassettes* are often used for data storage. The cassettes are just like those used for domestic audio systems.

    c. Data entry to the device is usually by means of a small keyboard, like a calculator keyboard, or by some special reading attachment.

10.43 A basic device, using only a keyboard for data entry, and able to transmit data, is effectively a portable terminal.

10.44 Popular attachments to both portable and static devices are the light-pen and **magnetic-pen.** These attachments resemble pens at the end of a length of electrical flex. More bulky hand held alternatives are sometimes called '**wands**'. They can read specially coded data in the form of either optical marks/characters, or magnetic codes, which have previously been recorded on strips of suitable material. A common version is the **bar-code reader** (see figure 10.6).

Figure 10.6 A bar-coded strip readable by a light-pen, light-wand or laser scanner

Tags

10.45 The use of tags as a data collection technique is usually associated with clothing retailing applications, although they are also used to some extent in other applications.

a. The original tags were miniature punched cards. Today most tags in use have magnetic strips (details below) on them instead of holes.

b. Using a special code, data such as price of garment, type and size, and branch/department are recorded on the tag by a machine. Certain of the data is also *printed* on the tag.

c. Tags are affixed to the garment before sale and are *removed* at the point of sale. At the end of the day's trading each store will send its tags (representing the day's sales) in a container to the data processing centre. Alternatively, the tags may be processed at the point of sale (see later).

d. At the centre the tags are *converted* to more conventional diskette or magnetic tape for input to the computer system.

e. Note that data is 'captured' at the source (point of sale) in a machine-sensible form and thus needs no transcription and can be processed straightaway by the machine (see figure 10.6).

Bar-coded and magnetic strips

10.46 Data can be recorded on small strips, which are read optically or magnetically. Optical reading is done by using printed 'bar codes', i.e. alternating lines and spaces that represent data in binary (see figure 10.6). Magnetic reading depends on a strip of magnetic tape on which data has been encoded. The data are read by a **light-pen**, **magnetic-pen** or **wand** which is passed over the strip. Portable devices are available that also include a keyboard. An example of their use is in stock recording; the light pen is used to read the stock code from a strip attached to the shelf, and the quantity is keyed manually. The data are recorded on a magnetic tape cassette. This technique is also used at check-out points in supermarkets. Goods have strips attached and stock code and price are read by the light pen. The data thus collected are used to prepare a receipt automatically, and are also recorded for stock control purposes (see the photograph later in this chapter).

By-product

10.47 All the systems described up to now have been designed specifically with data collection in mind but data can very often be collected as a by-product of some other operation. A good example is that found in some modern cash registers.

10.48 **Cash registers.** These are fitted with magnetic tape cassette units. A mass of statistical data is captured at source without any intermediate operation. The cassettes, etc, are forwarded to the data processing centre for input to a computer. Alternatively, the cash register may be connected on-line (see opposite).

Point-of-sale terminals

10.49 The Point-of-Sale Terminal (**PoS**) is essentially an electronic cash register that is linked to a computer, or that records data onto cassette or cartridge. In its simplest form, it may simply transmit the details of a transaction to the computer for processing. The more complex terminals can communicate with the computer for such purposes as checking the credit position of a customer, obtaining prices from file and ascertaining availability of stock. If the customers bank or credit account is debited this is **EFTPOS** (Electronic Fund Transfer at Point of Sale). The terminal usually includes a keyboard for manual entry of data. A bar-code reader may also be provided, typically to read stock codes.

10.50 The type of bar-coding shown in stylised form in figure 10.7 is used on packets of consumable products such as foods. The numbers are coded in bar-coded strips and printed in OCR characters. The code is called a **UPC** (Universal Product Code) in the USA and an **EAN** (European Article Number) in Europe. The left-hand digit, '5' in Fig 10.6 represents the country of origin e.g. '0' is the USA, '5' is the UK. The digits represent the manufacturer's code and the product number.

The IBM 3660 Supermarket System incorporates a high-speed optical scanner. As an item is pulled across the scanner's window a laser beam reads the European Article Number EAN (or Universal Product Code in the US) bar code printed on the side of the package, and the system automatically decodes and registers the information on the symbol. The item can be of any shape and size and the bar code can be passed over the window in any direction.

(Picture and details courtesy of IBM)

Figure 10.7 A stylised example of an application of bar-coding

10.51 Such details would not be asked for in an examination but serve as a good illustration of a specialised coding system. In figure 10.7 each digit is represented by a set of seven bit codes with a different code set being used depending upon the digit position and the country of origin. The example is based upon the UK EAN format.

Factors in choice

10.52 The choice of data collection method and medium may be influenced by the following factors:

10.53 **Appropriateness.**

a. **Magnetic Media** such as magnetic tape and magnetic disk are primarily storage media, but are often used at an intermediate stage of data input. For example, data may be captured onto a diskette or magnetic cassette and then converted to magnetic tape on one computer prior to final input to the main computer needing the data. These magnetic media are reusable and can be input at much higher speeds than direct keying by DDE. Moreover, key-to-diskette systems provide an advanced method of data collection, with facilities for checking and control as the data are keyed, plus reducing the need for verification on the main computer. Tape and diskette are relatively cheap.

b. **Character recognition.**

   i. **MICR** is largely confined to banking. It was developed in response to the need to cope with large volumes of documents (in particular cheques) beyond the scope of conventional methods. It is a very reliable but expensive method.

   ii. **OCR** is more versatile than MICR and less expensive. It is suited to those applications that use a turnaround system such as billing in gas and electricity where volumes are too high for conventional methods. It is limited to applications in which a 'turnaround' document can be used – e.g. a bill printed by the computer, part of which is returned with the payment.

   iii. **OMR** is very simple and inexpensive. The forms can however be prepared only by people who have been trained in the method. All character recognition techniques suffer from the possible disadvantage of requiring a standardised document acceptable to the document reader.

c. **Terminals** provide a very fast and convenient means of data collection and provide the main means of carrying out **Direct Data Entry**. They may also provide a fast means of output direct to the point of use. But costs are increased by the need to provide terminals at a number of different points and possibly by the additional use of data-transmission equipment.

d. **Special media** such as tags and bar-coded strips reduce costs, but are essentially tailored to particular types of application.

10.54 **Cost.** This must be an overriding factor. The elements of cost are:

a. **Staff** (probably the biggest).

b. **Hardware** (capital and running costs).

c. **Media** Paper-based source documents are *not* reusable and magnetic media can only be reused a limited number of times.

d. **Changeover** There is normally a cost associated with changing over to a new method of data input.

10.55 **Time.** This can be quite fundamental in the choice of method and medium and is very much linked with cost because the quicker the response required the more it generally costs to get that response. On-line systems will cut down this delay; so will methods, like OCR, that prepare source documents in a machine-sensible form.

10.56 **Accuracy.** This is linked with appropriateness and confidence, and is a big headache in data collection. Input must be 'clean' otherwise it is rejected and delays occur. Errors at the preparation stage also are costly. Substitution of the machine for the human is the answer in general terms.

10.57 **Volume.** Some methods will not be able to cope with high volumes of source data within a reasonable time scale.

10.58 **Confidence.** It is very important that a system has a record of success. This is probably why many promising new methods take so long to be adopted.

10.59 **Input medium.** The choice of input medium is very much tied up with data collection. Often it will be an integral part of data collection, e.g. on-line systems. Key-to-diskette methods have the advantage of collecting data on what is a fast input medium. These two examples are enough to demonstrate the way in which input medium is a prime consideration when looking at the collection of data.

The objectives of control

10.60 The objectives of control are:
   a. To ensure that all data is processed.
   b. To preserve the integrity of maintained data.
   c. To detect, correct and re-process all errors.
   d. To prevent and detect fraud.

10.61 The different controls are dealt with under the following headings:
   a. Manual controls – applied to documents prior to computer processing.
   b. Data preparation controls.
   c. Validation checks.
   d. Batch controls.
   e. Other controls.

Design considerations

10.62 Controls are a major consideration of the systems designer. They must be designed into the system and thoroughly tested. Failure to build in adequate control has caused many expensive system failures. Although the emphasis here is on data entry, many of the considerations also apply to other areas.

10.63 The need for controls must be clearly defined at the outset to enable the appropriate action to be taken to provide them. User staff and auditors should be fully consulted.

Importance of control

10.64 Control must be instituted as early as possible in the system. The quality of input data is of vital importance to the accuracy of output. Everything possible must be done to ensure that data are complete and accurate just before input to the computer.

Types of error

10.65 The systems designer must guard against the following types of error:
   a. Missing source documents.
   b. Source documents on which entries are omitted, illegible or dubious.
   c. Transcription errors (e.g. errors in copying data from one form to another).
   d. Data preparation errors (e.g. errors made when keying onto diskette).
   e. Program faults.
   f. Machine hardware faults.

   Note. Machine hardware faults are less common in practice than is often supposed. Modern computers are self-checking to a very considerable extent (e.g. parity) and usually signal any internal failure. The machine is very often blamed for what are really faults in systems design or programming.

10.66 **Verification.** The process of checking that data has been correctly transcribed is called **verification**. A common verification method is to compare a second transcription with a first. Password changes are often verified in this way.

Manual controls

10.67 Even in advanced systems, considerable checking of source documents is often necessary. Such checks may be:

a. **Scrutiny** to detect:
  i. missing entries.
  ii. illegible entries.
  iii. illogical or unlikely entries.
b. **Reference** of the document to stored data to verify entries.
c. **Re-calculating** to check calculations made on the document.

Data collection controls

10.68 The collection of data for processing involves transcribing it into a form suitable for machine processing. There is a very real possibility of error at this stage, and control must be imposed to prevent or detect transcription errors. The type of control depends on the method of data collection used.

a. **On-line systems.** These depend on the data displayed (by a VDU) or being printed and checked by the operator before being released for processing.
b. **Character recognition.** With these techniques, accuracy depends on the character reader detecting any doubtful character or mark. Some readers provide facilities for display of the character and its immediate manual correction by the operator. Otherwise, the document is rejected by the machine.

Validation checks

10.69 A computer cannot notice errors in the data being processed in the way that a clerk or machine operator does. Validation checks are an attempt to build into the computer program powers of judgement so that incorrect items of data are detected and reported. These checks can be made at two stages:

a. **Input.** When data is first input to the computer, different checks can be applied to prevent errors going forward for processing. For this reason, the first computer run is often referred to as validation or data vet.
b. **Updating.** Further checking is possible when the data input are being processed. The consistency of the input data with existing stored data can be checked by the program. It is possible to perform checks of this type during the input run if the stored data is on-line at the time.

10.70 The following are the main types of validation check that may be used:

a. **Presence.** Data are checked to ensure that all necessary fields are present.
b. **Size.** Fields are checked to ensure that they contain the correct number of characters.
c. **Range.** Numbers or codes are checked to ensure that they are within the permissible range (e.g. costs codes within the series allocated).
d. **Character check.** Fields are checked to ensure that they contain only characters of the correct type (e.g. that there are not letters in a numeric field).
e. **Format.** Fields are checked to ensure that the format is correct (e.g. that a part number contains the correct number of alphabetic and numeric characters in the correct sequence).
f. **Reasonableness.** Quantities are checked to ensure that they are not abnormally high or low (e.g. that the amount of a certain type of goods ordered is 'reasonable').
g. **Check Digits.** Use of a check digit enables a number to be self-checking. It is calculated using a mathematical formula and then becomes part of the number (see Appendix 3.3). When the number is input to the computer, the Validation Program performs the same calculation on the number as was performed when the check digit was generated in the first place. This will ensure that the number is correct, e.g. no digits have been transposed.

10.71 The checks described above are usually applied during a first processing run unless all the processing is being carried out on-line. Further checks may be made when the data is processed. Discussion of such checks is left later chapters.

Batch controls

10.72 Batch controls are fundamental to most computer-based accounting systems. The stages of batch control in a computer-based system are:

a. **Batching.** At an early stage in processing, documents are arranged in batches by being placed in a wallet or folder, or clipped together. The number of documents in a batch may be standard (e.g. 50) or may represent a convenient group (e.g. one day's orders from one sales office). A **batch cover note** is attached to the batch.

b. **Numbering.** Each batch is allocated a unique number, which is entered on the batch cover note.

c. **Batch registers.** Each department or section responsible for processing the batch records its receipt and dispatch in a register. It is thus possible to check that all batches have been received and dealt with, and to trace any batch that gets lost or delayed.

d. **Batch totals.** Control totals are obtained for each batch, usually using a desktop adding or calculating machine. The control totals comprise:

    i. the total number of documents in the batch,

    ii. totals of the fields that it is required to control (e.g. total value of invoices; total value of overtime payments; total quantities of orders).

These totals are entered on the **batch cover note.**

e. **Data preparation.** When input is prepared, the batch totals are included (e.g. if key-to-diskette is used, batch totals are typed in first and checked against the entered data).

f. **Reconciliation.** When the input data are read by the validation program, batch totals are reconciled. The input items are accumulated and the total agreed to the input batch control total. If the two totals do not agree, an error is reported. The report shows the two totals, the difference, and may provide a listing of all the items in the batch. The batch does not go forward for processing; it is re-input after the error has been found and corrected.

g. **Hash totals.** Batch totals are usually used to control the number of forms processed and the quantities they contain. It is also possible to apply the technique to numbers such as customer or payroll numbers. When batch totals are obtained the numbers are also added and entered on the batch cover note. The totals are input and reconciled in the way just described. Since the totals are meaningless and useful only for control, they are called 'hash' or 'nonsense' totals.

Other controls

10.73 It is essential to ensure that data is not only input correctly, but also maintained correctly and processed correctly right through the system. Further details of such controls will be given in later chapters.

Cost of control

10.74 The cost of control should be measured against the cost of *not* having it. It is possible to have too much control as well as too little. The inability of the computer to detect by itself faults in programs or data should always be kept in mind. Controls should be designed in relation to the consequences of an error going undetected, and after investigations into the types of error likely to occur. Controls should be inserted into the system at the point where they give maximum benefit. It is often necessary to adjust controls (particularly validity checks) in the light of practical experience.

Signature Verification System from NCR PC
(Picture courtesy NCR Ltd)

SIRRES is a Signature Recording and Retrieval System which enables specimen signatures to be stored on computer and called up immediately on a terminal screen for comparison with that being presented. It consists of an electronic camera kit to photograph the signature, software which runs on an NCR Decision Mate V personal computer to encode and transmit the signature to a central NCR I-series computer for storage. The signature is retrieved and displayed on the Decision Mate V screen.

Summary

10.75 a. Data collection is the process of getting data into a form suitable for processing against master files.

b. Data collection is accomplished in stages from source document through to actual processing against master files.

c. Data collection is a costly, time-consuming and, in many cases, cumbersome process. Therefore methods of reducing cost and of reducing the time involved will be worthwhile.

d. Remember the factors that influence choice of system:
   i.   Appropriateness or suitability.
   ii. Cost.
   iii. Time.
   iv. Accuracy.
   v.   Volume.
   vi. Confidence.

e. Specialist methods such as tags and strips are in the minority but are important in their particular fields.

f. Controls need to be designed into a system carefully.

g. Controls have been considered under the following headings:
   i.   Manual.
   ii. Data Preparation.
   iii. Validation checks.
   iv. Batch controls.
   v.   Other controls.

h. Control is costly. Consideration should be given to what *should* be controlled rather than what *can* be controlled.

Points to note

10.76 a. Many traditional methods require data preparation, e.g. Key-to-disk, key-to-tape, etc.

b. Many modern methods collect data in machine-sensible form thereby eliminating data preparation, e.g. character recognition, source capture, etc.

c. **Data collection.** The process of getting data to the computer in a machine-sensible form for processing.

d. **Data capture.** Sometimes used as a substitute term for data collection, but more specifically refers to data 'captured' in a machine-sensible form at its *source*.

e. **Tags.** A major manufacturer of systems based on punched tags is Kimball and thus you may find tags referred to as **Kimball tags**.

f. Note that data preparation is a part of the data collection process.

g. Data is often captured or prepared in one machine-sensible medium and converted to another before input to computer.

h. OCR and MICR 'readers' can be of the type that are used off-line or on-line to the computer. The off-line readers may be linked to a magnetic tape unit so that the optical character/magnetic ink documents can be converted to tape for much faster input.

i. Note the importance of detecting an error as quickly as possible so that it may be put right and the data re-enter into the system quickly.

j. Long delays are caused by rejected input. It has to 'go round again' and this can cause days of delay.

k. The unit of control for input is usually the batch.

l. Note the use of the check digit. Its use preserves the integrity of the number field and when used in conjunction with the record key it ensures a transaction is processed against the correct master record.

m. Note that good source-document design is important. It helps legible entries to be made and eases the task of the data-preparation operator.

n. This chapter deals only with system controls. Other types of control designed to ensure that the DP department functions efficiently and that its files are secure are dealt with later.

Questions

1. At what stages in data collection is control applied?
2. Distinguish between 'human-sensible' and 'machine-sensible'. Give an example of a form of computer input that is both machine sensible and human sensible.
3. What do you consider to be the advantages and disadvantages of the various methods/media of data collection?
4. Compare the relative advantages of a VDU and printer terminals for on-line computing.
5. Explain how the factors identified in this chapter could influence the choice of printer to be used on a system.
6. What is the difference between verification and validation in the context of data collection?
7. Name six types of error that can occur in data collection, and, for each type, give an example of one measure that can be used to prevent the error.
8. The data processing manager of a large computer installation is concerned about the high volume of printout from the installation's two printers and the subsequent paper storage problems in the user departments. As a consequence he is considering the use of 'Computer output on microform', COM (Microfilm or Microfiche).

   Explain what is meant by COM and the difference between microfilm and microfiche, give the advantages and disadvantages of the systems.

(CIMA)

9. Define and give TWO examples of the use of each of the following:

    MICR Bar Marking

    OCR Badge Readers

    (IDPM Part 1)

10. Details of payments to, and withdrawals from, a savings account are recorded on small paper slips. Each slip contains the following data.

    i.   Date
    ii. Account holder's name(s)
    iii. Account number
    iv. Amount (in pounds)
    v.   Account holder's signature.

    a. Suggest ways in which this data might be validated.

    b. Suggest a suitable layout for a simple batch control slip (batch cover note).

11. Describe the functions and operation of a ''batch total' control over computer systems input.

    (ICA)

12. Controls are invariably incorporated into the input, processing and output stages of a computer-based system.

    a. State the guidelines which should normally be followed in determining what controls should be built into a system.

    b. Identify and briefly describe one type of control which might be used to detect each of the following input data errors:

        i.   error of transcription resulting in an incorrect customer account code;
        ii. quantity of raw material normally written in pounds weight but entered in error as tons;
        iii. entry on a dispatch note for a product to be despatched from a warehouse which does not stock that particular product;
        iv. five digit product code used instead of a six digit salesman code;
        v.   invalid expenditure code entered on an invoice.

    (ACA)

13. Within the context of a data processing system, discuss the need for, and the advantages to be gained from, the use of a meaningful accounting code.

    (AAT)

14. What data preparation and data validation checks may be applied to input data to assist in ensuring that the data is reliable for processing? Give full details of each method described.

    (IDPM Part 1)

Human Computer Interfaces

This Part of the text returns to the issue of interactive on-line computing, but instead of just considering devices, as in Chapter 8, it examines the issues that concern making computers easy for users to interact with. This interaction between end-users and the computer is said to take place at the **'Human Computer Interface'** (HCI). The term 'Human Computer Interface' is meant to cover *all* aspects of this interaction, not just the hardware. Of particular interest is what makes one HCI better than another one. GUIs deserve particular attention in this subject area because they offer facilities which enable the creation of very effective HCIs.

11 Human Computer Interfaces

Introduction

11.1 The interaction between end-users and the computer is said to take place at the '**Human Computer Interface**' (HCI). The term 'Human Computer Interface' is meant to cover *all* aspects of this interaction, not just the hardware. Of particular interest is what makes one HCI better than another one. This chapter provides an introduction to issues concerning the HCI.

11.2 When computers were first developed the only people who could operate them were highly trained engineers and scientists. Today almost everyone operates a computer as part of daily life. Of course, individuals may not necessarily think about the fact that they are operating a computer as when, for example, they make adjustments to their digital watch or operate a cash-dispensing machine at 'the hole in the wall'. With so many people operating computers it is very important to make computers as easy to use as possible. Not only that, specialist users of computers, such as engineers in nuclear power stations, need to have an HCI available to them which will minimise the risk of them making mistakes when operating the computer systems under their control.

11.3 It is not surprising, therefore, that in recent years a great deal of research and development work has gone into gaining a better understanding of what constitutes a good HCI and how to create one. Despite all this effort much of what is and is not considered good practice is still a matter of opinion or experience rather than a matter of straightforward scientific result. What follows is therefore a set of important issues to consider rather than a set of hard and fast rules. Always remember that **the primary purpose of the HCI is to enable communication to and fro between the user and the computer.**

User friendliness

11.4 One of the most important features normally required in an HCI is that it be '**user friendly**'. As the name suggests, a user-friendly interface is one that the end-user finds helpful, easy to learn and easy to use. It is easy to recognise unfriendly interfaces but not so easy to design one that is certain to be user friendly.

11.5 What makes an HCI user friendly? There is no simple answer but the following points are important.

a. It should be relatively easy for the user to start using the system.

b. As far as possible, the system should be self-contained so that the user is not forced into accessing manuals or dealing with things that should be kept outside the system.

c. The amount of effort and information required of the user to get the system to complete required tasks should be kept to a minimum.

d. The user should be insulated from unexpected or spurious system actions. This includes protection against being the cause of a system failure and implies that the system should also be robust and reliable.

e. The system should be able to adjust to different levels of expertise between users, and as users grow in competence.

f. The user should be made to feel in control of what is going on.

g. The system should behave in a logical and consistent manner enabling the user, to reason about what is going on and apply what has been learned.

Of course these points are rather general in nature. We now turn to a number of specific practical issues.

Types of interface

11.6 There are many different types of user interface available. They may be broadly classified as follows:

a. Command Driven Interfaces

b. Menu Driven Interfaces

134

c. Direct Manipulation Interfaces

d. User Interface Management Systems (UIMS)

e. Special Purpose Interfaces

Note. In some situations two different kinds of interfaces may be combined, e.g. a menu interface with command options.

Command driven interfaces

11.7 One of the long-established methods by which users can interact with the computer is by the use of commands. The use of commands has already been introduced with an example of a simple command interpreter 4.74). Commands enable the user quickly and simply to instruct the computer what to do. However, they require the user to already have a knowledge of what commands are available, what they do and the rules governing how they should be typed, so they are more suited to experienced users than to beginners. For these reasons commands tend to be most popular in situations where the end-user is a technical person, such as a computer operator or programmer, or where the end-user continually works with the same program and therefore can gain mastery of the commands.

11.8 To make commands more user friendly the following points need to be observed.

a. The command words used should be VERBS that clearly and unambiguously convey the intended action, e.g. PRINT, COPY, DELETE.

b. Unique abbreviations should be provided for more experienced users, e.g. PRI, COP, DEL. Even better is the provision of a means by which users may define their own abbreviations.

c. The format for more complex commands or variations on a single command should observe a simple and consistent set of rules. For example, the command **PRINT** might be used in the following ways:

i. PRINT report1

i.e. print the document called report1 on the default printer.

ii. PRINT report1 report2 report3

i.e. print the three documents called report1, report2 and report3 on the default printer.

iii. PRINT -PprinterB report2

i.e. print the document called report2 on the printer called printerB.

If the end-user can guess from this example how to write the correct command to cause reports called report4 and report5 to be printed on the printer called printerC then the command language is working well. The command language is working better still if the end-user can also correctly guess how to type other commands, e.g. the command that will cause report2 and report3 to be deleted.

Note

i. In the example given, separate items on a command line are ALWAYS separated by space, i.e. the rule is simple.

ii. In the example given a **'switch'** or **'command qualifier'** -**P** is used to signify an alteration to the default meaning of the command. Without the use of -**P** the printer called printerA is used.

Menu-driven interfaces

11.9 Menus provide another popular form of user interface. There are many different alternative forms of menu. The simplest menus provide the user with a number of options and a simple means of selecting between them (see figure 11.1).

11.10 The user is presented with a choice and therefore does not need to have remembered any commands. The interface is therefore suitable for beginners and infrequent users. All the user has to do is make a choice.

11.11 In the example given the user is expected to type '1', '2' or '3', which would appear in the box next to 'OPTION'. Where only a single keystroke is necessary, as in this case, the keystroke itself may cause the **activation** of the menu, i.e. the system starts to act upon the information given. More generally, the pressing of an additional key is needed to activate the menu. Common choices of keys for menu activation are the keys called 'RETURN', 'ENTER' or 'DO'.

11.12 Suppose that the user has typed 1 and activated the menu. The activation causes the 'MAIN MENU' to be replaced by the 'PRINT MENU' (see figure 11.2). One box on the screen already contains the name of the printer to be used (i.e. the default printer). The contents of the box can be changed if required by moving the cursor to the box and then over typing the name of the new choice of printer. The cursor is normally moved by the use of arrow keys or by the use of the TAB key, which moves the cursor from one box to the next. Places on the screen where data items are entered or displayed, such as the boxes shown in figure 11.2, are called **fields**.

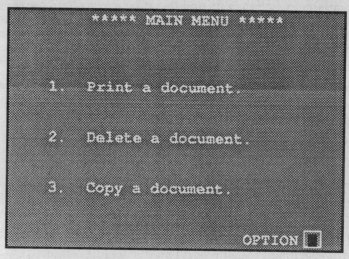

Note: the symbol ■ represents the cursor.

Figure 11.1 A simple menu

11.13 Another box on the screen shown in figure 11.2 contains a number of fields into which the names of reports may be typed. Figure 11.3 shows what the screen would look like once filled in, and before activation, if the user wanted reports called report2 and report3 to be printed on printerB.

11.14 Users like to be reassured of what is going on when they have activated a screen. In the example given, the activation of the PRINT MENU would cause the message Printing... to appear at the bottom of the screen.

11.15 **Help** is normally made available to the user of a menu-driven system by means of screens of information that can temporarily be called up and displayed on the screen during normal activities. It is best if the help information displayed is as specific as possible to the user's current activity. Help screens are normally activated by a special key. Some keyboards even have a key labelled 'HELP'. Similar facilities are often available in command-driven systems and are invoked by typing a command such as 'HELP'.

11.16 **Alternative methods of screen activation** are often available. The most common ones are:

a. The screen is activated by typing into the fields on the screen and then pressing an activation key (as per the example already given).

b. The screen is activated by pressing a function key associated with a desired choice of activation. For example, instead of typing 1, 2 or 3 followed by an activation key the user might press one of the function keys labelled 'F1', 'F2' and 'F3'.

c. The screen is activated by first moving the cursor until it is positioned at the desired choice and then pressing an activation key such as 'DO'.

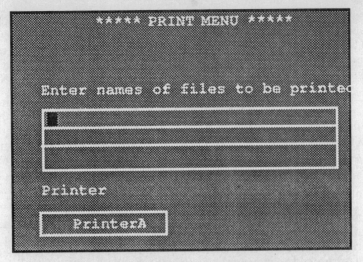

Note: the symbol ■ represents the cursor.

Figure 11.2 A screen for data entry.

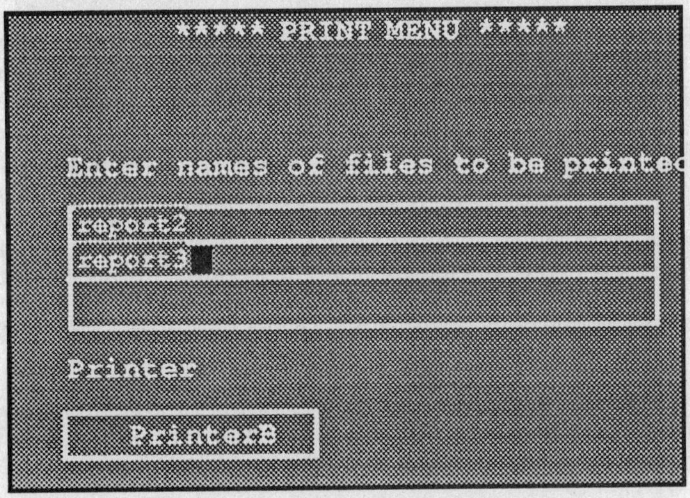

Note: the symbol ■ represents the cursor.

Figure 11.3 A screen after data entry

11.17 In large menu systems it is common to find several levels of menu, starting with a top-level main menu from which level-two menus can be activated, which in turn can activate level-3 menus. A lower-level menu is said to be **nested** inside the menu that activates it. The user normally returns from a low-level menu to the one from which the activation was made by means of an 'EXIT MENU' key. It is best not to nest menus very deeply because it can become difficult for the user to 'navigate' around the system.

11.18 **Pull-down menus** are a special type of menu used in windowing and were briefly introduced in 8.26d. Some variations on the same idea are **pop-up menus** and **pop-down menus**. As the names suggest these menus are made to appear above or below an item on the screen in order to elicit a choice from the user. A simple pull-down menu is shown in figure 11.4.

Figure 11.4 A simple pull-down menu

Direct manipulation interfaces

11.19 A direct manipulation interface is one in which the user *at all times* is made visibly aware of the options available and is provided with immediate visual responses on the screen to any action taken. Direct manipulation interfaces normally require bit-mapped screens and input devices such as mice used in conjunction with the keyboard. One of the most widely available software products using a general-purpose direct manipulation interface is the Apple Macintosh Hypercard system.

11.20 A typical direct manipulation screen presents the user with a set of options that are often represented by icons. The user uses the mouse to move the cursor until it is over the icon and then clicks the mouse button to select the option. It is common for the cursor to take on different shapes according to how it is being used. It might, for example, look like a pointer when being used to select icons, look like a vertical bar if it is used to mark a place in a data field and look like a paint brush or spray can when being used for graphical design work. A very simple direct manipulation interface is shown in figure 11.5. The cursor has the form of a pointing hand. The user can move the hand to point to a button to select one of three printers. The button with the solid centre signifies which has been selected. The pointing hand can also be used to select which action is required. For example, if a document is to be deleted, the hand may be pointed at the crossed-through document icon and the mouse button clicked to activate the delete. Alternatively, by clicking on the exit arrow the user can finish using the current screen.

11.21 The example given in figure 11.5 is deliberately simple in order to get across the basic ideas. However, most direct manipulation interfaces are more sophisticated in their design whilst at the same time being simple and effective from the user's point of view.

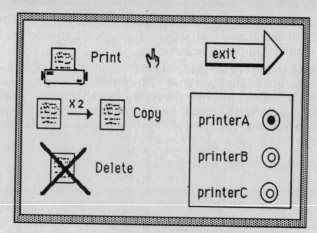

Figure 11.5 A simple Direct Manipulation Interface

User interface management systems (UIMS)

11.22 The aim of a user interface management system is the creation of a means by which a consistent interface with the same 'look and feel' can be provided for any number of different applications within the same system. In a full implementation, *every* user interface will have the desired properties. Examples of UIMS are the system used on the Apple Macintosh computer, OSF/MOTIF from the Open Systems Foundation and the 'Open Look' system developed by Sun for AT &T.

11.23 The UIMS achieves this goal as follows.

a. The UIMS provides a set of standard facilities for handling the user dialogue. These facilities are available to the programmer as a set of tools. Some tools, called widgets, provide the basic standard components of the interface, such as a facility to display a box on the screen for data entry.

b. The UIMS provides some standard software, which manages the way in which each application program uses the interface.

c. A set of rules governs the way in which various features should appear or behave. For example, there may be a strict rule about how the mouse is to operate, such as:

   i. A single click selects an item.

   ii. A double click activates an item.

   iii. Dragging the mouse along with the button held down selects all items passed over by the cursor.

11.24 Most general-purpose UIMSs are based upon windowing systems. Such a system might be built using X-windows and make use of some kind of WIMP. It is important to realise that, by themselves, windowing systems and interfaces like WIMPs do not necessarily provide a satisfactory interface because there is nothing to prevent such facilities from being used in an inconsistent and poorly organised way. It is the UIMS which provides and enforces the consistent interface.

11.25 Apart from the obvious benefits obtained from having a user-friendly interface the use of a UIMS also results in the saving of effort in programming and training. The savings in training are most noticeable when users come to learn their second application and discover they can already do lots of things because of its close similarity to the first application they learnt. The price sometimes paid for these benefits is the extra processing load placed upon the computer which may affect performance or require the purchase of more expensive hardware.

Special-purpose human computer interfaces

11.26 There are two main types of special-purpose HCIs.

a. A general-purpose computer may be used, BUT some parts of the HCI is provided by special hardware and software. For example, the computer may be used to control some industrial process and so there may be video monitors in use which simulate the appearance of traditional, pre-computerised instrument dials. Another example is the cash-dispensing machine used by banks and building societies.

b. The computer is embedded inside some special-purpose equipment and is controlled by an interface that is specific to that purpose. The interface used on a digital watch is a good example of such an interface, but not always an example of one that works well judging by the way in which some individuals have problems working out how to adjust their watches. If the interface was really good, there might be no need for an instruction book.

11.27 The use of embedded computers within a system should in principle make it easier to provide a better user interface. Sadly, this does not always happen.

Summary

11.28 The primary purpose of the Human Computer Interface is to enable communication to and fro between the user and the computer.

11.29 User friendliness is only achieved by taking great care over many different aspects of the user interface.

11.30 User interfaces may be broadly classified as:
   a. Command Driven Interfaces
   b. Menu Driven Interfaces
   c. Direct Manipulation Interfaces
   d. User Interface Management Systems (UIMS)
   e. Special Purpose.

Point to note

11.31 a. The term 'user interface' or even 'interface' is sometimes used instead of HCI when the context is clear, but take care not to use the term 'interface' by itself where it might be mistaken for a hardware device.

   b. There are many different types of menu but the methods of selecting items can be the same on the different menus. For example, a **full screen menu**, such as that shown in figure 11.1, may allow selection by means of: typing the option's number or letter; pressing a function key or using a mouse.

Questions

1. Name four types of human computer interfaces.
2. How might help be provided to the user of a command language?
3. What is a 'field' and how might it be activated?

Computer systems organisation

1. The next three chapters look at how computer systems are organised. Chapter 11 examines the ways in which the various hardware and software components can be organised to form a complete computer system.

2. Chapter 12 deals with the ways in which individual computers can communicate with one another either as independent systems or as a single integrated system.

3. Chapter 13 describes the operating systems which is the software at the heart of the computer system, controlling and coordinating the use of hardware by all other software.

12 Computer systems architecture

Introduction

12.1 Just as the basic elements of a human dwelling (kitchen, bedroom, bathroom, etc) are constructed and combined in ways which depend upon the type of dwelling required (flat, detached house, mansion, etc), so the basic hardware elements of a computer system are constructed and combined into 'architectural forms' which depend upon the type of computer required. So, the style of construction and organisation of the many parts of a computer system are its **'architecture'**. The computer counterpart to the single dwelling (e.g. the detached house) is a **'stand-alone machine'** with a single processor and no connection to any other computer. This chapter starts by describing the basic features of an individual processor, including the function and operation of its elements.

12.2 Human dwellings are often combined into larger structures (e.g. terraced houses, blocks of flats, etc) and likewise individual computers are frequently combined into large systems with multiple processors (e.g. 'distributed systems'). This chapter gives a description of the hardware features of the various types of modern computer system.

Basic features of the processor

12.3 The diagram of the elements of a computer system (figure 12.1) shows the processor as consisting of two primary elements and both are wholly electronic. They are:

a. The Control Unit (CU).

b. The Arithmetic and Logic Unit (ALU).

12.4 Although figure 12.1 provides a useful overview, the real situation is actually more complicated than that. The CU and ALU operate in conjunction with a number of additional processor components (details shortly). All components of the processor are *wholly electronic*.

12.5 The functions of the processor are:

a. to control the use of main storage to store data *and* instructions,

b. to control the sequence of operations,

c. to give commands to all parts of the computer system,

d. to carry out processing.

12.6 The processor controls the input of data and its transfer into main storage, processes data, and then sends the result to output units. At all stages data transmission is electronic.

Control unit

12.7 **Functions.** The Control Unit has been likened to the conductor of an orchestra, because of the coordinating and controlling function it carries out. It is the nerve centre of the computer, controlling all hardware operations, i.e. those of the input-output units, storage and of the processor itself.

12.8 **How it operates.** It *fetches* the requisite instruction from main storage, *stores* it in a number of special registers, *interprets* the instruction and causes the instruction to be *executed* by giving signals (or commands) to the appropriate hardware devices.

Arithmetic and logic unit (ALU)

12.9 **Functions.** The ALU has two main functions:

a. It carries out the arithmetic, e.g. add, subtract, multiply and divide.

b. It performs certain 'logical' operations, e.g. testing whether two data items match.

12.10 **How it operates.**

a. The various data items to be processed are taken from main storage as directed by the Control Unit, and stored in its registers. They then undergo the required operations (add, subtract, multiply, divide...). The results are placed back in main storage.

b. Logical operations are virtually the same as arithmetical operations, but the results (say of subtracting one number from another) will determine different course of action to be taken by the Control Unit. This gives the computer its decision-taking ability.

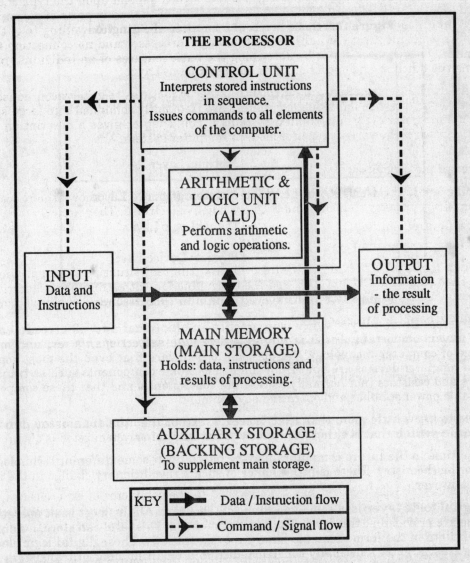

Figure 12.1 The elements of a computer system showing its 'logical structure'

Levels within computer architecture

12.12 There are a number of levels to the construction and organisation of computer systems. The simplest distinction between levels is that between hardware and software (figure 12.2). We may view hardware as the lowest and most basic level of the computer onto which a **'layer'** of software is added. The software sits above the hardware, using it and controlling it. The hardware supports the software by providing the operations the software requires.

12.13 The idea is easily extended by viewing the whole computer system as a **'multilayered machine'** consisting of several layers of software on top of several layers of hardware (figure 12.2). In this chapter we are primarily interested in the higher levels of hardware and the lower levels of software. A discussion of the higher levels of software is postponed until later chapters. However, in order to give an overall picture a brief description of all the layers is given below starting at the lowest layer.

| SOFTWARE LEVEL |
| HARDWARE LEVEL |

Figure 12.2 Basic levels of computer architecture

7.		Applications Layer
6.	SOFTWARE LEVEL	Higher Order Software Layer
5.		Operating System Layer
4.		Machine Layer
3.	HARDWARE LEVEL	Microprogrammed Layer
2.		Digital Logic Layer
1.		Physical Device Layer

Figure 12.3 Multilayered computer architecture

12.14 The **Physical device layer** which is in practice an **electrical and electronic component layer** is very important, *but it is largely outside the subject of this text* and more in the province of computer technology. We do need to be aware that even the most sophisticated modern computer devices are built from simple electronic components such as transistors, capacitors and resistors (not normally as discrete components) and that these components rely on suitable power supplies and operating environments.

12.15 We need to know little more than that, however, except that **the transistor can act as an electronic switch** that is either ON (binary '1') or OFF (binary '0').

12.16 At some time in the future computers may be based upon some different technology such as optics or biochemistry. There is little chance of such a revolutionary change in the immediate future, however.

12.17 The **digital logic layer** is of some importance to this text. All the most basic operations of the machine are provided at this level. The basic elements at this level can store, manipulate and transmit data in the form of simple binary representations. These digital logic elements are called **gates.** A gate is normally constructed from a small number of transistors and other electronic components.

12.18 The next two levels are more easily understood if considered together. The **microprogrammed layer** interprets the **machine language** instructions from the **machine layer** and directly causes the digital logic elements to perform the required operations. It is, in effect, a very basic inner processor and is driven by its own primitive control program instructions held in its own private inner ROM. These program instructions are called **microcode** and the control program is called a **microprogram.** They are one example of **firmware** (i.e. software in ROM).

12.19 There was no microprogrammed layer in the early generations of computers nor is there one in some of the small microprocessors of today. In machines without a microprogrammed layer the processor is constructed directly from a combination of digital logic components.

12.20 The use of a microprogrammed layer enables a manufacturer to produce a **family of processors** all of which process the same set of machine instructions at the **machine layer** but which differ in terms of construction and speed. In this way the manufacturer can offer a range of machines of differing power and price. Software can be moved from one machine to the next one in the range without alteration. As the technology is improved the manufacturer may replace an older model processor by a new one. So, the customer can **upgrade** the hardware without having to rewrite the software.

12.21 The details of this microprogrammed level of the architecture are not always disclosed by the manufacturers in order to protect trade secrets. For example, Motorola have not disclosed all details of the micro-programmed level of their MC68000 16-bit microprocessors. The details of the microprogrammed levels of larger computers, such as minis or mainframes, are sometimes published by the manufacturers. The microprogrammed layer is a special subject and further discussion is well outside the scope of this book.

12.22 As has already been indicated, the **machine layer** is the lowest level at which a program can be written and indeed it is only **machine language** instructions which can be directly interpreted by the hardware.

12.23 The **operating system** layer controls the way in which all software uses the underlying hardware. It also hides the complexities of the hardware from other software by providing its own facilities which enable software to use the hardware more simply. It also prevents other software from bypassing these facilities so that the hardware can only be access directly by the operating system. It therefore provides an orderly environment in which machine language instructions can be executed safely and effectively.

12.24 The **Higher Order Software Layer** covers all programs in languages other than machine language which require translation into machine code before they can be executed. Such programs, when translated, rely upon the underlying operating system facilities as well as their own machine instructions.

12.24 The **applications layer** is the language of the computer as seen by the person using the software, ie the '**end-user**'.

12.25 The underlying computer as viewed from each layer is sometimes called a '**virtual machine**'. For example, the operating system is a virtual machine to the software above it because, for practical purposes, it is the 'machine' the software uses.

Organisation of the computer

12.26 We now turn to a more detailed examination of some aspects organisation of the computer that were not covered earlier.

12.27 Designing and building a new computer from scratch is an expensive process. Also, the unit costs of individual components are high unless the components are mass produced. These factors cause most computer manufacturers to construct their computers from varied combinations of standard components. For example, many *different microcomputers* contain the *same microprocessors*.

12.28 This principle of **modular construction** applies to different levels of design. At one level it might be a matter of 'plugging in' one peripheral device instead of another. At a lower level it might be a matter of using one type of memory chip instead of another.

12.29 Standard components are much easier to interconnect if the means of interconnection is also standardised. One important method for doing this is using '**buses**'. A **bus** is a collection of parallel electrical conductors called 'lines' onto which a number of components may be connected. Connections are made at points along the length of the bus by means of connectors with multiple electrical contacts. There are two basic types of bus:

a. **Internal buses,** used within the processor and an integral part of its construction.

b. **External buses,** used to connect separate hardware elements together, e.g. connecting the processor to main memory.

12.30 Buses may be used to convey:

    a. data signals,

    b. data address signals,

    c. control signals,

    d. power.

12.31 One of the simplest architectures is one based upon a single **general purpose bus**. (figure 12.4). This arrangement tend to be used only on the microcomputer based systems. It is simple and effective but data transfers between the processor and memory can be held up by slower transfers involving input or output units.

12.32 **Note** that within the context of this discussion storage devices such as disk units and tape units are regarded as input and output devices. In what follows the common practice of using 'I/O' as a shorthand for 'Input or Output' is adopted.

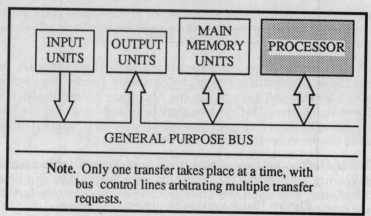

Figure 12.4 A system based on a general purpose bus

12.33 Most architectures are based upon two buses and follow one of the two basic alternatives shown in Figures 12.5 and 12.6 opposite. In both cases the bus used for data transfers between memory and the processor is separate from the bus used by input unit and output units. This reflects differences in speed. The data transfers between memory and the processor use a faster bus and are also not held up waiting for the slower devices used for input and output. Figure 12.5 shows a two bus arrangement commonly used on larger microcomputers and in many minicomputers. The processor has direct connections to both buses. Data only passes between memory and the (I/O) units via the processor. An alternative arrangement, more commonly found on larger minicomputers and mainframes, is that shown in figure 12.6 in which the processor only accesses data via the memory bus. In such arrangements the processor effectively delegates some of its detailed I/O controlling powers to subsidiary **peripheral processors**, also called **I/O channels**. Although details are not shown in figure 12.6 the processor still has overall control over I/O. The exact arrangements and terminology varies from one manufacturer to another but in all cases the aims are the same:

    a. to maximise the use of the processor by freeing it of the burden of controlling low level I/O operations;

    b. to maximise the speed and efficiency of I/O data transfers to and from memory.

12.34 Another factor affecting the speeds of data transfers is the **bus width** (ie the number of parallel lines it contains). In simple arrangements such as that in figure 12.4 the width of the data bus may only be 8-bits or 16-bit whereas in figure 12.6 the data bus width may be 32-bits or 64-bits.

12.35 **The influence of size on construction.** Three distinctly different forms of construction are, from smallest to largest:

    a. Single-chip computers.

    b. Single-board computers.

    c. Multiple-board bus-based computers.

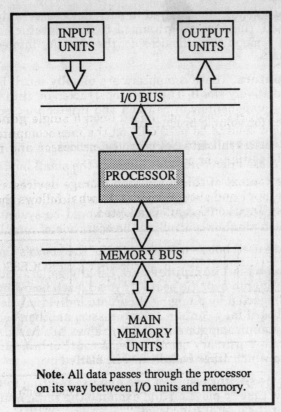

Note. All data passes through the processor
on its way between I/O units and memory.

Figure 12.5 A system based on two buses

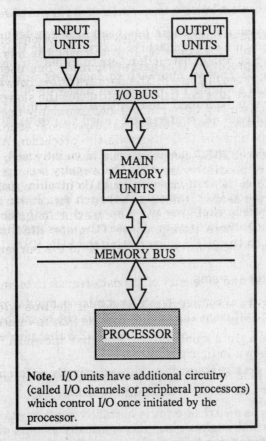

Note. I/O units have additional circuitry
(called I/O channels or peripheral processors)
which control I/O once initiated by the
processor.

Figure 12.6 Another system based on two buses

12.36 **Single-chip computers** are those found in such devices as watches, cameras, etc. The processors are specialised, they are programmed to do a specific task and, apart from the remarkable operations some of these devices do, they are not immediately recognisable as computers.

12.37 **Single-board computers.** These computers are usually much bigger than single-chip computers but are still relatively small. They are constructed on thin flat sheets of electrical insulator onto which the components can be fixed and interconnected. **Printed circuit boards (PCBs)** are often used for volume production.

12.38 The single-board computers fall into two broad categories:

a. Small general-purpose microcomputers such as the small home computers and many more basic PCs.

b. Small special-purpose computers, which are often used for applications involving the control of physical processes. Typical examples would be systems controlling a small-scale chemical distillation plant or controlling the operation of complex milling machines.

In both cases buses are used but as integral parts of the board's circuitry.

12.39 **Multiple-board, bus-based computers** are usually general-purpose computers. They are normally too large to fit onto a single board. Instead, each board has a particular function and all boards are interconnected by plugging them into individual slots on one ore more general-purpose buses. One board may contain the processor, another board may contain main storage, and so on. Many minicomputers and mainframes are based upon this type of construction. Sometimes there is a primary board, called a **motherboard**, for the processor and other main components into which other boards may be slotted.

12.40 Having considered some specific issues of size and use relating to the physical organisation of the computer it is now time to move on and examine the same issues in the broader context of system architecture at the digital logic level.

RISC and CISC

12.41 Over the last twenty years or so there has been a steady trend towards computers having more extensive and complex sets of machine instructions so that some 16-bit microprocessors in use today have more complex instruction sets than mainframes used in the 1960s. Within the last few years an alternative approach to designing processors has become popular in which the processor has a simple instruction set based upon a small set of instructions. The name for such machines is **Reduced Instruction Set Computers (RISC).** For the purpose of distinction the traditional alternatives are called **Complex Instruction Set Computers (CISC).**

12.42 Under some circumstances RISC computers can have very high performance compared with CISC computers, but comparisons are difficult to make because it may take many RISC instructions to do what one CISC instruction could do in some situations, so the number of instructions carried out per second is not a sound basis for comparison. Also, machine language programs on RISC machines contain many more instructions than their CISC equivalents and can therefore take much more storage space. Common RISC machines are IBM's RS6000 range and those based on the MIPS chip or using the SUN SPARC architecture.

Architecture of small computer systems

12.43 The architecture of a typical configuration for a microcomputer-based system is shown in figure 12.7. Provided that sufficient slots are present in the bus, other units may be plugged in.

12.44 **Memory organisation.** In a small system like that shown in figure 12.7 the main storage may be organised as shown in figure 12.8.

12.45 **Firmware.** Programs held in ROM are called **firmware.** They are stored permanently in the ROM and are ready for use when the computer is switched on.

12.46 When a microcomputer is switched on it is normally made to start executing the instructions held in ROM. This normally takes place automatically as part of switching on. Sometimes a 'boot' button is be pressed instead. This is known as '**booting up** the system'. The instructions in ROM sometimes perform a number of simple hardware checks such as finding out what RAM is fitted and working.

12.47 On most computers, not just microcomputers, the boot-up operation also causes a special **'loader program'** in firmware ROM to load a program into memory from predefined tracks on hard disk. On some microcomputers the program may be loaded from floppy disk instead of hard disk. This first program loaded into memory is that part of the operating system which takes primary control over the hardware and which contains the facilities for higher level software to use it. This software has several alternative names including the **kernel**, the **executive** and the **supervisor**. On some microcomputers it is sometimes rather vaguely called the **system**.

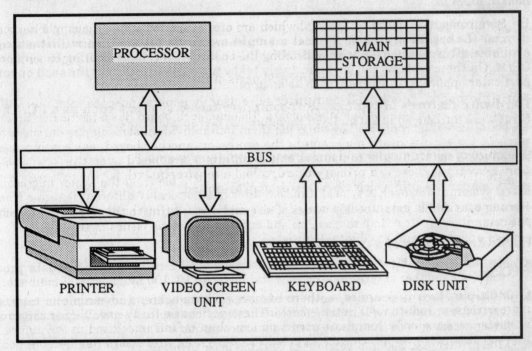

Figure 12.7 Simplified typical architecture of a small microcomputer-based system

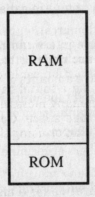

Figure 12.8 Organisation of main storage in a typical microcomputer

12.48 At some point the firmware program completes its loading operation and start the execution of the operating system kernel. Another file on disk sometime provides 'configuration information' which determines how the operating system uses the hardware resources available to it. For example it might specify how much memory the operating system may reserve for its own purposes. This configuration information often specifies which higher level program is the first to be executed once the operating system has completed its start-up procedures.

12.49 Normally the first program to be executed is a **shell** program. A shell is a high level program which sits above the operating system kernel and provides the user with a means to operate the computer. A common form of shell is a command language interpreter such as that used on MS-DOS or PC-DOS whereby the user types commands. Some shells provide a GUI instead of a command language as is the case with the Apple Macintosh 'Finder'. The terms 'shell' and 'kernel' draw on an analogy with a nut in which the shell surrounds the inner kernel. The shell is normally regarded as part of the operating system.

12.50 On the older 8-bit microcomputers the kernel and shell were sometimes both stored in ROM and were often know as the **monitor**.

12.51 Some microcomputers may have much more firmware in ROM, even to the extent of being able to accept, 'interpret' and execute programs written in a programming language such as BASIC. The microcomputer is then said to have 'BASIC in ROM'. GUI toolkits are sometimes held in ROM too.

12.52 On microcomputers designed for use by just one user at a time through a single keyboard and monitor the operating system operates a **single-user system** in which **multitasking** is not available. This is the case with MS-DOS, PC-DOS, Apple MACOS prior to version 7 and CP/M. On these systems the user effectively takes turns at either using the shell or running a particular applications program such as an applications package.

12.53 **Hardware features of typical microcomputer-based systems such as a PC.** These features were introduced in 2.3 and will therefore not be repeated here.

The architecture of minicomputer and mainframe computer systems

12.54 The smaller minicomputer systems can be indistinguishable from the larger microcomputer-based systems. However, a typical minicomputer has noticeably different features from a microcomputer and is essentially a scaled-down version of its 'big brother' the mainframe computer.

12.55 **Hardware features of a typical minicomputer system.**
   a. Medium-size 32-bit processor and main storage sufficient to handle the data processing needs of a number of terminals or workstations (e.g. 10–100 Megabytes of main storage).
   b. Multiple Hard disk units, both fixed and exchangeable, and magnetic tape storage (cartridge or reel-to-reel) in some cases. These devices typically have higher capacities and faster access speeds than those used on microcomputers.
   c. Line printer, e.g. 300 lpm versions or desktop laser printers.
   d. Multiple terminals, e.g. 20 VDUs or workstations.
   e. Standard means of interconnecting multiple machines via a network

12.56 It is also difficult to draw a line of demarcation between the larger minicomputers and small mainframe computers. The hardware in a mainframe may be similar to the hardware in a minicomputer, but there is usually much more of it, eg:
   a. Very large processors with massive amounts of main storage, e.g. hundreds of Megabytes.
   b. Large number of magnetic disk and tape units with very large capacities. For example, the disks have capacities measured in hundreds of megabytes or even gigabytes.
   c. High-speed line printers, e.g. 1,200 lpm.
   d. The ability to support large numbers of terminals, e.g. 100 or more VDUs.

12.57 **Front End Processors (FEPs).** Many mainframe computers incorporate minicomputers, which are used to handle input and output from various terminals, thus relieving the main computer of some tasks associated with input and output. The minicomputer being used for this purpose is called a Front End Processor (FEP).

12.58 The front end processor may not only deal with terminals close to the main computer it may also deal with *remote* terminals situated at the end of data transmission lines.

Other architectural features

12.59 **Cache memories.** These are high-speed RAMs, which work at speeds that match the processor. They are used to hold data that has recently been accessed from disk in anticipation of its use in the near future. Subsequent accesses, if they occur, will be fast because the disk will not require accessing again. The least accessed data in cache memory is replaced by newly accessed data. Alternatively, very high-speed cache memory may be used temporarily to store data read from main memory.

12.60 **Content Addressable Storage (CAS).** This storage works in a different way from normal storage. The principle will be explained by means of the following simplified example. Suppose that each word in memory can hold 4 characters and that location 200 contains 'FRED'. In normal storage the address, 200 would be used to load 'FRED'. In content addressable memory 'FRED' would be passed along a data bus and the memory would pass 200 back, indicating the location of 'FRED'. Thus a paragraph of stored text could be retrieved by supplying a word contained in the paragraph. CAS is very useful for rapid data selection or retrieval but is expensive at present. A variant on CAS is **Content Addressable File storage (CAF)** in which CAS logic is part of a disk unit's circuitry and storage set-up. For example, the processor may request the input to main memory of all text file lines on the disk contain the word 'FRED'. The disk unit finds the appropriate lines and transfers them into memory. The processor is saved the job of searching for the data. CAFs are gradually gaining ground. A leader in this field is ICL.

Multiprocessor systems

12.61 Here we are considering single computers with multiple processors as opposed to situations in which multiple computers are combined into a single system by means of networks and modern data transmission systems. Further details of the latter is left until Chapter 13.

12.62 Traditionally, multiprocessor systems have been very large computers with two or more main processors and large main storage that has been wholly or partially shared. This arrangement not only serves to handle a large processing load but also provides back-up in the case of breakdown (i.e. if one processor fails the system can continue to operate). Such systems are called **multiprocessing systems** (see figure 12.9).

12.63 In broad terms any computer containing more than one processor may be called a **multiprocessor computer**. However, the term is usually taken to imply processors that are sharing the same main memory. If the processors each have their own main storage but share disks and other peripherals the system is sometimes called a **clustered system**. The extra processors may be used as either of the following:

a. as additional main processors sharing the normal processing load,

b. as special-purpose processors catering for some particular function. For example, a **maths co-processor** may be used in conjunction with a single main processor to perform some standard complex computations.

12.64 Where there are a number of main processors, as in figure 12.9, there are two basic methods of using the processors:

a. **Asymmetric multiprocessing (AMP)** In an asymmetric multiprocessing machine one processor is the master processor and all other processors are subordinate to it. The master processor has special privileges over the operating system. These allow it to work in what is called **kernel mode**, which basically means that it is able to carry out specially controlled operating-system operations on the hardware that ordinary applications programs are not allowed to do. The subordinate processors are therefore limited to processing applications programs and may have to wait for the master processor if the programs require the operating system to carry out some operation on their behalf. This can potentially cause a processing bottleneck at the master processor.

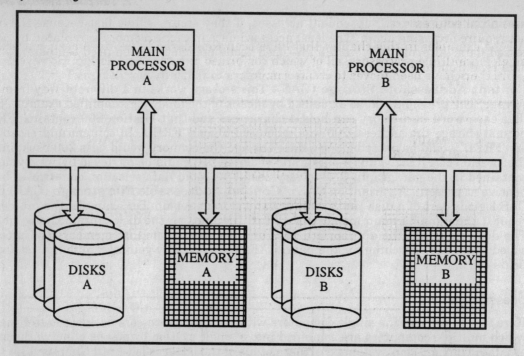

Figure 12.9 A multiprocessing system with duplicated disk storage and memory

b. **Symmetric multiprocessing (SMP)** In a symmetric multiprocessing machine all processors have equal status, with each one able to carry out kernel mode operations. This removes the processing bottleneck, which occurs with asymmetric multiprocessing. This major advantage means that symmetric multiprocessing is a much more popular option even though it is technically much more difficult to achieve. Examples of machines that perform symmetric multiprocessing are the Digital VAX 6000 series computers running under the VMS version 5 operating system and all computers made by SEQUENT.

12.65 It must be pointed out that both kinds of multiprocessing are very sophisticated and are currently only available from a few manufacturers.

12.66 **Local cache**. Some performance improvements may be gained in a multiprocessor machine by using a separate cache in close proximity to each of the processors. Thus, each processor has its own 'local cache'. Data can be read from main storage into the cache and then processed more quickly while it is in cache because of the higher access speeds. Any changes in the data must be written back to main memory before any other processor reads it. The accesses to main memory from the various processors can cause another bottleneck. Sophisticated methods of managing the cache, such as those used in SEQUENT computers, can help to alleviate these problems.

12.67 A further measure employed on such systems is to use **disk shadowing (also called disk mirroring)** whereby disks are used in pairs with the second disk storing exactly the same data as the first. If either disk fails for any reason the other one can continue operating so that no data is lost and the running of the system is not interrupted. This ability to continue despite a failure is called **resilience**. Figure 12.10 shows a multiprocessor system with local cache and shadowed disks.

12.68 Although the feature just described are quite sophisticated by general standards the components used can be quite ordinary. For example, one symmetric multiprocessing machine uses a standard Intel 486 microprocessor.

Alternative architectures

12.69 All the examples in this chapter that have been considered so far have been concerned with single or multiple processors, all of which conformed to same basic design. However, in recent years there have been moves to create computers to radically new designs.

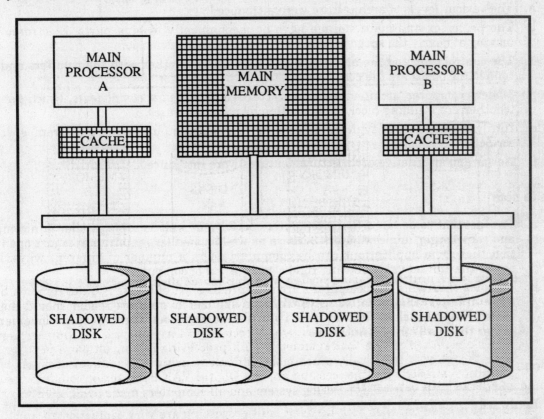

Figure 12.10 A Multiprocessing System local cache and shadowed disks

12.70 Many of these computers have been designed with the object of gaining greater computational speed. Two approaches that have had some measure of success are:

a. **Pipeline machines**.

b. **Array processors**.

12.71 In the **pipeline machine** architecture each stage in the fetch-execute cycle is handled by a *separate* machine hardware unit. This is similar in concept to the method of pipelining described earlier but is different in that the hardware is organised very differently to make maximum use of the method. The first unit fetches and instruction from memory. At any one time there may be four or five instructions within the processor each at different stages of execution in different units.

12.72 In the **array processor** there is one control unit but multiple ALUs, which are able to work in parallel with one another. They are particularly suited to applications in which sets of values require the same operation to be performed on each value, e.g. converting every value in a table to a percentage of the total.

12.73 **Parallel machines** A more general alternative to the array processor is the **parallel machine**, which is a multiprocessor machine able to carry out various operations in parallel *within a single program*. This contrasts with some ordinary multiprocessor machines in which several individual programs may run at the same time, but in which at any one time a single program is unable to use more than one processor.

12.74 In a simple case of parallel processing a computer might be taking a set of numbers in turn and for each number performing different operations on it at the same time using separate processors. The same arrangement can be used in situations where multiple input devices each provide instrument readings which need to be processed in parallel.

Summary

12.75 a. The various levels of architecture were introduced.

b. The processor and main storage have no mechanically moving parts. Electronic pulses moving at nearly the speed of light are used in data transmission.

c. The control unit and the arithmetic and logic units together with their buffers and interconnecting buses are the constituent parts of the processor.

d. Modern computer 'architecture' is characterised by *modular components*, which are linked together in a building-block fashion, often by means of *buses*.

e. Hardware features of typical microcomputers, minicomputers and mainframes were described.

f. Newer and alternative architectural features were introduced.

Points to note

12.76 a. The fact that some larger microcomputers perform as well as some smaller minicomputers and some larger minicomputers perform as well as smaller mainframes is just one indication that some applications can be computerised in a number of different ways. It also shows the limited value of using rigid classification of computers.

b. The idea of viewing the computer's architecture as a set of layers is quite common but the there are several alternative ways of classifying the layers. The reader should therefore merely take the classification used in this chapter as an example of a convenient one rather than as THE classification.

Questions

1. Define and distinguish between the terms:
    i. hardware
    ii. firmware
    iii. software
    iv. ROM
    v. RAM

2. Define the term 'Front End Processor'.

3. What are the essential differences between mainframe, mini and microcomputers? Give examples where each would be used to the best advantage.

(IDPM)

13 Data communications and networks

Introduction

13.1 This chapter covers the various aspects of data communications and networks. It describes the basic types of hardware used for communication between computer systems and also describes the ways in which the interconnections may be made. Descriptions of other forms of communication equipment are included where relevant. Later in the chapter the applications of this technology and specialist communication services are discussed.

13.2 The chapter starts with traditional forms of communication based upon the telephone system and then goes on to discuss more modern techniques including computer networks.

Data transmission and networks

13.3 Used in a general sense the term 'data transmission' refers to the movement of data from one location to another. Data in a physical form such as documents can be moved by dispatching through the post, by using a car or van, or by employing a courier service.

13.4 Nowadays, **'data transmission'** is usually understood to mean the movement of data by telecommunications systems. It is possible by this means to link a number of remote terminals to a central computer. Data and information can be transmitted between the computer and the terminals in both directions. The use of telecommunications facilities makes possible much faster transmission.

13.5 The basic components of a such a simple data transmission system are:

    a. a central computer.

    b. terminal devices.

    c. telecommunications links between **a** and **b**.

Traditional methods

13.6 Of the two long-established methods of telecommunications, telephone and telex, the one which has for a long time been used for a variety of forms of data transmission is the telephone system.

13.7 It will prove useful to remind ourselves of some of the familiar and significant features of the telephone system. Two key features are:

    a. It is a **circuit-switching system**, i.e. when a call is placed a circuit is established by the switching equipment in the exchange and then the circuit is maintained for the duration of the call.

    b. The electrical signal transmitted is the direct **analog** of the sound at the receiver, albeit of a quality far short of hi-fi!

13.8 The simplest forms of data transmission involve the connection of terminals to a computer via a telephone line. In order to use the telephone link the digital signals of the terminal and computer must be converted into analog form in order to be transmitted along the telephone line. This can be done by a device called a **MODEM**, short for **MOD**ulator-**DEM**odulator (see figure 13.1). The modem plugs directly into the telephone wall socket in the home, office or computer room.

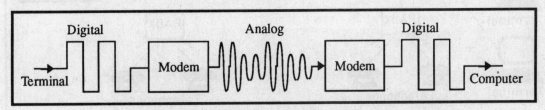

Figure 13.1 Data transmission and the use of MODEMs

13.9   In the absence of a modem in the vicinity of the terminal a portable device known as an acoustic coupler may be used instead (see figure 13.2). Modern **acoustic couplers** are very compact and can be very handy to use in conjunction with portable microcomputers or data-collection devices. However, they tend to be slightly more error prone than modems.

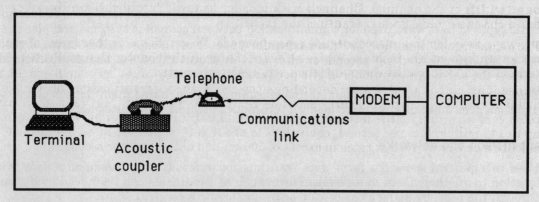

Figure 13.2 A communications link

13.10   A standard domestic telephone line used in conjunction with these simple devices is normally able to transmit data quite reliably at speeds up to about 30 characters per second. With relatively modest upgrading of the equipment and telephone line used it is possible to push the speeds up to approximately 120 characters per second.

13.11   Data transmission is not confined to the public telephone system. A private telephone system may be used too. Also, it is possible to set up permanently wired data transmission lines instead of dial-up lines. These lines, which are often leased or rented, can be set up to transmit data at much higher speeds than can be achieved over the standard telephone line, over 1000 characters per second in some cases.

13.12   Data transmission lines tend to be quite costly in comparison with the equipment used so there is a considerable advantage in using a technique called **multiplexing**, which makes it possible for the same line to be used for a number of separate signals at the same time. Signals are transmitted by a device called a **multiplexor** (also spelt multiplexer) and received by a device called a **demultiplexor**. There are many methods of multiplexing. One form of multiplexing involves a device known as a **concentrator**, which is typically used to connect a number of slow terminals in close proximity to a single transmission line i.e. the data to and from the set of terminals is *concentrated* into a single data stream (see figure 13.3). Data items are normally transmitted to or from the terminals' concentrator at irregular intervals and so the terminals to which they belong are identified by identification numbers transmitted with the data items.

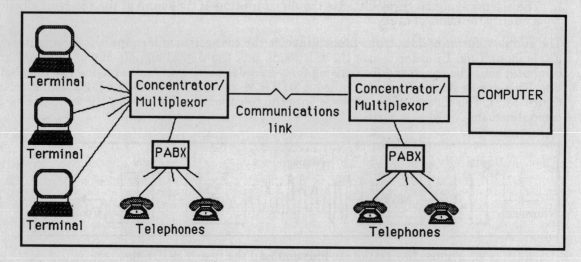

Figure 13.3 Data communications links using concentrators and multiplexing

Characteristics of data transmission lines

13.13 A data transmission link is normally called a **channel**. One very important characteristic of a channel is its capacity to carry data. This capacity is directly related to the range of frequencies with which it is possible to transmit bits along the channel, a characteristic known as the **bandwidth** of the channel. Channels with broader bandwidth, called **broadband** or **wideband** channels, have greater transmission capacities.

13.14 The actual rate of data flow, i.e. **'data transfer rate'**, is often expressed in terms of the number of bits transmitted per second, or alternatively a unit called the **baud**, which in simple cases is the same as the number of bits per second. It normally takes between 8 and 10 bits to transmit an individual character depending upon the method of transmission. So, for example, a 300-baud line will typically carry about 30 characters per second. Maximum data transfer rates vary according to the medium used. A **coaxial cable**, as used for a TV aerial, can carry up to 140 million bits per second, equivalent to about 2000 telephone lines, whereas an **optical fibre** can carry data at rates in excess of 500 million characters per second.

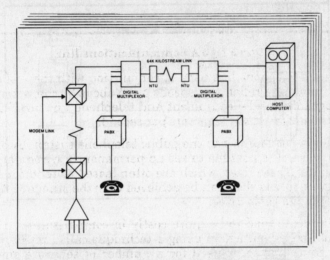

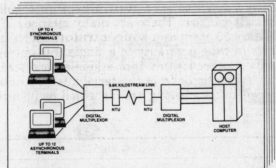

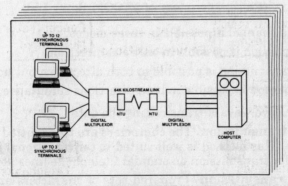

Figure 13.4
(Picture courtesy of MICOM-Borer Ltd)

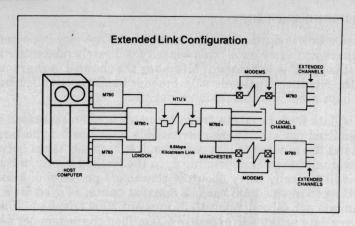

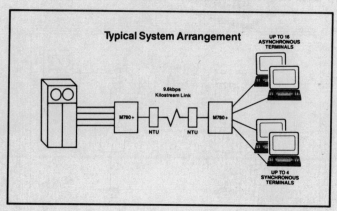

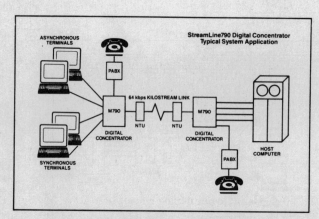

Figure 13.4 (continued)
(Picture courtesy of MICOM-Borer Ltd)

13.15 Transmission along a channel is possible in three modes:

a. **Simplex.** Transmission is possible in only one direction.

b. **Half duplex.** Transmission is possible in both directions, but not simultaneously.

c. **Duplex.** Transmission is possible in both directions simultaneously.

13.16 There are two alternative ways of transmitting the data:

a. **Asynchronous transmission.** The characters are transmitted singly, at will, at irregular intervals in time. This method is well suited to conversational interactions and is the one most often used for transmission on standard telephone lines at low baud rates.

b. **Synchronous transmission.** Prepared sets of characters are transmitted together as blocks at fixed rates. This method is more efficient at transmitting large quantities of data and is the one most often used at high baud rates.

The model M760 TDM attachment to 48k or 64k Kilostream links

**The model M790 Digital Concentrator supports both asynchronous
and asynchronous traffic simultaneously
(Picture courtesy of MICOM-Borer Ltd)**

13.17 All data transmissions have to be controlled by some kind of convention adopted between the sender and the receiver, just as the two-way radio operators use 'roger', 'over' and 'out'. These conventions are called data transmission **protocols.**

Digital communications

13.18 When considering the traditional telephone-based data transmission methods we saw that an important feature of these systems was the use of analog transmissions, i.e. the signals varied continuously in accordance with the sound waves to be transmitted. In digital transmissions the signals are at discrete levels corresponding to particular binary states, HIGH and LOW say. Digital transmissions are clearly more directly related to the binary-based data representations used in computers and are also superior to analog transmissions on a number of technical grounds. Therefore, digital transmission systems have been developed in recent years as alternatives to the traditional analog telephone systems.

13.19   Although these systems are designed primarily for data transmission they can also transmit speech if the signals are converted into digital form. This conversion is often handled by a **PABX (Private Automatic Branch Exchange)**.

13.20   There are a number of different digital transmission systems in existence. One example is the British Telecom Kilostream service, which has facilities to transfer data at rates up to 64 thousand bits per second. Figure 13.4 shows a number of typical applications of this equipment using the products by MICOM-Borer Ltd.

Message switching and packet switching

13.21   The traditional telephone circuits and modern digital circuit just described have one feature in common. They both employ fixed lines or circuit switching (13.7). In the case of circuit switching the data path has to be set up end-to-end *before* any transmission takes place and must be maintained throughout the duration of the call even if there are gaps in data transmission. Thus the system has some inherent delays and inefficiencies. Two alternatives to circuit switching which attempt to overcome its deficiencies are **message switching** and **packet switching**.

13.22   In a simple message-switching circuit the transmission is done in stages with the content of the whole transmission, that is, the message being sent along separate and successive sections of the circuit in turn. At the beginning and end of each section there is a computerised unit called an **IMP (Interface Message Processor)**, which is able to receive, store and forward the message to the destination to which it is electronically addressed. This is a form of **store and forward** system and has some inherent delay in it because of the need to assemble the whole message before transmission occurs at each stage.

13.23   A rather more versatile alternative is the **packet-switching system**. A packet consists of details of the sender, the intended destination 'address', a small portion of a message and other data used for control purposes. Each packet is transmitted in the same way as a whole message in a message-switching system. In particular, packets have a fixed upper size limit which enables them to be held in an IMP's main storage instead of requiring disk space as often happens with message switching. The duration of each packet's transmission is also limited which ensures more balanced access to communication channels. The packet size limit means that a packet switching system handles messages as multiple packets. The first packet can be forwarded before the second one has arrived which improves throughput. The packet itself enters and exits the circuit via a device called a **PAD (Packet Assembler-Disassembler)**.

13.24   Packet switching does not suffer from the inherent delay of message switching and also makes more flexible and efficient use of the transmission circuit because it only establishes each link for as long as it needs it to transmit each packet. The lack of delays means that packet switching systems may be used for conversational modes of transmission as well as for bulk data transmission.

13.25   The individual links, both in message-switching systems and packet-switching systems, tended to use digital transmission techniques.

Computer networks and distributed systems

13.26   An interconnected set of two or more computers may be called a **'computer network'**. However, if the computers in the network operate together as a single unit which to the user appears as a single computer, albeit physically dispersed, then the complete system is more accurately described as a **distributed system.** Therefore, although *any* interconnected set of computers is often conveniently referred to as a 'computer network', the use of the term often implies an interconnected set of *independent* computers and not a distributed system. However, it may be useful when considering a distributed system to be able to recognise the particular type of network on which it is based.

Note A computer that is *not* connected to other computers is a **'stand-alone system'**.

13.27 **Distributed systems.** Over recent years there has been a steady trend towards using computer systems that have several interconnected processors placed in separate locations. Each processor tends to have its own 'local' peripherals (disks, printers, terminals) in addition to any peripherals attached to some central processor (see figure 13.5).

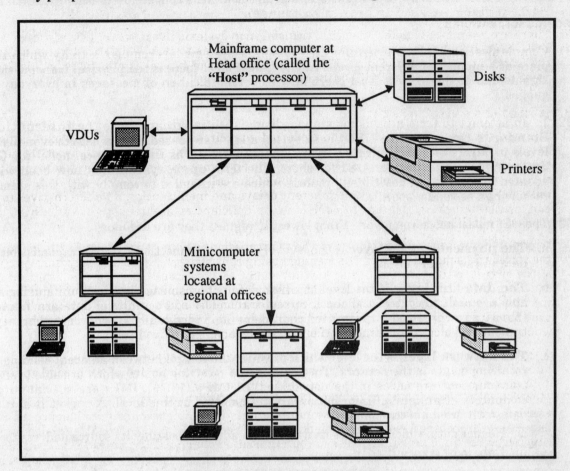

Figure 13.5 A Distributed System

13.28 Networks used to interconnect computers in a single room, rooms within a building or buildings on one site are normally called **Local Area Networks (LANs)**. LANs normally transmit data in a digital form using media such as coaxial cable or multi-stranded cable. The physical form of many LANs is **Ethernet**, which is a standard for handling low-level protocols and normally employs coaxial cables somewhat larger than that used for domestic TV aerials. Some ethernets use thinner wire or optical fibres. Sometimes multiple LANS are used on the same site. For example, there may be one LAN per floor in a multi storey building. Such LANs may all be connected onto one main network such as a **multidrop network** (figure 13.6) called a **backbone**. Alternatively, they may be individually connected one to another across a cabled link known as a **bridge**.

13.29 The networks which interconnect computers on separate sites, separate cities or even separate countries are called **Long Haul Networks (LHNs)** or **Wide Area Networks (WANs)**. LHNs tend to use packet-switching methods or message-switching methods and exploit optical fibre media and satellite transmissions in many cases.

Basic advantages of using networks

13.30 There are many possible advantages in using networks. The basic ones are:

   a. The sharing of resources (e.g. computers and staff) and information.

   b. The provision of local facilities without the loss of central control.

   c. The even distribution of work, processing loads, etc.

d. Shared risk and mutual support.

e. Improved and more economic communication facilities in general, e.g. including voice communication.

Standards for networks

13.31 Communication between interconnected computer systems is a complex activity which takes place at a number of different levels. At the lowest level there is the physical transmission of signals and at the highest level there may be communication of messages in everyday languages.

13.32 In an attempt to form a basis for standardising such interconnections the **International Standards Organisation (ISO)** has devised a standard based upon a set of seven distinct levels or layers of communication. This model is known as the reference model for Open System Interconnection, or **OSI** for short. The term **open system** has now been widely adopted as a means of describing products which are intended to comply with this standard rather than be vendor specific.

13.33 The OSI model has seven layers. From lowest to highest they are as follows:

a. **The physical control layer** is the level of electrical connections, signal transmission and data in raw binary form.

b. **The data-link layer** is the level at which data is transmitted in small units using suitable protocols to control and check correct transmission. The units of data are **'frames'**, that is, asynchronously transmitted characters (i.e. individually at will) or synchronously transmitted blocks of characters (i.e. at fixed intervals at a fixed rate).

c. **The network layer** is the level which provides the control between adjacent sending and receiving points in the network. The sending and receiving points which are able to *switch* transmissions are nodes in the network called **IMPs** (13.19). IMPs are special-purpose computers. **'Packets'** of information are transmitted at this level. A packet is a unit of data with two main components:

   i. Header data, which specifies its destination address (possibly its source address too).

   ii. Data to be transmitted.

d. **The transport layer** is the level which provides an **end-to-end** service between host computers. It deals with addressing, error controls and regulated data transfers.

e. **The session layer** is the level which handles the establishment of connections between hosts and the management of the dialogue. Messages created at this level are addressed by the transport layer and split into packets at the network layer.

f. **The presentation layer** is the level which handles the standard forms for presenting data, e.g. the layouts used for VDU displays.

g. **The application layer** is the level which the user has control over in determining what data is to be transmitted and how it is to be sent or received.

13.34 Separate standards are gradually being established to cover each of the separate layers. Work on standardising the lower levels is largely complete. It includes a series of standards numbered X1, X2, X3...etc. developed by the **CCITT** (Consultative Committee for International Telephone and Telegraphy) of which X25, for example, is a standard for packet switching.

Network structures

13.35 A number of standard network structures are shown in figure 13.6 The individual circles in Fig. 13.6 represent computers connected to the network in the case of LANs and represent IMPs to which computers are connected in the case of LHNs.

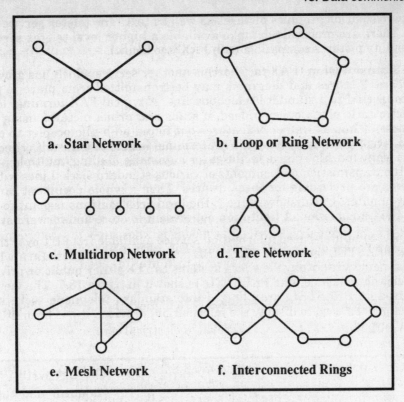

Figure 13.6 Standard network structures

Public services

13.36 In the UK the principal public data communication and network services are provided by **British Telecom (BT)**. Since BT was privatised and ceased to be a state-owned company operating a monopoly it now has competition for some services from other companies, e.g. **Mercury Communications**. Of the different types of services available the majority are still based upon the ordinary telegraph and telephone circuits, which are capable of carrying data as well as speech. However, the whole industry is going through a period of rapid change and there is every indication that the current situation may change significantly within a few years. Further legislative changes in the UK in 1989 were intended to allow greater competition.

13.37 **System X** is indicative of the changes which have taken place. It is a digital telephone exchange system developed by BT which has been installed across the whole country. It has provided better exchange facilities including higher performance data transmission facilities on its standard lines.

13.38 The long-established BT services for standard point-to-point data transmission have the trade name **DATEL**, with each individual service being identified by its own number – DATEL 200, 600, 1200, 2400, 4800, etc. The number corresponds to the transmission speed in bits per second (bps). Asynchronous transmission methods (12, 13) are used for transmission speeds up to 1200 bps and synchronous transmissions are made at speeds of 1200 bps or greater. Much higher speeds can be provided, up to 48,000 bps by using wideband circuits.

13.39 The DATEL services make provision for the use of public lines and privately leased lines. The latter tend to be used by organisations with significant amounts of data to transmit.

13.40 **TELEX** (short for telegraph exchange) is another well-established service. It is a public dial-up switched circuit system with over 80,000 users in the UK and over a million worldwide. The transmitter/receiver at each subscriber point of connection is a teleprinter, similar to a computer console typewriter.

13.41 A newer form of TELEX service has been developed in recent years. It is called **TELETEX** (a name easily confused with **Teletext** – to be described later). Teletex terminals are able to transmit low-resolution graphics pictures as well as text. The teletex service is still under development. There are proposals to make available a higher level teletex service which transmits high-quality pictures compatible with FAX (see below).

13.42 **Facsimile Transmission (FAX** for short) is another service which has grown in importance in recent years. Pictures and diagrams may be transmitted from place to place using FAX terminals connected to a standard telephone line. A typical FAX terminal looks like a small desktop electrostatic photocopier. Indeed, it scans and prints pictures using the same principles. Of course, it has a number of features not found on a photocopier to enable the transmission and reception of data. A basic FAX terminal is able to transmit or receive A4-size documents, but many machines have facilities for automatic dialling, multiple polling, call reservation and the transmission of documents of various standard sizes. Lines with speeds greater than 2400 bps are preferable for these devices. Then a whole document can be transmitted within a few minutes. One disadvantage is the need for a continuous point-to-point connection *throughout* the transmission. A limitation not present in store-and-forward systems.

13.43 **PRESTEL** is a computer-based information service available from BT over the telephone line with the aid PRESTEL terminals. PRESTEL is an example of **viewdata** which also has the international name **videotex**. Viewdata systems can be either public or private. An example of a public viewdata service, like PRESTEL, is shown in figure 13.7. The viewdata terminals, like those used on PRESTEL, are plugged into standard telephone sockets. In the home a television set may be used to display the information, provided it has been fitted with a special adaptor and keypad.

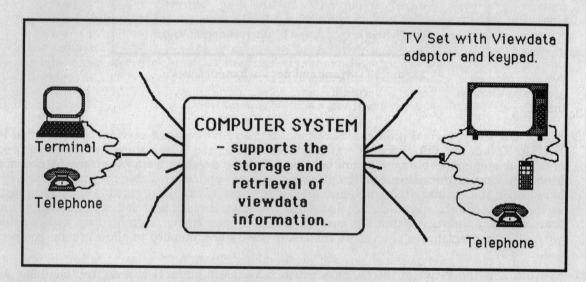

Figure 13.7 A Viewdata System

13.44 PRESTEL has been described as an 'electronic encyclopaedia for the home', but its main success has probably been in various business applications. There are currently over 60,000 PRESTEL users and over 1200 sources of information being used to provide PRESTEL with over 300,000 'frames' of information. A 'frame' is a screen-sized page of information. The information which has been most successfully exploited by business is that concerning subjects such as the money markets, the stock exchange, insurance markets, agricultural markets and travel information. Users pay a standard rental plus call charges and a charge for each page viewed. Some pages may be viewed freely others may cost several pence to view for a few minutes. Organisations may purchase frame space in order to provide information to PRESTEL users. The information is fed in via a PRESTEL terminal. PRESTEL is a two-way service so a user wishing to respond to information given (e.g. surveys, services or advertisements) is able to do so.

13.45 Do not confuse **viewdata** with **teletext**, which is also a computer-based information system, and which has some features in common with viewdata. The important difference is that whereas viewdata is a two-way system, teletext is a receive-only system. Teletext services are provided by the BBC *(Ceefax)* and ITV *(Oracle)*. In teletext the 'frames' of information are transmitted together with the TV signals using spare bandwidth. Provided the set has been fitted with a teletext adaptor it is able to decode the signals and display the frames of information on the TV screen. A hand-held control pad allows individual numbered frames of information to be selected. The methods used by viewdata and teletext for displaying frames of information are compatible with one another.

13.46 **PSS** is a packet-switching system provided by BT and operating in a network linking major cities. The PSS network has links with other major networks including several in Europe and North America. Many companies have become major users of this service since its introduction in the early 1980s and it is likely to expand even further. Each connection to the PSS network is called a PSS gateway and has an account number, which is rather like a telephone number only longer.

Private services

13.47 The public services just described have their private counterparts. So, just as BT has introduced System X, many companies have installed private digital telephone exchanges. There are also companies running private viewdata systems. For example, several travel tour operators provide a viewdata service for travel agents. The London Stock Exchange also runs its TOPIC service for financial institutions and private investors.

13.48 An important trend in recent years has been the move towards integrating the various kinds of services used within the organisation. For example, if a building is to be rewired so as to provide lines from a central computer to workstations in offices, it is possible to install one single digital transmission circuit containing a PABX which is able to handle both the data communications and the telephone communications. Even greater integrations of services can be achieved if LANs are used. Devices used for viewdata or FAX can be interconnected with the main computer system, or even personal computers, so as to form one large information system. In such a system orders collected by a private viewdata system can be automatically processed along with those collected by more conventional means or perhaps by a member of the sales staff equipped with a portable personal computer.

Electronic mail

13.49 As its name suggests electronic mail has some features comparable with those of the postal service. These features are given here in outline:

    a. Each user has a 'mailbox', which is accessed via a computer terminal or workstation within the system by entering an account number and password. Messages are drawn to the user's attention when entering the system, for example, by displaying message headings on the screen.

    b. When a message is sent it consists of two parts:

        i. A header which specifies the address of who it is to be sent to and the address of who it is from. The address may merely be another account number in simple cases.

        ii. The text of the message.

    c. The mailing system provides computerised ways of preparing and editing the text of the message.

    d. The mailing system also provides computerised ways of selecting messages to be read and then displaying them, saving them, deleting them, forwarding them or replying to them as required.

13.50 Electronic mail was originally devised as a means of communication between people using the same computer but it is an increasingly common facility to be found on LANs. On some LANs one computer may specialise in handling the electronic mail. Such a computer is called a 'mail server'. Users on the LAN always communicate with the mail server when dealing with mail. On other systems each computer takes a share of the work in processing the electronic mail.

13.51 Electronic mail on LHNs is transmitted using message-switching systems or packet-switching systems. There are already a number of private electronic mail systems which exploit public packet-switching systems. The sender's computer and receiver's computer do the work of assembling the message, making the transmission and disassembling the message. BT offers a public electronic mail system which will make use of their existing PSS system. There are international PSS systems too.

Summary

13.52 a. The long-established methods of data communication are based upon the telephone system and employ circuit-switching methods and analog transmissions.

b. Digital data transmission is technically superior to analog transmissions, akin to the data representations used in computers and is gradually replacing traditional analog methods.

c. Message switching and packet-switching offer advantages over circuit-switching systems.

d. Computer networks and distributed systems are becoming increasingly important in data processing because of the numerous advantages they offer over systems which are separate and autonomous.

e. Computer networks are of two basic kinds:
   i. Local Area Networks (LANs).
   ii. Long Haul Networks (LHNs).

The latter often exploit packet-switching system methods of data transmission.

f. The following services have been discussed:
   i. Digital telephone systems such as System X.
   ii. The BT DATEL service.
   iii. TELEX and TELETEX.
   iv. Facsimile Transmission (FAX).
   v. Viewdata (videotex) and BT's PRESTEL.
   vi. Teletext (BBC's Ceefax and ITV's Oracle).
   vii. The BT packet-switching system (PSS).
   viii. Electronic mail.

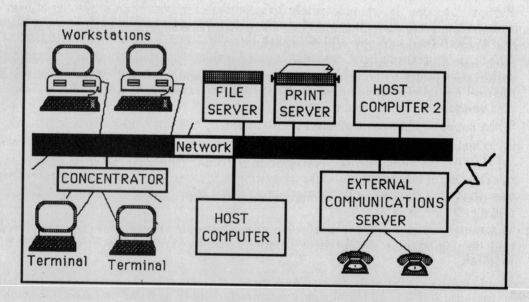

Figure 13.8 A Local Area Network (LAN)

Points to note

13.53 a. Wide-band circuits make possible high-speed bulk data transmission.

b. Some 'terminals' are in fact microcomputers. They are called 'intelligent terminals' because they have a small processor and can carry out 'local' processing as well as transmitting data. Banks use them as part of their system for linking branches with their computer centre.

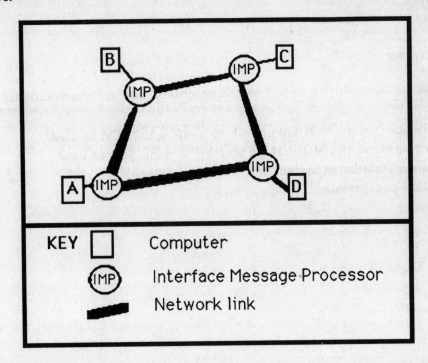

Figure 13.9 A Long Haul Network (LHN) (or Wide Area network (WAN))

c. It is also possible to use data transmission to link two large computers. One which is busy can then transfer work to the other. This is called 'load-shedding'.

d. In some situations the same service to the user may be provided by systems of differing design. For example, *one* moderately sized processor may support a number of user terminals *or* alternatively a number of single-user computers might be connected into a network. The former is called **'shared logic'** the latter is called **'distributed logic'**.

e. The term **'distributed processing'** is now widely used in relation to micro- and minicomputers. It implies of course that a processing facility is made available at a number of sites instead of at a single computer centre. The term can imply:

  i.   A number of micros and minis at different sizes, not linked to each other.

  ii. A network of micros and minis linked to a central mainframe computer.

  iii. A network of micros and minis linked to each other without a central mainframe.

f. Each of the services described is important in its own right in terms of its uses in data processing, but it is when these separate systems are integrated into a single information system that they can have a particularly significant effect on the way in which data processing activities are carried out.

g. A common low level protocol used on LAN rings is IBM's **token ring.** Another widely used but less low level protocol used on various LANs, including ethernet and token ring is **TCP/IP.**

Questions

1. What are the main problems that can arise in capturing raw data for use within a computer system? What solutions would you propose?

   (CIMA)

2. Explain any FIVE of the following terms used in data communication systems indicating their relevance to systems, and where applicable describe the hardware needed:

   a. LAN

   b. Baud

    c. Multidrop Lines

    d. Star network

    e. Asynchronous transmission

    f. Modem

    g. Acoustic coupler

(IDPM)

3. Explain the advantages which a packet switching system has over a conventional circuit switching system.

4.   a. What is the purpose of a MODEM and where would a MODEM be used?

     b. Name one alternative to a MODEM if a portable terminal is to be used.

5. Explain the terms 'Distributed System' and 'Computer Network'.

6. Why was the OSI model created?

14 Operating systems

Introduction

14.1 Computers are required to give efficient and reliable service without the need for continual intervention by the user. This requirement suggests that computers should monitor and control their own operations where possible. The software which performs these monitoring and controlling operations is normally called the '**operating system**', although very simple operating systems are sometimes called '**control programs**' or '**monitors**'. This chapter explains the purpose and facilities of operating systems. The characteristics of an operating system are introduced and the differences between the various common types of operating system are explained.

Control programs and operating systems

14.2 For most general purpose digital computers from PCs upwards at least two programs are within main storage. One may be an applications program, the other will be a **control program** which monitors, aids and controls the applications program. On small computer systems, such as PCs, the control program is sometimes called the '**system**' or **kernel**. Often, in addition to the kernel, there is a program which accepts commands typed in by the user. The commands cause the kernel to carry out general tasks such as printing out text files. This command interpreting program is often called the '**command shell**', or merely the '**shell**'. If the kernel and shell are combined into a single program, which is the case of very simple microcomputers, the combined program is often called a **monitor**.

Note. The terms kernel and shell come from an analogy with nuts since conceptually the shell fits around the 'inner' kernel.

14.3 In general the kernel is but one program in a whole suite of control programs which are able to allow a number of applications programs to run without the intervention of the user. This suite of programs is the **operating system**. The kernel normally remains in main storage. Other programs in the operating system are brought into memory when required, i.e. there are 'resident' and 'transient' parts to the **operating system.** The resident kernel on large systems is sometimes called the **Executive** or **Supervisor Program.**

14.4 **Definition.** An **operating system** is a suite of program which takes control over the operation of the computer to the extent of being able to allow a number of programs to be run on the computer without human intervention. The more advanced operating systems allow a number of applications programs to run *concurrently and in sequence* without the intervention of the user.

The purpose of an operating system

14.5 It can be seen from the definition of an operating system that the operating system controls the way software uses hardware. The purpose of this control is to make the computer operate in the way intended by the user, and in a systematic reliable and efficient manner. This 'view' of an operating system is illustrated in figure 14.1.

14.6 The intended use of the computer by the user will affect the character of the required operating system. For example in the traditional DP applications of computers, '**jobs**', comprised of user programs + data, need to be presented to the computer and processed in a way which will ensure that the maximum number of jobs get processed. At the other extreme, there are computer systems which essentially have one 'job', which is to control some process, eg. controlling the action of an automated engineering machine. Here a fast response to events must be ensured. Between events the hardware may be under utilised.

The functions of an operating system

14.7 In order to fulfil its purpose the operating system must carry out a number of functions. It has at its disposal, and under its control, the various system programs to accomplish this work.

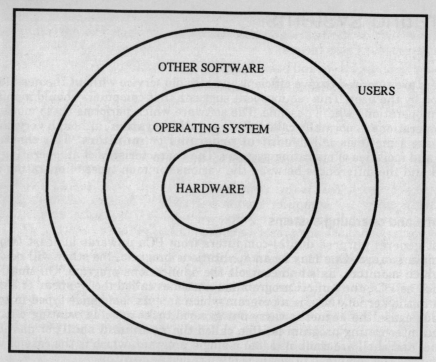

Figure 14.1 An Overview of a system showing the position of the operating system

The functions are:

a. The scheduling and loading of programs in order to provide a continuous job processing sequence or to provide appropriate responses to events.

b. Control over hardware resources eg. control over the selection and operation of devices used for input, output or storage.

c. Handling errors when they occur and using corrective routines where possible.

d. Passing of control from one program to another under a system of priority when more than one application program occupies main storage.

e. Protecting hardware, software and data from improper use.

f. Communication with the computer user or operator by means of terminals or consoles, and through the use of monitor commands and responses. The operator (details shortly) or user may also be able to communicate with the operating system by means of command language. Details follow later.

g. Furnishing a complete record of what has happened during operation. Some details of this log may be stored for accounting purposes.

Justification for having an operation system

14.8 In the early days of computing some of the functions just listed were entirely the responsibility of a person called an **'operator'**. A glance at the full set of operating system functions will show that with modern computers the task is beyond a human operator, simply by virtue of the speeds with which these functions must be performed.

14.9 The operator's task these days consists mostly of loading and removing I/O media from peripherals in response to messages from the operating system on the console typewriter. The justification for an operating system extends beyond operator limitations, the main reasons are:-

a. Modern computer systems are so complex and fast that they need internal control instead of human control.

b. The full system software facilities need to be readily available.

c. The complexity of systems demands that jobs are controlled in what they are allowed to do for the sake of security, although overall the user is provided with greater flexibility.

14.10 **Choice of Operating System.** The applications for which a computer is needed largely determine the choice of hardware and accompanying software. The operating system supplier will need to consider these factors.

   a. The hardware provision and basic design of the computer.

   b. The applications intended for the computer.

   c. The method of communication with the computer, eg. many or few peripherals.

   d. The method of operating the computer.

Methods of operating the computer and communication with it

14.11 a. **Multiprocessing.** This is the name for the situation which occurs if two or more processors are present in a computer system and sharing some or all of the same memory. In such cases two programs may be processed at the same instant. In the remainder of this discussion assume just one processor is used unless otherwise stated.

   b. **Multiprogramming.** This occurs when more than one program in main storage is being processed **apparently** at the same time. This is accomplished by the programs taking turns at short bursts of processing time. In its basic forms it merely involves low priority programs being able to exploit processor times unused by higher priority programs In its more advanced forms multiprogramming is sometimes called **multitasking** which usually implies a level of scheduling capable of supporting multiple users possibly running multiple programs. More details of multitasking are given later in this chapter.

   c. **Batch processing.** The job (program + data) is not processed until fully input. The jobs are entered and stored on a disk in a '**Batch Queue**' and then run one or more at a time under the control of the operating system. A job may wait in a batch queue for minutes or hours depending on the work load. No amendments are possible during processing.

   NB. The time which elapses between job submission and the return of results is known as the **turn around** time.

   d. **Remote job entry** refers to batch processing where jobs are entered at a terminal remote from the computer and transmitted to the computer eg. via telecommunication links.

   e. **Interactive Computing.** This occurs if the computer and terminal user may communicate with each other. (Also applies to computer communication with another device).

   f. **Conversational mode.** This is Interactive computer operation where the response to the user's message is immediate.

   g. **Multi-access.** This occurs if the computer allows interactive facilities to more than one user at a time.

   h. **Time-sharing.** Processor time is divided into small units called **time slices** and shared in turn between users to provide multi-access.

   i. **Real-time system.** A real time system is a computer system which is capable of processing data so quickly that the results are available to influence the activity currently taking place. There is often a need for multi-processing and a front end processor in these systems.

   k. **Virtual memory.** This is a technique whereby programs undergoing execution but exceeding their allocation of main storage can be held in a special area on disk. From there program sections must be loaded into main storage quickly when instructions within them are about to be executed.

Multiprogramming and time-sharing

14.12 Computer programs, if looked at in basic terms, can be seen to perform nothing more than a repetition of three steps:

   a. **Input**   —   reading into main storage from a peripheral device.

b. **Computing** – using the processor.

c. **Output** – writing out from main storage to a peripheral device.

14.13 In the very earliest of computers only *one* of the three steps could be performed at any one time and the processor was idle during input and output operations. The imbalance between processor and peripherals was improved with the concept of **simultaneity**, i.e. the simultaneous operation of two or more peripherals.

14.14 Nevertheless, developments along these lines were only concerned with processing one program in the computer at a time. In order to utilise the considerable processing power of the processor more effectively a way was found to have *more* than one program in main storage at any one time. These programs *share* the processor between them.

14.15 Programs generally will use various proportions of input or output (peripheral) time and computing (processor) time.

a. Programs which use a *lot* of peripheral time and very *little* processor time are referred to as being **peripheral bound** (a good example is the media conversion program, which does hardly any computing at all).

b. Programs which require *great* use of the processor and relatively little of peripherals are said to be **processor bound** (a good example is a program which is principally performing computations).

14.16 The ideal situation is to have one or more of each type of program in main store *at any one time* so that while one is carrying out an input/output operation another is using the processor. In this way the imbalance between the processor and peripherals is reduced and a balance between computing time and I/O time is achieved.

14.17 **Multiprogramming.** This term is used to describe the technique of having *more* than one program in main storage at any one time and *apparently* being processed at the same time. The kernel program will transfer control from one program to another so that when one is using the processor another is making use of peripherals. Skilful interleaving of programs increases utilisation of the processor.

14.18 **Partitions.** In order to achieve this *sharing* of the main storage, it is regarded as being divided into PARTITIONS. Each program will occupy a partition.

14.19 **Interrupt.** The control program (kernel) has the ability to *interrupt* a particular program to pass control to another. It is this power which enables the interleaving of programs. The applications program can request resources via interrupts. The interrupt concept is fundamental to the proper working of a multiprogrammed computer.

14.20 From the way in which multi-programming has just been described it should be clear how it can improve the throughput of batch jobs. When multi-access interactive users are to use a system, the multi-programming must take place under a strategy which gives each user both a fair share of processor time and conversational facilities. Time-sharing serves this purpose.

14.21 In a **time-sharing** system a clock is used to divide up processor time into 'time-slices' and these time-slices are shared between the users in an appropriate way. This 'scheduling' is described in more detail later.

Single user systems

14.22 As their name implies, these provide support for only one user at a time. They can be found on most PCs and on computers which are dedicated to a single function. They provide a simple command language, support for files, and I/O facilities for terminal, disk and printer. Some provide support for **multiprogramming**, ie. running more than one job concurrently, and this may be as simple as having one main job which runs in the **'foreground'** and a **'background'** job which is executed when the processor would be idle. Popular examples of this type of operating system include, MS-DOS (or PC-DOS) and CP/M all of which provide interactive facilities to the user.

Batch operating system

14.23 This is the oldest type of operating system and is characterised by a computer system which handles a batch of input which is collected over a period of time. Jobs are entered into a queue which is maintained by the operating system, and there is no provision for interaction by the user once the input has been submitted, although multi-programming may be used to optimise the use of peripherals.

Multi-access and time-sharing systems

14.24 A mainframe computer may support a hundred or more users simultaneously, whereas a typical minicomputer may support up to twenty or thirty. Time-sharing allows each user a time slice of less than a second, but in an interactive environment not all users will require service for each time slice: priority scheduling allows for a more rapid response. Multi-access operating systems use multiprogramming and often employ virtual memory, as described earlier. All aspects of control are more elaborate in these systems. Compare a single program system with picking up a ball throwing it into the air and catching it. Liken the ball being thrown to a program being processed, and liken the work of picking up throwing and catching to the operating system loading a program, executing it and then taking over control at the end. A multi-access time-sharing system compares with catching balls from all directions and juggling them.

Real-time systems

14.25 This type of operating system is characterised by speed of response. The system is able to respond very quickly to a change of circumstance and to initiate feedback. Examples include the control of a chemical plant, a space capsule or the monitoring of a patient's condition in hospital. In all cases, a rise of temperature would require a rapid response in order to maintain equilibrium. Reliability is very important in such systems, and hardware is often duplicated so as to be able to recover from hardware malfunction. The term **'fault-tolerant'** computer is used to describe this situation.

14.26 A real-time system which controls an engineering or manufacturing process is usually called a **Process Control System,** e.g. a system to control the operation of a chemical factory plant. Response to changes must be as fast as possible and reliability is essential.

Operating system features

14.27 Operating Systems should have the following features.

 a. efficiency, in terms of processor and resource utilisation, throughput of jobs, response time for multi-access systems, turn-round time etc.;

 b. reliability, in terms of being error-free and handling all possibilities in the execution of jobs;

 c. maintainability, in terms of enhancing facilities, modularity, correction of bugs etc.;

 d. small size, in terms of the amount of memory and backing store required.

 Clearly, some of these desirable features conflict with others.

14.28 Most operating systems are designed and written in a modular form. Many exhibit a structure which can be likened to the rings of an onion (see figure 14.1). A small central **'core'** (or **'nucleus'**, **'kernel'**, **'supervisor'**, **'executive'**) contains routines which are very time-critical, eg the interrupt handler and low-level scheduler or dispatcher. This is kept resident in memory at all times and maintains a variety of data structures to keep track of the status of other jobs running on the system.

14.29 The outer layers of the onion contain the other routines making up the operating system, and these are called into memory when necessary. A typical outer structure might be (in order of decreasing time-dependency); a memory management unit, input/output handling, file access, and scheduling and resource allocation.

14.30 The operating system interfaces directly with the hardware of the computer system. All other software makes use of the routines provided by the operating system, so there is no need for programmers to have detailed knowledge of how to control the hardware directly. These applications can be regarded as the 'skin' of the onion. Later in this chapter there are further details of how operating system functions are achieved.

Command language

14.31 A programming language used for communications with the operating system is called a command language. Most statements (commands) in the language are directives requiring immediate execution and are handled by a **command language interpreter**. These commands may also be called '**monitor commands**'.

14.32 **A Job Control language (JCL)** is a special command language used for batch processing. It is used to identify jobs and state their requirements to the nucleus.

Processes

14.33 A concept fundamental to the understanding of how an operating system works is that of a process. A **process** may be thought of as the *execution of a program*, and clearly the process will be carried out by a processor. However, there is rather more to the idea of a process than that because it is seldom the case that there is just one program assigned to a given processor for execution.

14.34 At this point it may help to use a simple analogy. Let us compare a processor executing a program with a student reading a book borrowed from the library. It will help if we think of the *process* of 'reading the book' as starting once the book is borrowed and ending when the book is returned. The student (processor) will have other things to do than just carry out the process of reading the book (program) and so at any one time the book may be waiting for the reader to start or continue reading it, or have the student in the act of reading it. Whenever the student sets the book to one side in order to do something else it will be necessary for the student to remember the point reached in the text and to remember any facts needed in order to be able to read on later. This is very like the case when the processor executes a program. The process may be in a state where it is waiting for the processor to continue execution or it may be in the running state. If running is suspended it will be necessary to save details of the point reached in the program and the state of any data being processed. On a multi-user system a single program may be executed by multiple users with each user having a separate process in its own stage and state of executing the program.

Storage management

14.35 On the more basic multiprogramming systems the operating system may organise main memory into blocks of convenient size called **partitions.** (See figure 14.2). In figure 14.2 the processes for the three programs in user spaces 1, 2 and 3 will each be given turns at processor time according to priorities determined by the operating system (details later). The need for reasonable performance will require all programs and system software to be held on disk so that overlays can happen quickly. With such a system it may be possible to overlay programs *or* subprograms and to make use of program segmentation.

14.36 The users' programs may be loaded into whichever partition is available, (such programs are called **relocatable programs**). On the more sophisticated systems the operating system is able to allocate, and reallocate, partitions of memory to system and user programs or subprograms and can do so continually and repeatedly in response to changes in the system. This is called dynamic allocation of main storage. As part of the **dynamic allocation** of main storage the operating system may copy programs onto disk, in a file called the **swap file**, when it suspends their execution. Then it will overlay the main memory space with another program. Later it may copy the program back into the same or a different part of main memory and resume its execution. This **swapping** from main memory onto disk and back in again is called **rolling out** and **rolling in.** Another term for it is **paging**.

14.37 **Virtual Storage.** The methods just described are extended on some systems so that the operating system will automatically segment programs and allocate memory to them so that the programmer may write programs with little regard for the main storage available. This is known as virtual storage since main storage can be regarded as bigger than its real size.

14.38 **Storage Allocation.** When dealing with the allocation of main storage space and backing storage space an operating system must keep track of how storage has been allocated. It must also protect the space allocated to one user from the accidental or deliberate interference of another user.

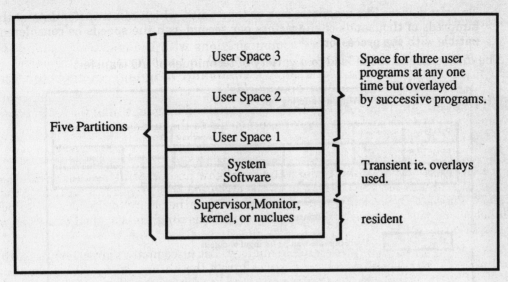

Figure 14.2 A simple multiprogramming system

Multi-tasking

14.39 Today, the term **multi-tasking** is most often taken to mean the multiprogramming of *user programs*. On a single-user computer *without multi-tasking*, such as MSDOS, the multiprogramming is primitive in that there is typically a very limited number of programs running together. These are: the operating system, *one* interactive user program and *possibly* a **background** (i.e. non-interactive) program running a printer queue. In a **multi-tasking system** there can be a number of interactive user programs being multiprogrammed together with the operating system and probably some background tasks too.

14.40 True multi-tasking is **pre-emptive** which means that if a process is interrupted it will not necessarily be resumed immediately after the interrupt has been serviced because other processes may have a higher priority. Modern general purpose minicomputers and mainframes have pre-emptive multi-tasking operating systems. In the case of **non pre-emptive multi-tasking** a single user process, if interrupted, will normally be resumed once the interrupt has been serviced and may therefore gain an unfair share of the processors time. It has the general appearance of multi-tasking to the user but provides a less smoothly balance performance between tasks. Non pre-emptive multi-tasking is sometimes called **pseudo multi-tasking**. Example of *non pre-emptive* multi-tasking are Microsoft Windows 3 running under MSDOS and the Apple Macintosh MACOS version 6 Multifinder. Example of *pre-emptive* multi-tasking are Unix, VMS, Apple Macintosh MACOS version 7 and Microsoft Windows/NT.

The management of input and output

14.41 **The Problems of speed differences.**

a. Communications between the processor and peripherals is fraught with problems caused by the differences in speeds between the two. To put this into context the following points may be considered.

i. A memory cycle takes less than one tenth of a microsecond ie one ten millionth of a second.

ii. Most instructions can be carried out well within 1 microsecond.

iii. Some printers can only print 300 characters per second when at maximum speed, so that in the time it takes for one character to be output the computer might comfortably perform 10,000 instructions.

iv. Even faster devices such as high speed printers make transfers of data at rates which correspond to dozens or hundreds of instructions. Compared to the processor they are slow.

v. Only for devices like magnetic disk or tape units, which can transfer data at the rate of hundreds of thousands of characters per second, can the speeds be considered as compatible with the processor.

b. The differences in speed lead to a variety of techniques of I/O transfer.

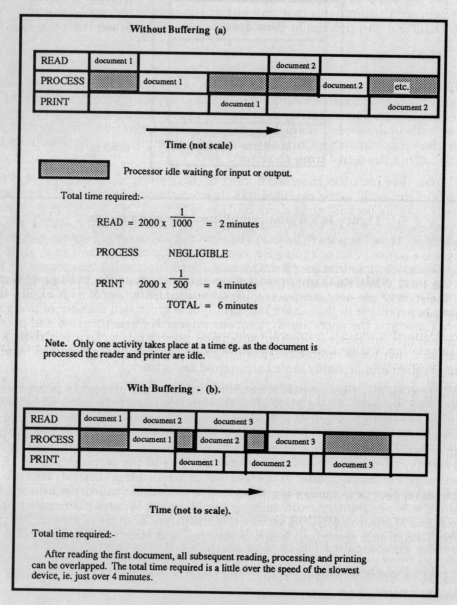

Figure 14.3 Buffering

14.42 The operating system has an I/O handler, ie. a number of programs and subprograms for handling input and output operations and which exploit a number of techniques. Some examples now follow.

14.43 **Buffering** is the name given to the technique of transferring data into temporary storage prior to processing or output, thus enabling the simultaneous operation of devices. This can only be achieved because of the autonomous operation of peripherals, which leaves the processor **free for other work.**

14.44 **Example.** Suppose 2,000 OMR documents need to be input and the details on the documents printed out on a line printer (one line being used for document read). The document reader operates at 100 documents per minute and the printer at 500 lines per minute. The processing cycle and time required would be as illustrated in figure 14.3a, if buffering were not used, and as illustrated in figure 14.3b, if buffering were used.

14.45 Another strategy for correcting for the large differences in speeds between the processor and input/output devices is to connect a large number of terminals to one computer. The processor is able to keep all the terminals in action just as one juggler can keep many balls in the air at one time. Details of how this can be done, by time-sharing, will follow shortly.

Scheduling

14.46 In multiprogramming systems the operating system must schedule the loading and execution of programs in order to provide a continuous job processing sequence or to provide appropriate responses to events. Time-sharing provides a popular scheduling method when multiprogramming with multi-access interactive users. In such a system a clock is used to divide up processor time into 'time-slices' and these time-slices are shared between users in an appropriate way , hence the term ' **time-sharing**'.

14.47 A typical time-slice lasts less than one hundredth of one second. At each pulse of the clock the user program currently being executed has its execution suspended. (The user will probably not be aware of this because time slices happen so frequently that within a second its execution is likely to be resumed.) Then the operating system checks the status of each user, in strict sequence, to see whether the user requires processor time. Some may not, for example they may have paused during typing for some reason. Once the operating system finds a user requiring processor time that user's program is allowed to continue execution for the duration of the time slice. When the end of the sequence of users is reached the operating system returns to the start of the sequence and repeats the sequence again. This is known as **polling** in a **round-robin.**

14.48 **Spooling** (**S**imultaneous **P**eripheral **O**perating **O**n-**L**ine). This method is used to get around the 'bottleneck' caused by the slow speeds of output devices in multiprogramming and time-sharing environment.

14.49 **Example.** A program which is to produce output for a line printer will actually direct its output to the disk. By doing so the program can complete its execution without being held up by the speed of the line printer. The program's output will join a queue to be output on the line printer when its turn comes. The queue may grow quite long at times when the computer is busy but will be reduced when the computer is less busy, this allows the line printer to spread its load over a longer time without holding up processing (See figure 14.4).

Operating systems on personal computers (PCs)

14.50 There are numerous manufacturers of PCs most of whom produce machines which are designed to be so similar to IBM PCs that they can use its operating system. They actually use an operating system called MS-DOS produced by Microsoft which may be described as a 'generic' operating system because it is used for a whole group or class of computers, namely those said to be '**IBM PC compatible**'. The popularity of MS-DOS means that it deserves a separate description here.

14.51 **MSDOS or Microsoft disk Operating System** is supplied by Microsoft Corporation for use on IBM PC compatible computers or '**clones**'. IBM's own version PC-DOS can only be purchased for use on IBM PC's.

14.52 It is a single-user, single-tasking operating system which is disk based. It was first introduced in 1981 but has been enhanced many times to include extra features. The large volume of IBM PCs and clones sold has helped to ensure that there is a vast amount of application software available, as well as utility programs and many programming languages.

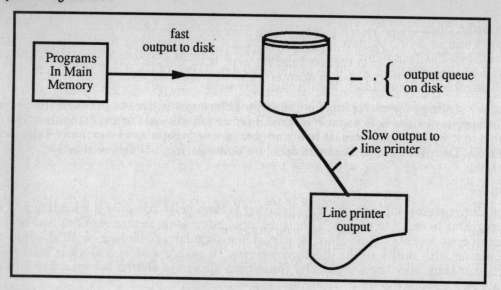

Figure 14.4 Spooling

14.53 MS-DOS provides a command line interpreter interface to the user enabling him or her to execute a program. It also handles input and output as well as managing files stored on disk. Examples of a few MS-DOS commands are given here:

FORMAT   – prepares a disk for use
COPY   – copies a file
DISKCOPY   – copies all files from one disk to another
TYPE   – displays the contents of a file onto the screen
DIR   – lists all files on a disk
DATE   – reports the current date and allows user to change it
CLS   – clears the screen

14.54 The operating system is split into a number of parts. Some of it is held in ROM, some of it is held on disk but is loaded into the computer's memory whenever the computer is turned on or reset, and the biggest part of it stays on disk and is loaded in to memory only when it is needed. The parts of the operating system which are resident in memory contain some of the most used commands, referred to as '**internal commands**', whereas the other '**external commands**' reside on disk.

14.55 MS-DOS organises files on a disk in a hierarchical manner in structure comparable to the family tree. The **root directory** on a disk is given the symbol \. All directories can contain up to 112 entries. An entry can be a file or another directory (known as a sub-directory). The names of files are limited to eight characters in length but these can also have a three letter extension to help indicate the type of file: TEST1.PAS, for example, may be the source code for a PASCAL program called TEST1.

14.56 The operating system was originally written for use on a 5 1/2' floppy disk drive, but has since been extended to include hard disks and 3 1/2' floppy disks. Disk drives are referred to by a letter followed by a colon. Drive A and drive B are usually reserved for floppy drives and drive C for hard disks.

14.57 A PC boots itself when first turned on, or reset, by undergoing a set sequence building up from simple programs to more complex ones. The '**bootstrap loader**' program is contained in ROM, and this is a simple program which loads and executes the file IO.SYS which must be present at a certain place on the disk.

14.58 This in turn reads parameters from CONFIG.SYS if it exists and then IO.SYS hands control over to the system, MSDOS.SYS. This assigns memory to COMMAND.COM, the command line interpreter. Finally, if the command file AUTOEXEC.BAT exists it is executed, otherwise control is passed to the user by indicating an A prompt (or C prompt if you are using a hard disk).

14.59 MS-DOS is command driven and has been criticised by many for being unfriendly. It is possible to provide a menu as a front-end to the operating system, and this is particularly valuable for inexperienced users. A further improvement is to provide a graphical user interface (GUI), such as WIMP (as introduced in chapter 2), whereby different functions or commands are represented by pictures or 'icons' on the screen. These can be selected by moving a pointer controlled by a mouse and 'clicking' on. This first became popular with the Apple Macintosh computer. Microsoft brought out a WIMP GUI for use with MS-DOS called **Microsoft Windows**, which was launched in 1990. It has since become very popular and continues to grow in popularity. It can not run on the older and less powerful PCs. It provides a form a pseudo multi tasking. For example, it allows the user to have several application windows 'open' at the same time.

14.60 As was just indicated, by reference to the Apple Macintosh, MS-DOS is not the only operating system used on PCs. Another generic operating system CP/M is used on 8-bit microcomputers although such machines are now overshadowed by 16-bit microcomputers such as IBM PC compatibles. The Apple Macintosh is probably the only main alternative machine design to the PC compatibles. Its operating system supports a very high standard user interface but is proprietary and therefore is only available on this machine.

Other operating systems

14.61 On larger computers full multi-user multi-tasking operating systems become available. A generic operating system which is gaining in popularity and which is available on a variety of different machines is UNIX (UNIX was developed by Bell laboratories). UNIX has a number of impressive features which have given rise to its widespread use. It is a full multi-tasking, multi-user time-sharing operating system written mostly in C, thereby making it relatively easy to port from machine to machine. It has a sophisticated and powerful command interpreter, called the **shell,** which is designed for used by computer professionals. For example, the one line command

```
'who | sort > mylist.txt &'
```

does the following. First shell runs the command 'who' to obtain a list of who is on the system. The symbol '|' signifies that shell must use the output of 'who' as the input to the 'sort' command which sorts the list into alphabetic order. The mechanism for the '|' is called a 'pipe'. The '>' signifies that output from 'sort' must be fed directly into a file called 'mylist.txt' , rather than to the terminal's screen. Lastly, the '&' signifies that the command line must be carried out as a background task.

14.62 Some versions of UNIX can also be run on the larger PCs. **SCO UNIX** is probably the most popular alternative for this. Almost all other operating systems in current use have been developed by computer manufacturers for use on particular machines, or ranges of machines, of a given make and type, ie they are **proprietary**.

Summary

14.63 a. Operating systems were defined.

  b. The purpose of an operating system was explained.

  c. The functions of an operating system were described.

  d. A number of important concepts were explained:

  i. Multiprocessing

  ii. Multiprogramming

  iii. Batch processing

  iv. Remote job entry

  v. Interactive computing and conversational mode.

  vi. Multi-access

  vii. Time-sharing

  viii. Real-time

      ix. Multitasking

e. The concept of a **process,** as the execution of a program, was introduced.

f. The uses of command language interpreters and Job Control Languages (JCLs) were explained.

g. The operation of various types of systems was explained.

h. Requirements affecting operating system functions were discussed.

i. Important operating system functions were discussed in more detail:-

    i. Storage management,

    ii. Input/Output management

    iii. Scheduling

j. Priorities, buffering, spooling and virtual storage were discussed.

k. Features of MS-DOS and UNIX were described.

Points to note

14.64 a. The operating system is usually the most complex and sophisticated software used on a computer. It is only natural therefore that this chapter only goes so far as to give an overview of operating systems even though a whole chapter is devoted to the topic.

b. The size and sophistication of an operating system will match the requirements of the overall computer system. At its simplest the operating system will be required to do little more than control the operation of the input, output and storage devices. Other computer systems will require the operating system to cope with such things as the simultaneous processing of many programs and checkpoint/restart procedures.

c. Take care not to confuse **time-sharing** with **real-time**. It is the response of a real-time system which distinguishes it from other systems. Systems controlling processes may not have multiple users but time-sharing by its nature shares time between multiple users. When many users are connected to a time-sharing system the response may be very slow and very unlike a real-time system.

d. Buffering enables better utilisation of equipment and faster throughput. Buffering is *one* method of overcoming the difference in speeds of hardware devices.

e. The term SPOOLING also applies to the conversion of *input* transactions from Document/Disk, etc, such operations being carried out in a multi-programmed computer as 'background' jobs. In this case it is called *Input* Spooling.

f. 'Simultaneity' is the name given to a computer's ability to carry out the simultaneous operation of more than one device.

g. **Multiprogramming and multitasking** are TECHNIQUES *not* items of software.

h. That part of the operating system which remains permanently in main store (i.e. Executive) is said to be 'RESIDENT', the rest of the operating system is 'TRANSIENT'.

Questions

1. Define multiprogramming. Discuss the hardware and software facilities necessary to facilitate multiprogramming.

(CIMA)

2. a. Briefly describe the following types of computer system:

    i. Word processing (6 marks)

    ii. Spreadsheet/financial planning (6 marks)

b. Under what headings would you seek to justify the implementation of the systems mention in (a) above? (8 marks)

(20 marks)
(ACCA)

Computer files

1. Files are named collections of stored data. They can be considered to be the framework around which data processing revolves, i.e. maintained data and input data are organised into files. Files tend to be too large to be held in main storage and are therefore held on backing storage devices such as magnetic disks and magnetic tapes. When data in a file is required for processing the file is read into main storage in manageable amounts.

2. Named programs are also often held on backing storage ready for use and may be regarded as 'files' too. In this Part of the text we are primarily concerned with file stored for data processing, which we may call **'data files'** to distinguish them from files containing programs.

3. Chapter 15 sets out the concepts of magnetic files. Chapter 16 describes the methods of organising a file on magnetic *disk* magnetic *tape* and how access is made to the records in such a files.

4. In the interests of clarity only two magnetic storage devices are used as a basis for discussing computer files. These are:

   a. Magnetic disk (hard or floppy) – Direct Access Storage (**DAS**).

   b. Magnetic tape – Serial Access Storage (**SAS**).

5. The *general* principles discussed with regard to magnetic *tape* or magnetic *disk* can be applied to other media according to whether the media are SAS media or DAS media.

15 Computer file concepts

Introduction

15.1 The purpose of this chapter is to look at the general concepts that lie behind the subject of computer files before going on to discuss the different methods of organising them. At all times the term 'file' will refer to computer data files. The term 'data file' in EDP is used to describe a collection of related data records. It should be recognised that all discussions of 'files' which follow is considered in an *EDP context*.

15.2 **Purpose.** A file holds data that is required for providing information. Some files are processed at regular intervals to provide this information (e.g. payroll file) and others will hold data that is required at regular intervals (e.g. a file containing prices of items).

15.3 There are two common ways of viewing files:

a. **Logical files.** A 'logical file' is a file viewed in terms of *what* data items its records contain and *what* processing operations may be performed upon the file. The user of the file will normally adopt such a view.

b. **Physical files.** A 'physical file' is a file viewed in terms of *how* the data is stored on a storage device such as a magnetic disk and *how* the processing operations are made possible.

15.4 A logical file can usually give rise to a number of alternative physical file implementations. These alternatives are considered in later chapters.

Elements of a computer file

15.5 A file consists of a number of **records**. Each record is made up of a number of **fields** and each field consists of a number of characters.

Clock number	Employee's name	Date of birth	Sex	Grade	Hourly rate
1201	P J Johns	06 12 45	F	4	850

Field   Field of characters 'P', 'J', 'J', etc

Notes:
1. Clock number is key field (15.10)
2. Grade is coded
3. Hourly rate is expressed in pence

Figure 15.1 Payroll Record (part only)

a. **Character.** A character is the smallest element in a file and can be alphabetic, numeric or special, (2.2).

b. **Field.** An item of data within a *record* is called a field – it is made up of a number of *characters,* e.g. a name, a date, or an amount.

c. **Record.** A record is made up of a number of related fields, e.g. a customer record, or an employee payroll record (see figure 15.1).

Alternative terminology

15.6 The terminology of 15.5 (i.e. record, field and character) is firmly established as a means of describing the characteristics of files in general situations. However, the use of this terminology can lead to excessive attention being directed towards physical details, such as how many characters there should be in a field. Such issues can divert attention from matters of high priority, such as what fields should be recorded in order to meet the information needs of the user. To overcome this difficulty, two alternative sets of terms have been developed, one set for physical files, and the other set for logical files.

They are:

- a. For physical files.
    - i. Physical record.
    - ii. Field.
    - iii. Character (a physical feature).
- b. **For logical files.**
    - i. Logical record – an 'entity'.
    - ii. Data item – 'attributes' of the 'entity'.

15.7 **Entities** are things (e.g. objects, people, events, etc.) about which there is a need to record data, e.g. an item of stock, an employee, a financial transaction, etc. The individual properties of the entity, about which data is recorded, are its **'attributes'**, e.g. the attributes of an invoice (entity) will include the 'name'; 'address'; 'customer order number'; 'quantity'; 'price'; 'description'.

A logical record is created for each entity occurrence and the logical record contains one **data item** for each **occurrence** of the entity's attributes, e.g. the 'customer's name' would be a data item and there would be **one** only in the logical record. Whereas the attributed 'quantity' would have as many data items as there are entries on the invoice.

15.8 The relationship between the various terms used is summarised in the following table:

Things about which there is a need to record data	Entities	❐ each entity has a number of *attributes*
How the data is recorded	Logical records (1 per entity occurrence)	❐ each logical record contains a number of *data items*
Physical details of how the data is recorded	Physical record (1 or more per logical record)	❐ each physical record contains a number of *fields*

Types of files

15.9
- a. **Master file.** These are files of a fairly permanent nature, e.g. customer ledger, payroll, inventory, etc. A feature to note is the regular *updating* of these files to show a current position. For example customer's orders will be processed, increasing the 'balance owing' figure on a customer ledger record. It is seen therefore that master records will contain both data of a static nature, e.g. a customer name and address, and data that, by its nature will change *each time* a transaction occurs, e.g. the 'balance' figure already mentioned.
- b. **Movement file.** Also called **transaction file.** This is made up of the various transactions created from the source documents. In a sales ledger application the file will contain all the orders received at a particular time. This file will be used to update the *master file*. As soon as it has been used for this purpose it is no longer required. It will therefore have a very short life, because it will be replaced by a file containing the *next* batch of orders.
- c. **Reference file.** A file with a reasonable amount of permanency. Examples of data used for reference purposes are price lists, tables of rates of pay, names and addresses.

Access to files

15.10 **Key fields.** When files of data are created one needs a means of access to particular records within those files. In *general* terms this is usually done by giving each record a 'key' field by which the record will be recognised or identified. Such a key is normally a *unique identifier* of a record and is then called the **primary** key. Sometimes the primary key is made from the combination of two fields in which case it may be called a **composite key** or **compound key.** Any other field used for the purpose of identifying records, or sets of records, is called a **secondary key.** Examples of primary key fields are:

- a. Customer number in a customer ledger record.
- b. Stock code number in a stock record.
- c. Employee clock number in a payroll record.

15.11 Not only does the key field assist in accessing records but also the records themselves can, if required, be *sorted* into the sequence indicated by the key.

Storage devices

15.12 Mention is made here of the two storage devices that will be considered in connection with the storage of files (i.e. physical files).

    a. **Magnetic or optical disk.** These are direct access media and are the primary means of storing files on-line.

    b. **Magnetic tape.** This medium has significant limitations because it is a serial access medium.

15.13 These characteristics will loom large in our considerations about files in the chapters that follow. Note then that they are inherent in the *physical* make-up of the devices and will clearly influence the *type* of files stored on each one, and how the files can be *organised* and *accessed*.

Processing activities

15.14 We will need to have access to particular records in the files in order to process them. The major processing activities are given below:

    a. **Updating.** When data on a master record is changed to reflect a current position, e.g. updating a customer ledger record with new orders. Note that the old data on the record is replaced by the new data.

    b. **Referencing.** When access is made to a particular record to ascertain what is contained therein, e.g. reference is made to a 'prices' file during an invoicing run. Note that it does *not* involve any alterations to the record itself.

    c. **File maintenance.** New records must be added to a file and records need to be deleted. Prices change, and the file must be altered. Customers' addresses also change and new addresses have to be inserted to bring the file up to date. These particular activities come under the heading of 'maintaining' the file. File maintenance can be carried out as a separate run, but the insertions and deletions of records are sometimes *combined* with updating.

    d. **File enquiry or interrogation.** This is similar in concept to referencing. It involves the need to ascertain a piece of information from, say, a master record. For example, a customer may query a Statement sent to him. A 'file enquiry' will get the data in dispute from the record so that the query may be settled.

Fixed-length and variable-length records

15.15 The question whether to use records of a fixed or variable length is one that usually does not have to be considered in manual systems.

    a. **Fixed.** Every record in the file will be of the same fixed number of fields and characters and will never vary in size.

    b. **Variable.** This means that not *all* records in the file will be of the same size. This could be for two reasons:

        i. Some records could have more *fields* than others. In an invoicing application, for example (assuming a 6-character field to represent 'total amount for each invoice'), we would add a new field to a customer record for each invoice. So a customer's record would vary in *size* according to the *number* of invoices he had been sent.

        ii. Fields *themselves* could vary in size. A simple example is 'the name and address' field because it varies widely in size.

15.16 It should be noted, however, that in the examples at 15.15b a fixed-length record *could* be used. In 15.15b.i the record could be designed in the first instance to accommodate a fixed number of *possible* invoices. This means the records with less than the fixed number of invoices would contain blank fields. Similarly in 15.15b.ii the field could be made large enough to accommodate the *largest* name and address. Again records with names and addresses of a smaller number of characters would contain blanks.

15.17 Fixed-length records make it easy for the programmer because he or she is dealing with a known quantity of characters each time. On the other hand they result in less efficient utilisation of storage. Variable-length records mean difficulties for the programmer but better utilisation.

Hit rate

15.18 This is the term used to describe the rate of processing of master files in terms of active records. For example, if 1,000 transactions are processed each day against a master file of 10,000 records, then the hit rate is said to be 10 Hit rate is a measure of the **'activity'** of the file.

Other file characteristics

15.19 Apart from **activity,** which is measured by hit rate, there are other characteristics of the file that need to be considered. These are:

   a. **Volatility.** This is the frequency with which records are added to the file or deleted from it. If the frequency is high, the file is said to be **volatile.** A file that is not altered is **'static'**. If the frequency is low, the file is said to be **'semi-static'**.

   b. **Size.** This is the amount of data stored in the file. It may be expressed in terms of the number of characters or number of records.

   c. **Growth.** Files often grow steadily in size as new records are added. Growth must be allowed for when planning how to store a file.

Data hierarchy

15.20 The data structure of a file forms part of a **data hierarchy,** as shown below.

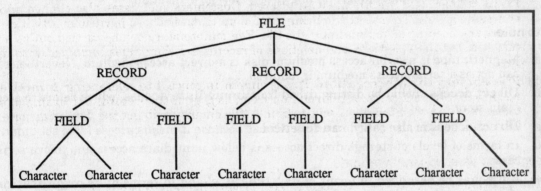

Other file types

15.21 **Document Files** were introduced in chapter 4 with particular reference to the simplest form of document file the **text file**. Other common forms of document files are those used in conjunction with word processors or desktop publishing systems. More generally, 'document files' may hold the files used by painting or drawing packages.

15.22 In a typical document file the records each have a single field of variable length and correspond to units of text such as lines or paragraphs. The records may not necessarily have key fields although a text line number is sometimes used as a key. A high-level language program may be stored as a text file.

15.23 Other types of files may also be referred to in the following ways:

   a. **Program file.** A file in which the 'data' held in the file is some item of software such as a simple program or collection of program parts.

   b. **Data file.** The types of file described so far, as opposed to program file.

   c. **Input and output files. Either** files formed from source documents but not sufficiently organised for use as transaction files (e.g. not sorted) **or** files holding processed data awaiting output.

d. **Work file.** A file created during an intermediate stage in processing.

e. **Scratch file.** A file no longer needed which may be overwritten.

Summary

15.24 a. A file is a collection of *related* records.

b. A file is made up of **records,** which are made up of **fields,** which are made up of **characters.**

c. It is often advantageous to distinguish between physical files and logical files.

d. Fields within logical records are normally called **'data items'** (or just **'items'**)

e. A record is recognised or identified by the record KEY.

f. Files can be broadly classified as master files, movement (or transaction) files and reference files.

g. The physical nature of the storage device will have a direct bearing on the way files are organised on it, and also the method of access.

h. The physical nature of the storage device will have a direct bearing on the way files are organised on it, and also on the method of access.

i. Four processing activities are: updating, referencing, file maintenance and file enquiry or interrogation.

j. Referencing is usually carried out during updating and is incidental to it.

k. Files can consist of records of fixed length or variable length. The decision on which is adopted is a question of programming ease v storage utilisation.

Points to note

15.25 a. Magnetic tape is a serial-access medium, disk is a direct-access medium. Nevertheless disk can act as a serial-access medium if required.

b. **Direct access** should be distinguished from **immediate access,** which refers to access to main store.

c. **Direct access** is also called **random access** because it means access in no set order.

d. In terms of levels of storage direct access is below immediate access and above serial access.

e. A file may be described in terms of its **'structure'** and in terms of its **organisation.** Its *structure* is determined by which data items are included in records and how the data items are grouped within records. Its *organisation* is determined by how the records are arranged within the file.

f. Files are not normally held in **primary storage** (i.e. main storage). They are normally held on an on-line backing storage (**secondary storage**) or on off-line backing storage.

Questions

1. a. Give your definition of the word 'file' as it is used in the context of data processing.

b. Distinguish between a master file and a transaction (or movement) file and explain the relationship between them.

c. List FIVE factors to be considered in determining how a master file should be organised.

(ACA)

2. Define the term 'key field'. Discuss the suitability of the following data items as key fields.

a. A person's surname in a personnel file.

b. A national insurance number in a payroll file.

c. A candidate number in an examinations file.

16 File organisation and access

Introduction

16.1 This chapter describes the ways in which files may be organised and accessed on disks and magnetic tapes. Before tackling this chapter the reader should be thoroughly conversant with the relevant hardware described in Chapter 7 including, in particular, the physical attributes of magnetic tapes (in the form of reels or cartridges) and disks (fixed exchangeable) plus the 'reading' and 'writing' devices called the tape units and disk drives.

16.2 Today most file processing is carried out using files stored on hard magnetic disks. Optical disks only have a minority use at present although they are being used increasingly for applications requiring large volumes of archived or reference data. Floppy disks are only used as the main file processing medium on very small microcomputers. The principles covered by this chapter concerning the use of disks are applicable to all disk types. Any relevant differences will be highlighted when appropriate.

16.3 There is still a significant amount of file processing carried out using files stored on magnetic tape but it is almost all done on mainframes in large commercial, industrial or financial institutions. Magnetic tape continues to be an important backup medium especially in its cartridge forms.

16.4 Magnetic tape is in most respects a much simpler medium than disk. Indeed, the simplest methods of organising and accessing files on disk are very similar to the standard ones use for magnetic tape. Therefore, throughout this chapter the descriptions relating to tape are give before the corresponding descriptions for disk.

16.5 **File organisation** is the arrangement of records within a particular file. We start from the point where the individual physical record layout has been already designed, i.e. the file 'structure' has been decided. How do we organise our many hundreds, or even thousands, of such records (e.g. customer records) on magnetic tape or disk? When we wish to access one or more of the records how do we do it? This chapter explains how these things are done.

Writing on tape

16.6 Records are 'written' in the first place from main storage onto the tape by the processor. Each record is written onto tape in response to a 'write instruction'. This process will be repeated until all the required records are written onto the tape, i.e. until the file is complete. Figure 16.1 illustrates what the tape will look like in diagrammatic form.

Cust. 1	Inter Record Gap	Cust. 2	Inter Record Gap	Cust. 3	Inter Record Gap	Cust. 4	Inter Record Gap	etc ...

Figure 16.1 Diagram illustrating records on magnetic tape

Note the inter-record gap (IRG), which is caused by the tape slowing down at the conclusion of one 'write' and accelerating at the beginning of the next.

Reading from tape

16.7 Having created (i.e. written) a file of records onto tape, we will later need to *process* the file. To do this, we take the reel of tape and mount it onto a tape unit. Records are now 'read' *from* the tape into the main storage. Notice that when 'reading', the tape automatically stops when the IRG is reached. It 'knows' when to stop *either* because the length of the record is known in advance *or* because control data recorded on the end of the record marks the end of the record.

Writing on disk

16.8 In order to process files stored on disk the disk pack must first be loaded into a disk unit. Records are 'written' onto a disk as the disk pack revolves at a constant speed within its disk unit. Each record is written in response to a 'write' instruction. Data goes from main storage through a read-write head onto a track on the disk surface. Records are recorded one after the other on each track.

Note. All references to 'records' in this chapter should be taken to mean 'physical records' unless otherwise stated.

Reading from disk

16.9 In order to process files stored on disk the disk pack must first be loaded into a disk unit. Records are read from the disk as it revolves at a constant speed. Each record is read in response to a 'read' instruction. Data goes from the disk to the main storage through the read-write head already mentioned. Both reading and writing of data are accomplished at a fixed number (thousands) of bytes per second.

16.10 We will take for our discussion on file organisation a '6-disk' pack, meaning it has ten usable surfaces (the outer two are not used for recording purposes). But before describing how files are organised let us look first at the basic underlying concepts.

Cylinder concept

16.11 Consult figure 7.3 where the disk pack is illustrated, and note the following:

i. There are *ten* recording surfaces. Each surface has 200 tracks.

ii. There is a read-write head for *each* surface on the disk pack.

iii. *All* the read-write arms are fixed to *one* mechanism and are like a comb.

iv. When the 'access' mechanism moves all ten read-write heads move *in unison* across the disk surfaces.

v. Whenever the access mechanism comes to rest *each* read-write head will be positioned on the equivalent track on *each* of the ten surfaces.

vi. For *one* movement of the access mechanism access is possible to *ten* tracks of data.

16.12 In the case of a floppy disk the situation is essentially the same but simpler (Figure 7.5). There is just *one* recording surface on a 'single-sided' floppy disk and *two* recording surfaces on a 'double-sided' floppy disk. The other significant differences are in term of capacity and speed.

16.13 Use is made of the physical features already described when organising the storage of records on disk. Records are written onto the disk starting with track 1 on surface 1, then track 1 on surface 2, then track 1 on surface 3 and so on to track 1 on surface 10. One can see that conceptually the ten tracks of data can be regarded as forming a CYLINDER.

16.14 Data is written onto successive cylinders, involving *one* movement only of the access mechanism for each cylinder. When access is made to the stored records it will be advantageous, in terms of keeping access mechanism movement to a minimum, to deal with a cylinder of records at a time.

16.15 Conceptually the disk can be regarded as consisting of 200 CYLINDERS. Cylinder 1 comprises track 1 on each of 10 surfaces; cylinder 2 comprises track 2 on each of the 10 surfaces and so on to cylinder 200, which comprises track 200 on each of the 10 surfaces. This CYLINDER CONCEPT is fundamental to an understanding of how records are organised on disks. An alternative term for cylinder is SEEK AREA, i.e. the amount of data that is available to the read-write heads as a result of one movement or SEEK of the access mechanism.

Hard-sectored disks and soft-sectored disks

16.16 The tracks on a disk are subdivided into **sectors** (see figure 16.2). There are two alternative design strategies for the division of tracks into sectors. One is called **soft sectoring,** the other is called **hard sectoring.**

In either case *whole* sectors of data are transferred between the disk and main storage.

Note. A disk said to have 'no sectors' is effectively a soft-sectored disk.

16.17 A **soft-sectored** disk has sectors that may be varied in length, up to some maximum value that is never more than the size of a complete track. Sector size and position is *soft* ware controlled, hence the term 'soft sectored'.

16.18 A **hard-sectored** disk has sectors of fixed length. There may be anything from 8–128 sectors per track. Sector size and position is predetermined by hardware, hence the term 'hard sectored'.

16.19 You may compare a sector with a physical record or block on magnetic tape (figure 16.1). In fact, it is common to use 'sector' and 'blocks' as synonyms. However, in the case of hard-sectored disks, blocks may be grouped together into larger units called 'buckets' or 'logical blocks'. It is therefore prudent to call a sector a 'physical block' so as to avoid any possible ambiguity.

Basic address concepts

16.20 As the disk is a direct-access device a record can be accessed independently of other records. To enable the disk to locate a record, the record must have some form of ADDRESS. The whole area of each disk can be subdivided to enable this to be accomplished.

    a. **Cylinder.** The major subdivision as we have seen is the cylinder.

    b. **Track.** Each cylinder is composed of a number of tracks (10 in our quoted example).

    c. **Block.** The smallest addressable part of a disk is a block (ie. a sector). This forms the **unit** of transfer between the disk and main storage.

    d. **Bucket.** When the block size is fixed (i.e. when the disk is hard sectored) a number of blocks (i.e. sectors) are grouped to form a larger unit of transfer. This unit is called a bucket or **logical block.**

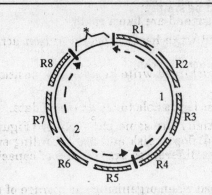

The start of each track is marked physically by a notch or hole. The start of each sector is marked by special data recorded there.

a. Soft-sectored disk

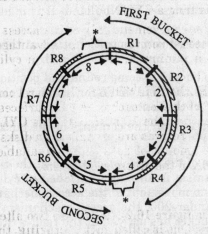

The start of each track and sector is marked physically by a notch or hole. There may also be recorded marks as on the soft-sectored disk.

b. Hard-sectored disk

Key

Sectors (i.e. blocks) are numbered 1, 2, 3, ...

Logical records are numbered R1, R2, R3, ...

* indicates wasted storage space.

Figure 16.2 Blocking records on magnetic disks

16.21 The block or the bucket is therefore the unit of input/output on disk. As on magnetic tape, records will be combined together to form one of these units. The optimum size for a block or bucket is determined by:

a. the need to optimise fillage of a track --- e.g. if a size were chosen for a variable-length block that did not divide exactly into the track size, space would be wasted, (see figure 16.2).

b. the need to minimise the number of transfers between main storage and disk storage. The larger the block or bucket size, the more records will be brought into main storage at each transfer, (e.g. in figure 16.2b, four records are transferred at a time).

c. the need to economise in the use of main storage. A large block or bucket may occupy so much main storage that insufficient space is left for other data and programs.

16.22 In basic hardware terms, the address of a record is given thus:

a. cylinder number

b. track number

c. block number (which will be the first block in the bucket if this concept applies).

Note. On a single-sided floppy disk the address would be simply

a. 'track' number

b. block number   } i.e. one of a number of concentric tracks

Thus the address 1900403 indicates

a. cylinder 190

b. track 4

c. block 3.

Access time

16.23 Access time *on disk* is the time interval between the moment the command is given to transfer data from disk to main storage and the moment this transfer is completed. It is made up of three components:

a. **Seek time.** This is the time it takes the access mechanism to position itself at the appropriate cylinder.

b. **Rotational delay.** This is the time taken for the bucket to come round and position itself under the read-write head. On average this will be the time taken for half a revolution of the disk pack. This average is called the **'latency'** of the disk.

c. **Data transfer time.** This is the total time taken to *read* the contents of the bucket into main storage.

16.24 Access time will vary mainly according to the position of the *access mechanism* at the time the command is given. For example if the access mechanism is already positioned at cylinder 1 and the record required happens to be in cylinder 1 no movement of the access mechanism is required. If, however, the record required is in cylinder 200, the access mechanism has to move right across the surface of the disk. Once the bucket has arrived at the read-write head, the transfer of data to storage begins. *Speed of transfer* of data to main storage is very fast and is a constant rate of so many thousand bytes per second. A hard disk will operate at speeds roughly 10 times faster than a floppy disk.

File organisation on tape

16.25 Organisation of a file on tape is simply a matter of placing the records one after the other onto the tape. There are two possible arrangements of files:

a. **Serial.** When records are written onto tape *without* there being any relationship between the record keys. *Unsorted* transaction records would form such a file.

b. **Sequential.** When records are written onto tape in *sequence* according to the record keys. Examples of sequential files are:

  i. **Master** files.

  ii. **Sorted** transaction files.

Tape file access

16.26 a. **Serial files.** The only way to access a serial file on tape is SERIALLY. This simply means to say that each record is read from the tape into main storage one after the other in the order they occur on the tape.

  b. **Sequential** files. The method of access used is still SERIAL but of course the file is now in sequence, and for this reason the term SEQUENTIAL is often used in describing serial access of a sequential tape file. It is important to note that to process (e.g. update) a sequential master tape file, the transaction file must *also* be in the sequence of the master file. Access is achieved by first reading the transaction file and then reading the master file until the matching record (using the record keys) is found. Note therefore that if the record required is the twentieth record on the file, in order to get it into storage to process it the computer will first have to read in *all* nineteen preceding records.

Note. These limited methods of organisation and access have led to tape becoming very much less common than disk as an on-line medium for the storage of master files. Tape continues as a major storage medium for purposes such as off-line data storage and back-up.

File organisation on disk

16.27 There are four basic methods of organising files on disk:

  a. **Serial.** As for tape. Records are placed onto the disk one after the other with no regard for sequence.

  b. **Sequential.** Again as for tape; records are written onto the disk but in a defined sequence according to the record keys.

  c. **Indexed sequential.** Records are stored in sequence as for 16.27b but with one important difference – an *index* is provided to enable individual records to be located. Strictly speaking the records may not always be stored in sequence but the index will always enable the sequence to be determined.

  d. **Random.** Records are actually placed onto the disk 'at random', that is to say there is no *obvious* relationship between the records as with 16.27b and 16.27c

  A mathematical formula is derived which, when applied to each record key, generates an answer, a bucket address (as illustrated in 16.22). The record is then placed onto the disk at this address, (e.g. one possible formula might be: given key = 36713. Divide by 193 giving 190 remainder 43. (Address is taken as cylinder 190, track 4, block 3.)

Access

16.28 a. **Serial files.** As for tape the only way to access a serially organised file is SERIALLY.

  b. **Sequential files.** As for tape also, in fact the comments under 16.26b apply equally to sequentially organised files on disk.

  c. **Indexed sequential files.** There are three methods of access:

  i. **Sequential.** This is almost the same as in (b) above; the complete file is read in sequential order using the index. The method is used when the hit rate is high. The method makes minimal use of the index, minimises head movement and processes *all* records in each block in a single read. Therefore, the index is used once per block rather than once per record. Any transaction file must be pre-sorted into the same key sequence as the master file.

  ii. **Selective sequential.** Again the transaction file must be pre-sorted into the same sequence as the master file. The transaction file is processed against the master file and *only* those master records for which there is a transaction are selected. Notice that the access mechanism is going forward in an ordered progression (never backtracking) because both files are in the same sequence. This minimises head movement and saves processing time. This method is suitable when the hit rate is low, as only those records for which there is a transaction are accessed.

iii. **Random.** Transactions are processed in a sequence that is not that of the master file. The transactions may be in another sequence, or may be unsequenced. In contrast to the selective sequential method, the access mechanism will move *not* in an ordered progression but back and forth along the file. Here the index is used when transactions are processed immediately – i.e. there is not time to assemble files and sort them into sequence. It is also used when updating two files simultaneously. For example, a transaction file of orders might be used to update a stock file *and* a customer file during the same run. If the order was sorted to customer sequence, the customer file would be updated on a *selective sequential* basis and the stock file on a random basis. (Examples will be given in later chapters.)

Note. In c.i and c.ii the ordered progression of the heads relies upon an orderly organisation of the data and no other program performing reads from the disk at the same time, which would cause head movement to other parts of the disk. In multi-user systems these things cannot always be relied upon.

d. **Random files.** Generally speaking the method of access to random files is RANDOM. The transaction record keys will be put through the *same* mathematical formula as were the keys of the master records, thus creating the appropriate bucket address. The transactions in random order are then processed against the master file, the bucket address providing the address of the record required.

Methods of addressing

16.29 For direct access one must be able to 'address' (locate) each record whenever one wants to process it. The main methods of obtaining the appropriate address are as follows:

a. **Index.** The record keys are listed with the appropriate disk address. The incoming transaction record key is used to locate the disk address of the master record in the index. This address is then used to locate the appropriate master record. We referred to this method in 16.28c.

b. **Address generation.** This is another method that was mentioned earlier, in 16.28d. The record keys are applied to a mathematical formula that has been designed to generate a disk hardware address. The formula is very difficult to design and the reader need not worry about it. The master records are placed on the disk at the addresses generated. Access is afterwards obtained by generating the disk address for each transaction.

c. **Record key = disk address.** It would be convenient if we could use the actual disk hardware address as our record key. Our transaction record keys would then also be the appropriate disk addresses and thus no preliminary action such as searching an index or address generation would be required in order to access the appropriate master records. This is not a very practical method, however, and has very limited application.

Note. Files organised as in 16.29b and 16.29c are said to be '**self-indexing**'.

Updating magnetic tape files

16.30 a. Because of the design of the tape unit it is not possible to write records back to the same position on the tape from which they have been read. The method of updating a tape file therefore is to form a *new* master file on a *new* reel of tape each time the updating process is carried out.

b. Updating a master file held on tape entails the following:

  i. Transaction file and master file must be in the same sequence.

  ii. A transaction record is read into main storage.

  iii. A master record is read into main storage and written straight out again on a new reel if it does not match the transaction. Successive records from the master file are read (and written) until the record matching the transaction is located.

  iv. The master record is then updated in storage and written out in sequence on the new reel.

The four steps are repeated until all the master records for which there is a transaction record have been updated. The result is the creation of a *new* reel of tape containing the records that did not change plus the records that have been updated. The new reel will be used on the next updating run (see figure 16.3).

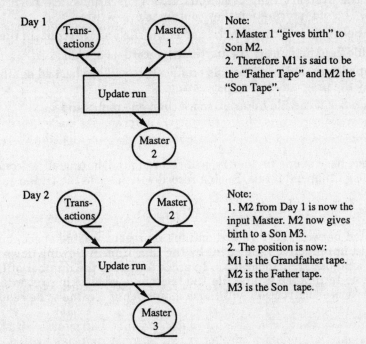

Figure 16.3 File security on tape – the father-son concept

Magnetic tape file maintenance

16.31 **File maintenance** is the term used to describe the following:

a. Removing or adding records to the magnetic file.

b. Amending static data contained in a record, e.g. customer name and address, prices of stock items following a general price change.

The term generally applies to master files.

16.32 Removing a record entails leaving it off the carried-forward tape reel, while adding records entails writing the new record onto the C/F tape reel in its correct sequence. Variable-length records present no problems because there are no constraints on the size of records that can be written onto tape.

File labels

16.33 In addition to its own particular 'logical' records (i.e. the customer or payroll records) each *tape file* will generally have two records, which serve organisational requirements. They are written onto the tape in magnetic form as are the logical records. These two records are usually referred to as LABELS. One comes at the beginning of the file and the other at the end.

a. **Header label.** This is the first and its main function is to identify the file. It will contain the following data:

   i. A specified field to identify the particular record as a label.

   ii. File name – e.g. PAYROLL; LEDGER; STOCK.

   iii. Date written.

   iv. Purge date – being the date from which the information on the particular tape reel is no longer required and from which the reel can be reused.

This label will be checked by the program before the file is processed to ensure that the correct tape reel has been mounted. definite policy with regard to how *many* generations are kept; Grandfather -- Father -- Son should be adequate. If an accident should befall M3 on Day 3's Update run then no matter, we can re-create it by doing Day 2's run again. The keeping of the Master and appropriate transaction files ensures security of the system's files. Notice as new 'generations' are born the oldest tapes are reused. The old information they contain is overwritten.

b. **Trailer label.** This will come at the end of the file and will contain the following data:

   i. A specific field to identify the particular record as a label.

   ii. A count of the number of records on file. This will be checked against the total accumulated by the program during processing.

   iii. Reel number if the file takes up more than one reel of tape.

Control totals

16.34 Mention is made here of one further type of record found on tape files – one which will contain control totals, e.g. financial totals. Such a record will precede the trailer label.

Blocking records

16.35 The gaps created between each record on tape represent wasted space, but more importantly they represent unproductive *time* spent by the tape unit in slowing down and accelerating in between each write and read operation. In order to reduce the number of IRGs and thus speed up the *total* time to process a tape file the technique of blocking records is adopted. Thus a single 'read' or 'write' instruction will cause a number of records to be read or written. See figure 16.4.

Buffers and buffering

16.36 The area of main storage used to hold the individual blocks, when they are read in or written out, is called a **buffer.**

16.37 In the example shown in figure 16.4 tape 2, where the blocking factor is 6, the buffer will be at least as long as 6 logical records because records are transferred between the tape unit and main memory one complete block at a time.

16.38 A program that was processing each record in a file in turn would only have to wait for records to be read in after processing the sixth record in each block when a whole block would be read in. The use of just one buffer for the file is called single **buffering.**

16.39 In some systems **double buffering** is used. Two buffers are used. For the sake of argument call them A and B and assume that data is to be read into main storage from the file. (The principle applies equally well to output.) When processing begins the first block in the file is read into buffer A and then the logical records in A are processed in turn. While the records in A are being processed the next block (block 2) is read into B. Once the records in A have been processed those in B can be processed immediately, *without waiting for a read.* As these records in B are processed the next block (block 3) is read into A replacing what was there before. This sequence of alternately filing and processing blocks carries on until the whole file has been processed. There can be considerable saving in time through using double buffering because of the absence of waits for block reads.

16.40 Note that single and double buffering are generally carried out by the operating system not by the application program. Further aspects of buffering and double buffering will be covered in later chapters.

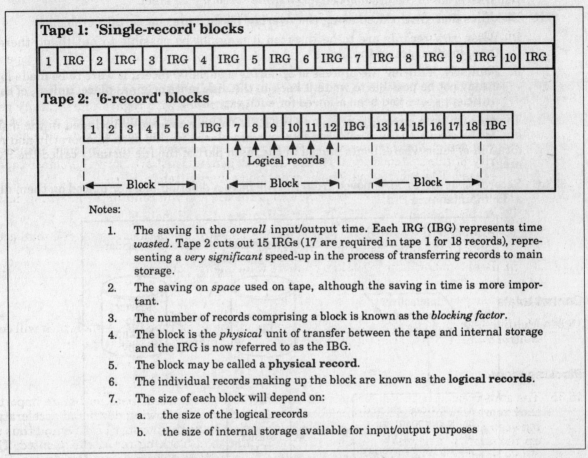

Figure 16.4 Blocking records on magnetic tape

Updating disk files

16.41 As individual records on disks are addressable, it is possible to *write back* an updated record to the same place from which it was read. The effect is therefore to *overwrite* the original master record with the new or updated master record. This method of updating is called **'updating in place'** or **'overlay'**. Note the sequence of steps involved:

a. The transaction record is read into main storage.

b. The appropriate master record is located on disk and is read into main storage.

c. The master record is updated in main storage.

d. The master record (now in updated form) is written from main storage to its original location, overwriting the record in its *pre*-dated form.

16.42 a. The method described can only be used when the *address* of the record is *known*, i.e. when a file is organised as indexed sequentially or randomly.

b. Files organised on a serial or sequential basis are processed in the same way as magnetic tape files, i.e. a physically different carry-forward master file will be created each time the file is processed. Such a new file could be written onto a different disk pack or perhaps onto a different area of the same disk pack.

16.43 The Grandfather-Son method of file security cannot be applied to 'update in place'. A common alternative is shown in figure 16.5.

File maintenance – disk files

16.44 a. If disk files are organised and processed in the same manner as magnetic tapes then the remarks made in the previous chapter apply.

  b. Disk files that are updated using the 'overlay' method present certain problems:

   i. When new records are to be inserted it may not be possible to put them, there and then, in sequence on the file.

   ii. Similarly, if during the process of *updating* a variable record it were to be made longer, it may not be possible to write it back to the disk in its original place, unless, of course, sufficient space had been allowed for such expansion.

  c To cater for such circumstances, an OVERFLOW area is usually included in the disk file and such records as those referred to above are placed in this area temporarily and an indication of their whereabouts placed in the main part of the file (usually called the HOME area).

  d. Records that are to be removed from the file have a deletion marker placed on them during a file maintenance run.

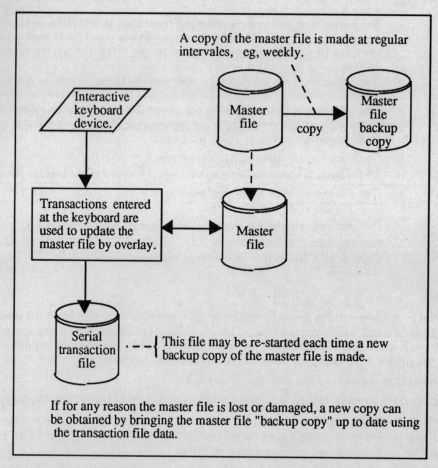

Figure 16.5 An example of file security for disk files updated by overlay

File reorganisation

16.45 As a result of the foregoing the number of records in the overflow area will increase. As a consequence the time taken to locate such a record will involve first seeking the home track and then the overflow track.

Periodically it will be necessary to reorganise the file. This will entail rewriting the file onto a new disk pack:

   i.   Putting the records that are in the overflow area in the home area in the proper sequence.

  ii.   Leaving off the records that have a deletion marker on them.

 iii.   Rewriting any index that is associated with the file.

Labels/control totals

16.46 Header and trailer labels and control totals – akin to those on magnetic tape – are used on disk files too.

16.47 In index sequential files there is some extra data included in the header label. The extra data is called the **primary index**, which is used to locate records on the disk. When the file is 'opened' the primary index is read into main storage and it is held there throughout the time the file is being processed. Each cylinder also contains its own **secondary index**, which supplements the primary index.

Other organisation and access methods

16.48 The methods of file organisation and access described so far are closely related to the physical features of the disk. It is now common practice for much of this detail to be 'hidden' from programmers or users of the system. Instead the operating system handles the physical levels of organisation and access, and provides standard *logical file* organisation and access methods.

16.49 **Some examples of logical file organisation.**

  a. **Sequential files.** A programmer need merely regard the file as a sequence of records, and need have no concern for their physical location. A program instruction to read the next record will result in the appropriate record being transferred into memory, i.e. the programmer's 'view' may just be like this.

R1	R2	R3	R4	R5	R6	etc

R1.... R6 are logical records.

  b. **Direct files.** These are files that provide fast and efficient direct access, i.e. they are normally *random files* with *one* of a number of appropriate addressing methods. A common type of direct file is the **Relative file.** The logical organisation of a relative file is like this:

R1	R2	R3	R4	R5	R6	etc
1	2	3	4	5	6	etc

R1.... R6 are *logical records* with *logical* keys 1....6.
A relative file may be accessed sequentially or randomly.

  c. **Index sequential files.** Logical versions of index sequential files are simpler than their physical counterparts, in that logical keys are used instead of disk addresses, and details of overflow are hidden from the programmer. The accessing methods are the same as those given in 21c.

Other direct-access media

16.50 The ability to access records independently of others within a file, i.e. at random or *directly*, has resulted in the term *direct-access* devices being given to those devices able to offer this facility. The **magnetic drum** is another direct-access device having one read-write head per track which reduces the elements of access time to rotational delay and transfer time (no seek time being involved as with disks). As electromechanical movement is a major part of access time, the elimination of seek time makes access to drums faster than to disks. However, drums are expensive to manufacture and have a much lower capacity than disks. Drums are therefore seldom used these days and do not merit further discussion.

Summary

16.51   a.   An inter-block gap is created after each block is *written* on tape.

b.   When the tape is being read the IBG terminates the 'read' operation (i.e. the transfer of the data in that particular block).

c.   Tape is a serial medium and can only be accessed serially.

d.   Updating is achieved by creating a physically different file each time.

e.   File maintenance involves adding and deleting records and the amendment of static data contained in records.

f.   Labels are provided for control/organisational purposes.

g.   A diagram showing the components of a tape file is shown in figure 16.6.

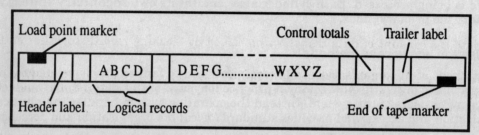

Figure 16.6 Diagram illustrating components of a tape file

h.   Conceptually the disk is regarded as being composed of so many concentric CYLINDERS.

i.   Disk is an addressable medium and therefore specific records can be accessed leaving the rest of the file undisturbed.

j.   Organisation on disk is by cylinder, track and bucket (or block).

k.   Access time on disk consists of three components seek time, rotational delay and data transfer time.

l.   The overlay or 'in-place' method of updating *can be* used on disk.

m.   Methods of file organisation on disk are:
  i.   Serial.
  ii.   Sequential (with or without an index).
  iii.   Random.

n.   Methods of access to disk files are:
  i.   Serial (for serial and sequential files).
  ii.   Selective sequential (for indexed sequential files).
  iii.   Sequential (for sequential and indexed sequential files).
  iv.   Random (for random and indexed sequential files).

o.   File maintenance on disk raises problems:
  i.   When inserting new records.
  ii.   When updating variable-length records.

p.   Special overflow areas are designated on disk to take new records and overlength records temporarily.

q.   A periodic file re-organisation run is required with disk files to place records residing temporarily in overflow areas into their correct sequence in the file and to leave off 'deleted' records. Any index also has to be reconstructed during this run.

r.   A summary of normally accepted methods of file organisation on disk and associated methods of access is given in figure 16.7.

File organisation method		Method of access	
1. Serial 2. Sequential	} (Sequential)	Serial Serial (sequential)	} (Sequential)
3. Indexed sequential		a. Sequential b. Selective sequential c. Random (Direct)	
4. Random (Direct or Relative)		Random (Direct)	

Figure 16.7 A summary of file organisation and access methods

Note. Terms in parentheses are alternative terms normally used at a logical level.

Points to note

16.52 a. Note the amount of data transfer *time* saved by blocking records together on tape (figure 16.4).

b. When we talk of 'transferring' or 'reading' from tape, we really mean *copying* it from tape because the data is still *there* on the tape. This concept holds good *whatever* the medium on computers.

c. Data can also be written onto tape 'off-line', i.e. by a transferring from another medium to tape, e.g. from diskette by means of a separate computer from that which will finally do the processing. Transaction files are generally associated with these methods of 'preparing' tape.

d. The size of blocks is limited by the amount of main storage available for the input/output area.

e. Tape labels are *magnetic* labels for use by the computer program.

f. The expression 'reading the master/transaction file' really means in effect 'reading *one* block into main storage'. A separate 'read' instruction is required for each block on each tape to be 'read' into main storage.

g. The use of the term 'generation' in connection with master files (figure 16.3).

h. Magnetic tape is *not* normally used as a storage medium for master files undergoing processing, unless the files are only updated infrequently and are not required for on-line access between updates.

i. Magnetic tape is the most popular storage medium for off-line 'back-up' of all kinds of files.

j. Some tape units may be operated in a mode in which data is transferred between the tape and main storage in a continuous stream for 'back-up' or 'recovery' purposes. This is known as **streaming.**

k. A file is 'open' for input once its header label has been read and checked, and it is 'open' for output once its header label has been written successfully.

l. The expression 'the disk' has been used in this chapter. It is probably more correct to use the slightly more verbose expression 'the disk pack'.

m. 'Seek area' or 'cylinder' constitutes the amount of data available at any one time to the read-write heads for only one movement of the access mechanism. Note, however that data can only be read or written for *one* read-write head at one time.

n. Although it is a direct-access device, the disk is very often used without making use of the particular characteristic of direct access for reasons that will be stated later.

o. Updating in place (overlay) is generally adopted in conjunction with *fixed* -length records.

p. The methods of file organisation and access were dealt with separately in the text for clarity. They are, however, very much related.

q. If you are asked a question about 'file organisation' the chances are you will be required to talk about the whole subject including, of course, access.

r. Although dealt with separately in the interests of clarity, file maintenance and file reorganisation are closely related and should both be included in an examination answer on either subject.

s. It is desirable to have a disk overflow area on the *same* cylinder as the home area. If the overflow area is on a different cylinder then the access mechanism has to move *twice* for one access; once to the home area and then to the overflow area. The second movement is not required if the home area and the overflow area are on the same cylinder.

t. Note the implication of an overflow area during the sequential access of an indexed sequential file on disk. Access is made to every record in their *logical* sequence, which may *not* be the same as the *physical* sequence because some of the records will be residing temporarily in an overflow area.

u. Index sequential access mode files (**ISAM** for short) are based upon a tree-like structures. One more advanced form of such a structure is called a **btree**. In a btree structured file the nodes of the index are split as the file grows so that the index maintains a balanced structure.

v. Details of file processing methods will be covered in later chapters.

Questions

1. What factors would govern the choice of storage media?

2. Explain the basic principles relating to the organisation of data on a disk pack and describe the indexed sequential method of file organisation.

(ACA)

3. A computer is sometimes described as having five basic elements. Other descriptions divide storage into two categories, internal and external, so making a total of six basic elements.

   Describe briefly the two categories of storage and explain fully the purpose which they serve.

(ACA)

4. a. Describe magnetic disc storage.

   b. Briefly outline the data storage and access methods which are possible on disc.

(IDPM)

5. Describe, with the aid of diagram where appropriate.

   a. how alphabetic and numeric data are coded onto magnetic tape, and

   b. the methods by which records are organised on a magnetic tape master file.

   c. Describe, with the aid of appropriate diagrams, how a master file held on magnetic tape is organised and processed.

(ACA)

6. In relation to Magnetic Tape, briefly explain the following terms:

Magnetic Storage	Content of frames	Parity
Records	Blocking	Inter Block Gap
Header record	Trailer record	Write protect
Read after write		

(IDPM)

Software

1. **Definition.** Software is the term used (in contrast to hardware) to describe *all* programs that are used in a particular computer installation. The term is often used to mean not only the programs themselves but their associated documentation.

2. There are numerous types of software. Chapter 17 is used to provide a detailed classification of the different types and a description of each type. The chapter also describes the features of programming languages. Other specialist aspects of software are covered in chapters in other Parts of this text.

17 Software types and programming languages

Introduction

17.1   This chapter provides on overview of software. It starts by explaining the difference between the various types of software and provides a description of each type. In a number of cases the reader is referred to other chapters for more detailed coverage. Later in the chapter programming languages are examined in detail and are classified by 'level'.

Types of software

17.2   From the introductory material given in chapter 1 (1.79–1.80) the reader may remember that the two basic types of software are:

   a.   System software.

   b.   Applications software.

17.3   **System software.** The user of a computer has at his or her disposal a large amount of software provided by the manufacturer. Much of this software will be programs which contribute to the control and performance of the computer system. Such programs with associated documentation are given the collective name **systems software.** Any one of these programs is a **systems program.** The **operating system,** described earlier in the text, is a suit of systems programs

17.4   **Applications software.** Applications programs may be provided by the computer manufacturer or supplier, but in many cases the users produce their own applications programs called **user programs** (e.g. payroll programs, stock control programs, etc). Most applications programs can only work if used in conjunction with the appropriate systems programs notably the operating system.

17.5   **Further sub-division.** A more detailed sub-division is as follows:

   a.   System Software.

      i.   Operating systems and control programs

      ii. Translators

      iii. Utilities and service programs

      iv. Database Management Systems (DBMSs)

   b.   Applications Software.

      i.   User applications programs

      ii. Applications packages (specialist and generalised)

17.6   The first half of this chapter discusses software under headings which correspond to this classification.

Operating systems and control programs

17.7   An **operating system** is a suite of systems programs which takes over the operation of the computer to the extent of being able to allow a number of programs to be run on the computer without human intervention. Very rudimentary or special purpose operating systems are sometimes called **control programs.** All but the more basic **operating systems** allow a number Operating systems were described in detail in chapter 14.

Translators

17.8   The earliest computer programs were written in the actual language of the computer. Nowadays, however, programmer writes their programs in programming languages which are relatively easy to learn. Each program is translated into the language of the machine before being used for operational purposes. This translation is done by computer programs called **translators.** Further details are given later in this chapter as part of the discussion of programming languages.

Utilities and service programs

17.9 Utilities, also called service programs, are systems programs which provide a useful service to the user of the computer by providing facilities for performing common tasks of a routine nature.

17.10 Common types of utility programs are:

a. Sort

b. Editors

c. File copying

d. Dump

e. File maintenance

f. Tracing and debugging

17.11 Sort This is a program designed to arrange records into a predetermined sequence. A good example of the requirement for this service program is the need for sorting transaction files into the sequence of the master file before carrying out updating. Sorting is done by reference to a record key.

a. **Parameters required.** It is a *generalised* program which must be *'specialised'* as it were, before use; this is accomplished by supplying the program with parameters which will be different for each application. Such parameters are:

   i. Key-size and number (if more than one).

   ii. Record size (length).

   iii. Peripheral units available for the sorting process, i.e. number of tape units, disk units, etc, which can be made available to the program.

   iv. Required sequence (ascending order of numeric or alphabetic keys, etc.).

b. How accomplished. The number of records to be sorted and limitations of main storage do not normally allow the sorting to be done in one attempt, so the sort is usually split into two stages:

   i. **String generation phase.** Manageable groups of records from the unsorted file are read into main storage. These groups are sorted into sequence and written as sequenced groups of **strings** onto other output disks or tapes.

   ii. **String merging phase.** During this phase strings are read into main storage, **merged** into larger groups (records are in sequence within groups) and written out to disk or tape. The process is repeated until the whole file is in one sequence.

   Note. Each repetition of the string merging is called a **pass**. The sorting within main storage is called **Internal Sorting** and is the type of sorting done during the **String generation phase.**

17.12 **Editors (also called text editors)** are used at a terminal and provide facilities for the creation or amendment of programs. These were described in chapter 4. The editing may be done by the use of a series of commands or special edit keys on the keyboard. If, for example, a source program needs correction because it has failed to compile properly, an editor may be used to make the necessary changes.

17.13 **File copying** (also called media conversion). This is a program which simply copies data from one medium to another, e.g. from disk to tape. The term **file backup** is more commonly used if the copying is performed so as to be able to recover the files if the originals are lost.

17.14 **Dump.** The term 'Dump' means 'copy the contents of main storage onto an output device'. This program is useful when an error occurs during the running of application programs. The printed 'picture' of main storage will contain information helpful to the programmer when trying to locate the error. It is also used in conjunction with a CHECKPOINT/RESTART program. This program stops at various intervals during the running of an application program and dumps the contents of main storage. If required, the Checkpoint/Restart program can get the application program back to the last checkpoint and restart it with the conditions exactly as they were at the time.

Note. 'Dump' is sometimes used to mean 'copy the contents of on-line storage onto an off-line medium', e.g. dumping magnetic disk onto magnetic tape for back-up purposes.

17.15 **File maintenance.** A program designed to carry out the process of insertion/deletion of records in any files. It can also make amendments to the standing data contained in records. File maintenance may also include such tasks as the reorganisation of index sequential files on disk.

17.16 **Tracing and debugging.** Used in conjunction with the debugging and testing of application programs on the computer. Tracing involves producing diagnostic information after obeying specified instructions so that the cycle of operations can be traced and errors located. Debugging is the term given to the process of locating and eliminating errors ('**bugs**') from a program.

Note. Well-written and tested programs will tend to be more reliable and will therefore require less debugging than badly written programs.

Database management systems (DBMS)

17.17 DBMSs will be described in chapter 27. A database is a single organised collection of structured data and a DBMS is the complex item of software which manages a database.

User applications programs

17.18 User applications programs are programs written by the user in order to perform specific jobs for the user. Such programs are written in a variety of programming languages according to circumstances, but all should be written in a systematic way such as that indicated in the part on programming.

17.19 For many applications it is necessary to produce sets of programs which are used in conjunction with one another and which may also be used in conjunction with service programs such as sort utilities.

17.20 For some applications it may be necessary to compare available software or hardware before writing the applications software. For example, the user may wish to compare the performance of two different COBOL compilers. Such a comparison may be made using a benchmark.

17.21 **Benchmarks.** A benchmark is a standard program, or set of programs, used to evaluate hardware or software. For example, a benchmark might be used to:

a. Compare the performance of two or more different computers on identical tasks.

b. Ascertain if the configuration provided by a manufacturer performs according to the claims made.

c. Assess the comparative performance of two alternative programs which can both perform the same task.

Application packages

17.22 These have already been introduced and examples given in chapters 3 and 4. A further noteworthy example is the **expert system**, sometimes called **Intelligent Knowledge Based Systems (IKBSs)**

17.23 An **Expert System** is a specialised computer package which can perform the function of a human expert. Some of the first expert systems to gain widespread publicity were those used for medical diagnosis. A medical consultant, assisted by his staff, took part in a lengthy exercise in which both the knowledge base required and the decision making procedures were transferred to the computer. Subsequently, the computer was able to ask the same questions and draw the same conclusions from the answers as the consultant, so that a relatively junior doctor, aided by the computer, could be as expert as the consultant!

17.24 There are many possible applications for Expert Systems, for example, company law, investment, finance and personnel. Products are gradually appearing on the market.

17.25 Expert Systems normally have the following features (a law Expert System will be used to provide examples):

    a. An organised base of knowledge – often in the form of a database (e.g. Acts of Parliament and Case law.)

    b. A user interface able to support diagnostic or similar discussions with the user (e.g. to enable the user to pose legal problems or to check the legality of an intended action).

    c. A facility to hold details of the status of the current consultation (e.g. the user, in consulting the Expert System, may have to go through a lengthy question and answer session and the system has to keep track of the state of the questioning).

    d. An Inference Engine, i.e. software which can use the knowledge base and current status of the consultation to either formulate further questions for the user or draw conclusions about what actions to recommend to the user, (e.g. a mechanism for formulating and sequencing appropriate questions about the user's legal problem.)

    e. A knowledge acquisition system, i.e. a facility to update the knowledge base. It is via the knowledge acquisition system that the human expert is able to endow knowledge to the expert system, (e.g. a suitable system for entering the relevant facts about company law).

17.26 Although these basic components are bound to vary from one discipline to another (e.g. the knowledge base for Company law is very different from the knowledge base for Personnel Management) the basic structure is the same. Therefore, an established method for developing an Expert System is to build the particular Expert System required from a standard non-application-specific basic system called a shell. It is possible to purchase a complete Expert System or merely a shell from which an Expert System can be created.

17.27 The user of the Expert System sits at a terminal, PC or work station and takes part in a question and answer session in which data about the problem is typed in. At various stages during the session, or maybe just at the end, the system makes an assessment of the problem and recommends actions to be taken. Expert System packages are not confined to large computers. Several are available on personal computers, e.g. Business Information Techniques 'Parys' system, which is used as an aid in Personnel Management.

17.28 This concludes the overview of the various types of software. Now we move on to consider programming languages.

Types of programming languages

17.29 There are three types of programming language:

    a. Machine language itself.

    b. Low-level languages.

    c. High-level languages.

17.30 It is **not** necessary for the reader to learn a machine or low-level language in order to understand data processing and IT. High-level languages merit more attention, but an understanding of pseudocode, together with an understanding of the details given in this chapter, should be sufficient for examination purposes.

Machine language

17.31 The basic features of machine language are illustrated here by means of a simple example. Part of a program is considered in which the larger of two numbers is determined. The procedure is first expressed in **pseudocode** (a precise notation akin to English). See figure 17.1 opposite.

17.32 Figure 17.2 shows the machine language version of the program shown in figure 17.1 together with the low-level language version. Some further details are given in Appendix 3.3 for the benefit of those readers who have a particular interest.

```
IF
        first_number > second_number
THEN
        larger := first_number
ELSE
        larger := second_number
ENDIF

NB.     This pseudocode is very similar to t he w ay
in which the procedure w ould be s tated in some
high-level languages.
```

Figure 17.1 A program fragment written in pseudocode

LOW LEVEL LANGUAGE	MACHINE LANGUAGE [in a 16 bit machine]	
	LOCATION ADDRESS	CONTENTS (BINARY)
.BEGIN		
FNO:	0	value of first number
SNO:	1	value of second number
LNO:	2	value of larger number
LDA FNO	3	0000000000000000
SUB SNO	4	0011000000000001
JAG FGT	5	1010000000001001
LDA SNO	6	0000000000000001
STA LNO	7	0001000000000010
JPU EIF	8	0110000000001011
FGT: LDA FNO	9	0000000000000000
STA LNO	10	0001000000000010
EIF: HLT	11	1110000000000000
.END	12	etc.

INSTRUCTIONS FORMATS

1.   Each machine language instruction is made up of an "operation code" and one or more "operands".

   a. **Operation Code.** The operation code is that part of the instruction which indicates to the computer what action is to be taken, eg, add, move, read, etc. When the instruction is fetched by the control unit the code will be identified and the necessary circuitry activated. The number of unique operations a particular computer is capable of performing is "wired" into the machine when it is built. In this example the left-hand four bits are used for the operation code, eg, in location 4 the operation code is "0011" for subtract.

   b. **Operand(s).** The operand is that part of the instruction which indicates the address of data to be worked on or indicates the "address" of a device used for input, output or storage. In this example the right-hand 12 bits are used for the operand, eg, in location 4 the operand code is "0000000000001", ie, address "1".

   Many modern computers have *two or more operands*. Multiple operands reduces the *number of* individual instructions required to complete a given task.

2.   The low level language instructions correspond to machine language instructions. They each have an optional label, an operation code and an operand, eg, in this example "FGT: LDA FNO" has the label "FT" followed by the operation "LDA" followed by "FNO", an address.

Figure 17.2 A low level language program with a corresponding machine language program

Machine execution

17.33 In order to follow through the discussion of machine language to its natural conclusion the following details of machine execution are presented here:

a. The instructions are automatically executed in the sequence in which they occur in main storage.

b. When its turn comes, each instruction is *fetched* from main storage by the control unit and placed in a register. Then the control unit interprets the instruction and causes its execution by controlling the actions of the appropriate hardware.

c. Some instructions prompt the control unit to switch to some other point in the instruction sequence for the next *fetch*, and thereby give a mechanism for selecting or repeating particular sequences of instructions.

d. There are five basic types of machine instruction:

    i. Input-Output – which control the transfer of data between peripherals and the processor.

    ii. Arithmetic – which perform additions, subtractions, etc.

    iii. Branch – which control repetitions and selections (see c).

    iv. Logic – which match and compare data items.

    v. Data handling – which move and manipulate data.

17.34 Writing in machine language is a tedious business and not done nowadays except on very few small computers. Just consider what it entails for the programmer.

a. All the machine's operation codes have to be memorised.

b. He or she would need to assign all memory addresses and keep a very careful track on them.

c. Instructions have to be written as they will eventually be obeyed, *in sequence*. Thus any insertions or deletions would entail the *relocation* of all succeeding instructions.

d. Subsequent revision of a completed program would be so impracticable as to almost require a complete *rewrite*.

17.35 The whole process is very time-consuming and inefficient.

Low-level languages

17.36 The first step towards easing the lot of the programmer came with the introduction of SYMBOLIC or low-level languages.

17.37 **Features of low-level languages**.

a. **Mnemonic codes** are used in place of the operation code part of the instructions, e.g. SUB for Subtract (see figure 17.2), which are fairly easy to remember.

b. **Symbolic addresses** are used in place of actual machine addresses. These would be appropriate to the particular application, e.g. 'GROSPAY' being a symbolic address in a payroll program. The symbol is chosen by the programmer and used consistently to refer to one particular item of data, (e.g. in figure 17.2 'FNO' is a symbolic address for First Number).

17.38 This symbolic language made program writing so much easier for the programmer, but clearly a program written in this form is not acceptable to the machine. Thus the symbolically written program has to be *translated* into machine language before being used operationally.

17.39 The translation process is actually done by the *computer* itself by means of a special translating program written and supplied by the manufacturer.

17.40 **Terminology**.

a. **Assembly.** The term used to describe the translation process, i.e. the production in machine code form of a program written in a symbolic language.

b. **Assembler program.** The manufacturer's specially written program (sometimes referred to as a processor) which the computer uses to produce a machine language program from a program written in symbolic language.

c. **Source program.** The name given to the program written in symbolic language.

d. **Object program.** The name given to the program in machine language produced by the assembly process.

17.41 The assembler:

a. Translates symbolic operation codes into machine code, and symbolic addressed into actual machine addresses.

b. Includes the necessary linkage for closed sub-routines (see Appendix 3.3).

c. Allocates areas of main storage.

d. Will indicate invalid source language instructions.

e. Produces the object program on disk or tape.

f. Produces a printed *listing* of the object program together with comments. Notice that one symbolic instruction is translated into one machine instruction (i.e. one for one), which is one feature which distinguishes a low-level language from a high-level language (see figure17.3).

17.42 **Macro instructions.** Notice that low-level languages made program writing easier, but the programmer had still to write out *every* single instruction in the source language. A macro instruction is a *single* instruction written as part of the assembly language which, when assembled, will generate *many* machine code instructions. These groups of instructions perform common sequences of instructions such as input/output operations and a whole library of 'Macros' (some written by the manufacturer, some by the user) will be kept on magnetic media. During the assembly process the macro instruction causes the group of instructions to be 'called' from the library (which will be available during assembly) to form part of the object program. You can almost regard them as sub-routines (open sub-routines) (see Appendix 3.4).

High-level languages

17.43 The development of high-level languages was intended to overcome the main limitations of low-level languages, which are:

a. Program writing is a relatively time-consuming business for the programmer because the assembly process produces machine instructions on a ONE-for-ONE basis.

b. Low-level languages are **machine oriented,** each conforming to the instruction set of the machine on which they are used and therefore restricted to use on that machine.

17.44 High-level languages are intended to be machine independent and are **problem-oriented languages (POLs)**, i.e. they reflect the type of problem solved rather than the features of the machine. Source programs are written in statements akin to English, a great advance over mnemonics.

17.45 The first high-level language to be released was FORTRAN (FORmula TRANslation) in 1957. Over the next few years many other high-level languages appeared and established themselves. In fact, new high-level languages have been coming into existence ever since. Most, but not all, have disappeared into obscurity.

17.46 The machine independence of high-level languages means that in principle it should be possible to make the same high-level language run on different machines and then write programs in that language that are portable. Such portability has a number of advantages.

a. A user of a program can change to a newer or bigger computer without the need to rewrite programs.

b. Users of different computers may be able to share or exchange programs and thereby reduce costs.

c. An organisation producing software for sale can sell the same program to users of different computers without the need to rewrite the program for each type of computer. Again, this reduces costs.

17.47 In practice, there are a number of obstacles to such portability. Perhaps the most serious obstacles are those resulting from variations that occur between different versions of each language. Each different *dialect* is usually the deliberate creation of a computer manufacturer, who will try to attract new customers with a 'better' product and who will then keep existing customers because their programs will no longer be portable to the computers of other manufacturers.

17.48 Despite these seemingly unavoidable variations, which have proliferated over time, the development of high-level languages has been accompanied by many successful moves to standardise high-level languages and the ways they are defined.

17.49 Standardisation is organised on an international basis. The international body is the **ISO** (International Standards Organisation). Member countries have their own representative bodies on the ISO committees. For example, in Britain the representative body is the BSI (British Standards Institution) and in the USA it is ANSI (American National Standards Institution). The standardisation of high-level languages has often been carried out in the USA. Subsequently the ANSI standard has become the ISO standard. Britain has produced some standards too, notably the standard for the language **Pascal.**

17.50 Every few years new versions of high-level languages appear in the form of new standards. For example, COBOL '68, COBOL '71 and COBOL '84 are versions of COBOL based on ANSI standards for those years.

17.51 **Features of high-level languages.**

   a. They have an extensive vocabulary of words, symbols and sentences.

   b. Programs are written in the language and whole statements are translated into *many* (sometimes hundreds) machine code instructions.

   c. Libraries of macros and sub-routines can be incorporated.

   d. As they are problem *oriented* the programmer is able to work at least to some extent independently of the machine.

   e. A set of rules must be obeyed when writing the source program (akin to rules of grammar in writing English).

High-level language translation

17.52 The translation of high-level language programs is carried out by compilers or interpreters, but they perform the translation in two completely different ways. It will be simpler to describe compilers first because interpreters are more easily understood by comparing them with compilers.

17.53 **Terminology.**

   a. **Compilation.** This is the term used to describe the translation process.

   b. **Compiler.** A compiler is a manufacturer's specially written program which translates (or 'compiles') a source language program.

   c. **Source/object programs.** Exactly the same as for low-level languages.

17.54 The compiler:

   a. Translates the source program statements into machine code.

   b. Includes linkage for closed sub-routines.

   c. Allocates areas of main storage.

   d. Produces the object program on disk or magnetic tape.

   e. Produces a printed copy (listing) of the source and object programs.

   f. Produces a list of errors found during compilation, e.g. the use of 'words' or statements not included in language vocabulary; or violation of the rules of syntax (see figure 17.3).

17.55 The **compiler** translates the whole of the high-level language source program into a machine code object program prior to the object program being loaded into main memory and executed. Contrast this with the **interpreter**, which deals with the source program one instruction at a time, completely translating and executing each instruction before it goes onto the next. Interpreters seldom produce object code but call upon inbuilt routines instead. Some intermediate code is usually produced temporarily, however.

17.56 If a **compiler** is used, the same program need only be translated once. Thereafter, the object program can be loaded directly into main storage and executed.

17.57 If an **interpreter** is used, the source program will be translated every time the program is executed. Executions carried out in this way may be ten times slower than the execution of the equivalent object programs!

17.58 Despite their apparent inefficiency interpreters are widely used, particularly for the programming language BASIC on small computers, because they are easier to use than compilers.

17.59 **Uses.** Interpreters are used for such things as:

a. Handling user commands in an interactive system.

b. Debugging programs as they run (i.e. removing program faults).

c. Handling software produced for or by a different computer. In this case the interpreter may be essential if:

    i. Two dissimilar machines are to be connected together for operation, or

    ii. If software produced on an old model and not yet converted had to be run on a new one.

Note. Interpretive routines have many uses, e.g. handling individual commands or directives.

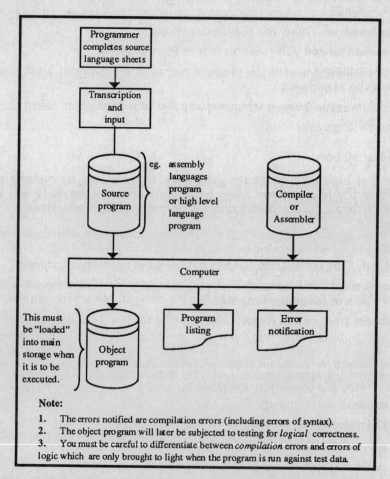

Figure 17.3 Using assemblers or compilers to produce object programs

17.60 **Simulation and emulation**

a. When an interpreter is used to allow a new computer to simulate the behaviour of an old computer this is often referred to as simulation. Interpreters can also be used to simulate a new machine not yet provided but for which software is already written. Note that both the interpreter and the applications program have to be accommodated in main storage when the applications program is 'executed' by the interpreter.

b. Sometimes the hardware of one computer can provide the same kind of facilities as those just described for an interpreter in which case the process is called **emulation**.

17.61 Other translation variations worthy of note are:

a. **Generators.** These are programs which create programs to a given specification. For example, the generator might be able to produce programs which print out the contents of the files on a choice of devices. The generator would be given data which specified such things as output device, type of file, name of file, format of output. The generator would then create the desired program.

b. **Compiler-Compilers.** Compiler-Compilers are generators which produce a compiler for a given language from a definition of the language. They are intended to save man-hours in compiler writing and speed up the production of compilers.

c. **Cross Compilers and Cross Assemblers.** Cross Compilers and Cross Assemblers are translators which are used on one computer in order to produce object programs for use on a second computer. Usually the computer used for the translation is a mini-computer or main frame and the object program is used on a microcomputer.

Types of high-level language

17.62 Five main types are:

a. Commercial languages.

b. Scientific languages.

c. Special-purpose languages.

d. Command languages for operating systems.

e. Multipurpose languages.

Commercial languages

17.63 These are of primary concern in DP and the most well known of them is COBOL (Common Business Oriented Language). A detailed knowledge is not required, but these paragraphs should be enough for examination purposes.

17.64 COBOL is an example of a PROBLEM-ORIENTED language. In other words its vocabulary reflects the type of *problem* to be solved rather than the type of *computer* on which the object program will be used.

17.65 It was intended that any program written in COBOL could be compiled and, within reason, run on any computer. This has not worked out in practice, however, and each manufacturer has its own version of the language *and* thus its own compiler. This applies to most high-level languages.

Some 'machine independent' versions are now available on small computers, e.g. 'CIS-COBOL'.

17.66 COBOL is a *high-level language* developed for *commercial* use. The *source program* is written using *statements* in a stylised but readable form of English. Every *COBOL* program is made up of *four divisions:*

a. **Identification division.** This contains the title of the program for identification purposes. It may also contain the date on which the program was written and the name of the author.

b. **Environment division.** Specifies the particular configuration (hardware) on which the object program will be compiled and executed, e.g. model of machine (IBM 4341), internal storage size needed for running the object program, peripheral units, etc.

c. **Data division.** All items of data to be used in writing the program are listed and identified. Names or labels are given for each *file* and any *records* or *fields* which are referred to later. Record/field *sizes* and *contents* (e.g. whether alpha or numeric) are also specified. Working storage areas are defined.

d. **Procedure division.** Contains the program instructions necessary to solve the particular problem indicated in the program flowchart. These are to be in the form of statements written in a type of English and which conform to the rules of the language (COBOL language). The statements written must use the data labels as defined in divisions 2 and 3. The compiler will report any inconsistencies. Also used are RESERVED WORDS which can only be used in a specific context because they convey a special meaning to the compiler (misuse of these words is reported by the compiler).

e. **Illustration of reserved words.**

'ADD TAX TO GRADPENS.' 'ADD' and 'TO' are reserved words indicating to the compiler that two items of data must be added together. 'TAX' and 'GRADPENS' are labels of two items of data defined in the Data Division.

f. **Examples of COBOL Statements.** (The statements are in block capitals; explanatory notes in small letters.)

   i. Peripheral instructions.

     OPEN INPUT-PAY-FILE (prepares a file for processing).

     READ PAY-FILE AT END PERFORM FIN (reads file into memory).

     WRITE PAY-LINE AFTER ADVANCING ONE LINE (print after throwing paper).

   ii. **Arithmetic Instructions.**

     MULTIPLY HOURS BY RATE GIVING BASICPAY.

     ADD BONUS TO BASICPAY GIVING GROSSPAY.

     SUBTRACT INCTAX FROM GROSSPAY GIVING NETPAY.

   iii. **Branch Instructions.**

     IF GROSSPAY GREATER THEN PERFORM EXCEPTION-RTN (conditional branch).

   iv. **Data Handling Instruction.**

     MOVE DEDUCTIONS TO DATAC (transfers a field to working store).

Scientific languages

17.67 The most well known:

a. ALGOL (**Alg**orithmic **O**riented **L**anguage). Used for scientific and engineering purposes and has particularly powerful mathematical facilities (ALGOL 68 is a more recent extensive version).

b. FORTRAN (**For**mula **Tran**slation). Mainly used for engineering applications but also of scientific use.

17.68 Features of these languages.

a. Extensive arithmetic computational ability.

b. Large library of inbuilt mathematical function.

c. Ability to handle mathematical expressions and procedures.

d. Array handling facilities.

Special-purpose languages

17.69 These are languages intended to be 'tailor made' for a particular type of problem, e.g. Machine Control, Wages, Simulation, Control Experiments. Examples are:

a. **CSL** which is a Simulation Language.

b. **Coral-66, IRTB** (Industrial Real-time Basic) and **RTL/2** which are used for real-time applications such as Process Control, i.e. the direct control of physical processes, e.g. Chemical plants and Power Stations.

c. **Ada**, a relatively new language for real-time and some general-purpose applications.

d. **Modula and Modula-2** This language is rather like an extended form of **Pascal** (see later) and is primarily especially suited to computer systems development work.

e. **SQL** (**S**tructured **Q**uery **L**anguage), **QUEL** (**QU**Ery **L**anguage) and **QBE Q**uery **B**y Example) are examples of database query languages. (Further details in chapter 27.)

Command languages for operating systems

17.70　These are languages used to control the operation of the computer. The required facilities will be apparent after you have read chapter 23. Most command languages are specific to the operating system of a particular manufacturer, for example, 'DCL' is the command language used on the DEC VAX/VMS operating system. Probably the two most widespread command languages are the command language used with MS-DOS and the 'SHELL', used with the UNIX operating system.

Multipurpose languages

17.71　These are languages which are intended to cope with a number of different types of application areas, e.g. business and scientific. Examples are discussed below.

17.72　**PL/1** was introduced by IBM as a language intended for use for business **and** scientific applications. It has been a very successful language except for the fact that its comprehensive multipurpose facilities have made it too large for use on small machines such as microcomputers and some other manufacturers have been reluctant to adopt it.

17.73　**BASIC** (**B**eginners **A**llpurpose **S**ymbolic **I**nstruction **C**ode). BASIC was created in 1964 by J.G. Kemmeny and T.E. Kurtz at Dartmouth College, USA. The language was originally designed as a simplified version of FORTRAN for use in teaching programming. From those simple beginnings the language has grown to become a very popular multi-purpose language available on a wide variety of machines but particularly microcomputers and minicomputers. Today more commercial programs are being written in BASIC than are being written in COBOL, although BASIC is still behind COBOL in terms of the volume of commercial code already in existence.

17.74　Early versions of BASIC, and sadly many versions in use on small computers today, deserve strong criticism for having features which encourage bad programming methods. However, some newer versions such as the product 'True-BASIC' devised by T.E. Kurtz and based upon the latest ANSI standard are very significantly better.

17.75　One language which has gained enormously in popularity in recent years is the language called 'C'. Originally, C was developed as a special-purpose language for **systems programming** on the UNIX operating system. C has not only spread with the growing popularity of UNIX, it has also became available on a wide variety of computers. Its widespread availability, and the fact that there is a remarkably high level of compatibility between the various versions, has resulted in it being adopted as a language in which portable software can be written relatively easily. It has thus become a popular multipurpose language, although it was never designed to be one. A new language based on C called 'C++' is also proving very popular for what is called '**Object Oriented Programming (OOP)**'.

17.76　Other languages which are regarded as multi-purpose languages include **Pascal** and **Modula**, which are both languages designed by N. Wirth and have features which support structured programming methods more readily than many of the older languages, such as COBOL or FORTRAN. Pascal and Modula are effectively their own pseudocode.

Other forms of high-level language

17.77　The language described so far in this chapter may be described as **procedural languages** because they describe **how** the computational procedures are to be carried out. There are radically different approaches to programming, however, which make use of languages which are non-procedural in that they assert *what* the required result is rather than how it is done. The details of *how* are actually handled as part of the language translation process. Two basic approaches to this assertional style of programming are:

a.　**Logic Programming**, for which one popular language is Prolog.

b.　**Functional Programming**, for which there are many languages available today, including **LISP, ML** and **Hope**.

Applications generators

17.78　Applications generators have been in existence for many years, but in their more modern forms they are often called **Fourth Generation Languages, 4GLs**, because they can often offer more cost effective alternatives to the high-level languages such as COBOL associated with the era of 3rd Generation Computers. Conventional high level languages such as COBOL, FORTRAN and C are often referred to as **3GLs**. 4GLs will be discussed more fully in chapter 28.

Summary

17.79 a. Software falls into two main categories:
   i. System software.
   ii. Applications software.

   b A further sub-division of software is as follows:
   i. Operating system and control programs which ensure efficient hardware use with a minimum of human intervention.
   ii. Translators which translate from one language to another.
   iii. Utilities and service programs which perform routine tasks for the user.
   iv. Data Base Management Systems which maintain data bases.
   v. User applications programs which are written by the user for a specific purpose.
   vi. Applications packages which are purchased by the user for a particular application.

   c. Application packages are suites of programs, with associated documentation, used for a particular type of problem or variety of similar problems and normally sold as complete products.

   d. Expert systems are an advanced form of package.

   e.

LANGUAGE	TRANSLATOR	INSTRUCTIONS GENERATED	ORIENTATION
Machine	None	N/A	N/A
Low-level (symbolic)	Assembler	1 for 1 (+ macros)	Machine
High-level	Compiler	Many for 1 statement	Problem

   f. Low-level languages are designed with particular machines in mind.

   g. High-level languages are generally problem oriented.

Points to note

17.80 a. Time spent in running systems software is really non-productive from an organisational standpoint.

   b. The operating system (especially the kernel) can be regarded as a 'Program which controls Programs'.

   c. The term **'Applications Package'** has been used in this chapter as a very broad category for software. Even so, not all software products sold as 'packages' would be called applications packages. For example, some database software is sold in very much the same way as applications packages but provides facilities 'on top of' those provided by the standard systems software and can be used by applications software. Such packages are often referred to as **'layered software products'** because of their position between standard systems software, which they add to, and the applications software.

   d. Applications packages may be broadly classified as
   i. Application Specific – e.g. a stock control package, or

ii. Generalised – e.g. a spreadsheet

e. As terminology is not completely universal in this area, a little thought is needed in examinations to decide what the examiner wants.

f. 'Translator' is the *general* term for an assembler, compiler or interpreter and you can use it as such.

g. The word 'Processor' is sometimes used instead of translator, but 'Processor' is used with two different meanings:

i. Here it refers to a Software Program.

ii. It is also an item of hardware.

h. If you get a question on languages generally and not a specific comparison of high- and low-level languages then base your answer on *high-level* languages.

i Note the use of the world *library:*

i. Meaning a *place* (room) where tapes/disks are kept.

ii. A collection of macros or sub-routines or other programs.

k The term 'Assembler Language' is often used instead of 'Low-Level Language'.

l. Applications Generators (and their more extensive variants called Fourth Generations Languages 4GLs) are growing in importance as alternatives to conventional high-level languages for many DP applications.

Questions

1. Distinguish between systems software and applications software and give further sub-classifications of each.

2. What is an editor and how might an editor be used?

3. Your company is installing a computer.

    Describe the types of software which you would expect a computer manufacturer to provide with his hardware and explain what purpose each serves.

    (CIMA)

4. What is an applications package?

5. Explain this statement. *'Spreadsheets are very valuable for carrying out "what if" calculations.'*

6. Briefly describe the features of an expert system.

7. When might the user of a computer consider using an applications package instead of writing programs from scratch?

    How would they be able to decide which package to use from among those available?

8. What are the advantages and disadvantages of high-level languages compared with lower level languages?

9. a. What are the characteristics of, and what advantages are claimed for, High-Level programming languages?

    b. Outline, with the aid of a diagram, how a program written in a High-Level language becomes a machine code program ready for operational use.

    (ACA)

10. a. Briefly list the main distinguishing features of high-level programming languages.

    b. Describe and indicate the purpose of the four divisions of a COBOL program. Illustrate your answer with a simple example of a statement which might be used in each division.

    (ACA)

Information systems development

1. This Part covers the activities involved in developing a new information system. Emphasis is placed within this Part on activities which are often broadly referred to as **'Systems Analysis'**. Systems Analysis may be defined as the methods of determining how best to use computers, with other resources, to perform tasks which meet the information needs of an organisation. The use of the word 'analysis' in the term is therefore misleading because 'analysing' is only *one* of the activities which are generally regarded as coming under the heading 'systems analysis'.

2. Chapter 18 gives an overview of the whole process, which is then amplified by the subsequent chapter.

3. Chapter 19 describes the methods used in systems development with the emphasis on the design stage and modern 'structured' methods.

4. In Chapter 20 the final stages of the development are described.

5. Finally, in Chapter 21 the Part ends with an examination of project management.

6. This Part gives an overview of common practice today rather than concentrating upon a particular approach.

18 The system life cycle

Introduction

18.1 New computer systems frequently replace existing manual systems, and the new systems may themselves be replaced after some time. The process of replacing the old system by the new happens in a series of stages and the whole process is called the 'system life cycle'.

18.2 This chapter provides an overview of the system life cycle. The individual stages in the life cycle are described in detail in subsequent chapters.

The life cycle in outline

18.3 The life cycle can be broken down into a number of separate stages. There are many different ways of doing this. In this chapter we are really considering a typical life cycle rather than 'the' life cycle. Figure 18.1 shows the major stages in a typical system life cycle.

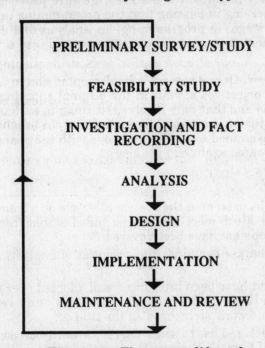

Figure 18.1 The system life cycle

18.4 The start of a new system life cycle is normally the result of some 'trigger' such as the perception of a business need, failures or limitations of the existing system causing dissatisfaction, or heightened awareness of modern developments. Whatever the reason it is management who will initiate the selection of a project for preliminary study or investigation.

18.5 **Preliminary survey/study.** The purpose of this survey is to establish whether there is a need for a new system and if so to specify the objectives of the system.

18.6 **Feasibility study.** The purpose of the feasibility study is to investigate the project in sufficient depth to be able to provide information that either justifies the development of the new system or shows why the project should not continue.

18.7 The findings of the feasibility study are presented to management in the form of a report, which will make appropriate recommendations. If the report finds in favour of the project then senior management may decide to move to the next stage.

18.8 **Investigation and fact recording.** At this stage in the life cycle a detailed study is conducted. This study is far more detailed and comprehensive than the feasibility study. The purpose of this study is fully to understand the existing system and to identify the basic information requirements. This requires a contribution from the users both of the existing system and of the proposed system.

18.9 **Analysis (also called Requirements Analysis).** Analysis of the full description of the existing system and of the objectives of the proposed system should lead to a **full specification of the user's requirements.** This **requirements specification** (also sometimes called a **requirements definition**) can be examined and approved before system design is embarked upon. In recent years greater emphasis has been placed upon this stage because of former expensive and frustrating experiences of designs that failed to meet requirements. The earlier in the system life cycle that a mistake is discovered the less costly it is to correct. It is quite common for the investigation and fact recording to be combined with analysis into a single stage.

18.10 **Design.** The analysis may lead to a number of possible alternative designs. For example, different combinations of manual and computerised elements may be considered. Once one alternative has been selected the purpose of the design stage is to work from the requirements specification to produce a **system specification.** The system specification will be a detailed set of documents that provides details of all features of the system.

18.11 **Implementation.** Implementation involves following the details set out in the system specification. Three particularly important tasks are hardware provision, programming and staff training. It is worth observing in passing that the programming task has its own 'life cycle' in the form of the various stages in programming, i.e. analysis and design occur at many different levels. The implementation stage is sometimes split into a **'build phase'** and a **'test phase'.**

18.12 **Maintenance and review.** Once a system is implemented and in full operation it is examined to see if it has met the objectives set out in the original specification. Unforeseen problems may need to be overcome and that may involve returning to earlier stages in the cycle to take corrective action. From time to time the requirements of the organisation will change and the system will have to be examined to see if it can cope with the changes. At some stage the system life cycle will be repeated again and yet again.

Methodologies

18.13 The preceding paragraphs presented the system life-cycle as a framework within which a new system can be developed. Much more needs to be added to that framework before all activities involved in such a development have been covered.

18.14 The remainder of this chapter examines the activities of analysis and design within the system life cycle.

18.15 Many of the methods that have been introduced and adopted over the last ten years or so are radically different from those used previously. They are often referred to as **'structured'** methods. Several have the word 'structured' in the title.

Although the term 'structured' is, to some degree, a word borrowed from the programming world by marketing staff to make their methods sound modern, these methods do indeed impose a structure on the development process by:

   a. providing a number of well-defined and complementary ways in which to represent information about important aspects of the system;

   b. providing a recommended series of tasks to be carried out so that the methods fit together as a whole;

   c. lending themselves to some degree of automation and the corresponding controls that go with it.

18.16 Such a system of methods, with its orderly and integrated collection of various methods, tools and notations, is often called a **methodology** so as to distinguish it from *mere* method.

Proprietary methodologies

18.17 A considerable number of methodologies are in use today and, although many are described in specialist texts generally available to the public, they are mostly sold as products composed of manuals, specialist training, consultancy services and automated aids. Among the better known methodologies are:

   a. Structured Analysis and Design by Yourdon.

   b. Structured Systems Analysis by Gane and Sarson.

    c.   Information Engineering from James Martin.

    d.   Jackson Systems Development (JSD) by Michael Jackson.

    e.   SSADM, originally produced by LBMS for the CCTA.

18.18   It is *not* the purpose of this text to describe any one of these methodologies in any detail. A number of general points deserve mention though.

    a.   Each methodology has its own overall method within which the various activities fit.

    b.   All of the methods make use of **charting techniques** whereby particular properties of the system are represented diagrammatically using an appropriate convention.

    c.   The particular kinds of property chosen for representation give each methodology its 'orientation'. For example, several methods place considerable emphasis on analysing the data within the system so as to represent its essential properties as it is stored, accessed or moved around the system, (e.g. SSADM, Yourdon, and Gane and Sarson.) Other methods place less emphasis on the data and greater emphasis on the processing activities and events that affect them (e.g. JSD).

18.19   An introduction to some of the more commonly used techniques is presented in the next chapter.

Requirements specification

18.20   An important aim of the analysis is to produce a **Requirements Specification.** The modern methods make it easier to produce a Requirements Specifications which present information in an implementation free form which is intelligible to the user. Not all the contents of the Requirements Specification may be intelligible to the user, however, because some parts of the requirement may be technical in nature and need to be expressed formally.

18.21   It should be clear by now that the Requirements Specification should present a clear, thorough and unambiguous description of WHAT the system is required to do and should NOT fall into the trap of ruling out possible design alternatives by specifying HOW the system should be designed and implemented. However, there are bound to be some limitations on the kinds of design which can be considered and some very specific and essential features about the design may be know right from the start. For example, there may be specific limitations on the budget available, the accommodation which can be used or the timescale in which events must happen. Also, it may be essential that the new system makes use of or is compatible with some existing equipment. Such information belongs in the Requirements Specification along with the implementation free descriptions which may be regarded as the 'high level' features of the design.

18.22   A Systems Analyst, with sound business knowledge, will discuss the Requirements Specification with the users. This analyst, aided by the Requirements Specification, will have the important task of bridging the gap between the system's user and the technical designer.

18.23   At the end of these discussions the Requirements Specification should be in an accepted form, estimates for alternative designs should be prepared, and the decision to proceed with a particular design can be made.

18.24   **Conceptual Models.** Within the documentation of the Requirements Specification is a system definition also expressed in an implementation free way ie. free of the constraints of any particular design alternative. Such a system definition is called a 'conceptual model', a term originally used in database design. Unfortunately, terminology is far from standard in this subject area and is made worse by the way in which those selling methodologies often use their own names for common methods for marketing purposes. 'Conceptual models' are often described as high level **logical models**. The key feature to note is the *implementation free* form of representation. At a later stage in the development process a **physical model** will be produced. Further variants in terminology refer to **logical designs** and **physical designs**.

18.25   The reader should not be put off by the terminology because most high level ways of representing the analysis in an implementation free way use some combination of three very natural components:

a. **a data model** which defines the data requirements, probably in terms of entities, attributes and relationships, for example, an entity such as an order contains attributes such as quantities required and has a relationship with other entities such as customers).

b. **a process model** which defines the processing requirements in terms of events and operations, for example, the event of an order arriving gives rise to operations such as the update of stock data and production of invoices).

c. **a system model** which defines functional areas and their interrelationship (eg. one functional area may deal with the reception of an order and then pass it to another functional area which processes the order).

It is also important to cross-reference these models to check for consistency and completeness

Areas of responsibility

18.26 Different types of staff are responsible for different stages in the life cycle. For example, the early stages will have significant involvement by senior management, the middle stages will be the responsibility of 'systems analysts' and a stage such as implementation will give major responsibility to programmers.

18.27 In the remainder of this Part those activities that are primarily the responsibility of the system analyst will be discussed. The responsibility of programmers will be discussed in later chapters.

18.28 It is during the design stage that the system developer is called upon to use his or her creative abilities. The implementation-free nature of the requirements specification means that *all* feasible alternative designs are open to consideration. By applying judgement, skill and knowledge an analyst can interpret the requirement specification to create one or more **system specifications** (or **system definitions**). A system specification provides *detailed* documentation of the new system, i.e. it gives the detail of a particular implementation, unlike the requirements specification, which is implementation free. A system specification requires acceptance by management just as the requirements specification does.

Design elements

18.29 We now deal with the detailed elements of design and the sequence in which they might be carried out. Design criteria are then dealt with and are followed by a description of a system specification. The design of a new system can be conveniently divided into the following elements:

a. User Interfaces.

b. Outputs.

c. Inputs.

d. Files or database components.

e. Procedures and programs.

18.30 **User interfaces.** Most modern systems have interactive users performing tasks on the system using PCs, workstations or terminals. The various screens have to be designed together with their associated processing operations. The methods of design vary according to the nature of the application and the type of devices used. For example, a GUI requires design methods which are different from those used with a simple character based VDU terminal.

18.31 **Outputs.** It is necessary to consider what is required from the system before deciding how to set about producing it. These requirements will have become clear as the project progressed. The analyst will need to consider form, types, volumes, and frequency of reports and documents. Choice of output media will also have to be made including when to use hard copy and when to use screen displays.

18.32 **Inputs.** Consideration of input will be influenced greatly by the needs of output, e.g. the necessity for quick response from the system would determine the need for an on-line type of input. Consideration would be given to:

a. Data collection methods and validation.

b. Types of input media available.

c. Volumes of input documents.

d. Design of input layouts.

18.33 **Files and database components.** These elements are very much linked to input and output. Input is processed against the stored data to produce the necessary output. Considerations involved in designing files are:

    a. Storage media.

    b. Method of file organisation and access.

    c. File security.

    d. Record layouts.

18.34 **Procedures and programs.** Procedures are the steps that unify the whole process, that link everything together to produce the desired output. These will involve both computer and clerical procedures. They will start with the origination of the source document and end with the output document being distributed. The design of the computer programs will constitute a major task in itself.

18.35 Because of their importance in the design of a new procedure the aspects of form design and internal checks are dealt with in some detail below. The reader should note that HCI design has already been discussed in chapter 11.

18.36 **Forms design.**

    a. **Introduction.** The design of forms and the design of procedures are very much linked. The completion of a form may be the first operation of a procedure (e.g. compilation of an order form); a by-product of an operation within a procedure (e.g. a receipt, as a by-product of posting to the cash book, in machine accounting); the end product of a procedure (e.g. reports to management); or the form may be completed at various stages within a procedure (e.g. invoice sets). Whether the requirements of the form dictate the procedure, or the steps in the procedure dictate the design of the form, is determined by individual circumstances. Very often, the justification for expensive machines brings in its wake the need for redesign of forms to fit the procedure.

    b. **Aim.** The aim is to keep forms to the minimum consistent with serving the needs of the system.

    c. **Features of design.**

        i. **Sizes.** Standard-size forms should be used, as it is more economic to do so, and *handling, filing* and *copying* are simplified.

        ii. **Types of paper.** The quality of paper used should be appropriate to requirements. Consideration should be given to such things as frequency of handling, storage needs, conditions under which forms are completed, and prestige requirements.

        iii. **Identification.** There should be a brief, self-explanatory title; copies should be identified by different colours or bold symbols; serial numbering may be required for internal check purposes.

        iv. **Common information.** If two forms are used in conjunction with each other, the common information should be in the same sequence and position.

        v. **Vertical spacing.** There should be adequate space for each item of entry (e.g. an invoice should have enough spaces to cover the normal number of items ordered). If a typewriter is being used in recording data on a form, consideration must be given to the normal vertical spacing requirements of the machine.

        vi. **Columns.** The length of column headings should be tailored to the width required by the information to be entered in the column.

        vii. **Pre-printing.** As much as possible of the common detail should be pre-printed, leaving only variable data to be entered.

        viii. **Clarity.** There should be overall simplicity of instructions. Material of a similar nature should be grouped together. A logical sequence for completion should be followed and unambiguous wording should be used. The size of the print should make for ease of reading.

        ix. **Miscellaneous.** There may be a requirement for perforation for subsequent bursting or pre-punched holes for subsequent filing.

        x. **Multi-part sets** Where more than one document is to be raised at the same time, consideration should be given to the method employed in carrying the image through all copies, e.g. carbon; no-carbon-required paper, carbon patches, etc.

18.37 **Internal check**.

    a. **Definition.** The arrangement of procedures and systems, and the allocation of duties so that there is an automatic check on what is being done.

    b. **Principle.** No one person should be placed in the position of having responsibility for all aspects of a business transaction. Thus the work flow is so arranged that the work of one person, or section, is independently checked by some other person or section.

    c. **Purposes achieved.**

        i. The possibility of fraud and error is reduced.

        ii. The responsibility for errors is determined.

        iii. Supervision is assisted (because of the built-in checks).

        iv. The work of internal and external auditors is reduced.

    d. Examples of the operation of internal check.

        i. The serial numbering of forms.

        ii. The requirements for two signatures on cheques.

        iii. The use of control accounts.

Design method and design sequence

18.38 Over the last ten years or so a number of design methods have become established, each with its own set of dedicated supporters.

18.39 The advocates of each of these methods naturally proclaim the advantages of their methods over the alternatives. Terms such as 'structured', 'hierarchical', 'top-down', and others are used to label the different approaches to design.

18.40 What all these design methods have in common is a recognition that large problems, such as those found in design, can only be tackled effectively if they are broken down into smaller, more manageable, tasks in some systematic way. The same ideas were first put into practice with considerable success in program writing, where terms such as 'structured' and 'top-down' suffer less ambiguity.

18.41 Without going into unnecessary detail about any particular method it is still possible to identify the following design sequence:

    a. The system is described at a logical level in terms of what it will do in the context of a particular design, i.e. a combination of design elements will be put together in a way that can meet the requirements in general terms.

    b. The 'logical model' is refined in a series of steps in which successive detail is added. Some steps may be re-traced as the emerging design is evaluated. Considerations of physical details are postponed as long as possible, because, for example, it is senseless to design a report document before it is decided exactly what the report should contain.

    c. Finally the physical detail is added to the logical detail so that the design shows not only *what* the system should do but also exactly *how* it should do it.

Criteria for design

18.42 **Purpose.** The purpose must be to meet the demands of the requirements specification and, for that matter, the objectives that were agreed at the beginning of the project. At one time, and still in some organisations, a requirements specification was not produced at the end of the analysis stage and so the system specification had to serve both purposes.

18.43 Some of the criteria outlined in the following paragraphs may be applied to the requirements specification. Where the criteria do apply it is a clear indication of the economic benefits of the requirements specification in catching errors earlier and saving inappropriate design effort and costs.

18.44 **Economical.** The costs and benefits of the new system should be compared with those of the existing system. This is not easy to do because of the difficulty of quantifying benefits such as 'better or more' information. It is important, however, that the attempt be made.

18.45 Work flows. The best work flows must be attained. This includes methods of transmitting data to and from the computer, the number of runs required, file organisation, the requirements of internal check, and the link with clerical procedures.

18.46 Specialisation, simplification and standardisation. The benefits to be derived from the practice of the 'three Ss' are well known. The analyst will have them in mind throughout the design stage.

18.47 Flexibility. Points to be considered here are:

a. **Integration of procedures.** Systems should be designed with possible integration of procedures in mind. This is particularly important as the centralised nature of computer processing makes possible the integration of many procedures carried out independently under conventional methods.

b. **Modularity of hardware.** It is important when choosing the hardware to ensure that it is capable of being expanded (units added) when the need arises.

c. **Peak periods/treatment of exceptions.** The system can be designed to cope with peak-period processing; an alternative arrangement is to use a bureau for the unusually high loads. Similarly, exceptional items (i.e. those not recurring frequently) could be designed into the system, but it may be more convenient to have them dealt with separately by conventional methods.

18.48 Exception principle. The principle of exception should be incorporated in the design of the new system, so that only deviations from plan are reported for management's attention. In a stock-control system, for example, warnings would be given of slow-moving stocks. The analyst must ensure that only necessary output is produced.

18.49 Reliability. The reliability of all the hardware and software must be considered. The analyst must ensure that facilities required for the new system have a proven record of reliability. Maintenance requirements, the expected life of the hardware and the back-up facilities (in case of breakdown) must be considered.

18.50 Forms. Data must be presented to the computer in a machine-sensible form. The analyst must consider all the methods of input and try to reduce the steps necessary between origination of data and its input. If output from one run is used as the input to another, the ideal medium for the subsequent input should be used. When output is required in a humanly legible form, choice of method of presentation is important. Methods available are visual display, printed copy, graphical, etc, and the needs of the person receiving the output will determine which one is appropriate.

18.51 Existing system. Consideration must be given to the existing staff, procedures, equipment, forms, etc, in the design of any new system. For example, if old-fashioned equipment is currently being operated, the procedures already exist for transferring the source data into a machine-sensible form, although it may well not be incorporated into the design of a new computer system.

18.52 Continuous control. As the majority of steps are carried out automatically, there is an even greater need for care in internal check. Audit trails (i.e. documentary records of various stages in processing that can be used to check that procedures have been carried out correctly) must be laid to the satisfaction of the auditors. Controls should be incorporated.

18.53 Time. The analyst must design the system to satisfy time requirements. Speeds of equipment, modes of access and processing methods must be considered. The length of the processing cycle is a most important consideration. The presentation of source data to the computer and the production of output documents will be subject to strict time constraints.

Systems specification (or systems definition)

18.54 The systems specification is the detailed documentation of the proposed new system. It serves two main purposes.

a. **Communication.** It serves as a means of communicating all that is required to be known to all interested parties; as follows:

    i. **Management** for final approval.

    ii. **Programmers** to enable them to write the programs necessary for implementation.

    iii. **Operating staff,** detailing all necessary operating procedures.

    iv. **Users,** as they will ultimately be responsible for running the new system. They must therefore be fully aware of the contents of the specification and their agreement is essential.

  b. **Record.** A permanent record of the system in detail is necessary for control. It will be used for evaluations, modification, and training purposes.

18.55 Different persons require to know only parts of the whole specification (e.g. programmers need to know the functions required and the file layouts, but will not need to know the timings for data preparation or numbers of staff required, etc). The specification is also produced at different stages of design *in outline* for top management, *in detail* for lowest levels. The specification is sectionalised to enable only the appropriate parts to be sent to the interested parties.

18.56 **Contents.** The following are the main items to be found in a systems specification.

  a. **Preliminary information.** This comprises contents, lists, names of recipients of particular sections, names of those having authority to change files, programs, etc.

  b. **Objectives of the system.** A brief statement is given of the aims indicating the departments and the main procedures involved. The benefits arising from implementation are also stated.

  c. **Systems description.** This will detail all procedures both clerical and computer using flow charts where applicable.

  d. Detailed specification of:

    i. All files together with specimen layouts.

    ii. Screen layouts and dialogue designs with specimen copies of each.

    iii. Source documents with specimen copies of each.

    iv. Output documents (e.g. reports) with specimen copies of each.

    Supporting narrative would accompany each item. Methods of file organisation and modes of access are detailed.

  e. **Program specification**. This contains:

    i. Details of screens, inputs, outputs and processes for each program run.

    ii. Test data and expected results.

    iii. Stop/start, file-checking and error-checking procedures.

    iv. Controls.

    v. Relationship between procedures and computer runs for batch programs.

  f **Implementation procedures**.

    i. Detailed timetable (using networks or other scientific aids).

    ii. Details of conversion procedures.

    iii. Change-over procedures, including systems testing.

  g. **Equipment.** All equipment including backup equipment and its maintenance arrangements.

  h. **User-department instructions.** These relate to the input to the system (i.e. times for forwarding source documents), the output from the system (i.e. dealing with documents and control totals, etc).

Summary

18.57   a.   The system life cycle is the series of stages involved in replacing an old system with a new one.

      b.   The life-cycle stages are:

          i.   Preliminary survey (preliminary study) – initiated by management.

          ii.   Feasibility study.

          iii.   Investigation and fact recording.

          iv.   Analysis.

          v.   Design.

          vi.   Implementation.

          vii.   Maintenance and review.

      c.   Some form of documentation accompanies all stages in the cycle. The following documentation is of particular importance:

          i.   Feasibility study report.

          ii.   User requirements specification.

          iii.   System specification.

      d.   The design stage is the creative stage in systems and analysis. All feasible design alternatives should be considered.

      e.   The systems analyst can use the requirement specification as the criteria against which to judge his or her designs.

      f.   The systems specification is important as a means of communication and a record of the detail design.

      g.   The idea of a **methodology** was introduced together with an explanation of what a structured method is.

Points to note

18.58   a.   'System analysis' takes place at all stages in the life cycle, not just the analysis stage.

      b.   Terminology is not universal. For example a 'systems specification' may also be called a 'requirement specification'. This is seldom a practical difficulty because the context normally prevents any ambiguity.

      c.   The terms *'specification'* and *'definition'* are used synonymously.

      d.   The systems specification acts as the *acceptance* of the design of the new system by all levels of management.

      e.   In reading this chapter on design, students should realise that much of the detail involved has been described under the appropriate headings, e.g. data collection, computer files, etc.

Questions

1. What is a 'methodology'?
2. What is a system specification.
3. What is the purpose of a feasibility study?

19 Development methods

Introduction

19.1 This chapter examines some methods which are commonly used in systems development.

Basic principles

19.2 Although it is very important to be familiar with the latest methods, and to be able to use them properly, it must also be recognised that most methods become dated eventually. Therefore, it is important to recognise any basic principles that apply whatever the method. In fact, there must be dozens of principles that apply to the process of systems development. Here are some important ones expressed as a set of recommendations.

a. Make sure you understand the problem.

b. Fully identify the requirements and get them agreed by the client.

c. Clearly document all work as you do it.

d. Have all work checked to an agreed standard of quality at every stage.

e. Be systematic.

f. Be creative but make sure it works.

g. Allow for future changes.

h. Make sure that all users find the system usable.

i. Break the problem down into manageable tasks and carry them out in a planned and methodical way.

j. Make sure that the final system is all there, in full working order, and does what it's supposed to do, **before** you say it's ready.

Data models

19.3 A data model is a representation of the properties of the data within an existing or proposed system. The basic elements from which a model is made are called **modelling constructs** and the complete process of constructing a data model from scratch is called data analysis.

19.4 **EAR Models.** The EAR model is one of the most common and successful types of data model around. Its basic elements are called **Entities, Attributes** and **Relationships**, hence the name EAR model, or occasionally **ER model**.

19.5 The modelling constructs are as follows:

a. **Entity.** An entity is any 'thing' about which data can be stored. For example, if the system needs to store data about customers or products, then the model would have customer or product entities.

   Note. Although the definition is stated in terms of what must be stored, in fact it is retrieval of the data that is the fundamental requirement.

b. **Attributes.** The attributes of an entity are those facts that need to be stored about the entity. For example, the attributes of a customer might include the account number, name, address and credit limit.

c. **Relationships.** Relationships exist between various entities within a system. For example, there may be a relationship between the customer and an order.

19.6 For such a data model to be considered **valid** it must conform to a set of rules. A valid data model is one that is **fully normalised** and the process of converting an invalid model into a valid one is called **normalization**.

19.7 **The aim of normalization is to ensure that each fact is only recorded in one place** so that facts cannot be inconsistent and the performance of updates cannot produce anomalies by updating one copy of the fact but not another.

19.8 This is not the place for a lengthy discussion of normalization, but here are some basic details. The rules may be expressed in more formal terms, but they are not considered suitable in a book at this level.

Each occurrence of an entity, for example each individual customer, must be uniquely identifiable by means of a key containing one or more attributes. The customer's full name or account number might serve as a key, for example. Other attributes (non-key attributes) may be regarded as facts about what the key stands for (e.g. facts about the customer). So given the key other facts relating to the key can be obtained.

The process of normalization ensures that in each entity of the final model every non-key attribute is a fact about *the key, the whole key and nothing but the key*.

19.9 To round off this description of data models here (figure 19.1) is a diagram of a simple EAR model concerning customers making orders for products.

In the diagram:

a. Entities are represented by round-cornered boxes.

b. Attributes are listed beside the entities. For example, CUSTOMER entity has the attributes listed as

' Account No., name, address, credit limit, credit'.

Keys are underlined. Note that the 'order detail' entity has a **composite key**, i.e. a key formed from more than one attribute. (It is assumed that each order number is unique and that each order can only be made by one customer.)

c. Relationships are represented by lines between entities. The 'bird's feet' at the end of the arrows are used to show the **degree** of the relationship. In the example, **one** customer places **many orders**. The bird's foot shows the 'many' end of the relationship.

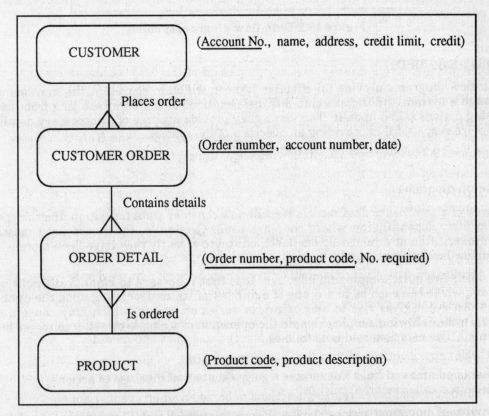

Figure 19.1 An EAR data model of an ordering system

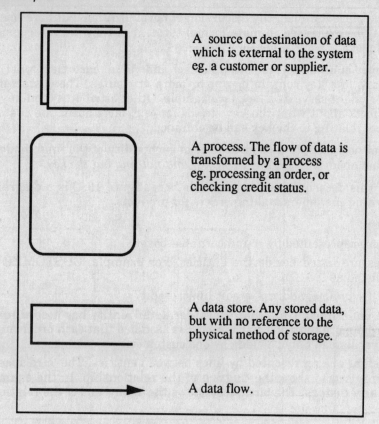

Figure 19.2 Data-flow diagram symbols

Data-flow diagrams (DFDs)

19.10 Data-flow diagrams provide an effective form in which to represent the movements of data through a system and the associated transformations of the data resulting from various processing actions taken upon it. The views they provide are free of unnecessary details and are therefore very useful in providing an overview of the system.

19.11 Diagrams 19.2 (above) and 19.3 (following page) illustrate their use.

State transition diagrams

19.12 By way of a contrast to data models we will now consider state transition diagrams, which differ in form depending on where they are used. Originally, they were used mostly in programming, often at a relatively low level, but more recently they have been more widely used as higher levels of design.

19.13 The ideas are quite simple and effective. It is first necessary to identify **objects** within the system, which can each be in any one of a number of states depending upon the **events** taking place. An event gives rise to an **action**, or series of actions, which may cause a change of state. In the following simple example the operation of a simple object, a conveyor belt, is represented. The notation used is as follows.

a. Circles represent states that the system may be in.

b. Labelled arrowed lines from states signify events that give rise to actions.

c. Round-cornered boxes represent actions to be taken when events happen.

d. Arrowed lines from actions show a change to another state, or possibly a further action to be taken before a change in state.

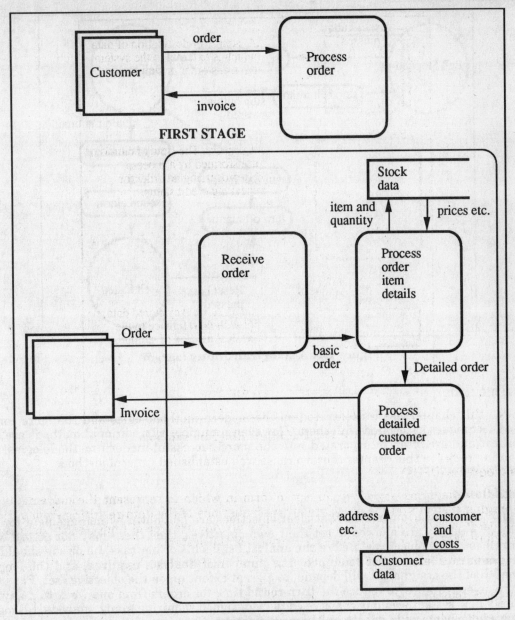

Figure 19.3 A data-flow diagram of an order processing system

Levels of modelling

19.14 The modelling process may take place at a number of different levels according to the stages in the life cycle. For example, the EAR data model, shown earlier, is called a **logical model** because it concentrates on **what** data is to be stored. A **physical model**, on the other hand, would provide detail on how the data was to be stored. For example, a physical model might be expected to detail the physical storage structures of files used to implement the system.

Validation and verification

19.15 It was mentioned earlier that for a model to be **valid** it must observe certain rules. In addition, it is most important to **verify** that the model is a correct representation of the system being modelled.

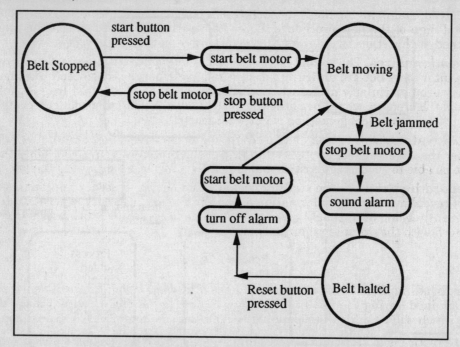

Figure 19.4 A state transition diagram

Traditional methods

19.16 So far this chapter has concentrated on the modern methodologies and the more commonly used techniques associated with them. However, a number of traditional methods are still important and are often incorporated into the more successful modern methodologies. The remaining topics in this chapter concern these well established general methods.

Terms of reference

19.17 It is of the utmost importance that clear objectives are laid down by management for all projects. If analysts are allowed to set their own objectives, then these may not accord with the overall company objectives. Before the analyst begins his or her task, he or she should, therefore, confirm the terms of reference. The number of analysts required, and the length and breadth of the assignment will depend, to a great extent, upon the objectives set. For example, if the objective were 'to reduce the turn-round time for orders from one week to a day' a completely new system would perhaps need to be designed requiring many analysts, taking a long time and having wide effects on the organisation. Conversely, the objective 'to reduce the number of clerks in the accounts department' may require a straight transfer of existing manual procedures to a standard computer package and would therefore take shorter time and less organisational disruption. The terms of reference may well refer to the standards which must be used for the project. It is increasingly common for organisations to adopt standard methodologies which must be used for all their systems development projects.

Fact finding

19.18 It is essential to gather all the facts about a current system to ensure that all strengths and weaknesses are discovered. Thus, when a new system is designed as many of the weaknesses as possible are eliminated, whilst retaining the strengths.

19.19 There are four general techniques available, those used depending upon the particular circumstances:

a. **Interviewing.** This is probably the most widely used technique and the most productive. Interviewing is an art not readily acquired. During interviews facts about what is happening come to light, together with the opinions of the interviewee regarding weaknesses in the system. The personal contacts are important in getting the cooperation of the people involved, and in giving them the feeling of having made a substantial contribution towards the design of the new procedure. It is vital to gain the confidence of the individuals concerned at this stage in order for all the facts to be gathered.

b. **Questionnaires.** The second technique is the use of questionnaires. They save the time of the interviews but are difficult to design and are generally considered irksome to complete. They are particularly useful when a little information is required from a great number of people. Moreover, when the study involves many different geographical locations they may be the only practicable method of gathering facts.

c. **Observation.** This is best employed in conjunction with other techniques and carried out after the observer has an understanding of the procedures involved. Only then will he or she be able to spot irregularities and generally apply a 'seeing' eye to the job.

d. **Record inspection.** The study of organisation charts, procedure manuals and statistics, can reveal much useful information about a procedure. However, a close study of the forms currently being used should give the best guide to current practice which may, or may not, accord with the original requirements.

Fact recording

19.20 **Fact recording.** Unless the investigator has formulated a plan for the keeping of notes of the facts obtained during the fact finding stage, he or she will end up with a mass of notes on all areas, which will be difficult to examine.

19.21 A good practice is to sectionalise notes into areas of investigation (eg. by department or operation) or by type of information (eg. organisation charts, interviews, forms, etc). Use should be made of the standard forms of presenting information about the system. This is where the newer methodologies can have a great deal to offer. Data flow diagrams can be used both to represent information about an existing system and to represent a proposed new system. EAR data models can often be drafted at the fact finding stage too. Later they can be amended and redrawn as the results are analysed. Some traditional charting techniques have their place too. Decision table and systems flowcharts are good examples of techniques which can capture the details of *how* the existing system works.

19.22 Note that at this stage no attempt is made at analysis or design since the existing system must be fully understood first.

Analysis

19.23 At this point, the analyst has gathered all the facts which are relative to the objectives set and has grouped them into a form suitable for analysis. The analysis stage is an important intermediate stage between investigation and design. The analyst must examine all the facts he or she has gathered in order to make a proper assessment of the existing system. He or she must resist the temptation to include ideas in the new system which have not been fully worked out. The aim of this stage is to ensure that all feasible alternatives are considered. According to the methodology used, there are different ways of dealing with this issue. As we will see shortly, many approaches attempt to present the information in a way which avoids making implementation decisions at this stage.

19.24 The present system may be criticised against the following **Principles of Procedure**, after which the strengths and weaknesses of the system should be apparent:

a. **Purpose.** Are the purposes being satisfied? Are they still necessary? Could they be achieved in any other way?

b. **Economical.** Is it economical? Benefits should be related to the cost of producing them. Are there more economical methods?

c. **Work flow.** Are the work flows satisfactory?

d. **Specialisation/simplification/standardisation.** Are the three S's being practised? Is the work capable of being carried out by computer? Can the complex procedures be simplified? Are standard practices observed?

e. **Flexibility.** Is the system flexible? What will be the effect on the system of a big increase of decrease in the volumes to be processed?

  f. **Exception principle.** Is the principle of exception being observed? Factors requiring actions should be highlighted and not submerged in a mass of routine detail.

  g. **Reliability.** How reliable is the procedure? What provision is there for such events as staff sickness, machine breakdown? Could more up to date equipment be justified?

  h. **Form.** Is the information being produced in the form best suited to the recipient? Is there a need for a hard copy?

  i. **Existing system.** If a change is made, what equipment and other facilities currently being used could be incorporated in the new procedure?

  j. **Continuous control.** What types of errors are occurring? Are the controls satisfactory? What other types of controls could be used?

  k. **Time.** Is the information being produced in time for meaningful action to be taken?

Prototyping

19.25 There are three activities which are sometimes described as of prototyping:

  a. **Mock-ups.** A 'Mock-up' of a proposed system or subsystem is produced for demonstration purpose at the early stages of a project so as to aid the users and designers to make decisions about what is required. Usually, the prototype has the appearance of the final system but lacks any real processing or storage capability.

  b. **Trial Prototyping.** A simplified working model of a proposed system or subsystem is produced. It may serve the same purpose as a mock-up but because it has some of the capabilities of a real system it can provide the opportunity to try out ideas and to investigate specific points of interest. Such a prototype might be used to design an appropriate user interface for a new system. Alternatively, it might be a prototype of a method of processing. Normally the intention is to throw away such a prototype at the end of the prototyping exercise. The results of the prototyping are fed into a conventional design life-cycle.

  c. **Rapid Prototyping.** (Also called **Rapid Applications Development (RAD)**)This is an alternative to the conventional life-cycle. It is most frequently used for small scale system which are required urgently and which will have a limited life. A simplified version of the system is built and then reviewed. At this early stages this is like method (b). Following the review the prototype is extended and upgraded to become version 1 of the new system. It is normally incomplete at this stage but may have all of the essential features in a simplified form. After a review the prototype is further upgraded, and so on. The rapid results provided by this method give rise to its name. The merits of the method is the short term gains of having a working system early. However, in the long run such systems can be come costly and difficult to maintain and tend to be less reliable than systems built by more conventional methods.

19.26 Of the three methods just described both (a) and (b) can be easily incorporated into the development life-cycle and have therefore become very popular in recent years because of the way they aid the work done in analysis and design. All three methods commonly make use of 4GLs.

Summary

19.27 a. Some commonly used methods were introduced:

   i. Entity-Attribute-Relationship (EAR) data modelling.

   ii. The use of data flow diagrams (DFDs).

   iii. The use of state transition diagrams.

  b. The terms of reference of an assignment must be clearly laid down.

  c. Fact finding, recording, and examination, are necessary to discover the strengths and weaknesses of the area under investigation.

  d. The analysis stage is important because of the need to ensure that:

   i. the requirements are fully understood and correctly specified.

   ii. all feasible design alternatives are contemplated.

It is an important breathing space between investigation and design.

    e. Prototyping methods were described.

Points to note

19.28 a. There is a tendency, in practice, for some analysts to neglect the analysis stage and to go ahead with the design of a new system based on a preconceived notion that he or she has held from the beginning. In this way the system produced may be neither what is required nor the most feasible alternative. The mandatory production of a Requirements Specification guards against such bad practices. Most of the modern methodologies contain within them mandatory stages and methods in the life-cycle to guard against this danger.

    b. Methods of analysis have been developed greatly over recent years. It is not necessary for you to   learn these methods but you should be aware of their importance in improving the quality and effectiveness of Systems Analysis.

    c. Improvements to the analysis stage have an impact on the design stage. The designer starts from a much stronger position if he or she has a Requirement Specification.

Questions

1. What is a 'methodology'?
2. Describe the basic features of a data model.
3. What are the modelling constructs of a state transition diagram?
4. What features might you expect to find in a 'structured' method?
5. Even if the objectives of an assignment indicate the need for a completely new system, it is still important to critically examine the present system. Why do you think this is so?
6. An important aspect of System Analysis is the 'fact finding' stage of a systems investigation. Depending on the circumstances and the system being studied, several different methods of fact finding may be used.

You are required to:

    a. state **three** methods of fact finding;

    b. give their advantages and disadvantages and the circumstances in which each might be used.

(CIMA)

7. a. Advances in programming languages (e.g. 4th generation) have made it possible to develop systems using prototyping techniques.

    Required:

    i. Describe prototyping in the context of systems development.   *(3 marks)*

    ii. List and briefly describe 3 benefits which can arise from the use of prototyping and 3 difficulties which it may present.   *(9 marks)*

    b. Approaches to systems analysis have changed in recent years to include 'structured methods' (or 'methodologies').

    i. What does the term 'structured method' mean?   *(4 marks)*

    ii. List and briefly describe 3 advantages of using such an approach for the development of business systems.   *(4 marks)*

(Total 20 marks)

(ACCA)

20 Implementation and post-implementation

Introduction

20.1 Implementation follows on from the detailed design stage. This involves the co-ordination of the efforts of the user department and the data-processing department in getting the new system into operation. A Coordinating Committee is sometimes formed for this purpose, having as its members the managers of the departments concerned and a representative from the computer department. The analyst responsible for the design of the new system will be an important member because of his thorough knowledge of the system.

20.2 Planning for the implementation will have begun early in the design stage. Details will have been stipulated in the systems specification.

They would cover the following:

a. Training of staff.

b. Programming.

c. System testing.

d. Master file conversion.

e. Changeover procedures.

f. Review and maintenance.

20.3 If new computers or networks are required for the new system this will require a separate implementation project which will have to be coordinated with the activities listed above. Whatever applications the computers are used for it is important to ensure that they are used effectively and not abused. This chapter deals with the issues involved.

Training of staff

20.4 The amount of training required for various categories of personnel will depend upon the complexity of the system and the skills presently available. The systems analyst would be required to ensure that all persons involved with the new system were capable of making it an operational success. The following aids would be used, as appropriate:

a. **Handbooks.** These will be produced as part of, or as a development from, the systems specification.

b. **Courses.** Either full-time or part-time courses, often run by the computer manufacturers.

c. **Lectures.** General background knowledge, or knowledge of specific areas, could be covered by means of lectures.

Programming

20.5 The programmer must design programs that conform to the requirements set out in the system specification. The stages in programming have already been discussed in earlier chapters.

20.6 The work of the programmer has already been discussed in chapter 18. Program implementation can pose problems of management in large computer departments where the programmers might specialise in certain areas of programming. These specialisms may be:

a. **Applications.** Applications programmers are the people who write the initial programs for each application.

b. **Maintenance.** Once the programs written by the applications programmer are operational they are handed over to a maintenance programmer, whose job it will be to carry out any amendments or improvements that may be necessary.

c. **Systems software.** This programmer will specialise in writing 'non-application' programs, i.e. systems software. These programs will supplement those supplied by the manufacturer.

20.7 In smaller installations, of course, a smaller team of programmers will have to turn their hands to any task that comes along.

System testing

20.8 There is a need to ensure both that the individual programs have been written *correctly* and that the *system* as a whole will work, i.e. the link between the programs in a suite. There must also be co-ordination with *clerical* procedures involved. To this end the systems analyst must provide the necessary test data as follows:

a. **Program testing.** The systems analyst will need to supply test data designed to ensure that all possible contingencies (as specified in the systems specification) have in fact been catered for by the programmer. *Expected results* of the test must be worked out beforehand for comparison purposes.

b. **Procedure testing.** The aim of procedure testing will be to ensure that the whole *system* fits together as planned. This will involve the clerical procedures that precede input; the actual machine processes themselves; and the output procedures that follow. Overall timings and the ability of staff to handle the anticipated volumes will be under scrutiny.

Master file conversion

20.9 It is necessary to convert the existing master files into a magnetic form. The *stages* of file conversion will depend on the method currently used for keeping the files (e.g. manually; in box files) but are likely to be:

a. Production of control totals by adding machine.

b. Transcription of all 'standing' data (such as account number, address, etc), to a special input document designed for ease of data entry.

c. Insertion of all *new* data required onto input document, e.g. account numbers where none were used previously.

d. Transcription of data from documents to magnetic media. This can be a major task in the case of a large manual system. Extra staff may need to be drafted in.

e. Verification of transcribed data.

f. Data is then used as input to a 'file-creation run'. A specially written computer program procedures the master records in the required format.

g. Printing out of files for comparison with old files.

h. Printing out of control totals for agreement with pre-lists.

i. At a date immediately prior to changeover, variable data is inserted in master files. (e.g. *balance* on accounts).

Changeover procedures

20.10 There are two *basic* methods of changing over to a new system:

a. Parallel.

b. Direct.

20.11 **Parallel.**

The old and new systems are run concurrently, using the same inputs. The outputs are compared and reasons for differences resolved. Outputs from the old system continue to be distributed until the new system has proved satisfactory. At this point the old system is discontinued and the new one takes its place.

20.12 **Direct.**

The old system is discontinued and the new system becomes operational immediately.

A variation of either of the two basic methods is the so-called 'pilot' changeover.

A 'pilot' changeover would involve changing part of the system, either in *parallel* or *directly*.

20.13 The features of the various methods of changeover are:

a. **Parallel**.

    i. It is a costly method because of the amount of duplication involved.

    ii. This method would mean the employment of extra staff or overtime working for existing staff. This can create difficulties over the period of the changeover.

    iii. It is only possible where the outputs from old and new systems are easy to reconcile, and where the systems are similar.

    iv. Its use does give management the facility of fully testing the new system whilst still retaining the existing system.

b. **Direct**.

    i. If the new system bears no resemblance to the old then a direct changeover is probably inevitable.

    ii. There must be complete confidence in the new system's reliability and accuracy before the method is used.

c. **Pilot**.

    i. Use of the variation of the two main methods is possible when part of the system can be treated as a separate entity, e.g. a department or branch might be computerised before the undertaking as a whole.

Review and maintenance

20.14 Once the system has become operational it will need to be examined to see if it has met its objectives. For example, the costs and benefits will be compared with the estimates produced at the system's inception. This particular activity is often known as 'post-audit'.

20.15 The system will also need to be reviewed and maintained periodically for the following reasons:

a. To deal with unforeseen problems arising in operation, e.g. programs may need to be modified to deal with unforeseen circumstances.

b. To confirm that the planned objectives are being met and to take action if they are not.

c. To ensure that the system is able to cope with the changing requirements of business.

20.16 The results of a systems review would be used in future systems-analysis assignments.

Operations after implementation

20.17 The day-to-day operations of the computer system rely upon a number of specialist staff including the following:

a. Operations manager. He or she is responsible to the computer manager for operation of the computer and ancillary equipment. Also under his control will be:

    i. Data-control section.

    ii. Data preparation.

    iii. Tape and disk library/ies.

b. Computer operator handles and operates the hardware in the computer room. He or she handles the input and output media (e.g. placing tapes onto tape drives), communicates with the operating system and tries to keep the installation running smoothly by stepping in when things go wrong to correct them immediately.

c. The layout of a typical computer room for a large installation requiring several operators is shown in figure 20.1 below.

This diagram shows the layout of a typical computer room. There is a separate room for the assembly of incoming work which contains a number of storage cabinets for stationery, etc, and a guillotine/decollator for handling output stationery.

Inside the computer room the various input/output devices face the console to minimise movement by the operators and to allow the senior operator to see what is going on. The processor, which the operators never touch, is out of the way at one end. In this example, the library of magnetic tapes and disks is kept in the computer room with a desk for the librarian.

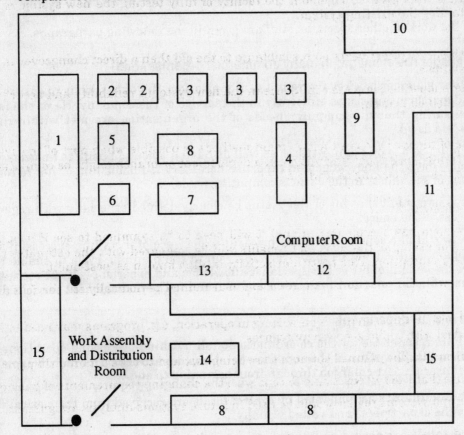

KEY.

1. Processor.
2. Magnetic Tape Drives.
3. Magnetic Disk Drives.
4. Line Printer.
5. Diskette Drives.
6. PABX.
7. Console.
8. Work Tables.
9. Librarian's Desk.
10. Magnetic Disk Cabinet.
11. Magnetic Tape Racks.
12. Diskette Cabinets.
13. Operators' and Engineers' Manuals.
14. Guillotine/Decollator.
15. Stationery Cupboards.

Figure 20.1 Layout of a computer room

Basis of organisation

20.18 The development and operation of a computer system requires careful organisation of the individuals involved and those individuals need to be suitably trained in the correct practices to follow.

20.19 The nature of several types of specialist work have been covered previously and do not merit repeating here:

a. Systems analysis.

b. Programming.

c. Operating.

Details of the work of other specialist staff are given in the following paragraphs.

The computer manager (DP manager in many commercial organisations)

20.20 The computer manager is a key figure in the organisation. His or her job is to ensure that the computer department functions efficiently in the service of the company. He or she is responsible for ensuring that the computer needs of the organisation are met within the policy guidelines laid down.

20.21 He or she must be a good administrator as well as having a sound business knowledge. He or she must also have the knowledge and expertise necessary to enable him or her to control his or her teams of specialists in the various computing fields.

20.22 **Status.** It is important that his or her status be clearly defined especially with regard to his right of access to the board.

20.23 Ideally one would like someone who has previous experience of installing successful systems, and the appointment should be made very early on in the planning cycle to enable the company to get the benefit of his or her specialist knowledge and experience. If not recruited from outside, the potential computer manager could be found in the management services division.

Data-control staff in a DP department

20.24 These staff are responsible for the co-ordination of all machine-processing operations and for ensuring a smooth flow of work through the operations department. In order to explain their work we will trace a particular job through from beginning to end.

20.25 a. **Source documents** accompanied by control totals are received from the clerical function (outside the department) and vetted visually.

b. **Control totals** are agreed and documents passed under this control to the data preparation section.

c. The data-preparation section prepares floppy disks or other media for source documents.

d. Source documents are returned to the clerical function and the floppy disks now represent the input for a particular run (job), e.g. 'invoice run'.

e. **The job-assembly** section 'make up' the run and prepare a run authorisation document. This will detail the various tapes/disks required and how the output is to be disposed of. This is then passed to the computer-room supervisor.

f. **Tape/disk library.** The librarian will provide all the tape reels and disk packs required for the particular job and will pass them to the computer room for the computer to process.

g. On completion of the computer run/s the tapes/disks, etc, go back to the library and all the documentation goes to the data control section.

20.26 **The control section** now scrutinises the control log to ensure all action has been taken correctly and to initiate any possible corrective action indicated. Control totals will be reconciled. These will now include totals of items rejected on the run/s, but all totals will need to be reconciled back to those compiled at the beginning of the job.

20.27 The output is dealt with; invoices, for example, will be despatched to customers and ware-houses, etc.

20.28 All necessary information will be fed back to the user department, e.g. copies of all output despatched, error lists, control totals.

Data-preparation staff

20.29 These staff are responsible for:

    a. Preparing floppy disks from source documents or preparation by other means, e.g. on-line data entry.

    b. Operation of ancillary machines such as floppy disk units, paper bursters, etc.

Tape/disk librarian

20.30 All tape reels and disk packs used in the installation are stored in a library adjacent to the computer room. The librarian issues tapes/disks to the computer room as per a run authorisation document from data control.

20.31 The librarian will maintain a register of all tapes and disks, noting the particular generations required for current use. Maximum security is observed and access is strictly limited.

Computer supervisor

20.32 The computer room is under the day-to-day control of a supervisor. Only authorised personnel are allowed entry. It is essential that anyone who has participated in the writing of the programs is forbidden for security and audit reasons to interfere with the operational running of those programs.

The control of computing activities

20.33 The use of computers imposes certain disciplines on those who work with them. Work has to be carried out in a uniform and orderly manner in the most efficient way. Staff and equipment will be well regarded if work is completed quickly and with the minimum of error or interruption. Well-defined standards allow the control of these activities to happen naturally.

20.34 Factors that aid control are:

    a. **Organisation,** i.e. all staff should know what their duties are and where they fit in the general picture (see Systems Development Part introduction).

    b. **Staff training.**

    c. **Supervision and working to plans.**

    d. **The use of documentation** to guide and assist work.

    e. **Clear procedures** for individuals to follow.

Data security

20.35 One important aspect of control is the control of data to prevent its loss, misuse or disclosure. This type of control is called 'data security'.

20.36 Data security is the protection of data. In some situations data security will be concerned with preventing the loss of data, e.g. in the file security method used during updates. In other situations data security will be concerned with preventing the misuse or unwanted modification of data, e.g. due to access by unauthorised persons. A third situation is the prevention of disclosure of data to unauthorised persons, e.g. where the data is important to national security.

20.37 Various measures can be taken to ensure all three types of security. Here are some common methods.

    a. The use of back-up copies of tapes or disks, e.g. in conjunction with generations of files.

    b. Physical prevention, for example:

       i. Write permit rings and similar devices.

      ii. Restricting the access of personnel.

     iii. Keeping data under lock and key.

    c. The use of passwords to prevent unauthorised use of computer terminals or unauthorised access to on-line files.

    d. constant checks of security.

20.38 People often demand higher standards of security from computer systems than they demand from manual systems. The reader might consider which is most secure, a folder of printed documents or a floppy disk holding the same information. A floppy disk can easily be damaged by dust or scratches so that its data is lost. On the other hand, specialist equipment and software will be needed to read its data, thus the data is more secure from those not trained in its use.

Even so, there has been a growth in computer crime in recent years, including an increase in **'hacking'** ie gaining unauthorised access to computer systems, often with ill intent.

Summary

20.39 a. Implementation is concerned with the coordinating and controlling of the activities necessary to put the new system into operation.

    b. Staff training, programming, testing, file conversion, changeover, review and maintenance are the stages in implementation.

    c. The systems analyst is needed at this stage because of his knowledge of the designed system and its implications.

    d. Careful organisation is needed to ensure that computers are used effectively and properly.

    e. The work of various specialist staff was described.

    f. The control of specialist work was discussed.

    g. Data security was defined and methods of data security were described.

Points to note

20.40 a. Note the difference between program testing and procedure testing.

    b. The responsibility for program testing lies with the programmers, who will be required to provide evidence of testing.

    c. The Part you are reading is entitled Systems Development because the term is generally used to describe the particular activities detailed in its chapters. In practical terms, however, the various stages will be undertaken as part of the system life cycle and a systems study carried out on instructions of top management.

    d. The emphasis throughout this Part has been upon systems development as it applies to commercial computer applications. However, the same basic principles apply to industrial applications. The most significant differences between systems development for commercial applications and that for industrial applications are:

       i. The systems being computerised (automated) in industrial systems tend to involve physical processes and are therefore well defined compared with commercial systems, which often rely on human sense and unwritten rules, which may be ill-defined.

      ii. Many industrial systems involve the time-critical processing of data read from instruments and this places a different emphasis on the whole analysis and design process.

    e. The more dependent people or organisations are upon computers the more important becomes the need for careful control and organisation of how the computer application systems are developed and the way they are operated.

Questions

1. What are the features of the various methods of changeover?

2. Define the term 'data security' and identify three types of data security.

3. If a manual system is scheduled for future computerisation what steps could be taken to alter the existing documents and procedures in order to make master file conversion more straight forward? (Hint: Apply your knowledge of methods of data entry.)

4. A company with 700 employees and labour cost analysed over 80 headings has decided to use a standard 'package' program to process its payrolls and provide labour cost analysis.

   a. What is a package program and what are the advantages of using one?

   b. Describe briefly the steps you would take to organise the transfer of the necessary records to the computer files.

   (CIMA)

5. a. What are the constituent parts which go to make up a typical systems analyst's assignment?

   b. Describe briefly the analyst's function in three of such constituent parts.

   (ICA)

6. What information would you expect to find in a well-prepared system specification?

   (ICA)

7. Explain how a systems analyst investigates a business system.

   (ACA)

8. Outline the main stages in the development of a systems project and briefly describe the work carried out by the systems analyst at each stage.

   (ACA)

9. What are the factors which govern choice of output media and device?

10. A computer has been installed in your company. You are involved in the design of the cost control information that will be provided by the computer.

    List the shop floor 'labour' control information that you have specified.

    Draft one of the relevant output documents produced by the computer.

    (CIMA)

11. An important factor in the efficient operation of any data processing system, whether manual, mechanical or computer based, is the design of the forms used.

    What are the major principles of good form design? Illustrate your answer, where appropriate.

    (CIMA)

21 Project management

Introduction

21.1 Good planning is a prerequisite of any business activity and computer systems development is no exception. This chapter deals with the planning and management of systems development projects by tracing the steps involved in the system life cycle.

21.2 The reader should recognise the fact that in this chapter we are primarily concerned with the management aspects of the system life cycle, whereas in earlier chapters the systems analysis aspects were considered.

21.3 In this chapter the assumption will be made that the company is not currently using a computer for the application concerned and that the size of the application is such as to make computerisation have a major impact on the organisation. It should be noted, however, that even for small applications, such as those requiring the use of a single microcomputer, the management task must still be done. Indeed, there is a particular danger when managing the development of many small systems that the development will end up happening in a piece-meal and fragmented way, which can subsequently create serious management problems.

Preliminary survey or study

21.4 There will come a time when the question of using a new computer system will arise. As a result, the board will decide to make an initial investigation into the possibility of using one. This will probably be carried out by one or two senior executives or consultants.

21.5 **Application areas.** More often than not a prima facie case can be made for a computer in a particular application area and it is this which will have prompted the board into carrying out the preliminary survey. There are likely to be other application areas to consider, in which case a long-term plan (including a list of priorities) will need to be drawn up.

21.6 **Outcome.** The preliminary study will determine whether or not to continue investigating the need for a computer. If so, *specific computer objectives* will be drawn up. It is important that the user should both agree to and sign the objectives to be met by the system.

Steering committee

21.7 When a project is established it is quite common also to establish a steering committee for the project. The purpose of this committee is to 'keep the project on course' so that it meets its objectives. The membership of the committee comprises management members and senior project staff such as analysts, so that the committee can carry out monitoring, controlling and consultative functions.

Feasibility study

21.8 Assuming the project is given the go-ahead, a study team will be formed to carry out a study of the application area or areas. This study team will be under the direction of the steering committee.

21.9 **Purpose.** The purpose of a feasibility study is to provide information in order to justify the use of a computer on three grounds:

a. Technical.

b. Economic.

c. Social.

21.10 **Study steps.** Steps in the study will depend on individual circumstances but generally will include the following:

a. The study team must be aware of the precise objective of the study.

b. Establish the requirements of the particular system being studied.

c. Make a detailed examination of the system to determine how these requirements are met. This will include details of volumes, information flows, time-scales, etc.

d. Note any improvements that can be made in the system as it stands as these may well be implemented at once.

e. Formulate the new design on the basis of the application of computer methods, considering various alternatives:

    i. Processing method (batch, on-line, real-time).

    ii. Choice of system (microcomputer, minicomputer, mainframe).

    iii. Centralised processing or distributed processing.

    iv. Methods of data entry, storage and output.

It must be stressed that the appropriate use of manual methods must not be overlooked.

f. Assess costs of possible new systems (staff, buildings, hardware, software, etc) over the life of the project.

g. Make comparisons with the present system.

h. Considerations of social factors, i.e. effect on staff relations, etc.

i. Make recommendations to the Board in the form of a Feasibility Study Report.

21.11 **Depth.** A feasibility study will be carried out in enough depth to enable the Board to make a decision on whether or not to proceed with detailed investigation and analysis. The contents of the report naturally will vary according to circumstances, but the main points on which information should be given are as follows:

a. **Aims and objectives.** It is important the aims and objectives be clearly stated. These should have been agreed with the line managers. The areas involved in the study should be defined.

b. **Cost/benefit comparison.** The alternative solutions will be outlined indicating the benefits to be gained from each and the costs involved. Comparisons with present methods will be attempted. Benefits that may accrue are:

    i. More timely information.

    ii. Better customer relations.

    iii. Improved cash flow.

Costs to be considered are development costs, capital outlay and operating costs.

c. **Outline of proposed system.** This will include details of:

    i. Inputs.

    ii. Stored data.

    iii. Outputs.

    iv. Processing activities from a business user's viewpoint.

    v. Programs and software.

The amount of detail assembled under each heading would be sufficient to enable a choice to be made between alternative solutions (if more than one is included in the report) and for the effects on existing procedures to be gauged.

d. **Effects on organisation.** The effects of the introduction of new methods and procedures on the organisation, in terms of change in posts, redundancy and staff re-training, will be included.

e. **Schedule of requirements.** Details of capital equipment, including costs, must be listed.

f. **Implementation.** the plan for the implementation of the proposed system will include a time-table. Methods of changeover will be stated.

g. **Recommendations.** These will recommend a particular solution which could conceivably be the adoption of conventional methods rather than computer methods to solve the company's problems.

Consideration of report

21.12 The board will consider the report and will want answers to the following questions:

a. Do the recommendations meet the objectives?

b. Do they still fit overall company objectives? (Note on 12a and 12b – some studies take so long that the original circumstances could have changed. The study itself could have led to a change in objectives.)

c. What is the effect on company profits going to be?

d. What is the effect going to be on company organisation and staff?

e. What are the costs involved and can the capital be obtained?

f. What is the time-scale for implementation?

g. Does it look sufficiently into the future, i.e. does the proposal allow for possible future expansion and modification?

21.13 **Decision.** The board may well ask for further information in certain areas. After the feasibility study report has been studied in detail a decision has to be taken whether or not to proceed.

Detailed investigation and analysis

21.14 Assuming that a decision is taken to proceed further, this stage continues the process started with the initial survey and feasibility study. At the end of the investigation and analysis a requirements specification is produced.

21.15 The production of a requirement specification provides the basis for a go/no-go decision between the feasibility study report and the full system specification.

Consideration of the requirements specification

21.16 The board will expect this report to answer the questions brought forward from their earlier considerations of the feasibility study report. In addition, the all-important question 'Does this specification give a full and accurate statement of the data-processing requirements?' must be satisfactorily answered.

21.17 **Decision.** Although the requirements specification is 'implementation free' it contains sufficient detail for the main design alternative to be identified. The board can approve the specification and decide whether or not to proceed with one or more designs. A balance has to be struck between the danger of eliminating a design alternative too soon and the cost of producing multiple alternative designs. It is also important when approving the specification to be sure that there is a clear technical (and in the case of outside contract, legal) basis for determining whether or not the specification has been satisfied when the system has been implemented.

Facility selection

21.18 The selection of one of the main design alternatives is effectively a selection of the kind of facilities to be used. For example, manufacturers and suppliers of particular products may be selected and asked to submit proposals that indicate how they can meet the requirements. Alternatively an independent firm of consultants may be requested to handle the problem.

Design

21.19 The design stage was described in Chapter 19. The outcome of this stage is the ultimate in documentation of the new system, the systems specification. This will contain full details of all clerical and computer procedures involved.

21.20 In the case of complete one-off systems the design stage will involve all the activities described in Chapter 19. However, in the case of many smaller systems, the design process may be largely a matter of matching what is available to what is required in order to find an acceptable match.

21.21 Each system specification is considered, along with any associated proposals from manufacturers or suppliers. After what may be a very long process one of the alternatives is selected and pursued.

21.22 It may well have been decided to use external consultants, in which case the following stages would not necessarily apply.

Resource planning

21.23 Whether the organisation is acquiring a small, medium or larger computer system a great deal of detailed planning and preparation now needs to be done in order that the installation of the machine and changeover to the computer-based system are achieved smoothly and efficiently.

21.24 Changing over to a system based on a microcomputer does not, however, have the same far-reaching effect on the organisation as that of a medium-sized machine. A medium-sized machine is assumed in the following paragraphs.

21.25 **Network.** The planning required up to the time of delivery of the machine and then on to the time the system is operational is normally so involved that it needs to be planned out using a chart that shows the 'network' of related activities and events that must take place and their interdependencies. The time-scale may well be linked to the date of delivery of the computer, and this could be many months. If there are many applications to be computerised, a schedule of priorities will ensure that at least one is ready for the computer soon after it is installed. **Estimation** of the time taken to complete tasks, and hence their related costs, must be done most carefully if any reliance is to be placed upon the network. Estimation is never easy but is improved in the long run by keeping records of time taken to complete various categories of task.

21.26 **Main resources.** The main resources requiring management's attention will be:

a. **Site.** This has to be chosen and prepared.

b. **Building.** A new building is to be erected or an existing one modified.

c. **Environment.** Requirements of the computer regarding humidity, dust control, etc, will need special attention.

d. **Standby equipment.** Arrangements will need to be made for such equipment in the event of a failure of the company's computer. In extreme cases involving 'mission-critical' systems this may involve the creation of an off-site standby system.

e. **Staff. Selection and training.** The decision has to be made on whether or not to recruit from within the company. Apart from the particular specialists who cannot be found in the company, it is generally found more satisfactory to recruit from within. At least such people will have a good knowledge of the company. Staff required will include:

i. Management (computer manager, etc).

ii. Clerical.

iii. Analysts and programmers – a few trained people recruited outside to help train company personnel.

iv. Operators – own personnel probably already employed in company as machine operators of some kind.

The manufacturer will often give assistance with training staff and also provide the temporary assistance of his own specialists.

f. **Finance.** Necessary arrangements will need to be made to ensure that the appropriate finance is made available. Detailed budgets will be drawn up for each area and strict control exercised over performance in accordance with budget.

Installation of computer

21.27 This will affect only a small number of people. The manufacturer's engineers will be responsible for installation of the machinery in conjunction with the computer manager or his representative. The machine is tested from an engineering point of view and handed over. The whole operation is usually accomplished in a matter of days.

21.28 **Maintenance.** Maintenance of the hardware and software will normally be the subject of an agreement and will ensure the machine is always in working order and spare parts available when required.

Implementation

21.29 This consists of:

    a. Training of staff.

    b. Programming.

    c. System testing.

    d. Master file conversion.

    e. Changeover procedures.

    f. Review (system evaluation) and maintenance.

Many aspects of implementation have already been discussed in chapter 46. Some additional points, regarding planning, are made here.

21.30 Planning this, the final and critical stage, would have started very early in the planning of the project as a whole. Indeed, quite often this particular stage will have a network of its own. This is the time when the computer system is going to take over from the old system and it is a very worrying time for everybody. There will be disappointments, setbacks and frayed tempers. It is a time of upheaval in the company and the value of good planning will be seen clearly during this period.

Program writing and testing.

21.31 Programmers will get on with the job of producing the computer programs from the systems specification. Individual procedures are programmed and compiled and then tested for logical correctness using 'dummy' data. After being tested individually the programs are tested as a complete system.

21.32 **Program testing.** It is the programmer's responsibility to ensure that each individual program meets its specification. Suitable test data must be used at each stage in programming. It is important that the programs are also subjected to independent testing.

21.33 The independent test data should be designed by people other than the program writers. The analysts in conjunction with the user department should do this job. This will ensure that every eventuality is designed into the test data pack and thus the programs are subjected to the most rigorous examination. All these eventualities must be considered before the specification is given to the programmer. It must be stressed, however, that the final testing is no substitute for good work practices and methods of quality assurance (QA), i.e. setting and enforcing standards of design, documentation, reliability, etc. All the evidence available shows that considerable benefits can be obtained from sound QA.

Review (system evaluation) and maintenance

21.34 Once the implementation process is complete and the system is operational there is a tendency to heave a sigh of relief, but it is just as important to follow up implementation with an evaluation process to ensure the original objectives are being met. This system evaluation is sometimes called **'post-audit'**.

21.35 It must be a properly mounted operation and its findings will be of help in future projects.

21.36 The need to keep abreast of new techniques is also important in order that the full benefits can be reaped.

21.37 In order that the new system continues to run efficiently it must be constantly monitored and maintained. This maintenance is bound to be necessary sooner or later and should be planned for.

Summary

21.38 a. The need for planning is vital because of the far-reaching effects of the changes that computers bring about.

    b. The stages in planning are:
      i.   Preliminary study.
      ii. Feasibility study.
      iii. Consideration of report.
      iv. Detailed investigation and analysis.
      v.   Consideration of requirements specification.
      vi. Facility selection.
      vii. Resource planning.
      viii. Installation of the computer.
      ix. Implementation.
      x.   Review (system evaluation) and maintenance.

    c. All possible alternatives should be explored in a feasibility study.

Points to note

21.39 a. The detail concerned with many of the points raised in this chapter has been covered in Chapters 43–46.

    b. The various steps do not follow neatly one after the other as in the text but overlap each other to a great extent.

    c. A feasibility study may be more correctly termed a justification study.

    d. Computer planning should not be geared to one application but should be designed to accommodate future applications when they arise.

    e. Note the different stages that involve a SYSTEM STUDY.
      i.   Initial study.
      ii. Feasibility study.
      iii. Detailed requirements study.
      iv. Detailed systems study.

    f. Each of these studies in e. above (or if you prefer, phases, in what will be a complete study in the end) will be conducted to the depth required to make a particular decision.
      i.   **The initial study** will only be made to the depth required for a decision to be taken on whether or not a prima facie case for a computer can be established.
      ii. **The feasibility study** will be in greater depth because it must provide the information that determines whether or not the use of a computer is justified to solve the company's problems.
      iii. **The detailed requirements study** will identify the precise data-processing requirement in an implementation-free way.
      iv. **Detailed systems study.** Further detail will be required to identify the precise hardware requirements and then to produce a systems specification for approval.

    g. You may need to make an assumption in an examination answer about the type of system the computer system is replacing, i.e. manual, computerised, etc.

    h. The term systems study can be applied to any of the four studies referred to in 21.39e so be careful in answering an examination question on systems studies to indicate the one you are talking about.

    i. The chapter has covered the various aspects of a large-scale project, but the same principles and basic practical issues are present irrespective of project size.

    j. The Part you have just read is entitled Information Systems Development because the term is generally used to describe the particular activities detailed in its chapters. In practical terms, however, the various stages will be undertaken as part of the System Life Cycle and a systems study carried out on instructions of top management.

k. The emphasis throughout this Part has been upon Systems Development as it applies to commercial computer applications. However, the same basic principles apply to industrial applications. The most significant differences between systems development for commercial applications and that for industrial applications are:

    i. The systems being computerised (automated) in industrial systems tend to involve physical processes and are therefore well defined compared with commercial systems which often rely on human sense and unwritten rules, which may be ill defined.

    ii. Many industrial systems involve the time-critical processing of data read from instruments and this places a different emphasis on the whole analysis and design process.

Questions

1. When acquiring an in-house computer system, which criteria are considered when deciding between the various manufacturers who have submitted tenders?

2. How do the contents of a feasibility study report differ from the systems specification?

3. What points would you include in the review of a newly implemented computer system?

4. The use of a computer is being considered by your company.

    a. Commencing with the preliminary survey, list all the steps you would recommend to be taken and briefly describe each of theses steps.

    You are to assume the ultimate purchase of a computer.

    b. The decision to go ahead is then taken. Summarise the remaining steps concluding with the systems evaluation.

(CIMA)

Software development

1. When a new computer system is to be developed, it becomes necessary to express the requirements in a number of ways. The requirements must initially be expressed in terms that the user can understand and agree to. Ultimately these requiremenst will be presented to the computer in the form of a set of instructions which the computer can obey, ie, a program. Any associated manual procedure must also be specified.

2. Over many years various methods have been developed to enable the clear and unambiguous expression of requirements and procedures. This Part examines these methods in detail.

3. In Chapter 22 a number of methods of specifying processing requirements and procedures are illustrated.

4 Chapter 23 explains how to produce decision tables and decision trees.

5. Chapter 18 deals with programming principles and practices.

6. The following definitions are given here in order to aid the reader's understanding of the following chapters:

   a. **Program.** A program is a series of *instructions* written in the language of the computer which specifies processing operations that the computer is to carry out on the data.

   b. **Programming**. The process of producing a computer program is called programming. In its simplest form it involves putting a series of instruction into the coded language of the computer. Generally, however, the term 'programming' implies some additional activities associated with producing the code, for example designing a solution and testing the finished program.

   c. The completed computer program is placed into main storage whenever its processing operations are to be carried out. Once in main storage the sequence of instructions is carried out *automatically*.

22 Program specification

Introduction

22.1   This chapter is primarily concerned with the methods of specifying processing requirements and procedures. However, it will be useful to consider the background to this activity in order to put it into context. Therefore, the chapter begins with a brief overview of software.

22.2   Following the overview the chapter goes on to deal with the traditional methods of specifying information-processing system, i.e. by the use of flowcharts. Flowcharts were widely used in the past. Some forms are still used and are important from an examination point of view. The second half of this chapter introduces modern methods which have superseded flowcharts in most circumstances. Some specialised methods, e.g. the use of decision tables, have been left for full discussion in later chapters.

22.3   As stated previously, **software** is the term used to describe programs and associated documentation. Compared with hardware, the software used on a given computer is relatively easy to change and it is that capability which gives computers their flexibility of purpose. The point is demonstrated well by the home computer used for playing games. Instead of buying a new machine each time a new game is wanted, as would be necessary if the game was solely hardware (i.e. wholly built into electronic components), all that is needed is for a new program to be 'loaded' into the machine each time a different game is needed. Better still, it is relatively easy to chop and change between games at will. This kind of flexibility is soon taken for granted, but it is in sharp contrast to most other items of everyday technology which have far less flexibility of purpose. It is this ability readily to change the computer's function which originally lead to the term '**soft**ware' being used. Additional flexibility is also provided by software because not only is it relatively easy to change from one program to another, individual programs can be changed too, although such changes cannot necessarily be carried out by the computer user.

The organisation of software in the computer

22.4   The following diagram (figure 22.1) gives a simplified illustration of how the various main items of software are organised and used in a general-purpose computer. At the top of figure 22.1 two types of computer user are shown above the software that they may directly access. Lower down, and not directly accessible, to the user, is the Operating System. As was discussed in Chapter 14, the operating system is a special suite of programs which controls the way in which the software above it accesses and uses the computer's hardware. At the very bottom is the hardware, which ultimately carries out the instructions it is given by the programs above it. Figure 22.1 may be interpreted as follows.

END USERS			
APPLICATIONS USERS		COMPUTER SPECIALISTS	
APPLICATIONS PACKAGES	SPECIALIST APPLICATIONS SOFTWARE	SYSTEMS FACILITIES	COMMAND INTERPRETERS
OPERATING SYSTEM			
HARDWARE			

Figure 22.1 How software is organised and used

22.5   The individuals who actually sit at computer terminals or at their own personal computers are called '**end-users**'. This distinguishes them from individuals who may be 'users' but who do not get personally involved with 'hands-on' activities. The end-users of a general-purpose computer may be broadly classified as either **applications users** or **computer specialists** according to the kinds of software they use.

a. An applications user is an end-user who puts the computer to some specific practical purpose by using **'applications software'**. An applications user is not normally technically knowledgeable about the computer but may be trained to use a particular **'specialist applications program'** designed for a specific purpose or an **'applications package'** which is a suite of programs, with associated documentation, used for a particular type of problem. In business organisations applications users most frequently use software to aid them in carrying out some clerical or administrative tasks. In industrial organisations applications users may use software which can monitor or control industrial processes for them, or may use software to perform complex computations.

b. Some end-users are computer specialists whose work it is to set up, control or monitor the computer, or to produce new systems. In an organisation using large minicomputers or mainframes there may be many such staff. They may have specific roles and job titles such as 'Computer Operator', 'Systems Manager' or 'Technical Support Officer'. Alternatively they may be involved in developing new software. The most common example of such a person is a 'programmer'. As might be expected, these individuals use software which is often very different in nature from that used by other end-users.

Note. In the case of small computers, such as home computers and personal computers, there may only be one end-user, who therefore may be both an applications user and, to some degree, a computer specialist.

22.6 In figure 22.1 the applications users are shown using either specialist applications software or applications packages. The computer specialists are shown using two types of software, which will now be explained.

22.7 **Command interpreters** are programs which provide a general-purpose means of instructing the computer to carry out operational tasks. For example, there will be commands which cause the computer to copy data from one magnetic disk to another. Other commands may cause particular information about the system or its users to be displayed on a VDU or printed out. Yet other commands may enable the computer to be set up so that applications packages can be used by particular end-users. More detailed examples will be provided later in this text.

22.8 The program is called a **command interpreter** because of the way in which it works. A user sitting at a terminal using the command interpreter will be able to type in simple standard instructions which the command interpreter will decipher and carry out straight away.

22.9 Figure 22.2 shows a VDU screen at which a user has typed a command. In figure 22.2 the letters shown in plain type are those which are generated by the command interpreter. Those underlined are the commands typed in by the user. The symbol '>' at the start of each line is called a **prompt**. Its purpose it to inform the user that the interpreter is ready to accept a command. The first command typed in, PRINT report1, tells the command interpreter to print a copy of a report called 'report1' on the computer's printer. The word PRINT is a special word which the command interpreter can understand. Such words are called **key words**. The command interpreter has responded to the command by transmitting a copy of the report to the printer. From the message the command interpreter has displayed on the VDU screen for the user, REPORT1 QUEUED TO SYSTEM PRINTER, it would appear that the report may have to wait its turn to be printed. Having completed that task the command interpreter has displayed a prompt signifying that it is ready for another command. The user has responded by typing a similar command, and so on.

```
>PRINT report1
 REPORT1 QUEUED TO SYSTEM PRINTER
>PRINT report2
 REPORT2 QUEUED TO SYSTEM PRINTER
>
```

Figure 22.2 A simple dialogue between an end-user and a command interpreter

22.10 **System facilities** include a variety of other items of **Systems Software** which were discussed in Chapter 14. Some additional points are worth considering here.

22.11 Most programmers make use of many different kinds of systems software, but one of the most common programs they use is an **editor**, which is a program that may be used at a terminal to create or amend programs.

22.12 A systems manager may use a special **authorisation program** to control which users may *access* the computer to use its facilities. Such a program will be able to keep track of named users, the programs they use, and the data they may look at or change. In particular, it may itself only be used by the systems manager. The operating system will make use of the information created by the authorisation program to determine whether or nor end-users may carry out particular actions. In practice, the systems software achieves part of this control by the use of *'user accounts'*, which are set up by the authorisation program. As with accounts in other situations, such as banking, a user must have an account before being able to use the facilities on offer. To use the software provided on the system the user must first **'log in'** to the system. Logging in is similar to using a command interpreter in that the system gives prompts to the user to which the user must type in appropriate responses. An example of logging in is shown in figure 22.3.

```
login : Bloggs
Password : typed in but not displayed

Welcome to the XYZ Ltd CompanyComputer

Please note the computer will close down at 18:30 today.

The time now is 09:15

> At this point the user will gain access to whatever software he or she has been authorised to use.
```

Figure 22.3 An example of an end-user logging in to a computer

22.13 In the example given in figure 22.2 the end-user typed his or her user name, 'Bloggs'. The system software controlling the login was able to check that 'Bloggs' was an authorised user, so then went on to prompt for a password. Bloggs then typed the password at the keyboard but, for security reasons, the letters were not displayed on the screen. Apparently the password was correctly typed because the system responded with a message and displayed the time.

Note. On many small computers, such as personal computers or home computers, such elaborate procedures may not be necessary. Some smaller computers operate as **turnkey systems**, which means that when they are switched on, perhaps by *turning a security key*, the computer automatically gives the user the use of just one particular applications program.

22.14 The **operating system** has a special role to perform, in that most other program are not able to work without it. In effect, the operating system provides facilities which enable the other programs to use the hardware in a safe and controlled way. The mechanisms by which this takes place are too complicated to discuss in detail at this stage but the ideas are simple. For example, a program which wishes to display some data on a user's VDU screen makes a request to the operating system, giving it the data concerned. The operating system then displays the data. The end-user is totally unaware of all this. As far as he or she is concerned a single program is being used.

22.15 Having considered the way software is organised and used we may remind ourselves what is expected of professionally produced software (1.83–1.85). Amateur programmers often consider that their job is done once they have produced a program which seems to work. Indeed, if the program is for their own private and personal use that may be perfectly satisfactory. However, most software that people use is produced as a product for sale and therefore must be more finished. We now turn to the subject of specification.

The need for the methods of specification

22.16 The general model of a DP system highlights the fact that in essence all a DP system does is perform processing operations on input data, or stored data, to produce information. The prospective user of a new DP system will tend to view the proposed system in those terms (e.g. 'I want to feed in the hours worked and get back a payroll cash analysis, among other things'). However, such requirements must be expressed in precise and clearly defined terms to ensure that when the system is developed it does what it is intended to do.

22.17 Computer specialists need to be able to analyse the user's information requirements, design suitable solutions, implement new DP systems and then maintain the systems. To do all this they need a number of 'tools' for the job.

22.18 Different 'tools' are used at different stages in the work. For example, the 'Systems Analyst', whose job it is to analyse the user requirements, must be able to express the requirements in terms that the user can understand and ratify, and must also be able to express the requirements in terms which aid the design process (we will see how charts and diagrams can be effective tools for this). At a later stage a programmer will need to break down design specifications of processing functions into simple, well-controlled operations on data. Well-proven and efficient methods are needed at all stages.

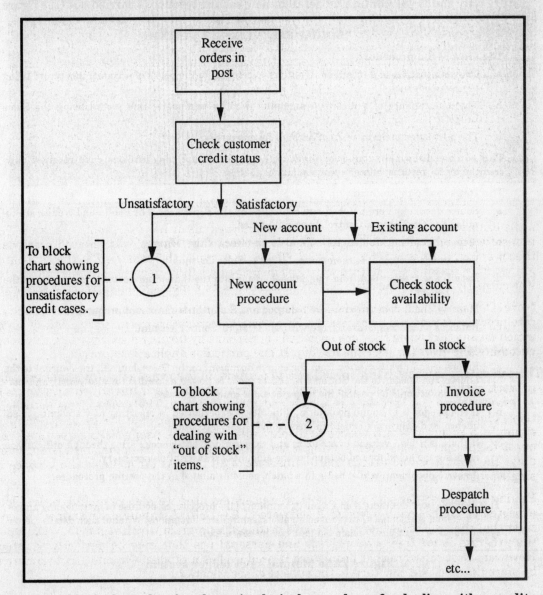

Figure 22.4 A block chart showing the main clerical procedures for dealing with a credit order

Flowcharts

22.19 Flowcharts are a traditional means of showing, in diagrammatic form, the sequence of steps in a system and the relationship between them. Various types of flowchart are described here.

Types of flowchart

22.20 We will consider flowcharts under four headings:

    a. Blockcharts (or diagrams).

    b. Systems flowcharts.

    c. Procedure flowcharts.

    d. Program flowcharts.

Block charts

22.21 The block chart (or diagram) shows the sequence of the main procedures in a system and can be regarded as the simplest form of flowchart. The object of such a chart is to give the broad picture only and it will contain no detail of how each procedure is carried out (see figure 22.4).

MANUAL SALES LEDGER SYSTEM

1. **The aims of the procedure**

    a. The maintenance of a record of all entries to be made to the books of account; this record being the Sales Journal.

    b. The maintenance of a record of amounts owed by customers; this record being the Sales Ledger.

    c. The production of Statements of Account for customers.

2. **The source documents** used for input to the procedure are copy invoices; cash received slips credit notes for returns; miscellaneous adjustment slips.

3. **The steps in the procedure**

    a. Source documents are batched and controlled by the supervisor. The debits and credits are to-talled and the Debtors' Control Account updated.

    b. Source documents are then sorted into the sequence of the ledger.

    c. Each source document is then entered into the Sales Journal.

    d. Details are transcribed from the Sales Journal into the individual customer's account in the Sales Ledger.

    e. Monthly, the Ledger Accounts are balanced and Statements of Account prepared.

    f. Balances on the ledger are agreed with the Debtors' Control Account.

4. **Limitations**

    a. Errors arise in *transcription* from the source document to the Sales Journal; the Journal to the Ledger; the Ledger to the Statement. *Debits could be posted as credits* (or vice versa); an *incorrect amount* could be posted; the *wrong account* could be adjusted.

    b. If the Ledger is in bound book form, difficulty is experienced in inserting new accounts, in sequence, and delays are caused in passing over 'dead' accounts.

    c. If there is a high volume of accounts and transactions, bottlenecks arise through difficulty in agreeing the accounts and because of the amount of transcription necessary.

    d. A source document, whilst being in a batch, could be missed in the posting procedure.

NB. This example provides more than a mere description of the procedures, because in investigating an existing system it is essential always to record all its features and limitations. Without such details the systems analyst could easily retain old faults in the new design.

Figure 22.5a Manual sales ledger system

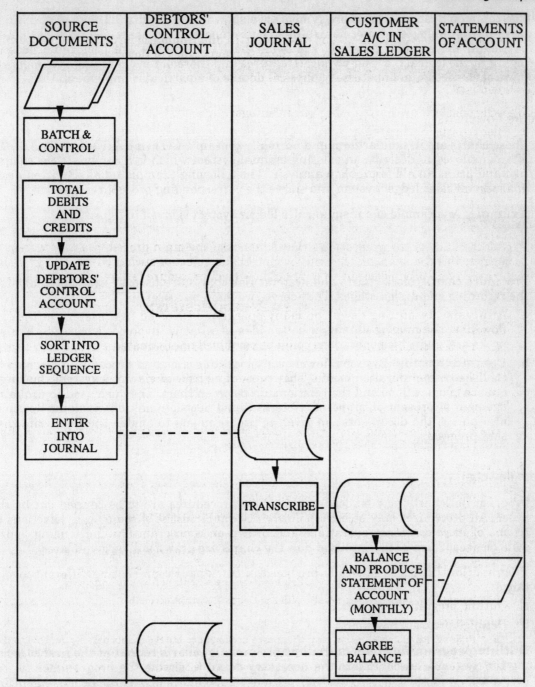

SOURCE DOCUMENTS	DEBTORS' CONTROL ACCOUNT	SALES JOURNAL	CUSTOMER A/C IN SALES LEDGER	STATEMENTS OF ACCOUNT

Figure 22.5b Outline procedure flowchart for a manual sales ledger system

Systems flowcharts

22.22 The systems flowchart shows in more detail the procedures outlined in the block diagram. It provides a picture of the processing operations in the system. The systems flowchart is concerned with the complete system (not just the part the computer plays in it) and will therefore include both clerical and computer operations. (The symbols are shown in Appendix 3.2.)

22.23 Because of the additional detail involved in constructing systems flowcharts they sometimes take up more than one standard sheet of paper. This is overcome by dividing up the flowchart, and linking the various parts by means of connector symbols. (Examples will be given in Chapters 20 and 21.)

22.24 The common Systems Flowchart symbols are shown in Appendix 3.2. Use of specific symbols for input, storage, etc, may be useful if it is important to show the physical details of a particular design, but generally speaking the NCC symbols are preferable because they highlight the logical (i.e. non-physical) features and therefore avoid hiding the important data flows of the design in unnecessary physical details of a particular implementation.

Procedure flowcharts

22.25 These charts are in tabular form and normally contain NCC symbols (Appendix 3.2). They are often employed to describe an existing manual system which is a candidate for computerisation and act as an aid to problem analysis. The following example takes a written description of a manual sales ledger system and shows the corresponding procedure flowchart.

22.26 **Example.** An example of a manual sales ledger system is given in figure 22.5.

Uses

22.27 Procedure charts, block charts and systems flowcharts are used by systems analysts during the recording and design stages. They serve two main purposes:

a. **Analysis.** By putting down the many operations involved in a system in the form of a flowchart the analyst obtains a better idea of what is involved, where the likely bottlenecks are, and which operations could be combined or eliminated.

b. **Communication.** Systems flowcharts, block diagrams and procedure flowcharts are established communication media. They present a pictorial view of a system showing the sequence of operations and the relationship between them. They are used to acquaint management of present or proposed systems to aid decision-making. Systems flowcharts are also part of the documentation given to programmers to enable them to write the necessary programs.

Program flowcharts

22.28 Program flowcharts may be used to show how procedures are to be carried out by the computer. All procedures may be broken down into combinations of sequences, selections or repetitions of basic computer operations and drawn on a program flowchart using appropriate symbols (see figure 22.6). Details of how the charts are drawn will be given later.

22.29 Program flowcharts are generally produced in two stages representing different levels of details:

a. Outline program flowcharts.

b. Detailed program flowcharts.

22.30 **Outline program flowcharts.** Outline program flowcharts represent the first stage of turning the systems flowchart into the necessary detail to enable the programmer to write the programs. As implied by the title they present the actual computer operations in outline only. (Figure 22.7a.)

22.31 **Detailed program flowcharts.** These charts are prepared from the outline charts and will contain the detailed computer steps necessary to perform the particular task. It is from these charts that the programmer will prepare his or her program coding sheets. Such is the amount of detail involved that these charts are often prepared by individual programmers each taking a segment of the outline charts (see figure 22.7b).

The limitations of flowcharts

22.32 Flowcharts were originally introduced as aids to a systematic process of analysing problems and developing suitable computer-based solutions. In recent years flowcharts have been heavily criticised as being cumbersome and inefficient tools for the job. Newer alternatives have been introduced and widely adopted.

22.33 Particular limitations of flowcharts are:

    a. Different levels of detail can easily become confused, e.g. details of a particular implementation can be inadvertently introduced too early in the design.

    b. There are no obvious mechanisms for progressing from one level of design to the next, e.g. from systems flowchart to outline program flowchart.

    c. The essentials of what is done can easily be lost in the technical details of how it is done.

    d. Program flowcharts, although easy to follow, are not such a natural way of expressing procedures as writing in English, nor are they easily translated into programming languages.

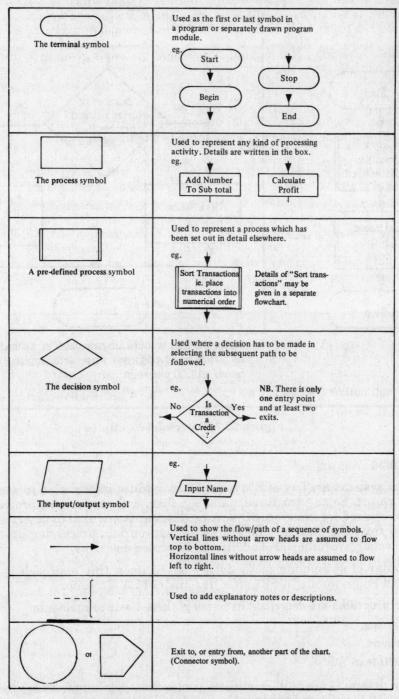

Figure 22.6 Program flowchart symbols

22.34 The remainder of this chapter introduces modern alternatives to flowcharts.

Data-flow diagrams (DFDs)

22.35 These are used in modern methods of systems analysis. They are simple, in that they use a convention with few symbols and rules, and avoid unnecessary technical detail. They aid the analyst in building a logical model of the system which is free of unnecessary detail, and in which the important data flows stand out. They aid the user in providing an intelligible picture of the system. They will be described in more detail in Chapter 29.

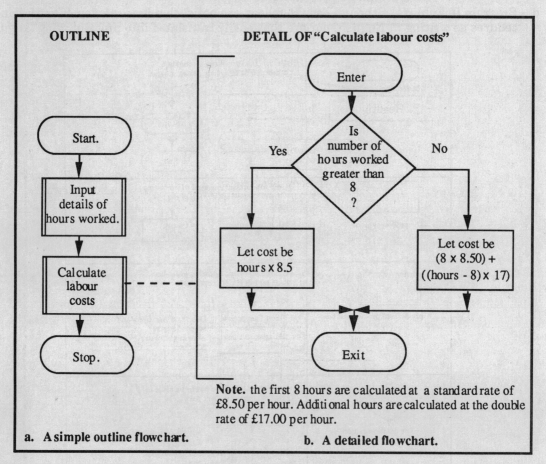

OUTLINE   **DETAIL OF "Calculate labour costs"**

Note. the first 8 hours are calculated at a standard rate of £8.50 per hour. Additional hours are calculated at the double rate of £17.00 per hour.

a. A simple outline flowchart.   b. A detailed flowchart.

Figure 22.7 Flowchart examples

Structure diagrams

22.36 Computer systems are frequently required to produce information in some 'structured' form, e.g. as a report. Some 'structured' data, e.g. files, will normally be processed in order to produce the required information. **Structure diagrams** are used to describe the structure of the data, and from the structure diagrams the appropriate processing procedures may be produced, normally with the aid of additional structure diagrams.

22.37 One popular programming methodology based upon this approach is known as 'Jackson Structured Programming' (JSP), after its founder M.A. Jackson.

22.38 Data and programs are described in terms of three basic components:

    a. Sequences.

    b. Selections.

    c. Repetitions.

22.39 Structure diagrams are built from these components working from top to bottom. Each line is *read from left to right* and expands the previous line into more detail (see figure 22.8).

Pseudocode

22.40 Pseudocode is a modern alternative to the program flowchart, but without the limitations of the flowchart (paragraph 19).

22.41 Pseudocode is halfway between English and a programming language. It is based upon a few simple grammatical constructions which avoid the ambiguities of English but which can be easily converted into a computer-programming language.

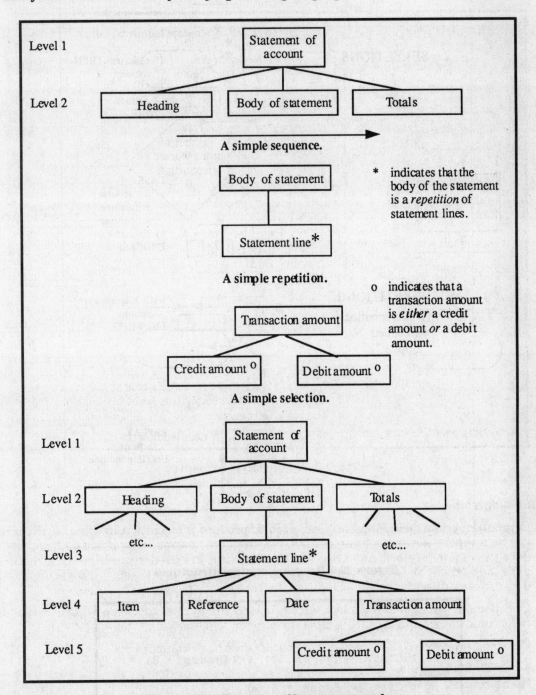

Figure 22.8 Structure diagram examples

22.42 All programming procedures, no matter how complex, may be reduced to a combination of controlled sequences, selections or repetitions of basic operations. This fact gives rise to the basic 'control structures' to be found in pseudocode. Figure 22.9 explains these control structures by cross-reference to program flowchart symbols. (Also see figure 22.10.)

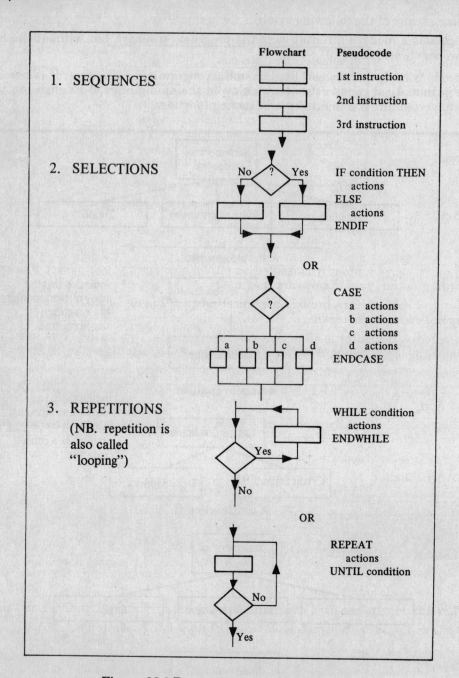

Figure 22.9 Program control structures

```
IF
      Hours > 8
THEN
      Cost := (8 * 8.50) + ((Hours - 8) * 17)
ELSE
      Cost := Hours * 8.50
ENDIF
```

The Pseudocode equivalent to Figure 17.7b

NB. * is used as a multiplication sign.

Note the meaning of the following symbols (figure 22.10).

Symbol	Meaning
>	"is greater than"
<	"is less than"
>	"is greater than or equal to"
<	"is less than or equal to"
<>	"is not equal to"
=	"is equal to"
:=	" is assigned the value of "

Figure 22.10 Pseudocode example and symbol details

Summary

22.43 a. End-users may be broadly classified as either applications users or computer specialists according to the types of software they use.

b. Command interpreters provide a general-purpose means of instructing the computer to carry out operational tasks.

c. Access to the computer is often controlled by software. One method requires the user to login and give a password. Another method involves the use of turnkey systems.

d. The operating system controls the way in which all other software uses the hardware.

e. Software was considered as a product to highlight the various requirements of the software user.

f. Basic methods currently used to describe data-processing requirements and data-processing procedures were introduced.

g. The methods included the use of:
   i.   Blockcharts.
   ii. System flowcharts.
   iii. Procedure flowcharts.
   iv. Program flowcharts.
   v.   Data Flow Diagrams (DFDs).
   vi. Structure diagrams.
   vii.   Pseudocode.

h. Different methods are used depending upon the stage in investigation, analysis or design.

i   Details of particular methods have been left until later chapters.

Points to note

22.36 a. With the hardware remaining unaltered the user can completely change the function of the computer merely by changing the software.

b. You should find the modern methods easier than the traditional ones, but be prepared to express examination answers in specific forms if required to do so.

Question

State four limitations of program flowcharts. Suggest one alternative to flowcharts.

23 Decision tables and decision trees

Introduction

23.1 In considering a particular problem it is sometimes difficult to see all the possible factors involved and how they interact. Decision tables are used to analyse a problem. The conditions applying in the particular problem are set out, and the actions to be taken as a result of any combination of the conditions arising, are shown. Decision trees are a graphical representation of decision tables. Their purpose is to aid the construction of decision tables.

23.2 Decision tables and trees are means of expressing process logic. They may therefore be used in conjunction with, or in place of, flowcharts or pseudocode.

23.3 This chapter begins with a very simple example of a commercial situation involving conditions and actions. The example is then used in the succeeding paragraphs to illustrate the concepts of decision tables and trees.

23.4 **Example 1.** A clerk, in assessing the amount of discount allowed on a customer's order is required to comply with the following policy:

'Any order of £500 or more received from a credit-worthy customer attracts discount of 5% and, similarly, orders of less than £500 attract discount of 3% Other circumstances must be referred to the supervisor for a decision'.

Now see this policy illustrated in the form of a decision tree at figure 23.1, and as a decision table at figure 23.2.

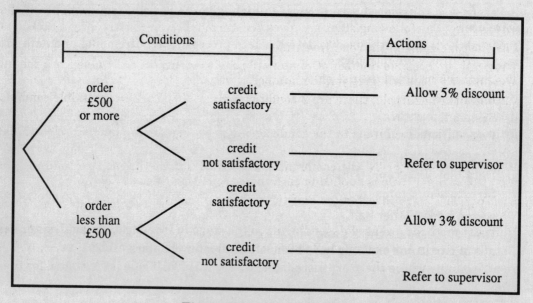

Figure 23.1 A decision tree

Format

23.5 Decision tables have a standardised format and are comprised of four sections (separated by double lines):

a. **Condition stub.** This section contains a list of all possible conditions which could apply in a particular problem, e.g. 'order of £500 or more', 'satisfactory credit'.

b. **Condition entry.** This section contains the different *combinations* of the conditions, each combination being given a number termed a 'Rule'.

c. **Action stub.** This section contains a list of the possible actions which could apply for any given combination of conditions, e.g. give discount of '3%', '5%', 'refer to supervisor'.

d. **Action entry.** This section shows the actions to be taken for each combination of conditions.

NB. The decision tree contains the same information but in a less formal way.

CONDITIONS	RULES			
	1	2	3	4
Is order for £500 or more?	Y	Y	N	N
Is credit satisfactory?	Y	N	Y	N
ACTIONS				
Allow discount of 3%			X	
Allow discount of 5%	X			
Refer to supervisor		X		X

KEY	
Y	YES
N	NO

Figure 23.2 A decision table

Method of preparation

23.6 In constructing a decision table from a narrative given to you in an examination, go about it in an orderly way. The following steps are given for you to follow in constructing a decision table.

a. List the conditions in the *condition* stub.

b. Work out the possible number of combinations of conditions, i.e. 2^n where n = the number of conditions. This will give you the number of rules.

In the worked example, there are 2 conditions, thus $2^2 = (2 \times 2) = 4$ possible combinations (rules).

c. Rule up sufficient columns in the condition entry section for the number of combinations, i.e. 4.

d. When entering 'Y' or 'N' the combinations must be unique (i.e. no two columns must be alike). The 'halve' rule is applied to each row of condition rules as follows:

i. **Row 1.** Y's are inserted for half the number of rules (2 in our case) then N's are inserted for the other half.

ii. **Row 2.** Alternate the Y's and N's, the groups being half the size of those in Row 1. (The group size in our example is 2 therefore the second row size will be 1, i.e. Y, N, Y, N.)

In an example where there are more than two rows, the half rule is continued for the other rows.

e. Enter the action stub.

f. Follow down each rule and mark in the appropriate action to be taken.

Note. The decision tree is drawn from left to right. Each question is filled in the same order as the corresponding decision-stub entry.

23.7 **Example 2.** The unit price of a particular product is £15 if less than 10 are purchased, £14 if between 10 and 49 are purchased, and £13.80 if 50 or more are purchased. If the customer also has preferred customer status then the purchase is subject to a discount of 10%

This policy is illustrated in the form of a decision table in figure 23.3, which is arrived at by setting out all 16 rules and then eliminating impossible cases leaving just the six shown.

Summary

23.8   a.   Decision tables are of standardised format and are used in conjunction with, or in place of, flowcharts.

Decision tables are divided into four sections:

CONDITION STUB	CONDITION ENTRY					
ACTION STUB	**ACTION ENTRY**					

	RULES					
CONDITIONS	1	2	3	4	5	6
order< 10	Y	Y	N	N	N	N
10 ≤ order ≤ 50	N	N	Y	Y	N	N
50 ≤ order	N	N	N	N	Y	Y
Preferred customer	Y	N	N	Y	N	Y
ACTIONS						
charge £15.00 per item		X				
charge £13.50 per item	X					
charge £14.00 per item				X		
charge £12.60 per item			X			
charge £13.80 per item						X
charge £12.42 per item					X	

KEY	
Y	YES
N	NO

Figure 23.3

Points to note

23.9   a.   The form of decision table dealt with is called LIMITED ENTRY because the *conditions* and *actions* are *limited* to the condition/action stub respectively. EXTENDED ENTRY tables are ones showing a *part* only of the condition/action in the *stub* with the balance in the *entry*, e.g. in the action *stub* of figure 23.2 the first two actions could be combined as 'allow discount' and in the action entry '3%' and '5%' shown in place of crosses. Limited-entry format and extended-entry format can both be used in a single table for individual conditions or actions. Where a table contains *both* types of format it is called a MIXED-ENTRY decision table.

   b.   Whether one type of format is used in preference to another depends on particular circumstances. In general terms, extended-entry and mixed-entry tables use fewer conditions and actions and are thus more compact, but are not so easily checked for completeness as are limited-entry tables.

   c.   It is possible to present processing requirements to the computer in the form of decision tables instead of programs, provided a special item of software called a 'decision-table processor' is available. Although some decision-table processors have been available for a number of years they have not been widely adopted.

Questions

1.   When invoicing customers, the invoice clerk has to work out the discounts allowable on each order. Any order over £200 attracts a 'bulk' discount of 7.5% A customer within the trade is allowed 15% There is also a special 5% allowed for any customer who has been ordering regularly for over 2 years.

   a.   Construct:

   i.   a flowchart.   ii.   a decision table.

   to illustrate the management's policy.

b. State the possible advantages and disadvantages of using:

    i.   flowcharts.

    ii. decision tables.

2. A company wishes to grade its employees in accordance with a new grading structure given below:

Grade 'A' employees must satisfy at least two of the following requirements:

a. they must possess acceptable academic qualifications;

b. they must have completed a training programme;

c. they must have the commendation of their department head.

    Failure to achieve a Grade 'A' rating automatically means a grading of 'B'.

    However, if employees qualify for Grade 'A' ratings but have not received their heads' commendations they are classed as 'Grade 'A' under review' and referred to the Personnel Officer for further investigation.

    Employees who are classed as Grade 'B' but who have obtained their heads' commendations are classed as 'Grade 'B' provisional' and are required to undertake further training.

You are required to:

a. prepare a limited entry decision table describing the grading system;

b. discuss the advantages and disadvantages of decision tables compared with flowcharts.

(CIMA)

24 Programming principles and practices

Introduction

24.1 Programming principles and practices are determined by recognised programming aims and the need for good programming methods. This chapter uses a simple programming exercise to illustrate these various aspects of programming.

24.2 The chapter is primarily concerned with *program writing*. Details of program execution are left until later chapters. The reader should note the difference between *program writing*, which is a once-only task and the *machine's execution* of a program, which occurs every time the program is placed in main storage, i.e. whenever there is a requirement for 'running' it on the machine.

The importance of good programming methods

24.3 Today, great reliance is placed upon computers for all kinds of applications, including banking, insurance, public and private administration, national defence, and so on. Computers are only machines and will slavishly follow the program instructions given them.

24.4 The costs of programming have risen because the shortages of skilled personnel, as required for programming, have pushed up labour costs, whereas the costs of hardware have fallen because of technical innovation and increased automation. It is a false economy to reduce programming standards in order to achieve greater programmer output, because of potentially damaging effects of errors, high correction and maintenance costs and difficulties experienced in transferring sub-standard programs from one computer to another.

24.5 The need for good-quality programming is greater than ever, but there is also a need to reduce programming costs. Experience has shown that it pays to put greater effort into program design rather than into trying to get a badly designed program to work. The longer an error goes undetected the more costly it is to correct and so the early stages of program design are very important.

Programming aims

24.6 These are summarised as follows:

   a. **Reliability**, i.e. the program can be depended upon always to do what it is supposed to do.

   b. **Maintainability**, i.e. the program will be easy to change or modify when the need arises.

   c. **Portability**, i.e. the program will be transferable to a different computer with a minimum of modification.

   d. **Readability**, i.e. the program will be easy for a programmer to read and understand (this can aid a, b and c).

   e. **Performance**, i.e. the program causes the tasks to be done quickly and efficiently.

   f. **Storage saving**, i.e. the program is not allowed to be unnecessarily long.

Some of these aims are in conflict with others, e.g. c and f.

Programming exercise

24.7 This exercise illustrates program writing.

24.8 **Requirement.** A simple program is required which will aid the checking of credit and debit totals in batches of cash transactions. A batch of 10 transactions (cash and adjustments) is to be input at a VDU keyboard. When all 10 transactions have been input, the total credit and total debit are to be displayed on the VDU screen.

24.9   System flowchart. A system flowchart for this problem is shown in figure 24.1.

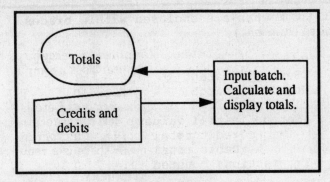

Figure 24.1

24.10   Planning the method of solution. There are a number of possible solutions, even for this simple problem, eg:

a.   **Method A**

Input all the numbers.

Calculate the totals.

Print the totals.

b.   **Method B**

Input the numbers, adding to the totals as each number is input.

Print the totals.

Method A has the advantage of separating out the different operations. Method B will be more instructive to consider first so it is adopted for this example.

24.11   Developing the method using suitable aids. The two main aspects to consider are:

a.   The operations to be performed on the data.

b.   The way the operations are to be combined into sequences, selections or repetitions.

24.12   Step 1. In outline method B can be represented as in figure 24.2.

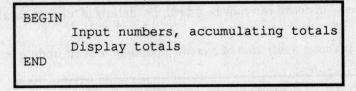

Figure 24.2 Step 1 in pseudocode

24.13   Step 2. We now fill in the next level of detail. 'Input numbers, accumulating totals' needs further consideration. At this step it helps to make a comparison with this method and the use of a pocket calculator. With a pocket calculator we can add up a set of numbers by *first* clearing the display and then *repeatedly* adding one number to the 'total' at a time. Here we do something very similar, except we have two totals, one for credits the other for debits.

24.14   In this problem there are 10 transactions which must be counted as they are entered.

24.15   Data Considerations. The data items used in the program can now be identified. They are:

a.   **Numerical constants** [Numbers of fixed value identified by name].

i.   Number-in-batch (Having the value 10 in this case).

b.   **Numerical variables** [Numbers identified by name but of changing value].

i.   Credit-total

ii.   Debit-total

iii.   Transaction-amount

iv. Transactions-counted.

```
NB.   Comments are enclosed within braces
thus:{comment}

BEGIN
    {Set up constant}
    Number_in_batch          :=     10

    {Set up initial values}
            Credit_total    :=      0
             Debit_total    :=      0
    Transactions_counted    :=      0

    {Input Numbers, accumulate totals}
    WHILE
        Transaction_counted < Number_in_batch
    DO
      Input Transaction_amount,
Transaction_type
      {Add one to transactions_counter}
      Transactions_counted :=
Transactions_counted + 1
      Update_totals
    ENDWHILE
    Display_totals
END
```

Figure 24.3 Step 2 in pseudocode

c. **Character Variables** [Characters identified by name but of changing value].

　　i.　Transaction type ('C' for Credit or 'D' for Debit).

24.16　The details of the stage can now be written (figure 24.3).

24.17　**Step 3.** The next level of detail can now be added, i.e. details of 'update-totals' and 'display-totals'.

　　a.　'Update-totals' involves a *selection* of a credit update or a debit update (see figure 24.4).

```
{NB. An alternative layout of IF...THEN...ELSE
is
 used here to aid clarity}

IF
    Transaction_type = "C"
THEN
    {Add transaction_amount to Credit_total}
    Credit_total := Credit_total +
Transaction_amount
ELSE
    {Add Transaction_amount to Debit_total}
    Debit_total := Debit_total +
Transaction_amount
ENDIF
```

Figure 24.4 Step 3 in pseudocode

b. 'Display-totals' involves displaying the value of the credit-total and the value of the debit-total. For the displayed values to have meaning, and hence provide information, some comments will need to be output with the data. The instruction:

DISPLAY 'CREDIT TOTAL', Credit-total

means display *literally* what is inside the quotation marks followed by the *value associated with* Credit-total. Thus 'Display-totals' consists of:

DISPLAY 'CREDIT TOTAL', Credit-total

DISPLAY 'DEBIT TOTAL', Debit-total

24.18 **The complete program** is shown in pseudocode in figure 24.5.

24.19 **Writing the instructions in a programming language.** As an example the pseudocode of figure 24.5 is shown transcribed into the computer-programming language BASIC. In figure 24.6 BASIC has been used for the example because of its widespread use. The use of BASIC here in no way implies that BASIC is particularly suitable as a data-processing language. Therefore, the reader should neither spend time studying the fine detail of this example nor consider it necessary to learn BASIC in order to understand Data Processing.

```
BEGIN
     {Set up constant}
     Number_in_batch            := 10

     {Set up initial values}
     Credit_total        :=     0
     Debit_total         :=     0
     Transactions_counted :=    0

   {Input Numbers, accumulate totals}

   WHILE
        Transactions_counted  <  Number_in_batch
   DO
        Input Transaction_amount, Transaction_type}
        {Add one to transactions_counted}
        Transactions_counted :=  Transactions_counted +  1
        {Update_totals}
        IF
           Transaction_type  =   "C"
        THEN
           {Add Transaction_amount to Credit_total}
           Credit_total := Credit_total  + Transaction_amount
        ELSE
           {Add Transaction_amount toDebit_total}
           Debit_total :=   Debit_total  + Transaction_amount
        ENDIF
   ENDWHILE
   Display  "CREDIT TOTAL",  Credit_total
   Display  "DEBIT  TOTAL",  Debit_total
END
```

Figure 24.5 The completed program

24.20 **Transcribing the instructions into 'machine-sensible' form.** Programs are input to the computer in the same way as data. Details of exactly how the computer interprets the program instructions and executes them are left to a later chapter. Initially the program is executed using test data to check that it works correctly.

24.21 **Testing the program.** The program needs to be tested to ensure that it has been written and transcribed correctly, and does what it is supposed to do. Test data is carefully selected for this purpose. For example, the program just described would need to be tested with a set of transactions including debits and credits so that all input, processing and output alternatives were tested.

```
100   REM    PROGRAM  EXAMPLE.
110   REM    AUTHOR  C S FRENCH.
120   REM
130   REM       THIS PROGRAM INPUTS A BATCH
140   REM       OF TEN CASH TRANSACTIONS AND
150   REM       PRODUCES TOTALS FOR THE
160   REM       CREDITS AND DEBITS
170   REM
180   REM    CONSTANTS
190   REM       N:  NUMBER IN BATCH
200          LET :  N = 10
210   REM    VARIABLES
220   REM       C:  CREDIT TOTAL
230   REM       D:  DEBIT TOTAL
240   REM       T:  TRANSACTIONS COUNTED
250   REM       A:  TRANSACTION AMOUNT
260   REM       T:  TRANSACTION TYPE
270   REM
280   REM    BEGIN
290   REM       SET UP INITIAL VALUES
300          LET C = 0
310          LET D = 0
320          LET T = 0
330   REM
340   REM       WHILE
350   REM           TRANSACTIONS_COUNTED
360   REM          < NUMBER_IN_BATCH
370          IF T  >  =  N  THEN  610
380   REM
390   REM          INPUT TRANSACTION AMOUNT
400   REM          AND TRANSACTION TYPE
410          PRINT  "TRANSACTION AMOUNT":
420          INPUT A
430          PRINT "TRANSACTION TYPE  (C  OR D)";
440          INPUT T
450   REM          NOTE PROGRAM DOES NOT CHECK FOR
460   REM          INVALID T INPUTS
470   REM
480   REM          ADD 1  TO TRANSACTIONS COUNTED
490          LET  T = T + 1
500   REM
510   REM          UPDATE TOTALS
520          IF T   = ``C" THEN  570
530   REM             DEBIT
540             LET  D  = D + A
555          GO TO 590
560   REM             CREDIT
570             LET  C = C + A
580   REM       ENDIF
590          GO TO 370
600   REM    ENDWHILE
610          PRINT  "CREDIT TOTAL";  C
620          PRINT  "DEBIT TOTAL";  D
630             END
```

NB. Lines starting with REM are merely remarks for the programmer's benefit and combination of the main operations on the data using standard control structures.

Figure 24.6

24.22 **Documentation** includes such things as a statement of the problem, flowcharts, pseudocode, test data and results, user instructions, etc. Documentation is a by-product of the program writing process which aids maintenance or modification of the program during its lifetime. Things such as comments or remarks in programs, and meaningful data names, are forms of self-documentation.

Program structure

24.23 There are two aspects to program structure:

a. Code-level structure.

b. Program-level structure.

It is easier to examine them in that order, but program-level structure is the more important of the two.

24.24 In figure 22.34 it was shown how the basic operations within a program may be organised and combined using standard control structures such as **While...endwhile, If...then...else and Repeat...until.** This is code-level structure, i.e. the organisation and combination of individual fragments of code using standard control structures.

24.25 In the early stages of programming the main **operations on data** within the program must be identified and combined using the standard control structures. This is program-level structure, i.e. the organisation.

24.26 **Structured programming** is the name given to program writing which employees such program structuring techniques. However, the term is often used very loosely to mean anything from happening to use standard control structures in a program to using very systematic design methods employing both code-level structures and program-level structures.

24.27 The **operations on data** mentioned in paragraph 24.25 take the form of **subprograms** (also called **subroutines** or **procedures**). A subprogram is a *named* component of a program which performs some *well-defined operation* on data. A subprogram is almost like a separate self-contained program except that the main program, of which it is a component, controls its operation. Data is 'passed to' the subprogram by the main program. The subprogram performs the required operations. Then results are 'passed back' to the main program by the subprogram. This may be compared with a manual procedure, e.g. where an unsorted batch of transactions is *passed* to a clerk, who sorts the transactions into order, creates a control total, and then *passes* them back.

24.28 The items of data passed to and from the subprogram are called its **parameters.** Once a subprogram's name, parameters and operations have been specified it can be written as if it were an independent program. Clearly, this is very useful when producing very large programs because it not only means that the task can be broken down into smaller, more manageable subtasks, it also means that the sub-tasks can be divided between a number of programmers. This is the basis of a popular programming method called **stepwise refinement**.

24.29 When using the method of **stepwise refinement** the whole programming problem is analysed and the main subprograms are identified and specified. The **top level** of the program design is then completed by specifying these subprograms and the program-level structure at the top level. The next step involves taking these subprograms and completing the same process again in each of them, i.e. identifying the subprograms and control structures from which they can be constructed. This process continues again at each level until the subprograms are so small that they can be written using simple code.

24.30 At each stage in the stepwise refinement process the individual subprograms are tested separately, which makes it much easier to find and correct errors than would be if all the testing was left to the end. Of course, the completed program has to be tested too.

24.31 In paragraph 24.10 'method A' lent itself to the method of stepwise refinement better than 'method B' because it allowed the program to be broken down into three separate and easily defined subprograms. To complete the first stage in stepwise refinement we must complete the task of specifying the subprograms and selecting the control structures.

24.32 The top level of the program is shown in outline in figure 24.7. There are three subprograms called 'Input-Transactions', 'Calculate-Totals' and 'Print-Totals', which are arranged into a simple control **sequence** enclosed between BEGIN and END. The direction in which the parameters are passed (IN or OUT) is indicated in the parameter description. The set of ten transactions is passed as a parameter which is a single data item called an ARRAY.

```
BEGIN
  Input_Transaction (OUT : ARRAY OF TRANSACTIONS)
    (*
        This procedure obtains the details of ten transactions
        from the user and then passes them OUT to the main
        program as a parameter, which is an array of ten records.
    *)
  Calculate_Totals (
                    IN  : ARRAY OF TRANSACTIONS
                    OUT : CREDIT TOTAL
                    OUT : DEBIT TOTAL
                    )
    *(
        This procedure is passed IN the array of ten transaction
        records as a parameter, calculates the totals and passes
        OUT the credit totals and debit totals as parameters.
    *)
  Print_Totals (
                IN : CREDIT  TOTAL
                IN : DEBIT TOTAL
                )
    (*
        This procedure is passed IN the credit totals and debit
        totals as parameters and displays them on the screen.
    *)
END
```

NB.   This example uses an extended form of pseudocode in which:

i.   The parameters of the subprograms are represented between parentheses "(" and ")" after the subprogram name.

ii.   Comments specifying what the subprograms do are enclosed between the symbols "(*" and "*)".

Figure 24.7 Outline top-level program design

Stages of programming

24.33   In the process of producing the necessary instructions making up a program, the following stages can be recognised:

a.   Understanding the problem.

b.   Planning the method of solution.

c.   Developing the method using suitable methods (details later) and notations, e.g. stepwise refinement and pseudocode.

d.   Typing the instructions into the computer using a programming language.

e.   Testing the subprograms separately as they are each produced and finally testing the program as a whole.

f.   Documenting all the work involved in producing the program. This documentation will be developed stage by stage.

24.34   If during testing the program an error is discovered, then *it is important to go back to earlier stages* in order to correct the error. If the error comes from misunderstanding the problem it will probably be better to start again from the beginning. An outline of what happens at each programming stage now follows.

24.35 **Understanding the problem.** The programmer needs to know exactly what the program is required to do and normally works from a **program specification.** This program specification is normally part of a **'system specification'**, which defines the whole system, of which the program may be only a small part. For example, the program might just be one of a suite of programs for use in a particular application.

24.36 Broadly speaking, the program specification will define the inputs, processing and outputs required. A good specification will normally specify *what* processing is needed by giving the exact relationship between outputs and the inputs from which they are derived rather than prescribing *how* the program should be written.

24.37 **Planning the method of solution.** Depending upon the extent of the task, the program preparation may be shared amongst many programmers. Such co-operation requires an overall plan. Large programs may require each programmer to write a separate part of the program. These separate parts are often called modules or segments. The modules may be prepared and tested separately, then linked together to be tested as a whole, a process known as **integration.**

24.38 **Developing the method by using suitable aids such as pseudocode.** Modern approaches to programming recognise the fact that complicated problems can be solved most easily if they are broken down into simpler more manageable tasks in a step-by-step fashion. At each step the problem is broken down further and consideration of details is put off as long as possible. This general approach is known as **Top Down Programming by Stepwise Refinement.** (More details later.)

24.39 **Typing the instructions in a programming language.** This may be regarded as the last step in stepwise refinement. The instructions written in pseudocode are written in a programming language. There are different types of programming languages and details will be given in later chapters. If programs have to be written in a very strict format, and are to be typed by someone other than the programmer, then they are first written on special forms called 'Coding Sheets'. The use of coding sheets is unusual today because most programmer-type their own programs using VDUs or workstations.

24.40 **Testing the program.** Once written a program has to be subjected to various tests to check that it has been written out and transcribed correctly, and does what it is supposed to do, i.e. it is correct. These tests invariably reveal errors which have to be corrected. This can be quite a lengthy, and expensive, process. Careful and thorough design in the early stages of programming will help to minimise these errors. The later an error is discovered the more expensive and troublesome it will be to eliminate it.

24.41 It is good practice to test each component of a program as it is produced as well as testing the completed program. There are several stages of testing:

a. **Unit testing**, which involves testing the separate components as they are produced.

b. **Integration testing**, which involves testing the separate components as they are put together.

c. **System testing**, which involves testing the whole program once it is in the final form in which it is to be used.

d. **User acceptance testing**, which involves the user of the program (possibly the customer) testing the program to see that it is what was required.

24.42 **Documentation.** It is very important that the work of the programmer in producing a finished program is fully documented. This documentation will include a statement of the problem (System Specification), pseudocode, coding sheets, test data and results. *Producing these documents should be done as part of each stage in programming and not as an afterthought.* If this is done the documentation will aid the maintenance of the program during its lifetime. Some programs have very long lives. For example, some programs written during the 1960s are still in use to day, although they may have been subjected to *regular maintenance*, e.g. modification or bringing up to date.

Software engineering

24.43 Although almost anyone can write a simple program in a language like BASIC, just as any reasonably competent individual may be able to erect a shed in the garden, the production of larger programs to suitable standards of reliability, maintainability, etc requires professional methods. The shed builder is hardly a civil engineer! The adoption of systematic methods and engineering principles to the specification, design, implementation and testing of programs, including the management of such activities, has in recent years been given the name **Software Engineering.** Although it may be argued that software engineering is no more than a new name for good programming principles and practices, it is nevertheless a useful term to use when wishing to indicate that what is meant is professional software development to industrial standards rather than amateur code-writing.

Computer staff

24.44 It is easier to see programming in context if at this stage we give some consideration to the work of the staff involved. An outline of the work is given in the following paragraphs. Greater detail will be given in a later chapter.

24.45 **Systems Analyst.** The main jobs of the analyst are:

  a. To examine the feasibility of potential computer applications.

  b. Analysis of existing systems with a view to their application to a computer.

  c. Design of computer-based systems, their implementation, and review.

24.46 It is very likely that systems analysts would work in project teams with a senior analyst in charge.

24.47 **Programmers.** Following the design process the job of programming begins. The programmer:

  a. Encodes the procedures detailed by the analyst in a language suitable for the specified computer.

  b. Will liaise very closely with the analyst and the user to ensure logical correctness of programs.

24.48 Programmers also frequently work in project teams.

Summary

24.49 a. Good programming methods are important for economic and other reasons.

  b. Programming aims include:

  i. Reliability

  ii. Maintainability

  iii. Portability

  iv. Readability

  v. Performance

  vi. Storage saving.

  c. Programming takes place in stages.

  d. Modern programming methodologies have been developed with particular regard for programming aims b.i. to b.iv. above.

  e. Structured programming and subprograms were introduced.

  f. The work of computer staff has been introduced.

Points to note

24.50 a. Good programs only come from good program design, and good program design only comes from giving sufficient thought and effort in the early stages of programming.

  b. The programmer cannot solve a programming problem satisfactorily if the problem has not been properly stated.

    c. Subprograms are also sometimes called 'Subroutines' or 'procedures'.

    d. One subprogram may be called upon several times, in different places within the same program.

Questions

1. Use a pseudocode to represent the management policy given in question 1 Chapter 17.

2. A key-to-diskette system is to be used for the entry of orders received by a mail-order business. What validation checks might be applied to the order details?

3. In the preparation of a program, from program specification to operational running, certain essential tasks have to be completed by the programmer.

    List and explain the main stages of the work undertaken by a programmer in achieving an operation program.

(ACA)

4. **You are required,** in the context of computer programming, to explain the following terms and to give an example of each:

    a. loop;

    b. conditional branch;

    c. sub-routine;

    d. unconditional branch;

    e. literal.

(CIMA)

File processing

1. The processing of files is of major importance in DP. This Part discusses the subject in detail.

2. In one sense computerised data processing is file processing, i.e. in practical terms data processing almost invariably involves the processing of files. In some situations files may be replaced by databases, as is happening in a growing number of organisations. Nevertheless, the basic principles of file processing apply. We may therefore leave issues specific to databases until later chapters (Chapters 27 and 28) and concentrate on file processing here.

3. The recognition of the major role of files (or their alternatives) in computerised data processing highlights some important points:

   a. File processing methods must be understood in order to understand the methods of modern DP.

   b. Understanding the fundamental purposes of file processing leads to a clearer understanding of the purposes of DP systems.

4. In order to understand file processing it is first necessary to have some prior knowledge of both storage devices and media, and programming, which is why the subject matter of this Part could not be introduced earlier in this book.

5. Chapter 25 is an introduction to file processing and explains the basic principles and concepts. In addition the chapter describes traditional methods of processing sequential files on DAS and SAS. The chapter also deals with important aspects of controlling file processing.

6. Chapter 26 describes the processing of non-sequential files with particular reference to DAS but not SAS. It describes more advanced batch processing methods and introduces the ideas of transaction processing.

7. The following notes are intended to serve as an introduction to this Part.

8. The maintained data within the DP system should correspond to what is happening outside the DP system. For example, in the case of Stock Master File we need the stored values of numbers of items in stock to correspond to the actual number of goods in the warehouse. Taking the example of the master file storing details of our own bank current account, we require that the balance corresponds to the actual balance of payments or withdrawals. Of course, we may be prepared to accept some delay between the time changes happen and the time the master file reflects them.

9. Since every data processing system is required to provide timely, accurate and appropriate information about the real state of affairs, there is a fundamental requirement for the state of the data-processing system to correspond to the real state of affairs, ie, the data-processing 'model' must be valid. File processing plays a major role in meeting these objectives.

25 File processing I

Introduction

25.1 The main purpose of this and the next chapter is to apply the basic ideas concerning storage media and processing requirements to file processing. This is a large subject area which is why the material has been split into two chapters. In order to place the subject matter in context this chapter considers factors affecting the choice of methods for file organisation and access. Methods associated with sequential file processing are discussed in detail in this chapter too.

25.2 Sequential file processing is an important feature of the simpler and long-established methods of batch processing. Such methods were established when magnetic tape was the main file-processing medium. Today, the same methods continue to be used but with magnetic disk as the usual choice of storage medium.

25.3 The examples given in this chapter relate to business and commercial applications but the principles illustrated are general. A brief mention is made of text files too at the beginning of this chapter.

25.4 The chapter contains three main examples of file processing. The first is used to explain how a sequential master file is updated. The second example is more general and typifies sequential file processing. The example is followed by a discussion of the advantages and limitations of magnetic tape as a file storage medium. The third example illustrates file controls, i.e. measures to ensure that data files are processed correctly.

Processing text files

25.5 Text files were introduced in chapter 4. They may be regarded as a special type of sequential file. It is often possible to write or and read text file one character at a time. The 'records' are the individual characters, and they have no key – just a physical order in the file. If this is the primary way of processing the text file it may be called a **stream file**. Normally, however, characters in text files are structures into variable length records as follows.

    a. Each line (or possibly a paragraph) in the text file is a variable length record containing one variable length field of characters.

    b. There may be no key as such for identifying individual records, although some text files may contain line numbers.

    c. Lines of text are written to the text file one after the other and may then be read back in the same order.

    d. It is normally possible to write or and read text file one character at a time too if required.

Choice of file organisation and access methods

25.6 **Factors affecting choice**:

    a. **Size**.

        i. Disks and tapes are both capable of storing very large files but very large files are stored more economically on magnetic tape. Small files can use disk space well if blocks are suitably sized and can be easily accessed, but may be troublesome to access if strung along magnetic tape because of the serial nature of tape.

        ii. The percentage of additions or deletions in file maintenance if low may allow satisfactory organisation of indexed or random files, but if high will make sequential organisation more attractive.

        iii. If a file is likely to increase in size then the design of an indexed or random file must allow for it.

    b. **Reference and enquiry.** If quick reference is essential then indexed or random files will be needed. If the file is only used for quick one-off reference then a random organisation may be best.

    c. **Hit rate.** This relates to b, in that low hit rates are suited by indexed or random files, and high hit rates are suited by sequential files. Putting together batches of enquiries to form a transaction file can raise hit rates.

    d. **Security and backup.** The 'Father-Son' concept is an aid to security when using sequential files. Indexed and random files are overwritten *during processing* so they may need to be dumped onto tape or another disk *between processing,* as well as keeping a copy of all transactions between dumps.

File-handling techniques

25.7   The techniques discussed in this chapter apply to the following file-handling activities.

    a. **File creation.** The creation of transaction files **after** the validation stage will be considered.

    b. **File updating** (amendment).

    c. **File maintenance.**

       The techniques described in this chapter apply mainly to sequential and index sequential file handling. During random file handling each record is handled separately, and so techniques used with sequential transaction files may either apply to single records or be irrelevant.

25.8   Prior to any sequential file update or maintenance it is necessary to get the transaction file into a suitable form. This usually involves:

    a. **File conversion**, i.e. converting from the input medium (e.g. diskette) to storage medium (e.g. magnetic tape say).

    b. **Sorting** i.e. the transaction file must be sorted into the sequence of the master file before processing can take place. The key fields of the transaction file may be sorted into either **numerical sequence** or alphabetical sequence according to the method used on the master file.

25.9   **Final sequencing.** A final check may be made to ensure that all records on the transaction file do lie in sequence.

25.10   **Collating.** Collating can also involve merging and matching, e.g. a transaction file is merged with a master file and unpaired records are removed, thus leaving only those records needed for updating.

Validation checks

25.11   When records on transaction files are matched with master files, further checks may be made. These are:

    a. **New records.** If a complete new record is input for insertion into the master file, a check is made to see that a record with the same key number is not already present.

    b. **Deleted records.** If input indicates that a record is to be deleted from the file, an error is reported if the record is not present on the file.

    c. **Consistency.** Before the master file record is amended, a check may be made to ensure that the new data is consistent with data already stored in the record (e.g. before updating a payroll record with overtime payments, the record would be checked to ensure that the employee was not a salaried member of staff not entitled to overtime).

Application example

25.12   In order to illustrate file-processing activities we will now consider a simple stock control system. This example will be used both in this chapter and again in the next one.

25.13   Details about individual stock items may be stored as logical records in a stock master file, i.e. a stock item is an 'entity'. One 'attribute' of the stock item entity will be the number of items in stock.

25.14 Events taking place in the organisation will change the actual stock. The master file must be made to reflect these changes so that the required information about stock can be produced from it.

25.15 Events such as the introduction of new stock items, or the discontinuation of existing items, correspond to the *insertion or deletion* of entities in the master file.

25.16 Events such as the delivery of items as they are sold correspond to *'debiting'* or *'crediting'* the attribute value of the number of items in stock.

25.17 Events such as price increases of stock items correspond to changing the attribute value of the stock item price.

25.18 From the cases just considered the following basic file-processing activities can be identified:

    a. **File maintenance** (Insertions, deletions and changes to values)

    b. **File update** (debits and credits)

In fact these activities are typical of most file-processing applications. The reader should be able to see the parallels in other applications, e.g. we may open or close an account, change a client's address or credit or debit the client's account.

25.19 Although file updating and file maintenance are different file-processing activities they are sometimes combined together for convenience. The term ' **master file update** ' is often used loosely to mean both update and maintenance and in the remainder of this Part the same meaning will apply.

25.20 **Transactions.** Relevant details of events need to be recorded and input to provide the data needed to update the master file. Since data is recorded about the events, the events are entities too. In traditional file terminology these entities are called transactions.

Processing strategies

25.21 There are two basic strategies for processing transactions against the master file:

    a. **Transaction processing** – i.e. processing each transaction as it occurs.

    b. **Batch processing** – i.e. collecting transactions together over some interval of time and then processing the whole batch.

25.22 One method of processing is no better than the other. It is a matter of 'horses for courses'. Details of the different methods of file processing will be discussed in the chapter following this one. The relative advantages and disadvantages of the different methods will be included in the discussion.

		TRANSACTION TYPE				
		INSERT NEW RECORD	DELETE EXISTING RECORD	CHANGE EXISTING RECORD	CREDIT EXISTING RECORD	DEBIT EXISTING RECORD
Key status prior to processing the transaction.	Allocated	X	✓	✓	✓	✓
	Not allocated	✓	X	X	X	X

Key: **✗** : a valid operation.
    ✓ : an invalid operation.
      eg, "Insert new record" is **not** a valid transaction if the key is already allocated, ie, present.
      Similarly, "Delete existing record" is **not** valid if the key is not allocated.

Figure 25.1

25.23 Transaction processing will be considered in the next chapter. Batch processing is most commonly achieved by sequential file processing, so batch processing will now be explained before we continue with an example of sequential file processing.

25.24 The majority of commercial computer applications are involved in batch processing. Transactions are accumulated into batches of suitable sizes, then each batch is sorted and processed. The concept is not new, in fact it is also adopted in most manual systems of data processing. By its very nature a batch-processing system will involve a degree of 'delay'. Generally, the result of processing a particular *item* of data will not be known until the results of the *batch* are known.

Example 1 – updating a sequential master file

25.25 This example illustrates the basic principles involved in the update of a sequential master file, by dealing with the update of a simple stock master file.

25.26 Each item of stock is an entity about which data is recorded in one logical record. Each logical record is identified by its own unique key (its stock number). At any one time only some of the set of available keys will be *allocated* to stock items, e.g. if an account number is a key some account numbers are not allocated.

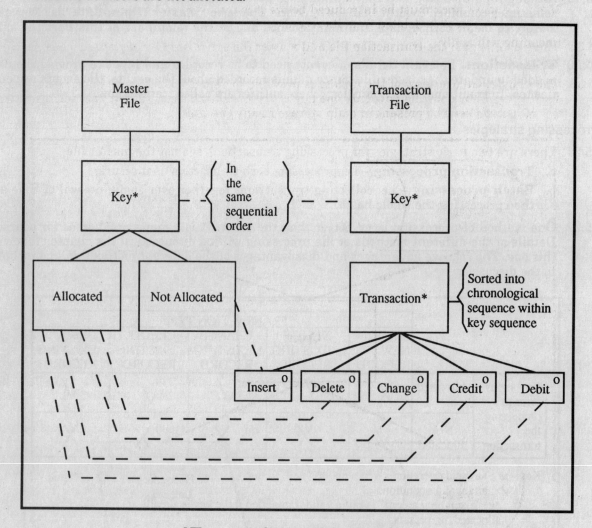

NB. – – – – indicates valid operations.

Note. Some master keys may not have any corresponding transactions.

Figure 25.2 Structure diagrams for the two files used in the update

25.27 It will aid a clearer understanding of the master file update if we think of the master file as the *complete* sequence of available keys, although only some keys will be allocated to stock items at any one time. The *status* of a key, i.e. allocated or not allocated, is signified by the fact that only allocated keys have records physically present within the master file.

25.28 **Processing operations.** There are different types of transactions, and each transaction corresponds to a particular operation on a master file record. The status of the key will determine whether or not the operation is a valid one in a particular situation. The possible combinations of valid and invalid operations are shown in figure 25.1.

25.29 **Batched transactions.** Batches of transactions of different types are accumulated together into a transaction file. The means by which these transactions are entered into the system have been covered in earlier chapters.

25.30 In the case of a sequential master file update, the transaction file is sorted into the same key sequence as the master file prior to processing. This enables the processing to be carried out in an orderly and efficient manner.

25.31 Within one transaction file there are likely to be multiple transaction records with particular key values, e.g. several debits from the same stock item. The sequence in which these transactions are processed should correspond to the chronological sequence of events that created them, e.g. new stock must be introduced before it is removed, and similarly a key must be allocated before stock is debited from its record.

25.32 The way in which the transaction file and master file are related by key sequence is shown in figure 25.2.

25.33 The update. An overview of the update is provided by figure 25.3. Figure 25.4 gives a further level of detail by showing how only one key is processed at a time, so that only a limited number of records need be present in main storage at any one time.

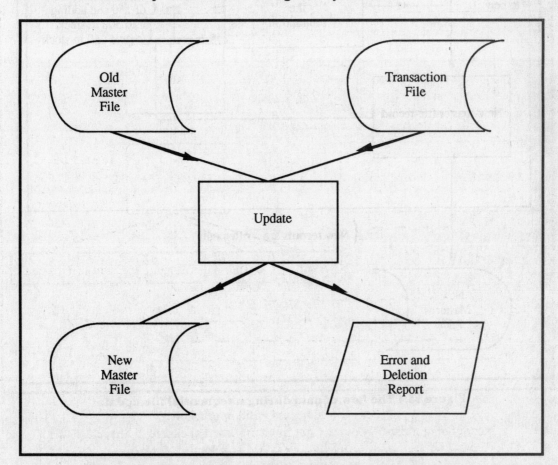

Figure 25.3 Sequential master file update – system flowchart

25.34 The procedure is given in outline in the structure diagram (figure 25.5) and in greater detail, in pseudocode, in figure 25.7. The procedure shown in these two diagrams may be easier to understand if read in conjunction with figure 25.6.

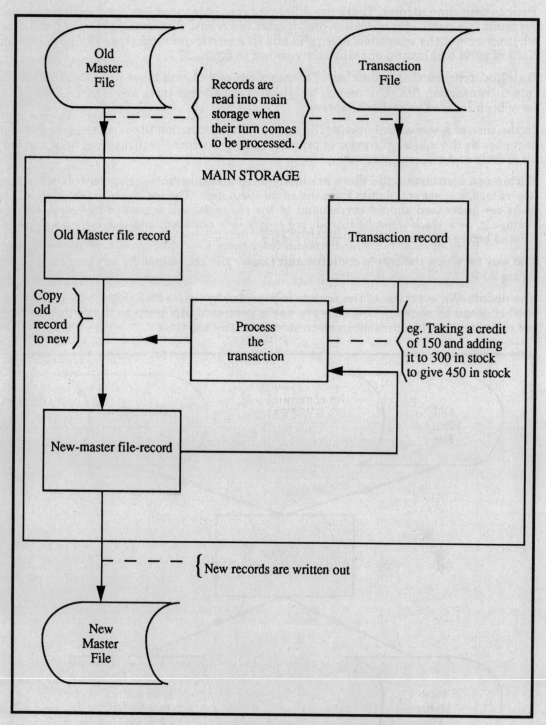

Figure 25.4 The flow of data during a sequential file update

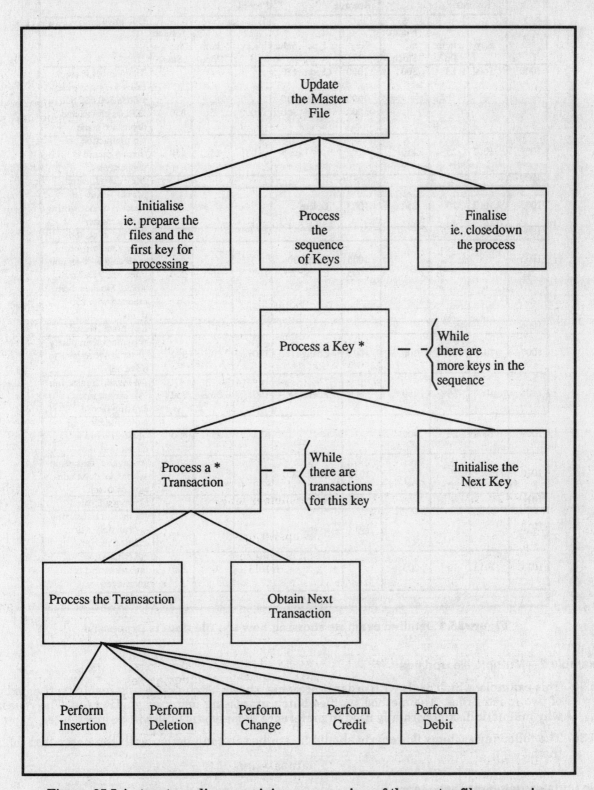

Figure 25.5 A structure diagram giving an overview of the master file processing

Key	Old Master File Records			Transaction File Records			New Master File Records			Comment
	Key	Item Price	Number in Stock	Key	Type	Value	Key	Item Price	Number in Stock	
1000	1000	15	300	1000	Credit	150				The number in stock takes the successive values 300 450 650 350, as credits and debits are made
				1000	Credit	200				
				1000	Debit	300	1000	15	350	
1001	1001	25	450				1001	25	450	No transaction, so master record is unchanged
1002										Key not allocated
1003	1003	20	250	1003	Delete					Master record is deleted by not writing to new master
1004										Key not allocated
1005				1005	Insert	30				A new master record is created with an item price of 30 and zero stock. Stock is then credited with 250 items
				1005	Credit	250	1005	30	250	
1006										Key not allocated
1007	1007	15	300	1007	Change	20	1007	20	300	Assume for simplicity that change applies to price only
1008	1008	30	350	1008	Insert	35	1008	30	350	An invalid transaction --- cannot insert existing record
1009	1009	25	400				1009	25	400	No transaction, so master record is unchanged
1010				1010	Debit	200				An invalid transaction --- cannot debit non-existent stock
1011										Key not allocated
1012				1012	Delete					An invalid transaction --- can only delete existing record
1013	1013	30	200				1013	30	200	No transaction, so master record is unchanged
............etc............										And so on ....

Figure 25.6 Detailed example showing how the file data is processed

Example 2 – Multiple file updates

25.35   This example, which deals with order processing, shows batch processing involving the update of two master files. The method typifies batch processing using magnetic tape. The reasons why magnetic disk is normally used in preference to magnetic tape will be given later.

25.36   The following systems flowcharts should be studied in conjunction with the notes that follow them.

File updates using magnetic tape

25.37   This chart illustrates the computer runs necessary to update the stock and customer files and to produce invoices. Orders are entered at a terminal and the stock file (held in stock-number sequence) and customer file (held in customer-number sequence) are stored on magnetic tape.

Magnetic tape

25.38 Having just considered an example in which magnetic tape was shown in use for file processing, this is an appropriate point for us to discuss the advantages and limitations of tape as a storage medium.

25.39 **Advantage of tape.**

a. It is relatively cheap, (e.g. approx. £10 per reel vs approx. £250 per disk pack).

b. It has high capacity, enabling it to store the largest files.

c. The data transfer speed is fairly high.

d. It requires no complicated systems software for its operation.

e. Industrial standards govern the way data is normally recorded on tape. This ensures compatibility between different computers and therefore allows bulk off-line data transfers between systems.

```
BEGIN    (* Main Program *)
    (* Initialisation *)
    Open_files
    Read_old_master_file
    Read_transaction_file
    The_key_to_process  :=   Min(Old_master _key,
Transaction_key)
    (* ie, The smaller of the two is assigned to
The_key_to_be_processed *)
    Initialise_the_key_to_process
        WHILE
            The_key _to _be _processed  <> Sentinel)
            (* ie, While there is a key to process *)
        DO
        WHILE
            Transaction_Key  =  The_key_to_process
            (* ie, While there is a transaction for
this key *)
        DO
            Process_the_transaction
            Read_transaction_file
        ENDWHILE
        IF
            Key_is _allocated
        THEN
            Write_new_master_record
        ENDIF
        The_key_to_process := Min(Old_master_key,
Transaction_key)
            Intialise_the_key_to_process
        ENDWHILE
    Close_files
END
```

Figure 25.6a

25.40 **Limitations of tape**.

a. The major limitation of tape lies in the fact that it is a serial non-addressable medium and many of the other limitations spring from this.

b. As tape is a serial medium all transaction files must be in the sequence of the appropriate master file. This involves a great deal of unproductive time spent in sorting and re-sorting input data.

c. Updating a master tape file involves reading and writing the complete file however small the transaction file may be. Notice that when the batches are very small (i.e. the hit rate

(20.18) is low) this will involve a high proportion of *redundant processing* (i.e. the reading and writing of the inactive records).

d. Because tape is a non-addressable medium a particular record cannot be accessed directly. Information required from a particular record is *not available* until the whole batch has been processed.

e. Several runs are required to produce output and this may result in some files not reflecting a *true up-to-date position* at a given moment (figure 25.11 Note 5).

```
(* Details of procedures given im Fig. 25.6a *)
PROCEDURE (Read_old _master _file)
    (*
    This procedure reads the next record from the master
    file.  If the end of file has been reached then this
    procedure will assign a "Sentinel" to the
    old master key.  A sentinel is a high value signifying
    the end of a sequence of numbers.  In this case the
    sentinel value of the key will be 9999.
    *)
PROCEDURE (Read_transaction _file)
    (*
    This procedure will be the same as "Read_old _master _file"
    except that it applies to the transaction file and its keys.
    *)
```

Figure 25.6b

```
PROCEDURE (Initialise_the_key_to_process)
BEGIN
    IF
        The_key_to_process <> Sentinel
    THEN
        IF
            The key_to_process  =  Old_master_key
        THEN
            Key_allocated := TRUE
            New_master_record := Old_master_record
            Read_old_master_record
        ELSE
            Key_allocated := FALSE
        ENDIF
    ENDIF
END
```

Figure 25.6c

```
PROCEDURE (Process_the_transaction)
(* NB. There are 5 types of transaction *)
BEGIN
CASE: Transaction_type
    INSERT:
        IF
            Key_allocated  =  FALSE
        THEN
            (* copy details from transaction to new master *)
             Key_allocated  :=  TRUE
        ELSE
            (* Print error - record already exists *)
        ENDIF
    DELETE:
        IF
            Key_allocated  =  TRUE
        THEN
            Key_allocated  :=   FALSE
            (* Write to deletion report *)
        ELSE
            (* Print error - record does not exist *)
        ENDIF
    CHANGE:
        IF
            Key_allocated =  TRUE
        THEN
            (* Make changes to new master *)
        ELSE
            (* Print error - record does not exist *)
        ENDIF
    CREDIT:
        IF
            Key_allocated  =  TRUE
        THEN
            (* Add transaction amount to  new master record value *)
        ELSE
            (* Print error - record does not exist *)
        ENDIF
    DEBIT:
        IF
            key_allocated  =  TRUE
        THEN
            (* Subtract transaction amount from new master record value *)
        ELSE
            (* Print error - record does not exist *)
        ENDIF
    ENDCASE
END
```

Figure 25.6d

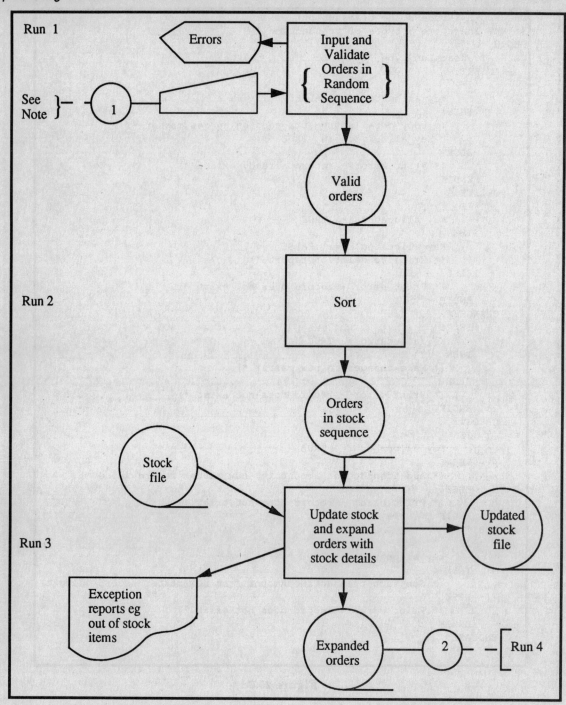

Note: Connector symbol 1 shows the link between this part of the systems flowchart and another part of the chart, which contains the clerical procedures involved in preparing the documents for input.

Figure 25.7

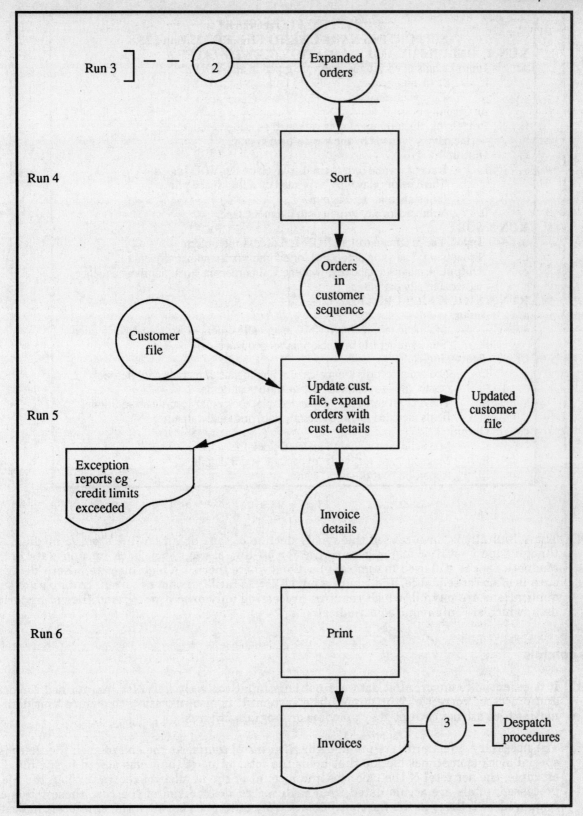

Figure 25.8

SYSTEM FLOWCHART
SUPPORTING NARATIVE TO FIGURES 25.7 and 25.8

RUN 1. DATA INPUT AND VALIDATION (KEY-TO-TAPE)

a.   **Input** Details of each transaction are typed in at a VDU:
      i.   Stock number
      ii.   Customer number
      iii. Quantity ordered.

b.   **Processing.** Each transaction is validated as it is entered,
      ie, the data is "vetted" by the key-to-tape system.

c.   **Output.**
      i.   Data of invalid orders are displayed on the VDU screen.
          These errors may also be printed on a low-speed printer
          (not shown in the diagram).
      ii.   Valid orders are written onto magnetic tape.

RUN 2. SORT

a.   **Input.** The magnetic reel at RUN 1. c.ii, ie, valid orders.

b.   **Processing.** The valid orders are sorted into stock-number sequence.

c.   **Output.** A magnetic tape reel with the valid orders in stock-number sequence,
      ie, sequentially organised.

RUN 3. STOCK FILE UPDATE

a.   **Input.**
      i.   Magnetic tape reel at RUN 2.c, ie, valid orders in stock-number sequence
      ii.   Stock master file in stock-number sequence.

b.   **Processing.**
      i.   The order records are matched with the master records and the stock
          master file is updated by the quantities of items.
      ii.   The order records are "expanded", ie, each order record has additional
          fields included for stock description, price and value

c.   **Output.**
      i.   Magnetic tape reel with updated stock file.
      ii.   Magnetic tape reel with "expanded" order details.
      iii.   Report on "out-of-stock" items.

Figure 25.9

25.41   These limitations have caused the steady decline of tape as an on-line storage medium, although tape is still of major importance for off-line storage, e.g. back-up and data entry. Magnetic tape is still used in some applications where there is a high hit-rate, where 'delay' as such is of no consequence, and where a direct-access facility is not required. Examples of such applications are payroll, which requires processing only once a week, and files of historical data, which are only required periodically.

File controls

25.42   It is essential to ensure that data are not only input correctly, but also maintained correctly and processed correctly right through the system. It is also necessary to ensure that data in master files are not corrupted by machine or program failures.

25.43   The necessary safeguards are provided by *file control totals*. At the end of each file there is a special block (sometimes blocks) that holds the total value of the items stored in the file. For example, the net total of the balances and a count of the number of records. When the file is processed, totals are accumulated from each record. At the end of the run, these totals are compared with those in the file control block. Any difference between the two totals indicates some error in processing or some corruption of data in the file.

RUN 4. SORT
a. **Input.** the magnetic tape reel at RUN 3. c.ii, ie, expanded order details.
b. **Processing.** The records are sorted from stock-number sequence into customer-number sequence.
c. **Output.** Magnetic tape reel with "expanded" orders in customer-number sequence.

RUN 5. CUSTOMER FILE UPDATE
a. **Input.**
   i. The magnetic tape reel at RUN 4. c.
   ii. Customer master file in customer-number sequence.
b. **Processing.**
   i. The order records are matched with the customer master records and the invoice amount calculated. The customer master records are updated by the value of the invoices.
   ii. Name and address details are extracted from master records.
c. **Output.**
   i.   Magnetic tape reel with updated customer file.
   ii. Manetic tape reel with invoice details.
   iii. Reports on credit limits being exceeded, etc.

RUN 6. PRINT OUTPUT
a. **Input.** The magnetic tape reel at RUN 5. c.ii, ie, invoice details.
b. **Processing.** the invoices are printed.
c. **Output.** Printed invoices on the line printer.

Notes:
1. The use of tape as the storage medium requires that each transaction file and appropriate master must be in the same sequence in order to carry out processing.
2. Consequently there is need for much sorting and re-sorting of the transaction file.
3. Two updating runs were required (ie, updating the stock file and the customer file) and a sort was necessary before each.
4. Not all the information required could be obtained in one RUN and thus 6 separate runs were necessary to produce the final output.
5. a. If an order is found to be unacceptable on Run 5 (for reasons of "credit" for instance) then the stock file shows a false position. The order will have been recorded during Run 3, thus reducing the balance of the particular produce. Notice that all subsequent orders for that product on Run 4 will be processed in the light of the stock having been depleted by the amount involved; a situation which in fact does not exist as Run 5 shows.
   b. The stock file is "put right" on the next run by means of a "receipt" transaction (ie, an adjustment voucher).

Figure 25.10

25.44 File-control totals are derived from batch totals, and the following paragraphs explain how this is done.

a. **Transaction files.** When batch totals have been reconciled, data are written onto a magnetic file for further processing. By adding all the correct batch totals for the run, a control for the transaction file is obtained. This total is used to ensure that the transaction file is correctly processed during subsequent runs, and that all transactions are processed when the master file is updated.

b. **Master file.** When the master file is updated from the transaction file, the processing of the transaction file is controlled as described above. The control totals in the master file are then adjusted by the amount of the transactions that have been inserted into it. Subsequent runs of the master file are reconciled to the control total.

c. **Clerical control.** It is possible to maintain an independent control on computer processing. Records are kept of the batch totals and are added to provide a run total, i.e. the total value of transactions passed to the DP department for processing. When the computer outputs are received the control totals printed by the machine can be reconciled to the original batch figures. Adjustments have to be made, of course, for individual items rejected by the computer because they fail validity checks.

Example – purchase invoice processing system

25.45 The operation of these controls is illustrated by the example that follows (figure 25.15) of a Purchase Invoice Processing System. Note that the system has been simplified for the sake of clarity. On the left, a system flowchart shows the main processing stages. On the right, the controls imposed at each stage are explained.

Summary

25.46   a. The factors affecting choice of file-processing method were discussed:
- i. Size.
- ii. Reference and enquiry.
- iii. Hit rate
- iv. Security and back-up.

  b. File-handling techniques applicable to sequential files were discussed.

  c. Sequencing and sorting are common techniques required to get transaction tapes in the sequence of the master file.

  d. Choice of sorting methods affected by:
- i. File size – whether or not two stages are necessary.
- ii. Main store size – whether or not two stages are necessary.
- iii. Degree of pre-ordering – the bubble sort is quicker.
- iv. Record size – whether the whole record or just the key is moved.
- v. For final sequencing a serial check is sufficient.

  e. Batch processing was explained.

  f. A detailed example of the updating of a sequential master file was given.

  g. Multiple file updates were explained by example.

  h. The advantages and limitations of tape as a file-processing medium were explained.

Points to note

25.47   a. Internal sorting is sometimes called **in-core sorting**, a term left over from the days when main storage was made from cores, a now obsolete form of storage.

  b. We say that the records are **sorted** but the file is sequenced.

  c. The example of file updating and maintenance shows a common method of combining maintenance with updating, thereby saving a separate run with low hit rate.

  d. Tape is no longer an important on-line storage medium because it is a serial access medium.

  e. Tape is very important as a low-cost, high-volume, off-line storage medium.

SYSTEM FLOWCHART

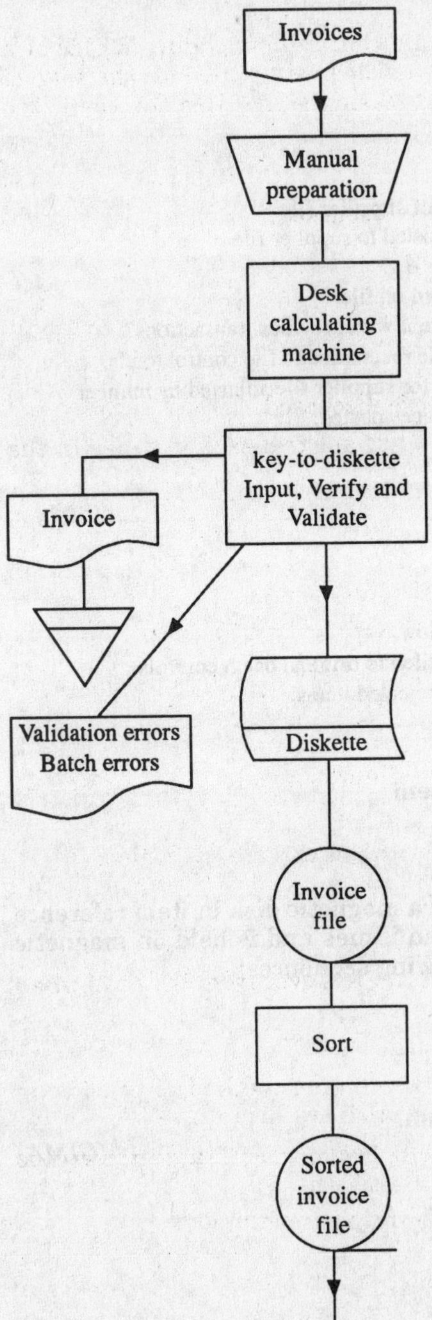

PROCESSING AND CONTROLLING STAGES

Receipts
Invoices received from suppliers

Manual preparation
1. Supplier number verified by reference to supplier file.
2. Invoice checked against purchase order and goods received note.
3. Invoice scrutinised for legibility.
4. Invoices arranged in batches.
5. Batch cover note attached and numbered.

Desk calculating machine
1. Invoice calculations checked (quantity x price, discount).
2. Batch total obtained for
   (a) number of invoices   (b) value of invoices.

Input and verification
1. Key in
   (a) invoice details   (b) batch totals
2. Data verified.
3. Errors corrected.

Validation
1. Validation checks e.g.
   (a) all fields keyed in correctly
   (b) supplier number (check digit)
   (c) invoice value reasonable
2. Batch control totals reconciled.
3. Valid data copied onto magnetic tape (invoice file).
4. Invalid data reported (subsequent reprocessing and re-input not shown).
5. Batch control totals accumulated to provide file control total.

Sort
1. Invoice details sorted to supplier sequence (sorted invoice file).
2. File control total copied onto new file.

Flowchart (left column, top to bottom):

- Invoices
- Manual preparation
- Desk calculating machine
- key-to-diskette Input, Verify and Validate
  - Invoice
  - Validation errors Batch errors
- Diskette
- Invoice file
- Sort
- Sorted invoice file
- (2)

continued...

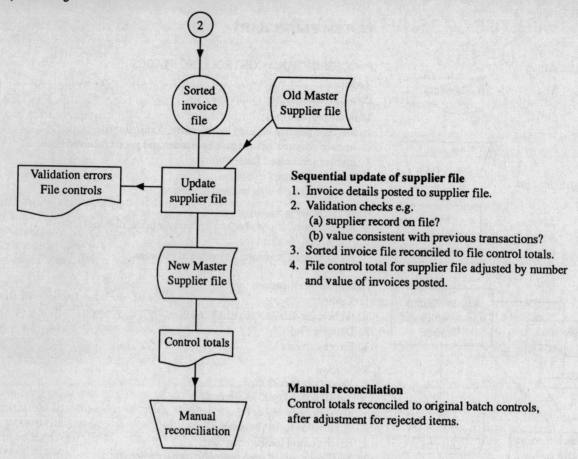

Sequential update of supplier file
1. Invoice details posted to supplier file.
2. Validation checks e.g.
   (a) supplier record on file?
   (b) value consistent with previous transactions?
3. Sorted invoice file reconciled to file control totals.
4. File control total for supplier file adjusted by number and value of invoices posted.

Manual reconciliation
Control totals reconciled to original batch controls, after adjustment for rejected items.

Figure 25.11 Purchase invoice system

Questions

1. Draw a program flowchart to update a stock master file held on a magnetic disk in item reference order. The input to update the master file includes receipts and issues and is held on magnetic tape which has been sorted by a previous program into the following sequences:

   Item reference:

   Receipts:

   Issues. quotation

   The control totals are the only items to be printed by this program.

   (CIMA)

26 File processing II

Introduction

26.1　The previous chapter introduced file processing by the use of examples that explained the basic methods of sequential file processing used with disk or magnetic tape. In this chapter we will see how the advantages of disk over magnetic tape make it possible to use disk for a wide variety of file-processing activities, including more sophisticated forms of batch processing. Several examples are used to illustrate the points that are made.

Magnetic disk

26.2　Disk is a direct-access storage medium and therefore overcomes the major limitation of tape. This gives it a very real advantage over tape in this respect. Disk does require the use of systems software, although this is not a serious problem with the current range of computers. It has a higher data transfer speed than most models of tape and effectively has a greater storage capacity. The cost of disk is much higher than that of tape but it is a cost users seem willing to pay for the benefits of its use.

26.3　Not all the limitations of tape are overcome by the use of disk. However, the facility of direct access helps to solve some of the problems and help to alleviate others. We will now reconsider the limitations of tape in the same order as previously outlined (22.43) and see how the use of disk helps overcome them.

　　a.　The question of access has been covered already and disk does overcome this limitation completely.

　　b.　Despite the fact that disk provides a direct-access facility it is often expedient to sort a transaction file into the sequence of the master file. For example an Indexed Sequential File processed Selective Sequentially makes use of direct-access while not involving the access mechanism in back-tracking, provided no other use is made of the disk by the other users while the file is being processed. If the same file were processed in a random manner (i.e. using an unsorted transaction file) a great deal more time would be spent by the access mechanism in moving to and fro across the face of the disk. The first method involves sorting time and seek time, the second involves no sorting but considerably more seek time. Individual circumstances will indicate the method to be used.

　　c.　If a very large file with a low hit rate is stored on disk then the direct-access capability makes it possible to access *only* those records requiring updating, thus eliminating the redundant processing that occurs with tape.

　　d.　Requests for information can be answered quickly. **File Enquiry** (as it is called) is accomplished by linking a terminal or workstation to the processor. A request for information can be answered by displaying the contents of a particular record on the screen. This could be done while the enquirer (a customer) is waiting at the other end of a telephone. Notice that by using a multiprogrammed computer (i.e. one that runs more than one program at a time), file enquiries can be answered during the running of another program, e.g. an updating program. (An example will be given later.)

　　e.　In the example in Figure 26.1 the use of disk storage solves the problem of a file not reflecting a true situation. The stock file is stored on disk and access is made to it at the same time as the customer file. Thus the two runs are combined and all the data required is available at *the same time*. The underlying principle is important because it represents a significant advance on tape processing.

　　　　Notice that the 'delay' problem is *still* present, because it is inherent in the batch-processing system itself.

26.4　Most small systems use either floppy disks or small hard disks and can exploit the direct-access capabilities of disks. However, few small systems can provide simultaneous file access by multiple programs as just described in d. although it is becoming more common on newer 16-bit or 32-bit microcomputers such as the Archimedes and those running the operating systems Unix or OS/2.

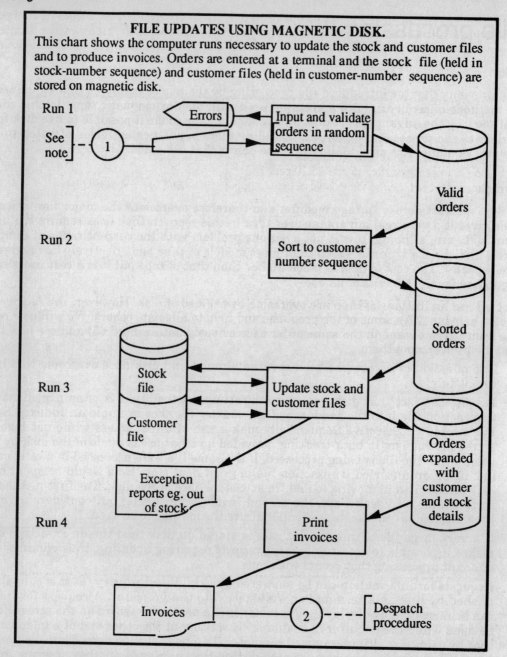

FILE UPDATES USING MAGNETIC DISK.

This chart shows the computer runs necessary to update the stock and customer files and to produce invoices. Orders are entered at a terminal and the stock file (held in stock-number sequence) and customer files (held in customer-number sequence) are stored on magnetic disk.

Run 1 — See note ① — Errors — Input and validate orders in random sequence — Valid orders

Run 2 — Sort to customer number sequence — Sorted orders

Run 3 — Stock file / Customer file — Update stock and customer files — Exception reports eg. out of stock — Orders expanded with customer and stock details

Run 4 — Print invoices — Invoices — ② Despatch procedures

Figure 26.1

Processing applications using disk storage

26.5 a. **File enquiry.** This has been mentioned already. The information required must be stored on a DAS medium. Random access would be necessary in this particular application in order to be able to deal with any enquiry as it arose.

b. **Random access.** Building societies and insurance companies have extremely large files with a very low hit rate. Random access is used in view of the small size of batches, thus saving the vast amount of redundant processing of inactive records which would be required with tape. Such files stored on tape can take some six hours to process completely, which will give you an idea of the problem.

c. **Simultaneous processing** of files. A customer file and stock file can be processed together provided the stock file is on a DAS medium.

26.6 So far we have considered the concept of batch processing purely in terms of computer processing and have seen how the use of disk storage can overcome many of the limitations of tape. We now want to extend our considerations to include the link with data collection so that we can see a more complete picture.

SYSTEMS FLOWCHART DISK PROCESSING - SUPPORTING NARRATIVE.

RUN 1 - DATA VALIDATION.
a. **Input.** See Figure 25.10 para 1a.
b. **Processing.** See Figure 25.10 para 1b.
c. **Output.** Onto disk instead of tape, otherwise the same as shown in figure 25.10.

RUN 2 - SORT.
a. **Input.** The magnetic disk used for output in Run 1.
b. **Processing.** Sorting of valid orders into customer-number sequence.
c. **Output.** Onto disk.

RUN 3 - UPDATE OF STOCK AND CUSTOMER FILES.
a. **Input.** The magnetic disk used for output in Run 2.
b. **Processing.** Access to the customer file is by the selective sequential values are calculated.
c. **Output.** magnetic disk with details of invoices and exception reports.

RUN 4 - PRINT OUTPUT.
a. **Input.** Invoice details.
b. **Processing.** Invoices are printed.
c. **Output.** Printed invoices on the lineprinter.

Notes:
1. Using disk as the storage medium it is not *essential* to sort each transaction file into the sequence of the master file.
2. Consequently, Run 3 combines updating of customer file (where transactions *are* in the sequence of the master file) with updating the stock files (where the transactions are *not* in the sequence of the master file).
3. Because of this, fewer runs are required than with magnetic tape, and the files show a *true* position.

Figure 26.2

Link with data collection

26.7 For many years the delay spoken of earlier in terms of batch processing was *aggravated* by the time it took for data to pass through all the stages of data collection prior to processing. Newer methods of data-collection have helped to reduce data collection times. The change to key-to-disk eliminated media conversion. The use of OCR/MICR eliminated the transcription process.

26.8 Although these methods of data collection add delay to the time cycle of the system, nevertheless this time lag is perfectly acceptable to many users, which is why this form of DP is still widely used.

On-line processing

26.9 The methods just discussed tend to involve some physical transportation of data or *manual intervention* in the data-collection process. The data source itself can be linked directly to the computer, in which case there is no manual intervention and the whole process is automatic. This 'on-line data entry' may take place by means of data transmission equipment or as part of a distributed system. By one means or another data arrives at the main computer where the processing is to take place.

26.10 On receipt at the main computer, the data (which may be coming from hundreds of remote terminals, is at once stored on disk and after a suitable interval sorted and then processed (involving data validation, updating and production of output). Notice that in essence all we have done is to dramatically speed up the process of data collection. The batch-processing concept *still* applies.

MULTI-USER SIMULTANEOUS FILE PROCESSING.

This chart shows the simultaneous processing of two files and file enquiry in a multi-user, multi-programming system.

1. It is a multiprogramming system because more than one program is running. In this example one program is the update program (as in Figure 26.1 run 3), another is the file enquiry program.

2. The stock file and customer file are each being processed by both programs so simultaneous file processing is taking place.

NB. Careful controls on file access are necessary in order to deal with situations where two different programs try to access the same record at the same time. One method, called **record locking**, enables the first program accessing the record to prevent access by the other programs until it has completed processing the records.

3. This requires direct access storage and a file organisation method that supports random access.

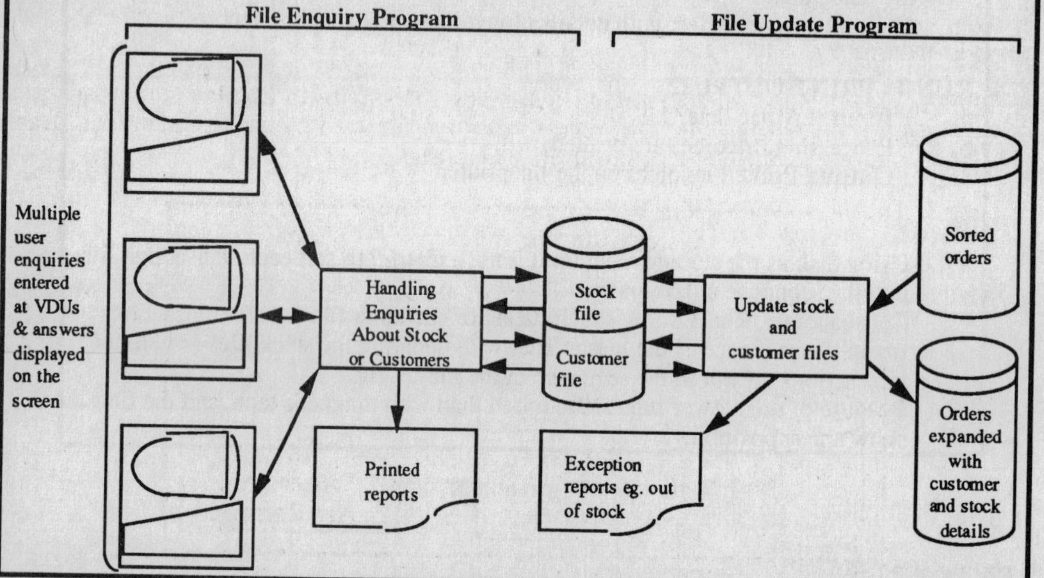

Figure 26.3

26.11 The advantage of 'on-line' processing is that data is less out of date on arrival in the computer. As a result, files reflect a much more up-to-date, more *real*, picture of a particular set of circumstances. Furthermore, the results of processing are available more quickly as they can be fed back to the same terminal if need be. Additionally the remote terminal can also be used for enquiries that arise at the source.

26.12 The major clearing banks have an on-line system of processing coupled with file enquiry.

26.13 It should be realised that on-line systems of batch processing are much more costly than the conventional method involving transporting the data by post. However the advantages lie in the time saved and the availability of more up-to-date information.

Transaction processing

26.14 We have just seen how the time lag in batch-processing systems can be reduced by the use of various data collection techniques and more especially by the use of the techniques of on-line processing (coupled with the use of DAS). Most businesses *do not* require their files of data to be right 'up to date' at all times and gear their activities to a time cycle that is acceptable.

26.15 There are situations, however, that require any data that arise to be immediately processed and the relevant file updated because any action taken must be based on the true current circumstances. Such a processing system is said to be working in **real time**. Real-time processing is the processing of data so quickly that the results are available to influence the activity currently taking place. Decisions are continually being made on the very latest information available because files are kept permanently up to date.

26.16 You could say that a single transaction becomes the batch, which is processed *on demand*. Thus the process of input, validation, updating and output must be gone through just as with batch processing, but for *each* transaction as and when it occurs. This real-time processing of individual transactions is known as **'Transaction Processing'**.

26.17 Transaction processing is just one kind of real-time processing. Other kinds of real-time processing are those concerned with the control of physical systems such as chemical plants or power stations.

26.18 Further details of transaction processing and its applications will be given in later chapters.

A simple practical example

26.19 The following examples shows random access to a disk file to display and view **or** display, view and update records singly. Old records are overwritten by updated records. Each record is identified by its key, which is keyed in at a terminal.

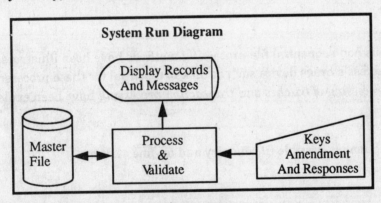

Figure 26.4

26.20 The following pseudocode outlines how the main processing is performed. Assume that:

a. The file has been opened for random input and output.

b. 'Key' is an integer, reply and response are strings, record-valid is Boolean and master record is a record containing a key.

c. The function key-allocated returns true when its argument has a record with that value in the file.

d. The procedure get has key as an IN parameter and master-record as an OUT parameter. It reads and returns the master record with the specified key from the file.

e. The procedure **put** has **key** and **master record** as IN parameters. It writes the master record to the appropriate position on the disk.

```
Repeat
    (* get a key value from the program user *)
    output ("which key?")
    input (key)
    if
        key_allocated(key)
    then
        call get(key, master_record)
        Output (master_record)
        Output ("Any changes? (yes or no")
        input (reply)
        if
            reply = "yes"
        then
            repeat
                (* input record amendments *)
                (* validate amendments *)
                (* display error messages where necessary *)
            until record_valid
            call put(key, master_record)
        endif
    else
        Output ("there is no record with this key")
    endif
    Output ("Any more records? (yes or no)")
input (response)
until response < > "yes"
```

Summary

26.21 a. The various non-sequential file-processing methods have been illustrated by example.

b. A direct-access storage device such as disk is essential for these processing methods.

c. *On-line processing of batches and transaction processing* have been explained.

Point to note

26.22 Note how DAS makes possible file enquiry and on-line systems.

Questions

1. a. Draw a system flowchart showing the **main** programs which would typically be required in a computer-based stock control system.

b. Give, and briefly explain:

i. Five examples of transaction or amendment data which would normally be input into such a system.

ii. **Five** examples of the kind of reports you would expect the system to produce, also indicating their frequency.

(ACA)

2. a. Explain the following terms as they relate to the organisation and processing of files held on magnetic disks:

i. cylinder,

ii. overflow.

b. What advantages do disks have over magnetic tapes as file storage media?

(ACA)

Database systems

1. This part introduces databases, how they are organised and the languages used to access them.

2. Chapter 27 concentrates on database architecture and related matters.

3. Chapter 28 concentrates on database query languages and related products called 4GLs.

27 Database architecture

Introduction

27.1 When organisations first began to use computers, they naturally adopted a piece-meal approach. One system at a time was studied, re-designed and transferred to the computer. This approach was necessitated by the difficulties experienced in using a new and powerful management tool. It had the drawback, however, of producing a number of separate systems, each with its own program suite, its own files, and its own inputs and outputs. The main criticisms of this approach are that:

a. The computer-based systems, being self-contained, do not represent the way in which the organisation really works, i.e. as a complex set of interlocking and interdependent systems.

b. Systems communicate with each other outside the computer. This proliferates inputs and outputs and creates delays. For example, input of a customer order to an order processing system might create an output of an invoice. This in turn would have to be converted back into input for activating the sales accounting system. Similarly, if the order reduced stock levels to the re-order level (i.e. the level at which they must be re-ordered so that ordered stock arrives before existing stock runs out) another output would be created, which would then have to be input to the production control and/or the purchasing system.

c. Information obtained from a series of separate files is less valuable because it does not give the complete picture. For example, the sales manager reviewing outstanding orders from customers has to get information about stocks from another file.

d. Data may be duplicated in two or more files, creating unnecessary maintenance and the risk of inconsistency.

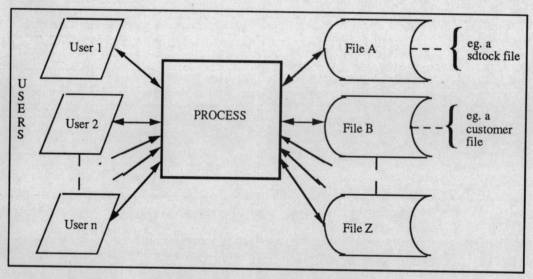

Figure 27.1 An integrated file system

Integrated file systems

27.2 Integrated file systems represent an approach to solving the problems just described by conventional means. In an integrated file system the data is pooled into a set of inter-locking and interdependent files, which are accessible by a number of different users.

27.3 When a transaction enters an integrated file system *all* the appropriate files are updated. The features of an integrated system are shown in figure 27.1.

27.4 A large number of integrated file systems are in use today. Many of them have been tailor-made to meet the requirements of particular organisations.

27.5 Integrated file systems do not provide a satisfactory answer to all the criticisms mentioned in paragraph 27.1, however. They tend to suffer from the problems caused by *data duplication* (27.1d) and from the fact that the task of maintaining the data is shared between the programs that access and maintain the data and therefore lacks proper central control.

Note. The idea of integrating the *processing functions* will be returned to later in this chapter.

Databases

27.6 Databases represent a radically different approach to solving the problems discussed so far in this chapter.

27.7 **Database definition.** A database is a single organised collection of structured data, stored with a minimum of duplication of data items so as to provide a consistent and controlled pool of data. This data is common to all users of the system, but is independent of programs that use the data.

27.8 The independence of the database and programs using it means that one can be changed without changing the other.

27.9 The users of a database may find it convenient to imagine that they are using an integrated file system like the one shown in figure 27.1. In reality the database is organised as in figure 27.2. A more detailed description of the organisation is given later in this chapter.

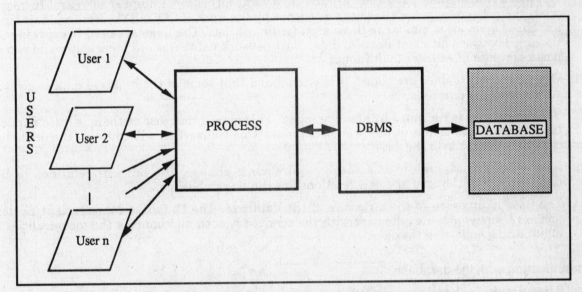

Figure 27.2 An outline view of a database system

27.10 Databases are normally set up in order to meet the information needs of major parts of an organisation. Although the long term goal may be to end up with a single database it is very common for an organisation to set a series of separate databases in the first instance because of the time, risks and costs involved in doing the whole job in one go.

27.11 It is not possible to construct a database in one single operation, it is usually built up section by section. During this process it is possible to:

   a. add new 'files' of data.

   b. add new fields to records already present in the base,

   c. create relationships between the items of data.

27.12 A database requires to be stored on large-capacity direct-access devices. The usual medium is the magnetic disk. For security purposes a copy of the database may be held on magnetic tape or disk.

27.13 It is often *wrongly stated* that there is no duplication of data in a database. Data may be duplicated, but it is important to realise the duplications are minimised and controlled. This is referred to as **'controlled redundancy'**.

27.14 Although, to the user, the database may appear as a collection of files, data in the database is organised in a more complex way than data in conventional files.

27.15 Databases may be classified according to the approaches taken to database organisation. The classes are:

a. Relational.

b. Network.

c. Hierarchical.

d. File inversions.

The last two are more basic, have a number of practical limitations, and do not merit further discussion here.

27.16 **Relational** databases use types of tables called **relations.** The terminology is initially confusing because of the use of the name 'relation' for a table and because relations are not the same as relationships. However, relational databases were developed from mathematically sound ideas, have an elegant simplicity and are likely to be increasingly important in the future. They are already the most common type of database to be found on minicomputer systems, and simplified versions of them are well established as the most common type on PCs. Leading independent suppliers include INGRES, ORACLE, INFORMIX and SYBASE. IBM's main relational database, which runs on its mainframes, is DB2.

27.17 **Network databases** have been around in several forms for a number of years. In recent years the network approach has been developed by the work of CODASYL. Network databases are based upon ideas similar to those used for linked lists. The links are used to express relationships between different items of data. Most network databases are proprietary and run on particular manufacturer's mainframes.

27.18 When new sets of data are added, it is often found that some of the required data is already stored for other purposes.

27.19 The database is maintained by a 'single input'. This means that just as there is little duplication of data, there is also no duplication of inputs. One transaction will cause all the necessary changes to be made to the data.

27.20 As the base is expanded, or as user requirements change, the links or relations in the database can be changed and new relationships can be established.

27.21 The user is unaware of the structure of the database. The Database Management System (details shortly) provides the user with the services needed and handles the technicalities of maintaining and using the data.

Communicating with the database

27.22 Some databases have their own computer languages associated with them which allow the user to access and retrieve data at a terminal. Other databases are only accessible via languages such as C, COBOL, Pascal, BASIC, Ada or FORTRAN, to which extra facilities have been added for this purpose.

27.23 Data descriptions must be standardised. For this reason, a **Data Description Language (DDL)** is provided, which *must* be used to specify the data in the base. Similarly, a **Data Manipulation Language (DML)** is provided, which must be used to access the data. The function of these two languages may be compared to the declarations and processing statement in a conventional programming language. As indicated by the previous paragraph DDLs and DMLs may be either free-standing or embedded in another language. The combination of a DDL and a DDL is often referred to as a **Data Sublanguage DSL.** Probably the most common DSL in use today is **SQL (Structured Query Language).** SQL will be discussed in the next chapter.

The database management system (DBMS)

27.24 The database management system is a *complex software system* that constructs, expands and maintains the database. It also provides the controlled interface between the user and the data in the base.

27.25 The DBMS allocates storage to data. It maintains indices so that any required data can be retrieved, and so that separate items of data in the base can be cross-referenced. As mentioned above, the structure of a database is dynamic and can be changed as needed. In what follows for the sake of generality and simplicity operations are described in terms of records and files. However, the reader should note that the actual structure and organisation of the data is not merely in the form of simple files but in terms of such things as rows, tables or nodes according to the database's type (e.g. Relational or Network).

27.26 The DBMS maintains the data in the base by:

a. adding new records,

b. deleting 'dead' records,

c. amending records.

In addition to these functions (which are performed by any file-maintenance program) it can expand the database by adding new sets of records or new data to existing records.

27.27 The DBMS provides an interface with user programs. These may be written in a number of different programming languages. However, the programmer need not be familiar with the structure of the database because the data his or her program requires is retrieved by the DBMS.

27.28 The DBMS provides facilities for different types of file processing. It can:

a. Process a complete file (serially or sequentially),

b. Process required records (selective, sequential or random).

c. Retrieve individual records.

It can also, as has been explained above, retrieve related records or related data within records.

27.29 The DBMS also has the function of providing security for the data in the database. The main aspects of this are:

a. Protecting data against unauthorised access.

b. Safeguarding data against corruption.

c. Providing recovery and restart facilities after a hardware or software failure.

The DBMS keeps statistics of the use made of the data in the database. This allows redundant data to be removed. It also allows data that is frequently used to be kept in a readily accessible form so that time is saved.

27.30 **Data dictionary.** The DBMS makes use of descriptions of data items provided by the DDL. This 'data about data' is called a **data dictionary.** Often the data dictionary is actually implemented as an additional database accessed by the DBMS.

27.31 Clearly, something so complex as a DBMS needs to be organised in a logical way. This logical organisation is achieved by having a number of distinct levels within the DBMS. At the top level, data is expressed in a form compatible with the view of individual users, (as applications files, say). At the middle level the data is expressed in global terms applicable to all applications. At the bottom level the data is expressed in forms that relate to the way the data is actually stored. The DBMS transforms data as it moves it from level to level.

Database system architecture

27.32 The growing importance of database systems in most office environments merits a more detailed discussion of how a modern database system is organised.

27.33 Figure 27.3 shows the organisation of a modern database system. The client application programs run by users are able to connect to a DBMS server. The DBMS server is normally a special program which is able to accept multiple connections from many client programs at the same time. It is therefore said to be **multi-threaded**.

27.34 The client program sends a request to the DBMS server using a DSL such as SQL. SQL will be used in this example but the ideas are completely general. The DBMS server treats the SQL statement as a request which it must translate and act upon. The client may request data to be defined, inserted, updated, deleted or retrieved depending upon the SQL statements issued to the server.

27.35 Once the DBMS server has translated the SQL statement it retrieves data from the database into a **Data Cache** where it can be access and manipulated more quickly and easily. The data will also be more readily available to any other client once it is in cache but the DBMS server has to manage any such multiple accesses to the data so that client programs do not interfere with each other's data.

27.36 A well know problem which has to be avoided is the **lost update** which occurs if two separate clients are allowed to update the same data value at the same time. Suppose that two clients 'A' and 'B' each wish to update an account balance by 100 and that the initial value of the account is 500. Suppose they follow the following sequence:

a. 'A' take a copy of the balance of 500.

b. 'B' takes a copy of the balance of 500.

c. 'A' adds 100 to its copy of the balance and replaces the balance with 600.

d. 'B' adds 100 to its copy of the balance and replaces the balance with 600.

e. the final balance is 600 *but it should be 700!*.

27.37 The DBMS server prevents this kind of problem from happening. The most common way is for it to use **locks**. When a lock is taken on data by a client it restricts what other clients may do. An alternative arrangement to the one above is as follows.

a. 'A' requests a **write lock** on the data which is granted by the DBMS.

b. 'B' requests a **write lock** on the data which is denied by the DBMS so 'B' must wait.

c. 'A' takes a copy of the balance of 500.

d. 'A' adds 100 to its copy of the balance and replaces the balance with 600.

e. 'A' releases its lock so the DBMS now grants 'B' the lock it requested.

f. 'B' takes a copy of the balance of 600.

g. 'B' adds 100 to its copy of the balance and replaces the balance with 700.

h. 'B' releases its lock.

i. the final balance is 700.

27.38 In the example given above a **write lock** was mention. A write lock is held by a single client to have exclusive access to data while it is being updated. An alternative kind of lock is the **read lock** that may be held by many clients wanting to read the same data. The clients share access to the date but by holding read locks they prevent any other client from taking a write lock and changing the data while they are using it. Now back to the processing of the SQL statement.

27.39 When data has been updated in cache it must be written back to the database. The changes may also be recorded in a log file from where they may copied into journal files. The reasons for this are to enable data to be recovered if the system should fail for any reason such as power failure. There is also the need to cover the bad case of a database being lost because of a 'disk crash'.

27.40 The **checkpoints** shown in figure 27.3 are 'snapshots' of the database before it was updated by clients and the **journal** hold details of the updates subsequently made. In the event of failure the **recovery process** can rebuild the database.

27.41 In subsequent diagrams the logging and recovery details are omitted for the sake of clarity.

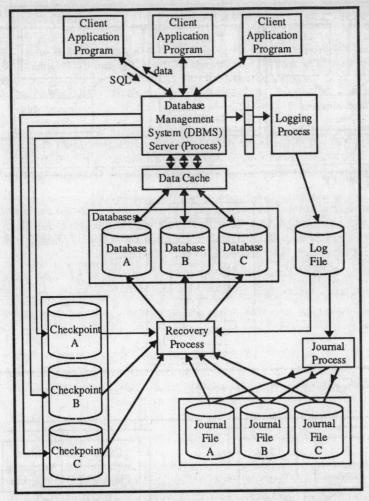

Figure 27.3. The organisation of a database system.

27.42 Figure 27.3 shows a database system as it might be set up on a single machine such as a minicomputer or mainframe. It is also very common to set up database system to operate in client-server mode on a network. Figure 27.4 shows such an arrangement. There are three workstations acting as clients and there is one server machine, a minicomputer say. The **communications process** enable the clients and server to communicate with one another just as if they were on the same machine. Such an arrangement is not only very flexible it also makes very good use of processing resources because the load is spread between clients and their server in a cost effective way.

27.43 Figure 27.5 shows a further more advanced arrangement where the clients are accessing a **distributed database**. There are two databases, A and B, on different machines each accessible by their own DBMS servers. However, the clients have **distributed database servers** which enables them to access both 'A' and 'B' at the same times as if they were a single database. The combined database is said to be distributed.

The database administrator (DBA)

27.44 The importance of a database is such that a special manager is often appointed, sometimes with a staff. His or her functions are described below. The DBA must have a sound knowledge of the structure of the database and of the DBMS. The DBA must also be thoroughly conversant with the organisation, its systems, and the information needs of the managers.

27.45 The DBA is responsible for ensuring that:

a. The data in the database meets the information needs of the organisation.

b. That the facilities for retrieving data and for structuring reports are appropriate to the needs of the organisation.

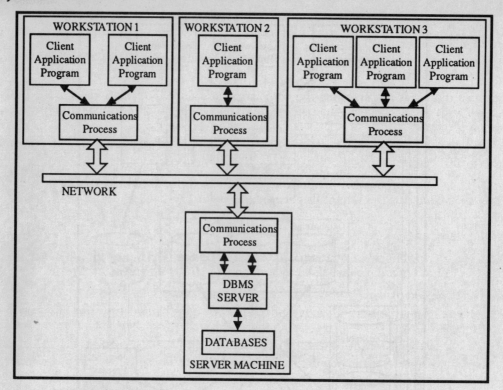

Figure 27.4 Client-server database access on a network

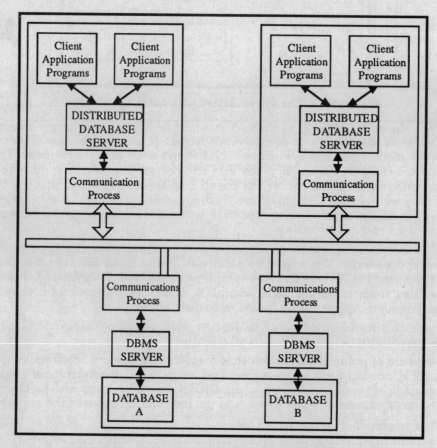

Figure 27.5 A distributed database system

27.46 The DBA is responsible for the following documentation:

    a. The data dictionary.

    b. Manuals for users describing the facilities the database offers and how to make use of these facilities.

27.47 Another function is to supervise the addition of new data. For this purpose, the DBA will have to liaise with the managers who use the data, and the systems analysts and programmers who develop the systems.

27.48 Security of the database is also the responsibility of the DBA and further, the requirements of privacy.

27.49 The DBA is also responsible for periodic appraisal of the data held in the base to ensure that it is complete, accurate and not duplicated.

Examples of a database

27.50 There are at present few organisations who have a really comprehensive database. An example is given here of a database used by a major computer manufacturer.

27.51 The database comprises:

    a. Records of customers who have purchased or who rented the manufacturer's computer equipment.

    b. Records of the different items of equipment, i.e. processors, peripherals and other devices.

    c. Records of spare parts showing the location where they are stored and the quantity held.

    d. Records of customer engineers responsible for maintenance and repairs.

27.52 The uses made of the database are too numerous to list completely, but a selection does give some idea of the facilities that a database can provide.

    a. **Accounting.** Customers are billed for maintenance and rental charges. Any change in configuration automatically causes the customer charges to be amended (the 'single input' principle).

    b. **Spares.** The database is used to control stocks of spares. It can also be used to find the location of a spare part nearest to the installation that requires it.

    c. **Modifications.** If a modification to a particular item of equipment is needed, all installations in which it is present can be quickly identified.

    d. **Engineering services.** The database shows which customers are served by which engineer (an example of the 'linking' or cross-referencing of records). Engineers can be allocated to cover absence or sickness or to assist at an installation that is in trouble. The records show which types of equipment the engineers are qualified to service.

Advantages of a database

27.53 The following are the advantages of a database:

    a. Information supplied to managers is more valuable because it is based on a comprehensive collection of data instead of files that contain only the data needed for one application.

    b. As well as routine reports, it is possible to obtain ad hoc reports to meet particular requirements.

    c. There is an obvious economic advantage in not duplicating data. In addition, errors due to discrepancies between two files are eliminated.

    d. The amount of input preparation needed is minimised by the 'single input' principle.

    e. A great deal of programming time is saved because the DBMS handles the construction and processing of files and the retrieval of data.

    f. The use of integrated systems is greatly facilitated.

Integrated systems

27.54 The database represents the integration of the data and information of an organisation. Associated with this concept is the integration of the systems that use the data. As has been seen, the development of separate systems increases the amount of external communication (inputs and outputs) between systems and is also likely to duplicate programming effort.

27.55 The concept is best illustrated by an example of three systems that are often integrated: order processing, sales accounting and stock control.

a. The basic input to the system is that of a customer order.

b. On input, the order is validated in the normal way. It is then

c. checked against the customer record to ensure that the credit position is satisfactory, and

d. checked against the stock file to ensure that the stock is available.

e. After the order has passed these checks, the files are updated. The stock level is reduced by the amount ordered. An invoice is generated, and the customer record is updated.

f. The documentation is distributed as necessary, e.g. the invoice is sent to the customer and the copies for despatch procedures sent to the warehouse.

g. If the supply of the order causes the stock level to fall below the re-order level, a report is printed indicating that replenishment of stock is necessary.

h. Subsequently, the monthly statement for the customer would be produced.

27.56 This example obviously represents only a small part of the total activities of the company. Possible future development would be:

a. In a manufacturing organisation, input of a customer order would generate the necessary works order. This would be the 'input' to the production-scheduling system, which would in turn generate the bill of materials.

b. The bill of materials would be 'input' to the stock-control system. The necessary stocks would be allocated. If purchases were necessary, an input to the purchasing system would be generated.

c. Subsequent receipt of the invoice from the supplier would cause another input to the purchase accounting system, resulting in checking of the invoice, notification of queries and eventual payment of the suppliers.

d. The production scheduling system would allocate the necessary machines and labour using and updating plant and personnel files.

e. At the due date, the production scheduling system would activate the production control system. Progress of the job through the factory would be controlled and actual inputs from the factory floor would be received to monitor progress.

On completion of the order, the documentation would be produced and the customer file updated with details of the invoice.

27.57 It will be realised of course that a number of new files would have to be added to the database to make this possible – resource files of plant and labour, supplier file, work in progress, etc. At the time of writing the above is somewhat *futuristic*, as very few organisations have constructed a *comprehensive* database and *fully* integrated their systems. A gradual approach, building up the database section by section and adding new systems one at a time is obviously desirable. There is really nothing difficult to understand in the concept; the approach is simply to move into the computer *all* the files, *all* the systems and *all* the communications between them, instead of using the computer for only the more straightforward work and linking the computer-based systems externally.

PC databases and file-management systems

27.58 A number of software products have appeared on the market in recent years that appear to offer *some* of the features of databases on even the smaller computers. These products, some of which claim to be 'database packages', are usually more correctly called 'file-management systems'.

27.59 Typical file-management systems usually have rudimentary DDLs and DMLs, which allow the user to set up and maintain a few files with a minimum of programming effort or skill. Facilities are often included that allow limited but extremely useful data retrieval functions such as sorting and selecting. A file-management system may therefore be thought of rather loosely as a 'computerised filing cabinet'.

27.60 Some of the more advanced and well established packages available on PCs may have started out as file management systems but have been developed into true database systems, almost always based on the relational database approach. In these packages the DBMSs are often quite simple because they seldom have to deal with large number of users. However, other features can be very advanced and sophisticated when it comes to such things as ease of use and ease of programming. Amongst the more advanced PC products are dBase, Paradox, FoxPro and Dataease.

27.61 When client-server computing is used the client application may run on a PC which is connected via a network to a server running on a minicomputer say. In this situation the PC client software is often supplied by the DBMS vendor, as is the case for INGRES and ORACLE.

TP monitors

27.62 **A Transaction Processing Monitor (TP Monitor)** is a specialist item of software which performs transactions for applications program's. Some TP monitors are sometimes used with conventional files but TP monitors are often used in conjunction with databases and the trend towards using TP monitors with DBMSs continues. TP Monitors, although specialised for particular instances of applications, normally conform to a basic standard in terms of how they receive and perform requests to execute transactions. A common standard for TP Monitors, established by IBM, is CICS.

27.63 One of a number of possible configurations is shown in figure 27.6. Applications 'A' and 'B' are using the database in a conventional way. They are connected directly to the DBMS server. They are passing SQL to the DBMS server and receiving results back. If a business transaction requires a series of SQL statements to be performed the application controls the necessary series of request to the server and the associated responses. Applications 'D' and 'E' are using the TP monitor. If they want a transaction to be performed they pass a request to the TP monitor. The TP monitor controls the necessary series of request to the server and the associated responses. Normally the requests from the applications are placed on a queue so that the TP monitor can process them one after the other in the order in which they are requested. The TP monitor is optimised to process the transactions quickly and efficiently. It removes processing load from the client applications and reduced the number of permanent connections that the DBMS server has to manage. It works best in situations where lots off applications are all repeatedly performing a small set of the same types of transaction again and again. For example, the transactions carried out at the ATM ('hole in the wall') machines used by banks are well suited to a TP monitor. TP Monitors are not aimed at managing complex ad hoc queries or long transactions associated with business analysis or reporting. In such cases the conventional direct connection, as in 'A' and 'B', will typically be more efficient. Client application 'C' in figure 27.6 has a direct connection to the database plus a connection to a TP monitor. This is likely to be the case when an application is performing a combination of simple routine transactions and a series of complex queries.

Summary

27.63 a. The development of separate systems with their own files is simple but does not make the best use of resources. Integrated files, databases, and integrated systems are more difficult to install, but have many advantages.

b. A database is a comprehensive, consistent, controlled and coordinated collection of structured data items.

c. **A Database Management System (DBMS)** is a software system that constructs, maintains and processes a database.

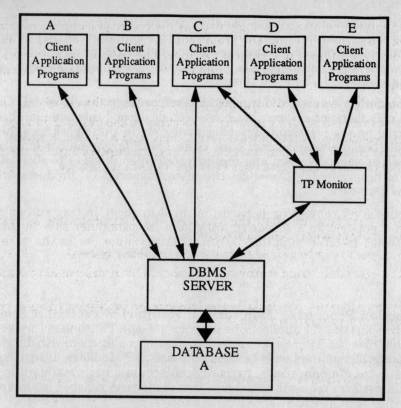

Figure 27.6 A TP Monitor used in conjunction with a database

d. Communication with the database is via the **Data Description Language (DDL)** and **Data Manipulation Language (DML).**

e. The **data dictionary** holds 'data about data' in the database.

f. Some of the more modern database systems may be set up using a client-server architecture which in some cases may enable distributed databases to be used.

g. Where there is concurrent access to a database the multi-threaded DBMS server must control access so as to prevent problems such as the lost update. One method is to use locks.

h. A **Database Administrator (DBA)** is the manager responsible for that database.

i. Integrated systems are a natural corollary to databases.

Points to note

27.64 a. Locks are commonly used to control concurrent access but they can also be problematical. For example, a client may hold a lock unnecessarily long causing other clients to wait too long. A further problem called **deadlock** can occur when two clients are each waiting for the other's lock and cannot finish their transaction and release their own lock until they get the other! The DBMS server must attempt to manage deadlock, for example by aborting one of the two deadlocked transactions.

b. Another term you may come across is '**data bank**'. This has a slightly different meaning to 'database'. An organisation constructing a database will put into it only data that it expects to use – for obvious reasons of economy. A 'data bank', on the other hand, is designed to contain any data that may be required – just as a librarian has to keep stocks of books, some of which may never be referred to. An example of a data bank is a file of legal cases; they all have to be there because enquiries cannot be predicted, but some may never be inspected.

c. The integrated system extends the database to include *all* information flows in a business and automates as many 'decisions' as possible to produce a comprehensive management-information system.

d. The computer is being increasingly used as the centre of a *communications network*. Many organisations are replacing the traditional centralised methods of data collection with terminal devices linked to a central machine. The flows of data (inwards) and information (outwards) are greatly accelerated, and there is considerable improvement in communication and control.

e. Integrated file systems are integrated systems without the use of databases.

f. For various reasons such as security or recovery in the event of damage suffered to a computer system there is sometimes a need to maintain a duplicate copy of a database as it is being maintained. The term used for this is **data replication.** Some of the independent relational database suppliers offer facilities for data replication.

Questions

1. Explain the term 'data base' and how the operation of a data-processing system using a database differs from one using conventional file structures.

    a. What advantages are to be gained from using a database system?

    b. What are the essential design features which should be incorporated into the system?

    (CIMA)

2. Some computer installations, particularly the larger more sophisticated ones, are using databases in which to store the organisation's data.

    You are **required** to:

    a. define a database;

    b. list and explain briefly **five** of the advantages claimed for a well designed database;

    c. explain briefly **three** of the major problems associated with the implementation and operation of a comprehensive database;

    d. distinguish between the logical and physical structure of data.

    (CIMA)

3. Distinguish between a database and a file management system.

4. Explain the terms:

    a. DDL

    b. DML

    c. DBMS

    d. DBA

    e. TP Monitor

    f. Distributed database

    g. Multi-threading

28 Query languages and 4GLs

Introduction

28.1   In recent years there has been a major increase in the use of relational databases. The increase has been accompanied by a number of different products that aid the development of new systems. These new products are often described as being **'Fourth Generation Languages (4GLs)'** because they are considered to work at a higher level than normal high-level languages such as COBOL, Pascal and C. The latter are often, consequently, called 3GLs. The actual facilities provided by 4GLs vary considerably.

28.2   Many 4GLs make use of relational databases, which themselves have query languages (DDLs plus DMLs), which perform operations at a very high level. Some 4GLs are actually the combination of a database query language and other facilities. For this reason query languages and 4GLs are both discussed in this chapter.

Query language features

28.3   A query language normally comprises a DDL and a DML all rolled into one. The name **query language** is therefore something of a misnomer since query languages do much more than handle queries to the database.

28.4   Query languages have two basic modes of operation:

   a.   **Terminal monitor mode**. The user is able to use the query language at a terminal, in much the same way as a command-language interpreter is used. The idea is for the end-user to formulate ad hoc queries in order to obtain useful information from the database. The importance of such facilities is greatly overrated, however, because in practice a great deal more control and care must be taken when accessing most databases. Nevertheless, such facilities can be of great value to those developing queries to be run in the other mode.

   b.   **Embedded query languages.** The query-language statements are included within the code of programs written in some other programming language, e.g. COBOL or C, and effectively becomes part of the program, hence the term 'embedded query language'.

28.5   In order to give more concrete illustrations of the features used, the following examples are all based upon what is undoubtedly one of the most widespread query languages, **SQL (Structured Query Language)**.

28.6   SQL is an international standard for database query languages and has been adopted by many computer manufacturers and database product suppliers, e.g. IBM, Digital, INGRES, ORACLE, SYBASE and INFORMIX.

28.7   **Tables.** Data in a relational database is stored in tables (sometimes called 'relations'). Each row in the table is broadly comparable to a single record in a file having simple records all of the same size. Another name for a row is a 'tuple'. An example is given in figure 28.1

A table called "CUSTOMER"				
Account No.	Name	Address	Credit Limit	Credit
A13245	John Brown	39 Graveside Gardens	1000	25
A13495	Robert Peel	21 Police Station Rd	1000	120
A13554	Anna Seed	15 Sweetbriar Rd	1500	500
A13782	Mary Christmas	22 Pundit Close	1200	200
A14854	Anita Dresser	99 Avenue Rd	2000	750

Figure 28.1 A relational database table

28.8   Each row should be uniquely identifiable by a suitable key. For a given table the key may be either a **simple key** consisting of the value in one column or a **composite key** consisting of multiple columns. In the example just given (figure 28.1) the account number is a simple key.

28.9   **To create a table** like the one given in figure 28.1 using SQL a statement such as the following could be used.

```
create           table customer
(
accountno        char(6)              not null unique,
name             char(20)             not null,
address          char(40)             not null,
creditlimit      smallint,
credit           smallint
)
```

The meaning of the statement is to a large degree self-explanatory. The layout has been chosen for readability, with the definition of each column in the table set out on a separate line in the order in which it is to appear in the table. The line 'accountno char(6) not null unique', states that the first column is to be called 'accountno', it can be up to 6 characters long, it must not be 'null' (i.e. it must have a value and not be left blank) and its value must be unique. The line defining the last column 'credit' merely defines the data type of 'credit' to be a small integer (i.e. low precision).

28.10   **To retrieve values from a table a SELECT statement is used.**

The following select statement retrieves rows from the table 'customer' displaying just the three columns 'accountno', 'name' and 'creditlimit'. The expression after the word 'where' defines what properties values in a row must have for the row to be selected. In this case the credit limit must be between 1000 and 2000.

```
select
         accountno, name, credit
from
         customer
where
         creditlimit > 1000
and
         creditlimit < 2000
```

This data is retrieved.

accountno	name	credit
A13554	Anna Seed	500
A13782	Mary Christmas	200

28.11   **To insert a row into a table an INSERT statement may be used.**

In this example a row is inserted in which three columns are assigned values and the other two left blank (i.e. have the value null). **Note.** The single quote mark is part of SQL syntax.

```
insert  into customer
      (accountno, name, address )
values  ('A14900', 'Simon Simple', '1 Pyman Close')
```

After inserting this row into the table given in figure 28.1 the table would be as shown in figure 28.2.

28.12   **To change values in one or more rows in a table an UPDATE statement may be used.**

In the following example the credit for account number A13245 (i.e. John Brown's account) is increased by 30 to 55. The use of the 'where clause' (i.e. 'where' followed by an expression) identifies just one row. Without the where clause the update would cause all rows to be updated. If no rows satisfied the where clause none would be updated.

```
update  customer
set
         credit = credit + 30
where
         accountno = 'A13245'
```

Account No.	Name	Address	Credit Limit	Credit
A13245	John Brown	39 Graveside Gardens	1000	25
A13495	Robert Peel	21 Police Station Rd	1000	120
A13554	Anna Seed	15 Sweetbriar Rd	1500	500
A13782	Mary Christmas	22 Pundit Close	1200	200
A14854	Anita Dresser	99 Avenue Rd	2000	750
A14900	Simon Simple	1 Pyman Close		

Figure 28.2 The table called customer after an INSERT

28.13 **To remove one or more a rows from a table a DELETE statement may be used**

In the following example 'Anna Seed's' details are removed from the customer table.

```
delete
from     customer
where
         account no 'Anna Seed'
```

After these updates and deletes the customer table would look be as shown in figure 28.3.

Account No.	Name	Address	Credit Limit	Credit
A13245	John Brown	39 Graveside Gardens	1000	55
A13495	Robert Peel	21 Police Station Rd	1000	120
A13782	Mary Christmas	22 Pundit Close	1200	200
A14854	Anita Dresser	99 Avenue Rd	2000	750
A14900	Simon Simple	1 Pyman Close		

Figure 28.3 The customer table after further changes

28.14 Now suppose that there are two further tables called 'ORDER' and ORDERLINE' as shown in figure 28.4a and figure 28.4b. Note how there is a relationship between ORDER and CUSTOMER because the customer account number appears as a column in ORDER. A customer may make many orders each with a different order number key. Also note that each order may have many order lines and that order number is part of a composite key for ORDERLINE. The complete key for ORDERLINE is the combination of the order number and product number. A simple **'data model'** showing these relationships is given in figure 28.5.

Order No	Account No	Order Date
X300000	A13245	1-MAR-1993
X300001	A13782	1-MAR-1993
X300002	A14854	2-MAR-1993

Figure 28.4a The table called 'ORDER'

Order No	Product No	Quantity Required
X300000	P20000	10
X300000	P25000	25
X300000	P24000	15
X300000	P20000	28
X300001	P21000	20
X300001	P23000	45
X300001	P24500	30
X300001	P25000	29
X300002	P25000	32
X300002	P25100	37
X300002	P24000	36
X300002	P23000	26

Figure 28.4b The table called 'ORDERLINE'

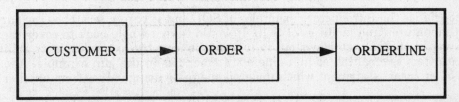

Figure 28.5 A simplified data model showing the relationships between the tables

28.15 By using the relationships between tables it is possible to retrieve cross referenced data from a number of tables. For example the following select statement performs what are called **join operations** across the three tables shown in figure 28.5.

```
select
        c.accountno,
        c.name,
        o.orderno,
        o.orderdate,
        ol.prodno,
        ol.prodqty
from
        customer c,
        order o,
        orderline ol
where
        o.accountno = c.accountno
and
        o.orderno = ol.orderno
and
        orderdate = '1-MAR-1993'
```

28.16 First some points on the syntax of the SELECT. In the lines following 'from' abbreviations for table names are defined which helps to simplify query writing. For example, '**customer c**' implies that 'c' may be used as a shorthand for the name of the customer table. Also not the use of the **dot notation** for specifying columns in tables which is essentially the same as the dot notation used for records. For example, '**c.accountno**' means the accountno column in the customer table. Now back to joins.

28.17 A first join in the query matches the order account number with the customer account number. This is expressed as

'o.accountno = c.accountno'.

317

The second join matches the order's order number with the order line's order number. This is expressed as

'o.orderno = ol.orderno'.

28.18 Figure 28.6 shows the result of the above join.

Account No.	Name	Order No	Order Date	Product No	Quantity Required
A13245	John Brown	X300000	1-MAR-1993	P20000	10
A13245	John Brown	X300000	1-MAR-1993	P25000	25
A13245	John Brown	X300000	1-MAR-1993	P24000	15
A13245	John Brown	X300000	1-MAR-1993	P20000	28
A13782	Mary Christmas	X300001	1-MAR-1993	P21000	20
A13782	Mary Christmas	X300001	1-MAR-1993	P23000	45
A13782	Mary Christmas	X300001	1-MAR-1993	P24500	30
A13782	Mary Christmas	X300001	1-MAR-1993	P25000	29

Figure 28.6 The result of SELECT with two joins

28.19 That concludes the introductory examples of SQL, but it barely scratches the surface in terms of all the features and facilities of SQL. It would take a whole book to cover them all. One of the strengths of SQL, not drawn out fully from the from the examples, is its ability to manipulate data from several tables in a single statement as in the join example. Another example would be an insert statement which updated one table using values from another.

Fourth generation languages (4GLs)

28.20 You may have noticed that one feature of SQL was the way in which the statements were expressed in a form that indicated 'what' result was required without specifying 'how' the result was to be obtained. That job is handled by the database management system. This very high level way of expressing processing requirements is one of the principal characteristics of a 4GL. For this reason SQL is itself sometimes described as a 4GL, although, as we will see, a 4GL normally has other important features too. However, some 4GLs use menu-driven user interfaces instead of a conventional 'language'.

28.21 4GLs may be regarded as the most modern form of **'applications generator'**, a type of software that has been in existence for many years. Those who promote or sell 4GLs claim that they offer more productive and cost-effective alternatives to the high-level languages such as COBOL associated with the era of 3rd generation computers, hence the name '4GL'. There is indeed some truth in these claims, although few current 4GLs are able to provide sufficient facilities to completely remove the need for 3GL in more than a narrow range of applications. Since there is such a variation in the features of products claiming to be 4GLs it is useful to define here those features that ought to be provided for the term 4GL to be used.

28.22 **Features of a 4GL.** A 4GL may be regarded as being a very high-level language that provides simple and powerful ways for the user to do such things as:
   a. Define data.
   b. Define what processing must be performed on the data.
   c. Define layouts of reports or screen based forms, including the formats of printed or displayed data.
   d. Define the processing operations to be carried out in the preparation of reports or in the user's interaction with screen-based forms.
   e. Define input data and validation checks.
   f. Select combinations of standard processing operations.
   g. Handle user queries.

28.23 Some 4GL have features aimed at supporting the development of applications which are based upon GUI interfaces, particularly WIMPs. A good example of this is 'Windows4GL' produced by Ingres.

28.24 Depending upon the way in which the 4GL has been designed it may either be used by the end-user directly or used by a computer specialist to 'build' an end-user system. Thus the 4GL either works by tailoring a generalised piece of software to handle a particular application or by using a general set of software tools to construct a particular application system

28.25 It is useful to distinguish between the following:

a. **A 4GL** – as described above.

b. **A 4GL tool.** A 4GL tool is an item of software that works *either* in the same way as a full 4GL but has more limited purpose *or* forms part of a full 4GL. For example, there are 4GL tools specially designed to handle the production of reports. Alternatively, SQL may be regarded as a 4GL tool.

c. **An applications generator.** Although a full 4GL is indeed an applications generator, the term applications generator tends to be more commonly used for simpler software products that provide flexible means of parameterising a general software package to deal with particular situations.

Summary

28.26 a. A query language comprises a DDL and a DML all rolled into one.

b. Query languages may either be used in terminal monitor mode or as embedded languages.

c. SQL is the most widespread query language.

d. A 4GL may be regarded as an advanced form of applications generator.

Points to note

28.27 a. The term **DSL (Data Sub-Language)** is sometimes used to mean the combination of a DML and a DML but the term query language is more common.

b. 4GLs may be used to build **prototypes** of new systems either as a means of investigating what is required or as a first step towards developing the whole system.

c. 4GLs are sometime used in conjunction with 'CASE tools'. CASE stands for Computer Aided Software Engineering. CASE tools are software packages which allows analysts or designers to specify databases and programs, often by means of a point and click GUI. The CASE tool generates such things as database table definitions (often in the form of DDL statements in SQL) and program code.

Questions

1. Explain the term 'embedded query language'.
2. What features would you expect a 4GL to have?

Computer systems

This Part looks at complete computer systems and how they are used. It deals with microcomputers, minicomputers and mainframes.

29 Computer systems

Introduction

29.1 This chapter examines the use of computers of different sizes from small to large. The three main topics considered are:

 a. microcomputers

 b. minicomputers

 c. large computer systems (including the use of mainframes).

29.2 The basic hardware features of microcomputers and minicomputers were described in Chapter 12. This chapter considers the use of these computers and examines where they fit in the overall picture of computer applications.

Microcomputers

29.3 Microprocessors are now to be found in a wide variety of devices from petrol pumps to wrist watches. Such devices are highly specialised and the computer systems within them are called **embedded systems.** In this chapter we are primarily concerned with general purpose computer systems rather than those just described.

29.4 The processing capability of the larger microcomputers is comparable to that of many mainframes of the 1960s. This fact should emphasise the major role that these small machines can play if properly utilised.

29.5 Until the early 1980s most microcomputers used for business purposes were 8-bit machines. During the 1980s 16-bit microcomputers took over from the 8-bit microcomputers and by far the most popular models were personal computers produced by IBM and those compatible with them, produced by other companies, e.g. Compaq. Probably the main competitor with the IBM PC and '**IBM compatibles**' was, and still is, the Apple Macintosh but the Apple Macintosh only has a small share of the total PC marketplace. Very powerful 32-bit microcomputers are now available which challenge the power of minicomputers. The following points apply to a typical microcomputer used as a personal computer in business.

29.6 **Software.** The system software available on these systems may be rather limited but this limitation is more than compensated for by the wide range of software packages available.

29.7 System software is usually made up of a simple operating system and a choice of programming common languages, e.g. C, BASIC, PASCAL, CIS-COBOL (A portable version of COBOL produced by Microfocus) and assemblers. More recently languages suited to programming the GUI windows based systems have become established. Amongst these are 'Visual Basic' from Microsoft and 'Windows4GL' from Ingres.

The operating systems used on 8-bit microcomputers are limited but effective. Probably the most common is CP/M. On 16-bit personal computers the predominant 'operating systems' are PCDOS, used on IBM PCs, and **MSDOS**, which is used on personal computers produced by other manufacturers who produce IBM PC-compatible products.

The more recent versions of PCDOS and MSDOS are broadly comparable in functionality to their minicomputer counterparts with **one big exception** – the PC operating systems are almost all single-user non multitasking systems. However, some newer operating systems, including the IBM's **OS/2** and Microsoft's **Windows/NT** are multi-tasking.

Another point, worthy of mention, is the growing number of '**laptop**' computers in use. These are portable microcomputers which are so small that they can be used when on a person's lap without discomfort. Even smaller forms of personal computers, close to the size of large pocket calculators are called '**notebook computers**'.

29.8 Software packages are available for an incredibly wide range of applications including:

 a. payroll

 b. stock control

 c. order processing, invoicing and sales ledger

    d. production control

    e. job costing

    f. information storage and retrieval

    g. word processing

    h. spreadsheets, etc.

29.9   A number of well-established software suppliers produce software packages that can be made to run on a wide variety of machines produced by different manufacturers, e.g. on the older 8-bit microcomputer Micropro's WORDSTAR package for word processing and Visicorp's VISICAL package for financial modelling are available. There are numerous 'portable' software products on PCs, e.g. LOTUS 1-2-3, dBASE, Word Perfect, Framework, EXCEL and Freelance.

29.10 **Multipurpose.** Many microcomputers are able to serve multiple purposes:

    a. They may be used as 'stand-alone' machines, i.e. working autonomously for a particular purpose.

    b. They may be connected to a LAN in order to share resources such as file servers and print servers.

    c. They may be used as 'intelligent terminals' within a distributed data-processing system by being connected to minicomputers or mainframes across a LAN.

29.11 The use of a LAN enables such machines to deal not only with data processing that is only of 'local' interest, but also with corporate data processing.

29.12 Advantages of a microcomputer include:

    a. A full configuration can cost less than £4,000, although it may cost much more.

    b. Cheap software packages arising out of the large volume of sales.

    c. It just plugs into the nearest mains socket.

    d. User-friendly 'menu-driven' programs mean that there is no need to employ specialist staff, the computer can be operated by general clerical staff provided they are properly trained.

    e. They brings computing within the budget of even the very smallest organisations.

    f. They allow a large organisation to implement distributed processing, with each department possessing its own independent processing facilities.

29.13 Disadvantages include:

    a. A lack of a multi-tasking operating system in many cases.

    b. Limited file store and memory capacity although this is *not* a problem on the more recent models.

    c. Smaller systems often lack a choice of languages.

    d. Purchased software other than standard packages is often of a poor quality.

    e. They are too often purchased by non-specialists who are too easily convinced by salesmen.

    f. They can lead to several departments duplicating the same procedures.

NB. 16-bit microcomputers with hard disks overcome 29.13a, and 29.13b is a problem of home computers rather than small business machines such as PCs.

Minicomputers

29.14 The hardware of a typical minicomputer system was described in Chapter 12.

29.15 Whereas the typical microcomputer is designed as a single-user system, the larger microcomputers and typical minicomputers are multi-user systems.

29.16 A user with an apparent need for multiple microcomputers at one particular location may be able to meet the same need with a single minicomputer.

29.17 Software. There is far more *system software* available on most minicomputers than there is on the typical microcomputer, but perhaps surprisingly there is not always such a good choice of applications software.

A Compaq laptop computer
(Photographs courtesy of Compaq Computer Ltd)

29.18 System software on minicomputers has been developed over many years and had its origins in the fast key-to-disk system. Some single-user systems are in use but the typical minicomputer has a time-sharing operating system such as Unix, plus some communications facilities. The latter reflect the fact that minicomputers frequently form part of a distributed system.

29.19 The choice of programming languages on minicomputers is usually better than that available on microcomputers and is very similar to that available on most main frames.

29.20 Software packages are available for use on most minicomputers, but they do not have the same importance that they have with microcomputers. The reasons are simply that the production of applications software for minicomputers has tended to take place using the same methods as those used for mainframe computers. That is, software is often written *by the user or for the user* in order to meet specific requirements rather than to meet the needs of some general market.

29.21 This situation is changing, however, as many packages first written for microcomputers have since been converted and extended to run on larger systems.

29.22 The applications dealt with by minicomputers include all those listed earlier under the heading of microcomputers but also include such things as:

    a. Retailing, e.g. point-of-sale systems.

    b. Banking.

    c. Life assurance.

    d. Stock Exchange dealing, etc.

29.23 **Multi-purpose.** Minicomputers may be used for several different purposes.

    a. As 'stand-alone' machines (often multi-users).

    b. As the central host computer in a small distributed system, e.g. with a number of microcomputers acting as 'intelligent terminals'.

    c. As a server machine on a LAN. For example, a minicomputer may act as a database server machine with workstations (including PCs) acting as clients.

    d. As the second tier in a larger-scale distributed system, e.g. acting as a local host to a number of microcomputers but also connected to some central corporate mainframe.

29.24 **Relative advantages and disadvantages of minicomputers** compared with other computers.

    a. They are more expensive than a typical microcomputer but much less expensive than a mainframe.

    b. They have systems software that is broadly comparable to that found on mainframes but they do not always have the same wide choice of applications packages found on microcomputers.

    c. They have greater file storage and memory capacities than most microcomputers and can cope with all but the largest data-processing problems.

    d. Their multi-user and communications facilities make them well suited to the integration of local data-processing activities and the provision of distributed processing facilities.

General considerations

29.25 **System support.** Generally speaking, smaller organisations buying microcomputers and minicomputers will not be able to justify economically the employment of the DP specialists required in mainframe installations. The supplier must therefore either be able to offer suitable applications packages or be willing to get more involved in program writing for the user. The latter is seldom an economic alternative in the case of microcomputers because the full development cost must be borne by the one user. The supplier will also be expected to provide considerable support for the user.

29.26 To understand the market situation, it is important to realise that many micros and minis are sold in what is called the **OEM** market, i.e. **Original Equipment Manufacturer**. That is to say, they are sold not to the eventual user but to another manufacturer who incorporates them into a larger system. Many manufacturers of micros and minis are wholly or partly dependent on this type of business. It was the decision of some of them to provide peripherals and software and to sell direct to the end user that created the explosion in 'mini' and now 'micro' sales.

Large computer systems

29.27 We now illustrate the use of large computer systems by providing a discussion of two applications:

    a. an airline booking system (a real-time system).

    b. a system used by a large corporate organisation.

29.28 The first application is specialised whereas the second application considers the typical general-purpose large system.

Application 1

29.29 **Airline booking system.** Records of seat availability on all its planes will be kept by an airline on a central computer. The computer is linked via terminals to a world-wide system of agents. Each agent can gain access to the flight records and within seconds make a reservation in respect of a particular flight. This reservation is recorded *immediately* so that the next inquiry for that flight (following even microseconds after the previous reservation) finds that particular seat or seats reserved. Notice the computer records reflect an accurate picture of the airline's seating load at all times because there is no time lag worth mentioning. The computer would then output information for the production of the customer's ticket and flight instructions, of confirmation on the booking by the customer, (see figure 29.1).

29.30 Each booking is a separate transaction and is processed immediately, i.e. not batched. This is therefore a **transaction-processing system**. A TP monitor may be used in such a system.

Features of real-time

29.31 **Response time.** The service given by a real-time processing system can be measured in terms of *response* time. This is the time taken by the system to respond to an input, e.g. the time interval between the pressing of the last key by the operator of a VDU and the display of the required (updated) information.

29.32 **'Traffic' pattern.** An important feature of real-time is the 'traffic' pattern, i.e. the *volumes* of data being input, the *times* at which they are input, the *types* of input and the *places* at which they are input.

29.33 **Reliability.** Because real-time systems operate automatically an extremely high standard of system reliability is required.

    a. Program protection. Many programs will occupy main storage simultaneously and the integrity of each program must be protected.

    b. File security. Duplicate files will probably need to be kept and in addition their contents will be dumped at intervals. These measures will aid reconstruction should the need arise. (Note the duplicate database in figure 29.1.)

    c. Standby machinery. In the airline application two processors would be required, one of which is operational and the other a standby machine. In the event of failure the standby machine would automatically come into use. (Again refer to figure 29.1.)

    d. Security. Confidentiality of information held on magnetic storage is achieved by the use of special code numbers allowing access to certain files only by certain people.

Hardware, software considerations

29.34 Implicit in the operation of real-time systems described are:

    a. A large main storage requirement to accommodate systems software and application programs. Also required will be an area to use as buffers for queuing of messages.

    b. Direct-access storage of large capacity as backing storage.

c. A sophisticated operating system to handle the many different operations being handled simultaneously.

d. A data communication system linking the many terminals with the processor.

Cost

29.35 Real-time systems are usually specially designed for a particular application and are extremely costly. Cost will vary with the service one wishes the system to provide. The better the service (i.e. the shorter the response time generally) then the more costly it becomes in terms of hardware and software, etc.

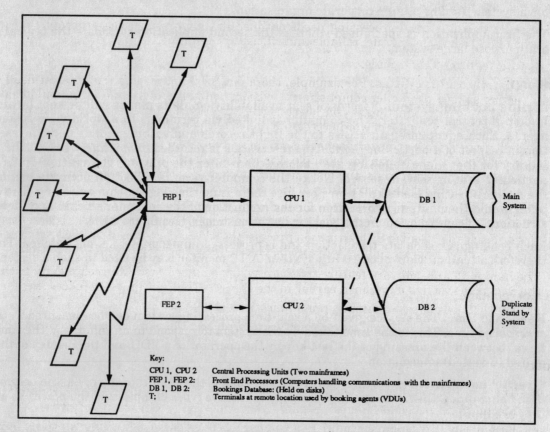

Figure 29.1 A real-time airline booking system

Application 2

29.36 **Systems used by large corporate organisations.** Such systems are required to meet the diverse information needs within the organisations.

29.37 Depending upon the type of organisation any number of the following functions of the organisation may be supported by the computer system:

a. Top-level management.

b. Finance and accounting.

c. Manufacturing.

d. Marketing.

e. Purchasing, stocking and distributing (i.e. logistics).

f. Personnel.

g. Administration.

29.38 Levels of computer support vary from function to function but particularly distinctive levels are:

a. Automation of basic clerical procedures such as those found in ordering, invoicing, payroll production and bookings. Batch or transaction processing will be used as appropriate.

b. Office automation and communication to support the administrative functions, e.g. by the use of word processors and electronic mail.

c. Automation of management-control operations such as the control of stock, production, materials, distribution, accounts and personnel.

d. Automated aids to strategic planning such as financial modelling, linear programming and other analysis methods.

Features of these systems

29.39 In order to support the processing needs outlined in the previous two paragraphs these systems must be large, versatile, reliable and efficiently organised.

29.40 Specific features may include:

a. **Distributed facilities.** For example, there may be a mainframe computer at head office acting as host to smaller computers at divisional offices. A divisional office could deal with marketing or production say. A lower level of the distributed system might handle office automation by means of word processors linked to the main computers across LANS.

b. **Integrated files of databases.** The advantages of integrated file processing or databases can be exploited so that, for example, the receipt of orders may *automatically* give rise to the ordering of materials, the movement of stock, the scheduling of production, the control of production and the distribution of manufactured goods.

c. **Combinations of different processing methods.** Run-of-the-mill stock control and payroll production may take place by batch processing while enquiries, orders, bookings, etc are being handled by transaction processing. Additional processing loads, such as those used for financial modelling, will also be placed upon the system from time to time.

29.41 The hardware and software features of these systems have comparable complexity to those of the real-time systems mentioned earlier in the chapter. The principal differences are:

a. The distribution of processing, communications and data.

b. The use of many different types of software to support the varied processing needs.

Summary

29.42 a. There is no difference in principle between a 'micro' or 'mini' and the larger computer.

b. Machines described as 'micros' or 'minis' vary widely in specification and price.

c. Essentially, the 'micro' or 'mini' is a smaller, cheaper, slower machine which is, however, acquiring an increasing degree of sophistication.

d. Although the typical microcomputer is noticeably different from the typical mini computer, the larger microcomputer and smaller minis are indistinguishable for most practical purposes. In answering examination questions, concentrate on typical features first and then mention any overlap.

e. 'Micros' and 'minis' play an important part in computer networks.

f. Software is usually supplied by the manufacturer as part of a complete system.

g. Applications cover a very wide range, and include all conventional accounting tasks.

h. The microcomputer is even smaller and cheaper than the 'mini'.

i. The two large-scale applications described in this chapter all use large amounts of hardware. The first system must have fast response times in order to satisfy the needs of the users. The second system must strike a balance between response and processing throughput. The airline booking system has essentially one large job to handle, but the other system has many different jobs to handle.

j. Real-time involves the processing of data as it arises, thus providing records that are permanently up to date.

k. Response time, traffic pattern and reliability are major features.

l. The hardware and software requirements are complex.

m. The system in a large corporate organisation will:

    i.   Have distributed processing, communications and data.

    ii.   Use many different types of software.

    iii.   Exploit integrated files or databases.

    iv.   Use a variety of processing methods.

Points to note

29.43 a. In the case of a transaction-processing system such as the one used by the airline the following points apply:

    i.   The accurate assessment of response time and traffic pattern is very difficult but of vital importance, as errors can be very costly in terms of size of processor, sophistication of software and transmission line capacity. (Unlike batch processing, where overtime or an additional shift might be possible, real-time processing depends upon the system being able to cope at the time required.)

    ii.   Because of the difficulties of accurate assessment, applications are normally implemented on a 'pilot' basis (e.g. with the airline reservations system – no pun intended – a few branch offices would have access initially).

    iii.   The essence of a real-time system is that it should provide an up-to-date (real) picture of events as they occur. Therefore a retrieval system is generally associated with it. It is possibly for this reason that students give undue prominence in examination answers to this latter function, forgetting that they are dealing with a system of *processing* just as they were with batch systems.

b. Other areas where real-time applications of computers are applied are automated process control and production control.

c. Most large-scale organisations are now totally reliant upon systems like the one described in the second example in the chapter.

Questions

1. Describe a typical microcomputer and a typical minicomputer. Why is the distinction between a microcomputer and a minicomputer hard to make in some cases?

2. a. Construct the systems flowcharts to show the processing runs for a nominal ledger system.

    b. i. Specify the input and indicate which input could probably be automatically provided by other computer systems

      ii. List the validation checks you would apply to the input.

(CIMA)

3. Name seven functions within a large organisation which could be supported by a computer system.

4. Explain what is meant by the 'configuration' of a computer system.

5. a. What is meant by the term 'real-time' processing?

    b. Explain the hardware and software facilities which are required for the operation of a real-time system.

(ACA)

6. Distinguish between on-line and real-time processing. Give an example of a commercial data-processing application where real-time processing would be applicable and explain what characteristics make it necessary to consider this type of processing.

(CIMA)

Information systems management

1. With the knowledge of the various elements that go into making up an information system, particularly with reference to the specific DP and IT issues, the reader is now in a position to consider the management of information systems.

2. The chapters in this Part draw on material from earlier chapters in the text to cover various aspects of the management of information systems. Chapter 30 deals with operational issues, in contrast chapter 31 deals with more general management considerations.

3. Chapters 32 and 33 discuss the control and audit of data processing activities respectively.

30 Operations management

Introduction

30.1 In most companies there is a separate department that controls computer-based data-processing activities. It has become more common for this department to have 'IT' in its title, rather than just calling it the 'DP department', thus reflecting the changes in technology and computer usage. The purpose of this chapter is to look at a typical 'IT department' and the people who staff it.

30.2 In larger companies it is often found as part of a Management Services Division. A progressive company with a big reliance on IT may have a director of IT on the board. Titles given to people who perform the functions of an IT department vary between installations. However, the more commonly used titles are used here. An organisation chart for a typical large IT department is shown in figure 30.1. In a smaller organisation some of the functions may be combined under a single heading.

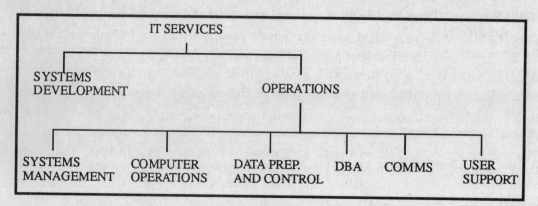

Figure 30.1 An outline organisation chart for IT services

30.3 There are alternative ways in which IT activities may be organised. For example, staff may be grouped into **project teams**, comprised of different types of specialist, or they may be grouped according to job function.

IT manager

30.4 The IT Manager is a key figure in the organisation with responsibility for all IT services. His or her job is to ensure that the IT department functions efficiently in the service of the company. He or she is responsible for ensuring that the IT needs of the organisation are met within the policy guide-lines laid down. At this point it should be pointed out that in cases where not all of the various IT services are under a single management structure the older title of 'DP manager' is more likely to be used.

30.5 He or she must be a good administrator as well as having a sound business knowledge. He or she must also have the knowledge and expertise necessary to enable him or her to control the teams of specialists in the various IT fields.

30.6 **Status.** It is important that his or her status be clearly defined, especially with regard to right of access to the board. As indicated above, in some companies there is an IT director.

30.7 Ideally one would like someone who has previous experience of installing successful systems and the appointment should be made very early on in the planning cycle to enable the company to get the benefit of his or her specialist knowledge and experience. If not recruited from outside, the potential IT manager could be found in the Management Services Division.

30.8 In figure 30.1 a structure is shown in which the IT services are split into two main functional areas:

a. **Systems Development.** This covers all the development activities of the organisation and therefore contains analysts, programmers and project leaders. It is common for this area to have responsibility for the development of new systems as well as the maintenance of existing systems. Software produced in this area is 'released' from the development environment to the production environment.

b. **Operations.** This covers all the activities associated with maintaining IT facilities and services, from the operation of the computers themselves to provision of personal computers or even telephones.

Systems development

30.9 It is common for the various specialists within a systems development group to be organised into project teams each run by a **'project leader'** or **'project manager'**. Depending upon the size of the department they may be a single **projects manager** or **systems development manager** with overall responsibility for all the projects. The project management tasks were discussed in chapter 32 so the role of the projects manager will not be discussed further here. Other key tasks in systems development are described in the following paragraphs.

Systems analysts (see Chapters 18–20)

30.10 The job of the systems analyst has already been described, but can be briefly stated as follows:

a. To examine the feasibility of potential computer applications.

b. Analysis of existing systems with a view to their application to a computer.

c. Design of computer-based systems, their implementation and review.

30.11 It is very likely that systems analysts would work in project teams with a senior analyst or project leader in charge.

30.12 The chief systems analyst will work very closely with his counterparts in other sections and the IT manager, and will assist in forward planning and overall project control.

Programmers (see Chapters 22–24)

30.13 Following the analysis and design process, in which senior programmers and database specialist may play an important role, the job of implementing the programs begins. The programmer:

a. Encodes and tests the procedures detailed in the design in a language suitable for the specified computer.

b. Will liaise very closely with the analyst and the user to ensure logical correctness of programs.

30.14 **Specialisation.** In a large IT department programmers might specialise in certain areas of programming. These may be:

a. **Applications.** Applications programmers are the people who write the initial programs for each application.

b. **Maintenance.** Once the programs written by the Applications programmer are operational they are handed over to a maintenance programmer, whose job it will be to carry out any amendments or improvements that may be necessary. The applications programmer then moves on to fresh fields.

c. **Systems software.** This programmer will specialise in writing 'non-application' programs, i.e. systems software. These programs will supplement those supplied by the manufacturer.

30.15 In smaller installations, of course, a smaller team of programmers will have to turn their hands to any task that comes along.

Quality assurance (QA)

30.16 In some organisations there is a manager responsible for Quality Assurance (QA) whose job it is to establish standards for the development of systems and to set in place suitable mechanisms to promote and enforce the standards. The job of checking and enforcing the standards is normally called **Quality Control (QC)**.

Operations manager

30.17 The Operations Manager is responsible for all the activities associated with maintaining IT facilities and services. Traditionally this role has been primarily concerned with the operation of the computer and ancillary equipment. Today the role is often much broader and may include responsibility for :

    a. **Systems Management.** This covers all aspects of installing, upgrading and maintaining the various computers which the organisation has. The work can range from installing new versions of the operating system on large computers to installing software packages on PCs.

    b. **Computer Operations.** This covers the day-to-day operation of the computers in the computer room and associated work such as the use of the library of tapes and disks.

    c. **Data preparation and control.** This area of activity has tended to contract in recent years as more and more data is input directly on-line by end-users. Nevertheless, many organisations provide central facilities for the input of data and the associated controls relating to the production and distribution of documents, including such things as turn-around documents.

    d. **Database Administration (DBA).** If an organisation uses databases there is normally a small group of specialist staff responsible for database administration (26.31).

    e. **Communications.** This area has responsibility for all data communications and network facilities within the organisation. It is common for this responsibility to be extended to include matters relating to telephones, and fax machines too.

    f. **User support.** Given that an IT department provides a service to the organisation it is common for there to be a specialist area dedicated to the support of users. User support is sometimes sub-divided further as will be explained later in this chapter.

30.18 Where it is merited the above functions will be described in more detail in the following paragraphs.

Data-control staff

30.19 These staff are responsible for the co-ordination of all machine-processing operations and for ensuring a smooth flow of work through the operations department. In order to explain their work we will trace a particular job through from beginning to end.

30.20 a. **Source documents** accompanied by control totals are received from the clerical function (outside the IT department) and vetted visually.

    b. **Control totals** are agreed and documents passed under this control to the Data Preparation Section.

    c. **Data preparation** section prepares floppy disks or other media from source documents.

    d. Source documents are returned to the clerical function and the floppy disks now represent the input for a particular run (job), e.g. 'invoice run'.

    e. **Job assembly** section 'makes up' the run and prepare a Run Authorisation document. This will detail the various tapes/disks required and how the output is to be disposed of. This is then passed to the computer-room supervisor.

    f. **Tape/disk library**. The librarian will provide all the tape reels and disk packs required for the particular job and will pass them to the computer room itself for the computer to process.

    g. On completion of the computer run(s) the tapes or disks go back to the library and all the documentation to the Data Control section.

30.21 The Data Control section now scrutinises the control log to ensure all action has been taken correctly and to initiate any possible corrective action indicated. Control totals will be reconciled. These will now include totals of items rejected on the run/s, but all the totals will need to be reconciled back to those compiled at the beginning of the job.

30.22 The output is dealt with; invoices, for example, will be despatched to customers and warehouses, etc.

30.23 All necessary information will be fed back to the user department, e.g. copies of all output despatched, error lists, control totals.

Data-preparation staff

30.24 These staff are responsible for:

    a. Preparing floppy disks from source documents or preparation by other means, e.g. direct data entry on-line.

    b. Operation of ancillary machines such as floppy disk units, paper bursters, etc.

Operator

30.25 The operator handles the hardware in the computer room. The operator also handles the input and output media (e.g. placing magnetic tapes onto drives), communicating with the operating system via a console. The operator tries to keep the installation running smoothly by stepping in when things go wrong to correct them immediately.

30.26 The operators work under the direction of the computer-room supervisor.

Computer-room supervisor

30.27 The computer room is under the day-to-day control of a supervisor. Only authorised personnel are allowed entry. It is essential that anyone who has participated in the writing of the programs is forbidden for security and audit reasons to interfere with the operational running of those programs.

Figure 20.1 showed the layout of a typical computer room. You may find it useful to refer back to it at this point.

Tape/disk librarian

30.28 All tape reels and disk packs used in the installation are stored in a library adjacent to the computer room. The librarian issues tapes/disks to the computer room as per a Run Authorisation document from Data Control.

30.29 The librarian will maintain a register of all tapes and disks, noting the particular generations required for current use. Maximum security is observed and access is strictly limited.

User technical support

30.30 With the Data Processing equipment no longer being always concentrated within the IT department and operated by specialists but often being distributed throughout the organisation and being operated by all kinds of staff it is necessary for the IT department to provide the necessary support. Technical support is basically concerned with ensuring that the hardware continues to operate correctly. This includes not only routine tasks of maintenance and cleaning but help in the provision of consumables, such as floppy disks, reconfiguring and upgrading machines, and fault detection and correction. Smaller organisations often rely on their computer supplier for these services.

User operations support

30.31 Operations support is basically concerned with helping the users of devices such as Workstations, Personal Computers and Word Processors. The help takes the form of assistance in the installation and use of applications packages and interactive software, training in the correct use of devices, media and software, and dealing with problems or queries as they arise.

30.32 This kind of support is most vital when the user is gaining his or her first experience of using such equipment and serious problems can arise if it is overlooked; for example, if staff are not properly instructed in the care of floppy disks and ways of doing disk back-ups vital data may be irretrievably lost.

Summary

30.33 a. An IT department is headed by an IT Manager (or IT director) and consists of analysts, programmers, operations staff and support staff.

   b. Security measures are extremely important.

   i.   With regard to magnetic files.

   ii. In forbidding unauthorised entry to the computer room and tape library.

Points to note

30.34 a. The IT department is responsible for the processing of data, but ultimate responsibility for the application systems themselves rests with the user departments served by them.

   b. Many computer installations work on a shift basis, in which case a *shift leader* will act for the operations manager outside 'normal' working hours.

Questions

1. 'Much publicity has been given to the impact of computers in business, yet 'it is still true that management's real functions remain unchanged'.

   Discuss this quotation

   (CIMA)

2. Draft the organisation chart of a large computer department and outline the main duties of the sections reporting to the operations manager.

   To whom do you think the data processing manager should be responsible? Give your reasons

   (ACA)

31 General management considerations

Introduction

31.1 Having some knowledge of the activities of an IT department you are now in a position to understand the management considerations which are the subject of this chapter.

Top management involvement

31.2 One of the major reasons for the lack of success of so many computer installations can be attributed to the failure of top management to become involved *right from the outset*. The company as a whole must be made aware of the Board's determination to see computerisation succeed, so that full co-operation will be forthcoming all along the line.

31.3 The need for top management involvement is seen when one considers the issued involved:

a. High capital investment.

b. Major organisation upheaval.

c. Effects on personnel both managerial and operative.

d. Reliance on computers for management information and basic business functions which affect the viability of the organisation.

IT policy must be formulated as carefully as any other sectional policy and its effect on the long-term objectives assessed. Top management knows what information it wants; thus it is up to them to see that the computer provides it.

Computer objectives

31.4 They must be clearly stated in order that the evaluation process which follows implementation can be meaningful. In particular application areas these can be stated precisely, e.g. in stock control 'a 15% reduction in stock holdings' and in invoicing 'to despatch invoice within 36 hours of despatch of goods'.

Education

31.5 a. **Management.** In order for a management to appreciate what the computer can do for the company and what is involved in its introduction, it must have the necessary knowledge. Selected members can be sent on courses and use could be made of the experience of other companies in the EDP field. Company seminars are a good way of communicating the kind of information which management need to be equipped with in order to provide the basis for decision-making.

b. **Staff.** It is very important that staff are fully prepared for what is to come. The computer brings with it new thinking, new disciplines and new methods of working. Training must begin early and everyone made aware of what is required under the new system. Action must be taken to dispel any fears that may precede the coming of the computer. There is a great *human* problem associated with the introduction of computers and it must receive due consideration.

c. **Users. These must be involved from the outset.** The computer is the servant of the user, but the user must be educated to make the most efficient use of this new management tool. He must be involved with the new system from the analysis stage to ensure that his requirements are designed into the new system. This sense of involvement in the design is important also because users will be responsible for operating the new system eventually.

Application selection

31.6 Applications which give immediate and real benefits should be chosen first. These will be found in the field of management information and control and include:

a. Stock control.

b. Production planning and control.

c. Business forecasting.

d. Cash-flow analysis.

31.7 What is important is that introduction of EDP methods in these areas can have a major effect on the firm's profitability. Reductions in stock holdings can release badly needed cash. Better production planning can result in more economic batch sizes, etc, etc. Administrative applications such as payroll and order processing are important but in themselves don't result in the same dramatic benefits. Priority of application will often be dictated by a firm's particular problems.

31.8 The accusation has been made that in the past computers have been nothing more than glorified accounting machines (and very expensive ones at that). The real value of a computer is in its ability to sift large volumes of data quickly and accurately and provide timely and meaningful information on what decisions can be made.

Composition of study teams

31.9 Teams should be headed by an experienced systems analyst, preferably one who has previous practical experience of a successful project. He or she should have a number of analysts to do the detailed work. Also in the team should be a representative of the area being studied. This is important because detailed knowledge will be required and also the user department must be identified with the project from the outset because it will be responsible for its efficient running eventually. The auditor too will need to be consulted early in the design stage in order to incorporate his particular requirements in the new system. It is essential that the team has sufficient status in order to carry out its tasks effectively and it must have the backing of top management.

Cost of feasibility study

31.10 This will be one of the factors considered in the Preliminary Survey. Cost will depend on the size of team and length of study but nevertheless it could be quite considerable. The time taken to carry out the study is nearly always underestimated. A timetable must be planned but should be flexible. Once the cost of the study has been authorised the study goes ahead. The detailed examination carried out during a feasibility study invariably brings about improvements to the existing system as it stands. It is sometimes found that the cost of the study can be recovered as it were from the savings presented by the elimination of the faults which have been brought to light. Studies vary in length from weeks to many months depending on the objectives set and their complexity.

Use of consultants

31.11 Opinions are divided on this question. A survey showed that more firms used outside consultants during the *first* involvement with computers then subsequently. Consultants have much IT knowledge and experience and if used properly they can be of immense help. However, it is vital that the company has someone who himself has enough IT background to be able to communicate in the consultant's language. The consultant must be given clear terms of reference and management must be prepared to make the necessary decisions the consultant requires during the various stages of his work. It should be remembered, however, that consultants can only advise, the company must make the decisions based on his or her advice.

Having a computer already

31.12 Previous chapters were concerned with the situation where a company had no computer and the feasibility study was used as the basis for acquisition. Once a computer is installed and working requests for computerisation of new applications or extension of existing ones will be received in the DP department. Each should be subjected to a preliminary survey and a feasibility study, in order to decide whether or not to put the application on the company's computer. There will come a time when the present hardware will need to be replaced or additional modules purchased. Again the requisite studies will determine the requirement.

Summary

31.13 a. Top management involvement and complete identification with computerisation is vital to its success.

b. A complete IT policy must be evolved and applied.

c. The computer can only be exploited to the full by people who have the requisite knowledge and experience. Thus education and training play a large part in successful computer development.

d. The human problem must not be overlooked.

e. Applications giving the greatest returns should be selected first.

f. Involve line management in study teams.

g. Do not hesitate to use consultants if the requirement arises.

Points to note

31.14 Do not hesitate to make use of your costing and accountancy knowledge in DP.

Questions

1. As a management accountant you are asked to identify the areas of cost of a proposed new computer system. List the major items in those areas.

2. Your company is about to embark on a feasibility study. What do you understand by a feasibility study?

    State the main points on which information should be given in a feasibility report.

    (CIMA)

3. When should a systems survey or study take place? Summarise

    a. The main steps and

    b. the work involved: in a systems study.

    Assuming that you are a project leader conducting a systems study covering all commercial activities in the company, who would you include in your study team and why? State the industry for which your selection would be suitable

    (CIMA)

4. Your company has decided to install a computer. In your capacity as Finance Director draw up a time-table for a seminar to be given to other Board Members.

    Explain the steps involved and the individuals who a should participate.

    (CIMA)

5. It has been said computer based systems are ideally suited to the application of management by exception techniques.

    a. State briefly when you think this statement is true and give and example of a specific application of management by exception using a computer.

    b. List the factors you would observe to ensure that a management by exception computer system is a viable one.

    (CIMA)

6. 'The list of unsuccessful computer installations is a long one and there is no doubt that many organisations are disappointed with the way their computer projects have developed.'

    What, in your opinion, are the principal reasons for the failure of computer projects?

    (ACA)

32 Control of data processing activities

Introduction

32.1　This chapter deals with control of the organisation and work of the IT Department. This control is established and maintained by setting 'standards'. Standards ensure that:

a.　work is carried out in a uniform and orderly way.

b.　criteria are provided against which the performance of personnel and machines can be measured.

General

32.2　**Organisation.** There should be complete division of responsibility between the sections described in chapter 30, with the possible exception of systems analysts and programmers. There should be no overlap of duties between the development and operations staff, and the operations sections should be self-contained! Organisation has become a more complex task in recent years with the increased use of computers by non-specialists throughout the various departments involved with DP equipment.

32.3　**Training.** All staff should be fully trained, and the effectiveness of training should be assessed by monitoring performance on the job. It is important to keep training programmes under constant review and to provide additional training so that staff are kept up to date with the latest developments in IT.

32.4　**Scheduling.** Schedules of work should be prepared so that:

a.　The various activities of the operations section are coordinated.

b.　A check can be kept on the progress of systems development.

c.　The introduction of a new system is properly coordinated between the development and operations functions.

d.　Delay can be quickly detected and corrective action taken.

32.5　**Supervision.** High standards of supervision should be maintained in all sections.

Systems analysis

32.6　a.　**Consultation.** Management must ensure that users are fully consulted about systems being designed for them, and that their views and criticisms are given due weight.

b.　**Evaluation.** All proposals should be fully evaluated, on a quantitative (i.e. cost) basis whenever possible.

c.　**Documentation.** All systems-development work must be fully documented, but the following are particularly important.

i.　documentation of the existing procedure on completion of the fact-finding stage.

ii.　documentation of the agreements between user management and the DP department as to the form the new system will take.

iii.　the Requirements Specification.

iv.　the Systems Specification.

d.　**Performance.** It is difficult to measure the work-rate of systems analysts, but some control can be kept by requiring regular (e.g. monthly) reports on work done and by regular meetings at which progress is reviewed. In practice, managers often assess performance on the basis of the success (or otherwise) of systems previously developed.

Programming

32.7　a.　**Documentation.** Program documentation must always be complete and up to date. Considerable difficulties may otherwise occur when an operational program fails or has to be amended.

   b. **Testing.** All programs must be thoroughly tested before being released for operational use. The role of the auditor is especially important.

   c. **Performance.** Measurement of the work-rate of programmers is not easy, since the output in terms of number of instructions or statements written may vary with the difficulty of the task. Standards can however be established for:

      i. the style and content of the documentation produced

     ii. the program design method used

    iii. the methods of testing and test plans.

    iv. the time required to complete the various stages of program development.

     v. the number of instructions statements written.

    vi. the number of program errors made.

   vii. the amount of program testing time used.

Data control

32.8 a. **Documentation.** All work done by the section should be supported by written instructions and job manuals.

   b. **Progress.** The section should maintain records to control the punctual receipt of incoming work, its progress through data preparation and computer processing and the eventual distribution of outputs. These records may be in the form of wall-charts so that they are available for inspection by the DP management.

   c. **Errors and queries.** Records should be kept of errors and queries raised in the course of processing so that:

      i. correction and re-processing can be controlled.

     ii. abnormal error rates can be taken up with the department responsible.

Data preparation

32.9 a. **Documentation.** Manuals or charts should be maintained containing specimen source documents, indicating what data has to be transcribed.

   b. **Performance.** Records should be kept of the output and error rates of each operator and of the section as a whole. Note that with Key-to-Disk systems this can be done by the program automatically. Standards can be established for the larger tasks.

   c. **Procedures.** Clear-cut procedures should be established and enforced for encoding, verification and error correction (if a separate stage).

   d. **Supervision.** Close supervision and high standards of discipline are needed to maintain satisfactory output.

   e. **Working conditions.** Good working conditions are essential to maintain output and to promote morale. Particular attention should be paid to:

      i. adequate space.

     ii. heating and lighting.

    iii. noise levels.

Computer room

32.10 a. **Documentation.** Full Operating Manuals must be provided for every program. Restart procedures should be covered in detail.

   b. **Logs.** Records should be kept of computer usage. These are used for:

      i. charging user departments.

     ii. controlling machine, operator and software performance.

c. **Operation.**

    i.   two operators should always be present

    ii. ideally duties should be rotated so that no operator is always responsible for the same run, but in practice this is not always feasible.

d. **Access.** Access to the computer room should be restricted to operating staff. The room should be locked when no manned.

e. **Fire precautions.**

    i.   there should be an automatic fire-detection system

    ii. adequate fire-fighting appliances should be provided.

f. **Stand-by** arrangements should be made for the use of a 'stand-by' machine so that essential work can be done if there is a prolonged breakdown or other mishap. These arrangements should be tested.

Note: This is often a reciprocal arrangement with another use of a similar machine.

Tape/disk library

32.11   The controls dealt with here come under the general heading of FILE SECURITY. It is important to realise that:

a. vital and irreplaceable files may be stored on magnetic tape or disk.

b. reels of tape and disk-packs are physically identical and the risk of confusion is very real.

c. the standard practice of re-using tapes and disk by 'over-writing' with new data can, if not properly controlled, result in the loss of files through operator error.

d. magnetic storage media are very easily damaged by an unsuitable environment.

32.12   a. Every reel of tape or disk-pack must be clearly labelled with a unique reference number.

b. A visual record (e.g. a card file or register) must be kept showing the current contents of each tape or disk.

c. Tapes and disks must be stored in an orderly fashion on suitable racks.

Security of tape/disk files

32.13   What we are mainly concerned with here is the security of master files. These are very valuable commodities holding as they do such information as is vital to the everyday conduct of the company's business. The contents can be damaged or destroyed by erroneous overwriting by machine or program error, or by sheer bad physical handling of the reel or pack.

32.14   **Tape files.** The method of file security is linked to the processing method. Remember a physically different c/f file is created on each updating run. The c/f file and the transaction records which were used to update it are retained for a period so that if an accident befalls the c/f master we can re-create it by processing the transactions that we have retained against the original (b/f) master. Security is then a simple matter of keeping tapes for a specific number of processing cycles.

32.15   **Disk files.**

a. If the same processing method is adopted as for tape then the file security arrangements will be the same.

b. File security of disk files where the overlay or 'in situ' method of updating is adopted is more difficult. There are two methods, sometimes used separately but often used together for maximum security:

    i.   One consists of dumping (copying) the disk file onto a tape *before* processing and then at *intervals* to provide back-up should anything happen to the disk pack. Notice the appropriate transaction files are kept also so that processing can be repeated as with tape.

    ii. During updating, those master records which are updated are dumped onto a tape before and after the particular record has been updated, thus a 'before and after' copy is held should anything go wrong.

32.16 **Fire.** The best safeguard against fire is to store the tape reel or disk-pack in a remote section or in a fire-proof safe within the computer centre itself.

Software protection

32.17 A considerable measure of protection is provided by the kernel Program of the Operating System. Each file has a standard label block at the beginning which identifies it and contains an 'expiry' date before which the file may not be overwritten. At the beginning of each run, the label is checked to ensure that:

i. if *reading* the correct file has been loaded,

ii. if *writing* the expiry date is not later than the current date (which is stored within the machine).

32.18 The manufacturer provides these checks as part of the standard software and users must avail themselves of them. Some users build additional checks into their programs.

32.19 In a multi-programming environment, the Operating System protects files from mutilation by other programs. Each program is restricted to its own files.

Write rings

32.20 A magnetic tape file is read or written during a run, but rarely both. It is possible to prevent accidental overwriting by the use of a 'write ring'. This is a plastic ring which fits into the back of a reel of tape,. If it is *not* fitted, it is impossible for the tape drive to perform a write, although the tape can be read. Protection can therefore be provided by leaving the ring off. The insertion and removal of these rings is part of standard operating procedures.

Confidential files

32.21 There are two aspects to the protection of confidential information against unauthorised inspection.

a. If the installation is completely in-house, protection can be provided by conventional methods. Confidential files (e.g. payroll) can be kept in locked storage and issued only under proper authority and supervision.

b. The problem becomes much more acute when a number of users have access to a single machine via terminals. Protection is provided by the Operating System. Each user identifies himself or herself by a 'password', without which he or she cannot gain access to the machine at all. He is then restricted to the inspection of authorised files, and this inspection may in turn be restricted to only some of the information in that file. Maximum security in the design of the Operating System is obviously of the utmost importance.

NB. Legal requirements in matters of confidentiality will be covered later in chapter 34 under the heading of Data Protection.

Summary

32.22 The following controls and standards are of particular importance.

a. Division of responsibility.

b. Training.

c. Scheduling.

d. Supervision and discipline.

e. Documentation – particularly of system and programs.

f. Performance measurement – particularly of data preparation.

g. File security.

Points to note

32.23 You may be asked why documentation is so important. The main reasons are:

a. Completion of systems and program documentation acts as an important *control* on the work of the staff responsible.

b. Documentation is important as a means of *communication* within the DP department, and between the DP department and users.

c. It provides a means both of recording *standards* and of measuring *performance* against those standards.

d. It is a vital safeguard against loss of key staff, whose knowledge may otherwise leave with them.

e. *Records* are essential for the efficient performance of many activities.

32.24 Many DP departments do not have a good reputation for control, and perhaps for this reason questions on the subject occur frequently in examinations.

32.25 When using a *computer bureau*, investigations should be made to ensure that its standards and controls are satisfactory. Particular attention should be given to controlling the flow of work to and from the bureau, and to establishing satisfactory communications.

32.26 An important general aspect of control is **'Data Security'**, i.e. the control of data to prevent its loss, misuse or disclosure.

32.27 Closely related to data security is the issue of 'Privacy'. Privacy is largely a matter of ethics, but many influence moral or legal requirements concerning the manner in which data security is implemented. (There is further discussion of this subject in chapter 44.)

Questions

1. Define briefly, and illustrate with an example, when appropriate, any six of the following electronic data processing terms:

   Check digit
   Limit check
   Parity check
   Password
   Tape mark (reflective spot)
   Conversational mode
   Batch mode
   Turn around document

   (CIMA)

2. As the financial controller of your company, one of your responsibilities is the data processing department.

   List the procedures and controls necessary to ensure that the department is run efficiently.

   (CIMA)

3. Benchmark tests are widely used for testing the performance of computers.

   What is meant by a benchmark test? In what circumstances are they used and what are their advantages and disadvantages?

   (CIMA)

4. **Either**
   a. i. What dangers are associated with storing information in magnetic form on tapes or on disks?

      ii. Describe the safeguards that should be adopted to guard against these dangers and draw a diagram to illustrate one of these safeguards.

   Or
   b. i. Name three computer output devices, each using a different concept.

      ii. Describe the features of each of the three devices named, and give an example of an application in which the use of each is relevant.

   (CIMA)

5. A file containing highly confidential information is held on magnetic tape.

   Discuss in detail the procedures which should be adopted to:

   a. ensure the confidentiality of the data on file;

   b. protect the data from loss or damage.

   (CIMA)

6. Due to a combination of an inexperienced operator and an electrical fault the main master file of 150,000 policy holders' records was destroyed.

   Describe what precautions should have been taken so that the above situation could be retrieved in the case of:

   a. a tape based installation;

   b. a disk based installation.

   (CIMA)

33 Auditing of data processing activities

Introduction

33.1 This chapter deals with the audit of computer-based systems and DP departments.

Knowledge of electronic data processing

33.2 The first task of the auditor is to acquire a knowledge of electronic data processing. Without this, he or she cannot hope to tackle a computer audit successfully. In particular, he or she should be familiar with:

    a. Organisation and responsibilities of the DP department.

    b. Data collection and validation techniques.

    c. File organisation and processing techniques.

    d. Systems controls.

    e. Methods of control of systems development, programming and operational activities.

33.3 This is a formidable amount of knowledge to master. Some teams of auditors now include members who specialise in this area. This trend is likely to increase as the use of computers spreads and computer systems become more complex and all-embracing.

File organisation and processing

33.4 The techniques used to organise and process computer files make conventional methods of audit difficult and sometimes impossible to use. The following points are of particular importance to the auditor:

    a. **'Invisible' files.** Files stored on magnetic media cannot be directly inspected in the way that, for example, a hand-written ledger can.

    b. **'Historical' data.** A complete record of previous transactions is not usually maintained in files. For example, a customer file stored on magnetic tape will often hold details of the last month's transactions only, earlier details having been deleted to keep down the length of records.

    c. **Sorting.** Source documents are often left in random order, sorting is left until data have been input and the computer can do it. The tracing of source documents can thus be difficult if sufficient attention has not been paid to the audit trail.

Division of responsibility

33.5 Computerisation means the *centralisation* of the processing of many of the applications previously carried out by *different* departments. The traditional safeguard of 'division of responsibility' can therefore be eroded. One suite of computer programs may deal with work previously carried out in several different departments. One small team of computer operators may be responsible for the processing of large volumes of work. It is essential that the auditor is aware of the dangers inherent in such a concentration, and of the safeguards that are required.

Nature of errors

33.6 The type of error which occurs in computer processing undergoes a fundamental change. Computers are usually very reliable and have extensive self-checking facilities; hardware failures which go undetected are rare. Random errors of the type made by clerks (e.g. in arithmetic and copying) are almost unknown. On the other hand, a fault in systems design or programming produces *repetitive errors*; in a given set of circumstances the same fault will occur.

33.7 It follows that much more attention must be paid by the auditor to systems development and testing. If the auditor satisfies himself that the programs are correct and that controls are adequate, less time need be devoted to checking routine operational processing.

344

Involvement in systems development

33.8 It is essential for the auditor to involve himself in the development of a system. By doing so, he or she can assure himself that:

a. The system is properly controlled.

b. Audit requirements are met.

Early involvement (beginning at the latest at the stage of system design) is important. Subsequent amendment of the system to meet audit criticisms is expensive and time-consuming.

33.9 A good working relationship must be established with systems and programming teams. Some explanation of the rights and duties of the auditor will often be needed at first. The auditor must have a sound knowledge of the appropriate control techniques, and be prepared to specify his own requirements at an early stage.

'Auditing around the computer'

33.10 One auditing technique concentrates on inputs and outputs to/from the computer and disregards the way in which such results are achieved.

It is adopted for one of two reasons:

a. The system is such that adequate checks can be made without examination of computer processing.

b. The auditor's knowledge of data processing is insufficient for him to carry out an effective audit.

33.11 In a fairly simple system, it may be possible to reconcile the outputs without reference to computer processing. For example, payment advices produced by a purchase ledger system may be reconciled with the original invoices by checking batch and file controls and sampling individual payments. This approach does become less effective as computer systems become more advanced. For example, in a sales-ledger system it will work quite well if the actual value of orders is input. But if the prices are obtained from a stock file, for example, it becomes impossible for the auditor to verify the accuracy of invoices and statements without investigation of the computer processing.

Test packs

33.12 Another auditing technique depends on the preparation of a set of test data by the auditor. Usually, a number of specimen source documents are prepared and the DP department is asked to process them. Tests are devised to ensure that:

a. Correct items are properly dealt with.

b. Errors (deliberately inserted by the auditor) are detected and reported.

33.13 Test packs may be used:

a. To test a system before it goes 'live'. The successful processing of an audit test may be a prerequisite of 'going live'.

b. To check that a system is still functioning properly after amendments have been made.

c. In the course of normal operational running, to make sure that no unauthorised alterations have been made.

33.14 The development of an *effective* test pack is a considerable undertaking and requires detailed knowledge of the system. Once available it may be re-used with little extra effort.

Audit packages

33.15 Standard software packages are now available for audit purposes. Properly used, they can save the auditor a great deal of routine work and increase the effectiveness of the audit considerably.

33.16 The packages are all essentially file-processing programs. The main facilities available are:

    a. Verification of file controls.

    b. Verification of individual balances in records.

    c. Verification that all necessary data are present in records.

    d. Selection of records according to parameters specified by the auditors: e.g.

        i.   random samples of a given percentage of the file

        ii. data outside specified limits, e.g.

            ❏   overdue accounts,

            ❏   non-active records,

            ❏   payments above a certain value. quotation

    e   Analysis of file contents: e.g.

        i.   debts by age or type of customer,

        ii. payments by size or type,

        iii. stock holdings by value.

    f.   Comparisons of two files (reporting any differences) to verify the accuracy of file maintenance.

33.17 The main considerations in selecting a package are:

    a. Cost.

    b. Facilities provided.

    c. Ease of use.

    d. Efficiency (in terms of machine time needed).

    The auditor requires a reasonable amount of computer time to run packages and other tests that he considers necessary.

Constructing an audit trail

33.18 The conventional audit trail relies on visible records, but because computer processing is carried out electronically and the files themselves are in machine-sensible form the trail disappears. It can be constructed to some extent by arranging for print-outs of data and files at intermediate points in processing (i.e. between the input of data and production of outputs). Audit packages may be used for the purpose. Alternatively, the systems designer may be asked to provide for special audit reports, either routinely or on demand. Such reports may be produced for:

    a. Exceptional transactions.

    b. Random samples.

    c. Sections of files (for detailed audit).

    d. Intermediate file-control totals.

On-line and real-time systems

33.19 These systems increase the difficulties of the auditor, because:

  a. The input of data from a number of remote points is not easily controlled.

  b. Source documents are not always readily available for inspection and sometimes may not exist at all (e.g. orders taken by telephone).

  c. Some control techniques (e.g. verification of keyboarding, batch controls) cannot be used.

  d. Unauthorised use of the computer or unauthorised inspection of its files may be possible.

  e. Immediate processing of transactions through all stages in real-time systems may make an audit trail impossible.

33.20 It becomes even more important for the auditor to check the system software thoroughly. He or she must pay particular attention to:

  a. Validity check of input.

  b. Protection against unauthorised inspection of files.

  c. Proper identification of terminal users by passwords.

  d. Reporting of exceptional or suspicious transactions or enquiries.

33.21 A useful technique is the monitoring of terminal activities by the central machine. All traffic for a certain period for a selected terminal can be recorded and audited. It is also possible for the auditor to make unannounced visits to terminal locations.

Systems development and programming

33.22 An audit of systems development and programming may be made by:

  a. Inspecting systems and program specifications and program documentation. Systems specifications should be made available to the auditor as a matter of routine.

  b. Inspecting system and program tests to ensure that thorough testing has been carried out.

  c. Reviewing an operational system to ensure that:

   i. Specified objectives are being achieved.

   ii. Costs are not excessive.

   iii. Users are satisfied with the service received.

   iv. The number of errors is not excessive.

  d. Inspecting records of the progress and output of systems analysts and programmers.

Operational sections

33.23 The auditor can check the efficiency of operational sections by:

  a. Inspecting records: e.g.

   i. Computer logs.

   ii. Output and error records of the Data Preparation operators.

   iii. Work progress and error records kept by the Data Control Section.

  b. Verifying the accuracy and punctuality of computer processing with user departments.

  c. General observation of standards of discipline, tidiness, punctuality, etc.

Check lists

33.24 Check lists are a useful aid to the auditor who has to deal with a DP department. They consist of comprehensive questionnaires covering all aspects of control. Standard lists are available from, for example, The Institute of Chartered Accountants and appear in other auditing publications.

Summary

33.25 The auditor must familiarise himself with data-processing techniques and the work of the DP department.

33.26 He must always bear in mind:
    i.   the novel features of computer-file organisation and processing.
    ii. the concentration of responsibility within the DP department.
    iii. the repetitive nature of computer-system errors.

33.27 The main audit techniques are:
    i.   involvement in systems development.
    ii. auditing round the computer.
    iii. test packs.
    iv. audit packages.
    v. construction of an audit trail.
    vi. check lists.

Points to note

33.28 a. If you are using this book to prepare for an auditing paper, do not limit your reading to this chapter. Study also:
    ❏ Chapter 10 (Choices and Practices)
    ❏ Chapter 38 (Control of Data-Processing Activities) quotation

     b. Auditors are not expected to understand programs. However, they should have enough knowledge of system and program documentation to be able to scrutinise it intelligently.

The social aspect

In the first Part of this text the reader was asked to bear in mind that IT systems have an important role to play in enabling the organisations they serve to meet their goals. The reader should, having read this far, be able to see how IT systems, with particular reference to DP, can play such a role. The following chapter returns to a somewhat broader view by looking at DP and IT not only within organisations but within society as a whole.

34 Computers in society

Introduction

34.1 The role of computers in society is a large subject to consider and this chapter merely highlights some important issues. Computers are just one example of automation although they have many special features. In a society which relies heavily on all forms of automation and on the automated handling of information, computers are bound to be very important. Issues related to jobs and privacy are particularly significant.

Computers in information technology

34.2 It is generally recognised that we live in an industrial society in which the efficiency of production of wealth depends heavily on various kinds of automation. Computers are special in that they *automate many methods of processing information*. Computers are also playing an ever increasing role in many other forms of automation.

34.3 Computers, telecommunications equipment, and other technologies associated with automation come under the general heading of **Information Technology (IT)**. Information Technology is having an impact on individuals, organisations and society. Various aspects of this impact will be discussed in the remainder of this chapter. Particular reference will be made to computers, and some key issues, notably privacy and employment.

The general background

34.4 Prior to industrialisation approximately 90% of the labour force was engaged in agriculture, i.e. society was agrarian. Methods of communication were limited and a very small proportion of the labour force was involved with the processing, storage and retrieval of information, which in any case merely involved manual paper-based methods or word of mouth.

Industrialisation produced a major shift in the labour force, with the proportion involved in agriculture falling below 10 in the UK. With industrialisation came the beginning of Information Technology and the start of a series of IT developments taking us right up to the present day: Telegraph, Telephone, Radio/TV, Computers, Microelectronics, etc.

34.5 These new forms of IT, and other developments, produced new forms of work. The larger scale of organisations has given rise to large administrative structures in which there are large numbers of clerical workers and people with technical and managerial skills collectively known as 'white collar workers'. Computerisation has mainly affected white collar work so far.

34.6 In addition to changes in the type of work there has been an increase in the number of organisations involved in activities other than manufacture. Some such organisations, for example those in the power industries, contribute to manufacturing and provide a general service. As a result of this change only 25% of the labour force remained in organisations directly involved in the manufacture of goods. For a number of reasons, not particularly related to IT, that 25% has fallen to 20% in the last few years and levels of unemployment have risen.

34.7 The fact that so few remain in manufacture, although manufacturing continues to generate most wealth, has lead to society today being called 'Post Industrial Society'.

34.8 Looking at the whole of the national and international community, and at the way organisations are run, highlights the fact that modern society is heavily dependent on the communication, processing and storage of information. It is claimed by some that we are moving towards an 'Information Society' in which the majority of the labour force will be engaged in information processing and the use of 'Information Technology'.

34.9 It is a mistake to imagine that technological innovation is what causes such changes. Such changes are the collective result of actions taken by those people able to control and influence the use and distribution of resources, within their own organisations, or within society at large. The uses of resources are determined by the goals that are being pursued. The next section looks at these issues.

Organisations

34.10 The uses of computers in various kinds of organisations have been discussed in a number of earlier chapters. The term 'organisation' was used fairly informally. However, it is possible to be more formal in defining what an organisation is and doing so highlights some significant points.

34.11 An organisation is a human group which has been deliberately constructed with the aim of seeking specific goals. An organisation will be reconstructed, from time to time, so that it can continue to seek its goals effectively.

34.12 The goals sought will depend on the organisation.

Examples.

a. The owners of commercial organisations may have profit as their goal with themselves as the main beneficiaries, e.g. in private or public companies.

b. The goals of many organisations are to provide 'services' to their clients or the general public, e.g. medical services, schools and colleges.

c. Other organisations have the mutual benefit of their members as goals, e.g. clubs or trade unions.

34.13 Any organisation needs to be controlled and co-ordinated and to be able to plan ahead. To do so it will need information and facilities to communicate.

34.14 In most organisations, and particularly in large ones, Information Technology can aid in the processing of information and thereby help the organisation to meet its goals. Whether or not an organisation uses such technology will depend on its evaluation of the technology in relation to its own goals.

Evaluation of information systems

34.15 There are many methods of evaluating new methods and technologies. In the area of computerisation the main methods are those used in Systems Development (chapters 43-47). A proposed computer system is evaluated in terms of how well it can meet objectives which will enable the organisation to meet goals such as optimum service or optimum use of resources.

34.16 The results of such evaluations determine whether organisations invest in computers. This in turn promotes or limits technological developments.

34.17 Large organisations such as government bodies or large corporations can have a major influence in this way. For example the US government attached a high importance to micro-electronics and silicon chip technology because of the goals of providing national defence. That depended on having miniaturised electronic circuitry in rockets, planes, etc. The necessary research and development costs were provided from the defence budget.

Computerisation and work

34.18 When computers are introduced into organisations because of the benefits they can provide, it usually affects the work of staff within the organisation. Some jobs are changed, some may be created and some may be lost. This creates a demand for training and retraining.

34.19 Any loss of jobs due to computerisation can give rise to alarm, particularly at a time of high unemployment. However, such job 'losses' probably signify yet another shift in the work of the general labour force, as has happened many times in the past.

34.20 Only a very small proportion of the current level of unemployment is directly attributable to new technology. In certain particular applications jobs are likely to be lost, notably:

a. some office jobs, e.g. caused by Word Processing.

b. Factory production where industrial robots may replace production-line workers.

34.21 Whether these job losses will result in permanent unemployment is another matter. It depends on the process of redeployment of labour and labour retraining. It may help to consider an example at this stage.

34.22 In the USA in the early 1970s there were proposals to introduce bar-coded PoS equipment into supermarkets. This appeared to be an attractive proposition because a saving of millions could be achieved if such equipment was introduced into 5000 stores.

34.23 Initially there was alarm from the trade unions, who predicted 20% job losses by 1975, the date at which implementation was due to be completed.

34.24 These fears were unfounded for two reasons. First, the rate at which the new technology was introduced was much slower, which allowed staffing changes to be dealt with by redeployment and natural wastage. By 1979 only 803 stores had equipment installed. Very different from the predicted 5000 by 1975. The trade unions were also able to negotiate an automation deal with their employers. This protected their jobs. The store owners were still able to make large savings by the introduction of the equipment, and to redeploy staff in ventures which improved and extended company activities. (In Britain the banks have also used automation to allow them to redeploy staff in broader and better services.)

34.25 Since these early difficulties were overcome the introduction of the equipment has continued smoothly in the USA and at an increasing rate. In Britain this kind of supermarket automation is still some way behind the USA.

Privacy

34.26 Another consequence of higher levels of computerisation is the increase in the use of computer-based equipment to store large quantities of data about individuals. Some of this data is of a particularly personal or private nature and there is a natural concern that it should not be misused. There is also concern that individuals may have personal information stored about them without their knowledge or control, and that it may be hard or impossible to find out whether such information is accurate.

34.27 In 1975 a government white paper considered this issue and in 1976 a committee was set up chaired by Sir Norman Lindop. The idea was that systems dealing with records containing personal details should be controlled.

34.28 The Lindop Report appeared about two years later and was well received. It established a number of principles, e.g. that stored data should only be used for the purpose for which its use was originally authorised and intended. The report suggested that a **Data Protection Authority (DPA)** should be set up which would enforce codes of conduct for different types of systems.

34.29 At about the same time, the Council of Europe set up a 'Convention for the Protection of Individuals with regard to Automatic Processing of Personal Data'. Each country signs twice, one to agree to legislate and the second time when it has legislated. Britain had only signed once by early 1984 and computer organisations such as the BCS (British Computer Society) and CSA (Computer Services Association) had expressed fears that delays could cost the UK dearly in terms of lost international contracts through failure to introduce legislation.

34.30 Such legislation is the primary responsibility of the Home Office, itself an important user of computer data banks of an unusual kind, e.g. those concerned with police records like those held on the Police National Computer at Hendon (North London).

34.31 A further government white paper appeared early in 1982. It only covered some aspects of data protection. In April 1983 a bill began its passage through Parliament but ran into initial trouble over the issue of confidentiality. The bill was lost when the general election was called. It was reintroduced, in a slightly modified form, becoming an Act in 1984.

The 1984 data protection act

34.32 The 1984 Data Protection Act was intended 'to regulate the use of automatically processed information relating to individuals and the provision of services in respect of such information'. What is immediately apparent is that the Act does not cover manual records. This fact is not only a disappointment to those concerned with freedom of information but may also be a discouragement to the use of computers for some applications.

34.33 The Act defines a number of terms including 'Data' (information in a processable form), 'Personal Data' (data relating to identifiable living individuals) and 'Data Subject' (the living individuals concerned).

34.34 The Act requires those using personal data to register with the **Data Protection Registrar**. The end of April 1986 was set as the deadline for initial registrations for existing users.

34.35 There are a number of general and specific exemptions. These exemptions are the subject of considerable controversy and practical difficulties. At the general level there are exemptions for a number of government departments for reasons stated to be related to national security and covering some aspects of criminal records, immigration, health and social security. More specifically, there are exemptions for work such as word processing, pensions, accounting and payroll. However, these exemptions are rather weak in that if the system under consideration carries out other tasks it may not be exempt. For example, if the payroll system is used for anything more than calculating and paying wages it will not be exempt.

34.36 An organisation may easily make a genuine mistake in interpreting these rules but will still be liable to criminal prosecution. Therefore, it is not surprising that many organisations have appointed an expert whose sole responsibility is to deal with matters concerned with the Act. The title for such a post is normally that of **Data Protection Officer.**

34.37 In future, it will be important for all staff involved in data processing to have an awareness of what the Act covers so that they know when to consult a Data Protection Officer for specific advice.

34.38 The main points covered by the Act which need to be borne in mind are:

    a. Data about individuals which is held for processing must have been obtained fairly for a specific lawful purpose.

    b. The data must only be used for the specific purpose and may only be disclosed in accordance with the specific purpose.

    c. Data must not be excessive for the purpose but merely adequate and relevant.

    d. Data must be accurate, up to date and kept no longer than necessary.

    e. The data must be protected and held securely against unauthorised access or loss but must be accessible to data subjects on request.

Computer crime

34.39 Three aspects of computer crime are often reported in the media and deserve a mention here because of their social importance.

    a. Hacking and Computer fraud

    b. Computer viruses

    c. Copyright piracy

34.40 Originally the term **'hacker'** meant a programmer who worked in an skilful but undisciplined way. More recently the name has become associated with individuals who make a hobby of making unauthorised access to computer systems, especially via dial-in lines or across computer networks. Although the individuals concerned often regard their activities as a game this antisocial behaviour often leads to loss and inconvenience to the individuals affected by the hackers. Legislation has now been passed in many countries, including the UK, to make hacking illegal in most cases. The methods used by hackers to bypass system security are often very similar to those used by individuals concerned in computer fraud. Those working with computer systems have a responsibility to make their own systems as safe and secure as possible.

34.41 A **computer virus** is a piece of software which attaches itself to an another program on a system in order both to spread itself to other programs and to have some undesirable affect on the programs it becomes attached to. The parallels with the way in which a biological virus affects other organisms gave rise to the term 'computer virus'. Computer viruses usually infect system by being introduced via disks which have already been infected. When a virus infected program is run the virus, which has modified its host, is able to replicate itself. Some viruses are merely annoying, such as the one which causes a small dot to wander randomly on the screen. Others are downright nasty like those which cause data on disks to be corrupted or deleted. There are many virus detection packages on the market today.

34.42 **Software Piracy** occurs when individuals use unauthorised copies of software. It is just like any other breach of copyright and the individuals or companies responsible can face stiff penalties.

The future

34.43 The current rapid rate of computerisation and technical innovation has lead some people to talk of a 'microelectronics revolution'. To others these changes are merely viewed as another phase in the process of automation which started with the industrial revolution. Either way it seems reasonable to expect change and yet more change in the future.

34.44 The 'fifth-generation' super-computers may well be here by the end of the century if current research and development programmes keep to schedule. Who can say whether these computers will cause delight or dismay? The answers do not rest in the technology.

Summary

34.45 a. The place of computers in Information Technology was discussed.
  b. The general background to the current state of computerisation in society was given.
  c. Organisations were defined and their role in computerisation was discussed.
  d. Computerisation and its impact on employment was discussed.
  e. Privacy and recent development in data protection were discussed.
  f. The future was considered briefly.

Points to note

34.46 Computerisation is not just a matter of technological innovation and development. It is a process which involves individuals, organisations and society in general.

Case exercises

1. The case exercises in the following chapter comprise questions on particular application systems. The questions, which will probably take over an hour to answer, are accompanied by suggested solutions and author's notes.

2. Although the questions are primarily taken from the examinations set by CIMA, they should also prove useful to students preparing for other examinations for which this book is used as a text.

35 Case exercises

Introduction

35.1 The questions given in this chapter are quite long by normal examination standards. In fact an examination candidate would have one hour and twelve minutes to devote to producing an answer. The answer would be worth a maximum of 40% of the marks obtainable in the three-hour examination.

35.2 It takes some time to understand these questions and it would be quite reasonable to spend fifteen minutes, or more, in reading the question and planning a solution.

35.3 You may find it helps you to understand each question better if you try to sketch a systems flowchart on a second reading and if you also underline what appear to be important facts given in the question.

35.4 Suggested solutions follow each question. Do not be alarmed if your answers are different. Questions of this kind are open to a variety of interpretations. As long as your answer is well thought out and properly takes into account the details given in the question you have little to worry about. However, by comparing your answers with those suggested you should be able to improve the quality of your answers and build up your confidence.

35.5 In order to be as instructive as possible some non-essential detail has been added to the solutions.

Question 1

A company manufacturing and selling a range of 200 standard stationery products is planning to employ a mini-computer for its routine administration, accounting procedures, and stock and production activities.

The computer configuration will comprise a processor, 10 megabytes of disk storage, a 150 lines per minute printer and three visual display units.

The first application envisaged is an integrated order processing, finished stock control, sales invoicing and accounting, and sales analysis system.

The majority of orders are received by telephone and will be input interactively on a visual display unit sited in the sales office. Facilities will be provided for the checking of credit status and the determination of product availability.

Each day all orders received up to 4.00 pm will be accumulated and documents printed out before 5.00 pm. These documents will be sent to the despatch department for the packing and despatch of goods the following day.

Despatch data will be input on a visual display unit located in the despatch department. This will update the order position and will generate data for invoicing purposes. Invoices will be produced in batch mode once per day.

In the context of the above, **you are required to**:

a.   identify the transactions which will be required to be input for this system;

b.   describe briefly the contents of the main files;

c.   list in sequence the processes associated with order input, emphasising the interactive nature of this part of the system;

d.   produce system run flowcharts of the batch procedures involved in the production of daily invoices and periodic sales analyses (assume two analyses, one by product within area sequence and one by customer type).

[(a) and (b) 5 marks each, part (c) 10 marks and part (d) 20 marks = 40 marks]
(CIMA)

Answer 1

1. Author's preliminary notes

a. You are only required to produce system run flowcharts for batch procedures, but a quick sketch of the systems flowchart of the *whole* system may help your understanding of the question.

b. Since the question mentions an 'integrated' system we should envisage a system in which data items should not need to be re-input for each processing procedure.

c. The 'interactive' features of ordering require that master files must be kept up to date throughout the day.

d. The 'batch' nature of the despatch procedures suggests that products and customer credit committed to orders are held pending until the despatch procedure takes place.

2. Suggested solution

a. **Required input transactions:**

    i. Customers' orders.

    ii. Cancellations or changes to Customers' orders.

    iii. Despatch data for orders.

    iv. Product receipts, amendments, insertions, deletions and returns.

    v. Customer cash receipts, credits, debits, insertions and deletions.

b. **Contents of main files:**

    i. Products master file:

        Product number

        Product description

        Total quantity in stock ⎫ Difference, i.e. 'free' stock could be stored
        Stock allocated to orders ⎬ or calculated

        Unit selling price (ex VAT) ⎫ **Current and Previous**
        VAT rate ⎬

        Reorder level

        Quantity on order from production.

    ii. Customer master file:

        [NB. This single logical file will probably be split into several physical files.]

        Customer account number

        Customer name and address ⎫ Alternative addresses for
        Area code ⎬ deliveries/invoices, etc, may be recorded

        Customer type

        Credit limit

        Current balance excluding non-despatched orders

        Current balance including non-despatched orders

        Date and number of last order (despatched and non-despatched)

        order details

        details of receipts

        etc.

iii. Pending orders file:

> Order number (generated automatically
> on creation)
>
> Customer account number
>
> Customer address
>
> Total value (ex. VAT) (inc. VAT)
>
> Product number
> Product description
> Quantity required } Repeated for each product
> Unit price
> Total selling price (with and without VAT)

iv. Despatched Orders file – as for pending orders

v. VAT master file:

> Order Number
>
> Invoice Number
>
> Customer account number
>
> VAT amount (at each rate)
>
> Total amount

vi. Sales analysis file:

> Product number
>
> Invoice number
>
> Order number
>
> Customer type
>
> Area code
>
> Quantity despatched/returned.

c. **Order input**

i. All orders will be entered via a VDU by a clerk. The majority of orders are telephoned in and it is the handling of these orders which exploits the interactive facilities of the system.

ii. The customers will identify themselves to the clerk by giving their account number and name when they telephone. The customer account number will be keyed in by the clerk. The customer details will then be displayed on the VDU screen so that the clerk can confirm names and addresses and check credit status. If at any stage in creating the order the credit limit it reached the clerk will have to adopt the appropriate credit control procedure, e.g. reference to a supervisor. The order number will be generated by the computer.

iii. The customer will specify which products are required by reference to a catalogue or similar document. The clerk will assist the customer as necessary and will key in the product number. Product details will be displayed on the screen, including the free stock available. The clerk will key in the quantity required unless there is insufficient stock available, in which case some appropriate action will be taken, e.g. order an alternative, or accept order despite the delay.

iv. The customer and products files will be updated to reflect the current state of affairs, e.g. current balance and allocated stock will require changing.

v. Different screen displays will appear at each stage of order entry according to whether the customer is confirming addresses, enquiring about products, deciding upon quantities required, or asking for unit or total prices.

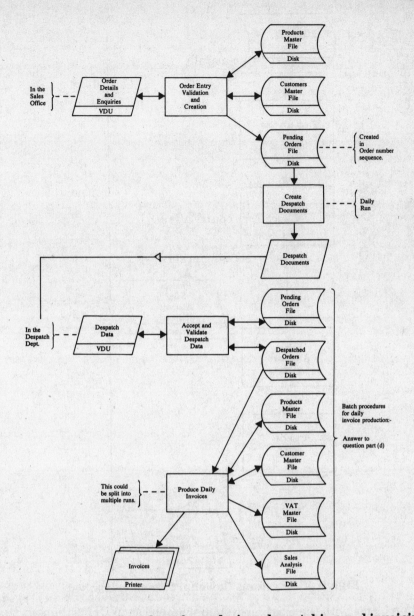

Figure 35.1 Systems flowchart for ordering, despatching and invoicing

[NB. In the absence of any evidence in the question to the contrary it is assumed that the
disks have the capacities and software necessary for simultaneous file processing.]

Question 2

A car spares wholesaler supplies several hundred small garages with spare parts by a daily van
service.

There is a stock of approximately 10,000 different spare parts and an average of 200 orders are dealt
with daily with an average of five items on each order. Most orders are received by telephone and
when ordering each garage invariably asks about the availability of the parts required and the
delivery position.

The orders are made up by the stores department and a van driver takes the goods and an advice
note to the garage. The invoice is sent by post later.

At present there is a manual system based on card-index files, hand written order forms, and daily
stock updating which is done by an evening shift. The invoices are typed from the stores notes and
the sales ledger is maintained by a keyboard accounting machine.

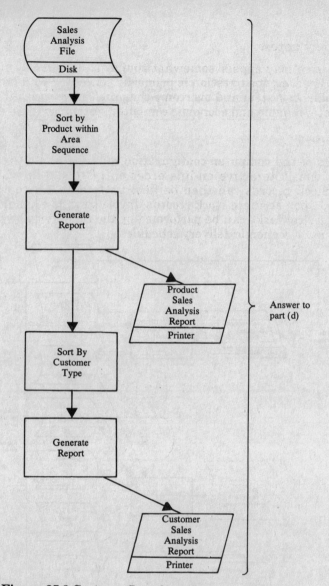

Figure 35.2 Systems flowchart for sales analysis

There are several problems with the existing system, namely:

i.   overload at several points in the system causing delays, for example, in stock record updating and in invoice preparation;

ii.   inaccurate stock records;

iii.   uneconomic stock control procedures;

iv.   uneconomic delivery schedules.

The wholesaler is considering installing a computer to deal with order handling, stock control and invoicing procedures.

You are required to:

a.   describe briefly a suitable computer configuration together with a rationale for the equipment chosen;

b.   draw a systems flowchart showing how the computer would handle the wholesaler's procedures, with sufficient narrative to explain your system;

c.   give specific examples of ways in which a computer based system could increase the organisation's efficiency.

[(a) 10 marks, part (b) 25 marks and part (c) 5 marks = 40 marks]
(CIMA)

Answer 2

1. Author's preliminary notes.

At face value this question may appear somewhat similar to question 1, in that it also deals with a stock-control system. However, the question is primarily concerned with how a computer system can be used to replace a manual system and overcome the problems associated with the manual system. A fast, efficient, accurate, reliable and economic computer system is required.

2. Suggested Solution.

a. i. The features of the computer configuration must help to overcome the problems of the existing system. Interactive on-line order entry should be effective in overcoming the problems. Stock records can then be kept up to date. Customers will be able to make orders based upon accurate stock records. Invoicing can be handled efficiently and quickly. Repetitive clerical tasks can be performed by the computer and the computer can be used to generate more economic delivery schedules.

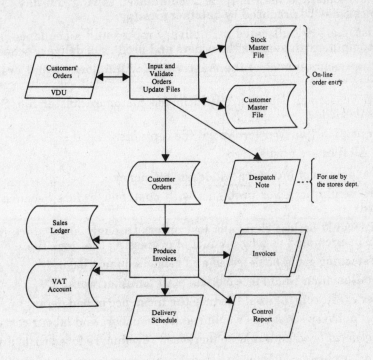

Figure 35.3 Order entry and invoice creation

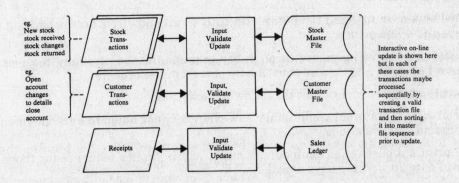

Figure 35.4 Outline system flowcharts for the remainder of the system

ii. Interactive order entry suggests that VDUs should be used, and since an average of 200 orders per day must be entered, which corresponds to 25 orders per hour in an 8-hour day, several VDUs will be needed. Given that other data will also need to be entered, 6, or possibly more VDUs may be necessary.

iii. Disks are essential for file storage in an on-line system. The size of the stock file suggests that in order to provide suitable disk storage two or more large disk drives are needed. Having at least two disk drives also makes disk file security more straightforward.

iv. The number of despatch notes and invoices required can be produced on a line printer. There may be some merit in having an additional printer, accessible from the stores, which can be used to produce despatch notes as the orders are created.

v. The peripherals and processing functions identified so far suggest that a minicomputer system is required to handle the work. Such a system should have sufficient main storage and the appropriate system and application software.

b. i. Orders are entered on-line (see answer to question 1) (figure 35.3).

ii. The customers' orders may be accumulated during the day (or half day) and then the invoices may be produced by batch processing.

iii. If customers are allocated set delivery routes and a sequence position on the route then the computer can analyse the orders and produce a delivery schedule for the driver.

iv. Routine maintenance of the master files will follow normal practice (see notes on figure 35.4).

v. 'Static' customer details are held in the customer master file. Sales details are stored in the sales ledger.

vi. See question 1 answer for typical file contents.

vii. **NB.** All files are on disk.

c. Specific examples of increased wholesale efficiency.

i. There would be fewer problems with customer orders because of the accuracy of stock records.

ii. There would be less change of lost orders through out-of-stock items because re-ordering could be prompted as a by-product of processing the stock file.

iii. Overstocking could be detected and remedied more easily.

iv. The automation would free clerical staff for other work.

v. Better credit control would reduce the incidence of bad debts.

vi. Better delivery schedules would reduce transport and labour costs.

vii. The *general benefits* would be increased revenue, reduced costs and improved services.

Question 3

An insurance company specialises in motor business and operates through a network of approximately 100 brokers.

The company has a medium sized computer with both serial and direct access backing storage, key to disk encoders, and a line printer.

All communications to customers are through the brokers and the company receives amendments, premiums, new risks and all other information by post from the brokers.

The data processing system deals with the following activities:

a. Daily processing of input comprising: new clients, client amendments, payment receipts, file amendments and deletions.

b. Daily print out of renewal reminders in client within broker sequence for those clients with a renewal date 20 working days ahead.

c. Weekly processing of agreed claims; production of claim payments, claims statistics and updating of client files.

d.   Weekly print out in client within broker sequence of payments overdue, of part payments and of clients whose insurance has been automatically terminated. An insurance is automatically terminated if a communication has not been received on or before the fourteenth working day after renewal date.

e.   Monthly analysis of premiums received and claims made by vehicle category within occupation code within zone code.

f.   Monthly analysis of new business, cumulative premium income, claims made, commission due or earned (monthly and cumulative year to date) for each broker.

The major items contained in the main client file are as follows:

    Client number
    Client name
    Client address
    Client date of birth
    Vehicle make and registration number
    Vehicle category
    Client occupation code
    Insurance category
    Voluntary excess
    Restrictions on use
    Zone
    Premium
    Premium renewal date
    Last premium paid date
    Claims record
    Broker reference quotation

You are required to:

a.   draw a systems run flowchart or flowcharts to deal with the activities specified above: your flowchart(s) must contain sufficient narrative to identify clearly what work is being carried out and in particular the major items contained in any files used other than the client file which is already specified;

b.   discuss briefly ways in which the time delays inherent in the existing batch processing system could be eliminated or reduced.

[(a) 30, (b) 10 = 40 marks]
(CIMA)

Answer 3

1. Author's preliminary note.

In answering this question pay particular attention to where data is stored, when data is entered and when data is used to provide reports. This will help you to identify the main processing activities needed and what other files are needed within the system.

2. Suggested solution.

a.   i.   Since 'all communications with customers are through brokers' the client master file has been organised as a sequential file in client within broker sequence.

    ii.   A brokers' master file is considered necessary. Since direct-access backing storage is available the brokers' file has been organised as an index sequential file (processed randomly in figures 35.5–35.8 and sequentially in figure 35.10).

    iii.   The brokers' master file contains the following items:

        Broker's reference

363

Broker's name and address
Number of clients
Number of new clients
Number of clients lost
Premiums received
Number of claims made
Value of claims made

} This month and year to date

iv. The systems flowcharts figures 35.5–10 have been annotated so as to reduce the supporting narrative.

v. The clients' master file is a sequential file (which may be stored on disk or tape).

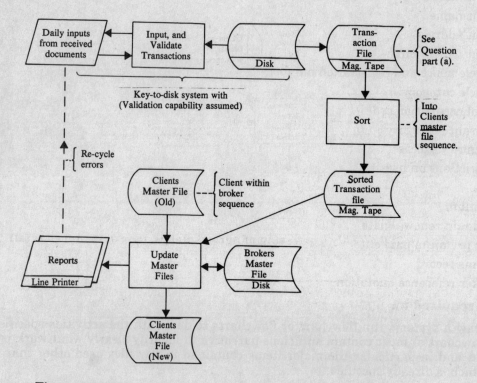

Figure 35.5 Daily input and update. (See question part (a))

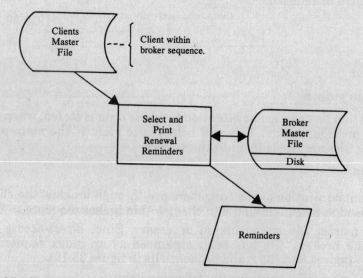

Figure 35.6 Daily printout of renewal reminders. (See question part (b))

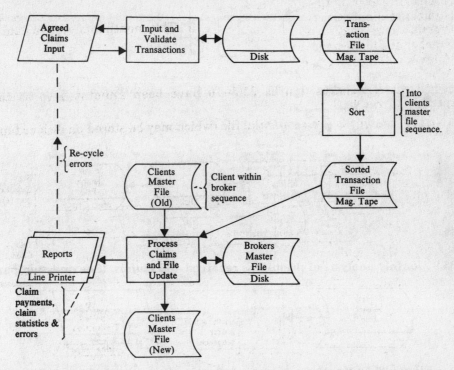

Figure 35.7 Weekly processing of agreed claims. (See question part (c))

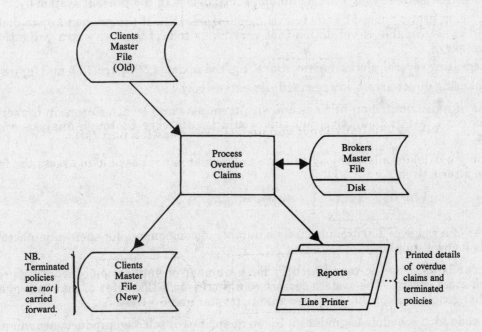

Figure 35.8 Weekly processing for overdue claims. (See question part (d))

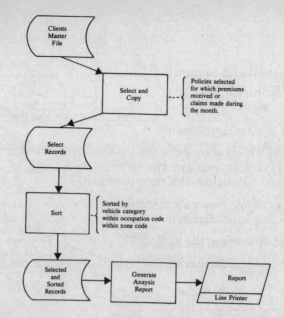

Figure 35.9 Monthly analysis of premiums received and claims. (See question part (e))

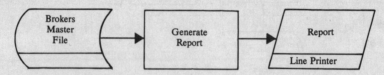

Figure 35.10 Monthly analysis of brokers. (See question part (f))

b.   An interactive on-line system could eliminate time delays in the present system by:

i.   Reducing delays caused by the re-cycling of errors. [NB. If the present key-to-disk system used is not capable of validation (not very likely today) then an extra validation run is necessary.]

ii. Integrating several processing functions, e.g. the updates of figure 35.5 and figure 35.7.

iii. Exploiting direct-access storage facilities extensively.

The use of a distributed on-line system with terminals and local printers in brokers' offices could be very fast and effective, but this would need a very thorough analysis and design process.

Since only partial details of the system are provided it is not possible to assess the feasibility of these alternatives.

Question 4

A manufacturer of a range of 200 products uses a number of components for their manufacture. Each component has its own supplier.

A mini-computer is used by the manufacturer for a number of applications including production scheduling and stock control. The system comprises a processor, 512k bytes of main storage, two 60 megabyte exchangeable disks, a 300 lines per minute printer and 6 VDUs.

Each week a production schedule is produced. Given quantities of selected products are input and the required quantities of components for each product are printed in a report. The products master file is structured so as to facilitate this processing. Without any further data entry, a report is produced which lists the components in sequence, details the total number of components used and identifies any products affected by insufficient component stock. Production is changed if necessary. The major items in the components file are as follows:

   Component number
   Component description

Supplier code

Unit cost

Quantity in Stock (actual and committed)

Reorder details e.g. reorder level

Quantity on order

Quantity used (year to date) quotation

a.   Draw systems flowcharts which show how the various processing procedures are carried out. Provide sufficient narrative to explain the system and indicate clearly the major items contained in any files used other than the components file.

b.   When component prices change how can the affected products be identified? What changes to the system would make this identification simpler.

c.   Suggest possible ways of improving the system.

[(a) 25 marks, part (b) 10 marks and part (c) 5 marks = 40 marks]
(CIMA)

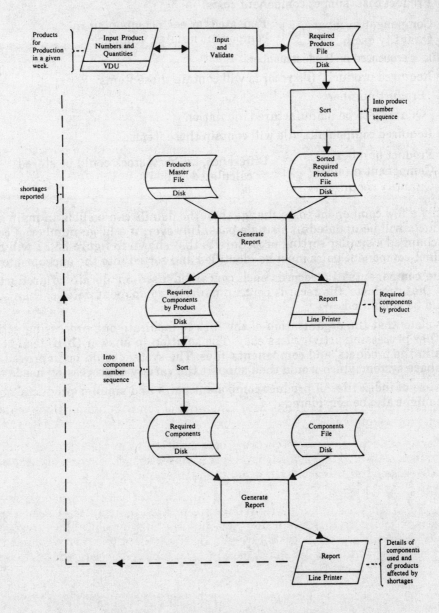

Figure 35.11 Systems flowcharts. (See question part (a))

Answer 4

1. Author's preliminary notes.

a. Only part of the whole system has been described, so this will be reflected in the answer to part (a) of the question.

b. It is the fact that there are many products, each containing many components, which causes the file organisation and processing problems in this application.

2. Suggested solution.

a. i. The products' file 'facilitates' the production of the first report and is therefore assumed to have the following structure:

Product number

Product name

Product description

Product stock details

Product cost (sum of component costs)

Component number ⎫ Repeated for each component in
Quantity used ⎭ component number sequence

The file is sequenced on Product number.

ii. The Required products' file records will contain these items:

Product number

Quantity to be manufactured. quotation

iii. The Required components' file will contain these items:

Product number ⎫ Difference, i.e. 'free' stock could be stored
Component number ⎬ or calculated
Quantity required ⎭

b. i. If only a few component costs change then the details can be held in main storage and the products will be updated in a single pass. However, if a large number of component costs are changed a similar sorting procedure to that shown in figure 35.11 will be required, i.e. product-component pairs must be identified and sorted into the appropriate sequences.

ii. If the components' file records each contained 'used-on' details of products, in the same way that products' file records contain multiple component details, then some processing would be simplified.

iii. It is clear that the organisation of the files to facilitate one processing activity can make another processing activity less easy. The solution in answer (b)ii. leads to replication of data in the products' and components' files. The system could be improved by the use of a database system which would then support the variety of processing needs more easily.

The use of index files of product-component pairs and simpler products' and components' files might also be considered.

Appendix 1 Answers to questions at chapter ends

Chapter 1

1. (1.6).
2. (1.5).
3. (1.21c)
4. (1.28)
5. (1.31)
6. a. (1.34) b. (1.40)
7. (1.84)
8. (1.80a)

Chapter 2

1. (2.3b)
2. (2.14 – 2.15)
3. (2.7)
4. (2.7d)
5. a. (2.29 b. (2.27) c. (2.35)

Chapter 3

1. (3.9).

Chapter 4

1. (4.8 – 4.22)
2. (4.42).
3. (4.56 – 4.57)

Chapter 5

1. (5.3)
2. **Possible advantages of batching**.
   a. Processing data in batches tends to be more efficient and economical than processing single transactions.
   b. Batching provides manageable units for control purposes.
   c. Processing can be left until slack times in some cases.

   Possible disadvantages of batching.
   a. Delays in obtaining information.
   b. Correct transactions being delayed still further because of errors in other transactions in the same batch.
   c. Uneven loads on the processing facilities.

Chapter 6

1. a. (6.11)   b. (6.18)   c. (6.14b)   d. (6.18)
2. (6.16 – 6.19).

Chapter 7

NO QUESTIONS

Chapter 8

1.   (8.3 & 8.11)

Chapter 9

1.   (9.19)

2.   (e.g Desktop laser printer, daisywheel printer, NLQ printer)

Chapter 10

1.   ALL stages (10.10)

2.   Human sensible – readable by a human.

   Machine sensible – readable by a machine.

   OCR and MICR are examples of human sensible and machine sensible input methods.

3.   **Introduction**

   It must be noted that advantages and disadvantages are relative. Also in many cases a user will disregard certain disadvantages of being of no consequences, or will be obliged to adopt a method despite its disadvantages. Finally, as has already been pointed out in the text, some methods will be better suited for certain applications than others.

   Magnetic tape cassette

   Possible advantages:

   a.   Can be prepared as a by-product.

   b.   Inexpensive.

   c.   Easily transportable.

   Possible disadvantages:

   a.   Slower input than 0.5' tape.

   b.   Smaller capacity of cassette.

   Key-to-diskette including preparation on pcs

   Possible advantages:

   a.   Data is encoded directly onto the diskette.

   b.   There is no document handling involved.

   c.   Error correction is easy.

   d.   Diskettes are easily transportable.

   Possible disadvantages:

   Diskette needs careful handling.

   OCR

   Possible advantages:

   a.   No transcription is required, thus there are no errors in the data preparation stage.

   b.   Characters are both human and machine-sensible.

   c.   Documents prepared in OC are suitable for use as turnaround documents.

Possible disadvantages:
- a. A high standard printing of optical characters is required.
- b. High document standards are needed to keep down error rejections.
- c. The cost of readers/scanners is relatively high, especially those used on-line to the computer.

MICR

Advantages and disadvantages as for OCR except that print tolerances are much stricter.

Possible disadvantage:

Very high degree of accuracy required in forming characters.

Bar coded strips and magnetically coded strips

Possible advantages:
- a. Data is captured at source.
- b. Data collection is done mainly by machine (handling excluded).
- c. Sales attendant's job is simplified as data is already recorded.

Possible disadvantages:
- a. There are limits to the amount of data which can be stored on the strip.
- b. Problems arise if (in retailing) goods are marked down in price.
- c. The strips have to be printed or stuck onto every item sold singly.

Plastic badges

Possible advantages:
- a. Plastic badges are able to withstand much handling and are suitable for shop floor systems are ordinary employees can operate the machines.
- b. The collection system is mechanised.
- c. The data recording machines can be linked directly to the computer.

Possible disadvantages:
- a. Limited scope.
- b. The recording machines are operated by the workers themselves.

On-line systems.

Possible advantages:
- a. Transcription can be eliminated.
- b. Speeds up entry of data to the computer and return of processed information.
- c. Cuts down delays in dealing with error rejections.

Possible disadvantage:

Cost is considerable.

4. Relative advantages.

VDU	Printer Terminal
No stationery costs	Produces permanent copies
Faster maximum speed	Not limited to length of screen when viewing
Quieter than most printers	Nicer to read than a vdu screen
Very reliable: no moving parts except the keyboard	
Parts of an output layout can be changed without redisplaying the whole screen	

5. Appropriateness — the need for a hard copy. Multiple copies would prompt the use of an impact printer. A quiet environment would prompt the use of a non-impact printer, etc.

   Cost — High speeds and extras raise the price.

   Time output. — High-speed printers may be needed if there is little time to produce

   Accuracy — Printer accuracy in positioning characters varies greatly. Impact line printers often produce slightly smudged and uneven lines of characters whereas daisywheel printers and good-quality matrix printers produce clear and accurate print.

   Volume — Total volume of output in a given time is limited by printer speed.

   Confidence — Well-proven printer types such as line and matrix printers tend to be favoured.

6. Both verification and validation involve checking. Verification is the checking for transcription errors, validation is checking that data conforms to rules that apply to it.

7. (10.65)

8. (6.25 – 6.27).

Possible advantages.

a. Saves storage space.

b. Saves the expense of printed output, as does a VDU, but has permanence.

c. Cheaper to distribute than bulky paper.

Possible disadvantages.

a. Can only be read by special viewer.

b. Cannot be annotated or corrected by hand.

c. Cost prevents frequent updates.

    MICR — Bank Cheques, Insurance returns.

    OCR — Giro Cheques, Billing.

    BADGE READERS — Product Pricing for PoS, Employee clock recording.

    BAR MARKING — PoS, Library Cards.

9. a. i. Data can be checked to ensure that each part of the date is valid, e.g. if the month is given as a number it should be in the range 1...12.

    ii. The account holder's name can be cross-checked with the name assigned to the account number.

    iii. The account number can be checked for character type (numeric say), format and range. A check digit check may also be used.

    iv. Amounts in pounds should be numeric.

    v. Signatures can be checked manually against a given copy.

    NB. One-day pattern recognition techniques may allow this check to be computerised.

b.   e.g.

```
┌─────────────────────────────────────────────────────────┐
│                   BATCH CONTROL SLIP                     │
│                                          Date – – / – – / – – │
│                                               dd   mm   yy  │
│   Number of documents in this batch   ☐☐                │
│                                                         │
│   Total of all amounts in this batch  ☐☐☐•☐☐           │
│                                                         │
│   Total of all account numbers (hash total) ☐☐☐☐☐☐☐    │
│                                                         │
│   Sent by _____                               │
│   Received by _____                              │
└─────────────────────────────────────────────────────────┘
```

11.   (10.72d)

12.   (10.67 – 10.73)

13.   **Coding Systems.** Coding of items, for ease of identification, is well established in many areas independent of the use of Computers. A popular type of coding system is the 'Facet Code' where, the characters of the code are sub-divided into groups, each of which has a meaningful interpretation. Take, for example, the postal codes assigned to every address in the U.K. The first two characters indicate the district, e.g. So for Southampton, BH for Bournemouth, the next two digits identify the local area within the district, and so on down to a group of houses. This is also an example of a heirarchical code.

The Need for Coding Systems. The computer is unable without very sophisticated programming, to match successfully names or descriptions. This can be seen quite easily by considering the type of name which may be given to accounting codes. Even allowing for misspelling, names may vary when in common use, either by abbreviation or by paraphrase so it is better to assign a unique code which will not vary and is also, as a general rule, much shorter than the corresponding description.

Advantages from the use of Meaningful Codes.

a.   As already discussed there is recognition without ambiguity.

b.   The code may assist in computer file organisation. For direct access files a pat of the code number may be used to generate the sector or bucket address. For serial access files, the code may be used to determine the sorted sequence of the file and hence assist in the organisation of the tabulations by ensuring that items are grouped together in respective categories.

c.   A meaningful code assists the user in assigning the correct identifier to a transaction.

d.   In addition, the user may undertake, possibly unknowingly, a feasibility check on the code if, say, goods are being supplied to a code which indicates something other than a customer.

e.   The elements of the code may be further subjected to validation by the computer input program. This may extend the feasibility checks mentioned in the previous point and also include tests for format, range and check digit.

14.   Validation (10.70).   Data prep. (10.10 – 10.11).

Chapter 11

1.   (11.30)

2.   Help command

3.   (11.13 & 11.16)

Chapter 12

1. i. (1.14)   ii. (12.18)   iii. (1.15)   iv. (6.7)   v. (6.6)

Chapter 13

1. **Introduction**

    Data has to be presented to the computer in a form which is acceptable as input (so called machine-sensible form). This *capturing* of data can be accomplished in many ways, using different input media. A summary of the main methods and media is given below:

No.	Method of data capture	Media used
1	on-line (to computer)	data transmission terminals, plastic badges etc.
2	character recognition	source documents using ocr; micr or omr.
3	manual encoding	magnetic tape (using encoders).
4	manual encoding	magnetic tape via disk (using computer-controlled data entry systems)
5	by-product	cassettes/diskettes, paper tape, tally rolls with cash registers, typewriters, etc.

    Stages involved in data capture

    a. Clerically produced source documents.
    b. Transcription into machine-sensible form.
    c. Verification of transcription stage.
    d. Getting source data or input to processing centre.
    e. Finally input to computer (possibly not *strictly* regarded as data capture as such).

    Basic problems

    a. **Accuracy and validity** of data when finally input to computer.
    b. **Form of source data** which in many cases means a clerically produced document and indifferent document standards.
    c. **Cost** of machinery, operators and buildings etc. which sometimes equals that of the computer system itself.
    d. **Time.** Many of the methods outlined are cumbersome and very time consuming.
    e. **Volumes of data.** Increasing volumes of data, indicating the need for more sophisticated methods of data capture.
    f. **Movement of data** (in raw or transcribed form) to the central processing point present problems of packaging, delay, loss etc.
    g. **Control.** With so many stages involved with some methods the problem of controlling and coordinating the whole is far from easy.

    Discussion of problems and solutions

    a. **Accuracy.** This problem is most acute with method 3 which requires *verification* to reduce errors made by punch operators. Even so errors will creep through and there is a necessity for a computer check of input. Limited *validity* checking can be carried out by the computer. Methods 4 and 5 (especially 5) claim increased accuracy and certain validity checks can be done *off-line* .
    b. **Form of source data.** On-line systems can do away with source document, which is the ideal solution. Method 2 (character recognition) avoids the need for transcription especially with the use of the ' *turn around* ' document. Method 6 (By-product) also enables the source data to be produced in a machine-sensible form. (Example – Cash Registers equipped with Paper Tape rolls which capture data as sale is entered). Kimball tags also obviate the need for a manually scribed document.

c. **Cost.** Each method is going to cost a great deal but Computer-controlled Data Entry is probably more cost effective in large installations than its predecessor – Manual Key Punching (fewer operators, but higher machine costs).

d. **Time.** Method 1 gets over this problem by capturing data at source and putting it *directly* into computer. The methods which employ more machinery and fewer humans are likely to be more efficient in this respect.

e. **Volumes.** Similarly increased volumes point to the choice of on-line systems, Character Recognition, or Computer-controlled Data Entry as appropriate.

f. **Movement.** The solution is the use of on-line system or something approaching it.

g. **Control.** The methods which eliminate the most stages in data capture will be the This points again to on-line systems and to a lesser degree Character Recognition, and Computer-controlled Data Entry (and possibly By-product).

Conclusion

The capture of raw data for use within a computer system is a time-consuming and costly affair. The basic underlying problem is the interface of the slow human with the high speed computer.

The ultimate solution must be to capture data at its point of origin in a machine-sensible form, thus eliminating the many stages involved at present in getting it into such a form.

However it is as well to appreciate that very often *cost* and the *appropriateness* of a method of data capture to a particular application will be very important factors influencing choice.

Data Communication is concerned with the physical transportation of both input and output data or information as well as the automatic transmission of digital data over telephone networks to remote location either on-line or off-line.

The context of the question is assumed to be the latter. Off-line transmission means data transmission by equipment not under the control of the central processor. For example, a branch office may use by-product paper tape as the means of data capture in an order processing system. At the end of the day, and using cheap rates for transmission, the tape may be loaded into a paper tape reader and transmitted to the central office for a daily sensitive sales analysis. On-line transmission implies that the equipment is under the control of the central processor, for example the many airline and hotel reservation systems.

The equipment is shown in the diagram and consists of a terminal device, a modem, transmission lines, and a multiplexor or front-end processor.

Terminals may vary from the conventional teletypewriter and visual display units through the complete range of input and output peripheral devices to the use of small computers themselves as terminals as, for example in the British Rail TOPS system where remote minicomputers are used in marshalling yards for local processing as well as being used as intelligent terminals for the receipt and transmission of information on-line to the central computer.

Transmission Lines fall into three main categories, a local line which is sometimes termed 'hard-wired' since it is a direct line from terminal to computer although it will almost certainly have a plug on each end for possible exchange with another system. This line is only suitable for distances of up to a hundred feet or so, the quoted distance varies between sources and is really a matter for local conditions to determine in practice. The second type of line is the BT telegraph line on the Telex system either using the public network or a private line which may be cheaper for heavy use and less prone to interference in signal. This service is called datel 100 and is, in practice, limited to speeds of about 10 characters per second. The third type of line is the STD speech network, again either on a public or a private line and this will cope with much faster transmission speeds but requires a special interface unit called a modem.

Modems are required for transmission of data over the STD network. Their basic function is to convert the signal from the terminal or computer into different form suitable for transmission over long distance on the STD line, essentially into a sound. The models of modem vary in specification and price according to the required transmission speed.

Multiplexor, although having a special meaning, is a general term used to describe the special piece of hardware required on the computer to receive and decode the messages received from a number of different terminals and, when a complete message has been collected, to pass it on to the central processor for action. This function may be very complex and on some systems there is a separate computer processor devoted to this activity and this is called a 'front-end processor'.

The use of this equipment is, by no means, confined to bureaux and is used extensively in banks, airlines, schools and colleges for processing student programs, and in many large companies with branches linked to a central computer service.

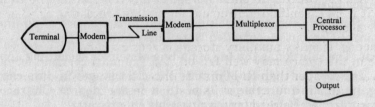

2. a. (13.28) b. (13.14) c. (Fig. 13.6) d. (Fig. 13.6) e. (13.16) f. (13.16) g. (13.9)

3. (13.23)

4. a. (13.8) b. (13.9)

5. (13.26)

6. (13.32)

Chapter 14

1. (14.12 – 14.21)

2. a. i. (4.19)   a ii (ch3)

    b. Any justification is likely to be based upon a satisfactory investigation of costs vs benefits. However, the key points likely to be considered for these systems are: productivity, improved quality of work, extra functionality not possible with manual methods (hence possible business advantages through newer technology), flexibility of use, faster production of documents, improved security and reliability.

Chapter 15

1. a. (15.1)   b. (15.9)   c. (15.10 – 15.18)

2. (15.10)

    a. May not be unique so not suitable.

    b. Unique and usable (if known) but might be unnecessarily long.

    c. Unique and usable. Specially designed for the job.

Chapter 16

1. The main types of storage are:

    (IAS) Immediate access storage e.g. RAM.

    (DAS) Direct access storage e.g. magnetic disk.

    (SAS) Serial access storage e.g. magnetic tape.

    The tasks that they are best suited to carry out are:

    a. **Immediate access.** Because of its unique electronic properties giving extremely quick access to stored data this type of storage is used as the computer's *main storage* . Access to individual characters/bytes is completely independent of their position in store. It is in the main storage that the programs are held during processing so that their instructions can be executed swiftly. Also the particular data currently being worked on is held in main storage. Ideally, IAS would be used for storage of all data because it is fast in operation. This is not practicable because of cost and its use therefore is limited to main storage. Thus some alternative form must be found for storing the files and data which are not immediately required by the program.

b. **Direct access** . One such alternative is DAS. Storage capacity can vary from thousands to hundreds of millions of characters. DAS has the important facility of allowing direct access, that its records can be accessed independently of each other. It is thus suitable for files being processed in a selective manner, also for storing programs and systems software which are required to be called into main storage at any time during the running of an application program. It is an essential requirement for on-line processing or where file-interrogation facilities are needed.

c. **Serial access.** If bulky auxiliary storage is required and the need for random access is not present then the choice may well fall on SAS the most common form of which is magnetic tape. It is also cheaper than RAM disk or drum. Because of its inherent serial nature, access to a record on tape is a function of its position on the tape. Therefore every preceding record on a master file must be read (and written out onto the new tape) before the required record can be located. Nevertheless millions of characters can be stored very cheaply.

Conclusion

IAS is the ideal storage medium but is very expensive. If bulk storage is required combined with facility for random access then the less expensive DAS is indicated. If the limitations of Serial Access are no serious hindrance then the cheapest form of store ie. SAS can be used.

2. 'Basic Principles' 16.11 16.26 (NOTE. cylinder concept in key).

'Index Sequential' 16.27 16.28.

3. See 1.

Note: Internal Storage (Immediate Access Storage).

External Storage (DAS and SAS)

4. a. 7.4 – 7.21 b. 16.27 16.28

5. a. (Fig. 7.10) b. (Fig. 16.1)   c. (Fig 16.1 & Fig 16.3)

6. (Fig. 7.22)   (Fig. 7.10)   (Fig. 7.10)

(Fig. 16.1)   (Fig. 16.1)   (Fig. 16.1)

(Fig. 16.33)   (Fig. 16.33)   (Fig. 7.24)

Chapter 17

1. (17.5)

2. (17.12)

3. (17.5 (a–c))

4. (17.22)

5. (3.9)

6. (17.23)

7. A package would be used whenever it was able to satisfy the requirements, because it would be more cost effective. Evaluating packages relies on having a set of criteria against which to judge them. A list of prioritised requirements should be drawn up on which essential and designed features are listed. Packages may be compared against this list. Matters such as reliability of supplier, cost etc will also need to come into the decision making process of course.

8. The advantages and disadvantages of high level languages are:

Advantages:

a. Program writing is less complex because of the use of vocabulary which is relatively simple to learn.

b. As program writing takes less time, programmers are therefore more efficiently utilised.

c. Amendments during program writing are easily incorporated and subsequent revision of the whole program is readily accomplished.

d. Extensive use of macros and sub-routines (both those of the manufacturer and the user) is permitted.

e. High level languages are independent of the computer compared with low level languages.

f. Source programs can be understood by people other than the person who wrote them.

Disadvantages:

a. A large number of rules have to be adhered to.

b. Object programs tend to be less efficient in terms of main storage utilisation and running time. (This occurs because of the generalised nature of the compiler's operation).

9. a. 'Characteristics of' – 17.51. 'Advantages of' – See 8.

    b. Fig. 17.3

10. (17.51 and 17.66)

Chapter 18

1. (18.16)

2. (18.10)

3. (18.6)

Chapter 19

1. (18.16)

2. (19.3 – 19.5)

3. (19.3)

4. (18.15)

5. A critical examination is needed because there are reasons for carrying out each step in the present system. These reasons must be discovered and questioned to see if they *need* to be incorporated in the new system.

6. a. Three from:
   i. Interview.
   ii. Questionnaires.
   iii. Observation.
   iv. Record inspection.

   b. (19.19).

7. a.
   i. A prototype is a first version of a system built as as a working model on which to base the final system, either through subsequent enhancement or by building another version from scratch which incorporates the features selected from the prototype. Often a prototype is used to explore requirements with the intended user of the system, for example, my creating an experimental human-computer interface which the user can try out. 4GLs are often used a tools for prototyping.

   ii. Benefits include: better understanding of requirements thus avoiding costly mistakes in development; rapid development of a usable system; better user involvement in the development process;

   Difficulties include: evolving a final system from a prototype can prove costly in the long run because of accumulated changes and re-working; if the prototype needs to be 'thrown away' and replaced the costs may be hard to justify; expertise may be unduly tied up in a prototyping project because of the high level of participation which it tends to produce.

   b. i. (18.15)   ii. (18.15)

Chapter 20

1. (20.10 – 20.13).

2. (20.35 – 20.37).

3. The process can be made simpler if, well in advance, the manual documents are re-designed so that when the time for conversion comes they will be easy to transcribe. Better still, they will have been designed to exploit document-reading methods such as OMR or OCR.

4. a. What is a package program?

   To take advantage of the similar information needs of large numbers of businesses, generalised packages have been developed by computer manufacturers and software houses.

   An application package is a program or set of programs of a generalised nature designed to solve a particular problem. The package is so designed that it can be used by a large number of organisations.

   The programs can be supplied in media such as punched card, magnetic tape, or disk and are accompanied by comprehensive documentation to assist the user.

   Advantages of using a package program.

   i. All the programming effort that is entailed in writing a custom-built program is saved. This gives savings in cost and manpower.

   ii. The user has a tried and tested set of programs, free of error and which can be used with confidence. It follows that a lot of computer time which is associated with the testing of programs is saved.

   iii. Following on from ii. above, good reliable information can be available very quickly.

   iv. A side-effect, which can be construed as an advantage, is the discipline enforced on those responsible for input procedures.

   It should be remembered, however, that because some packages are designed for a wide range of users, it may well be necessary to modify the package to suit the user's needs, (in this case the '80 heading analysis').

   A compromise would be to alter the company's information requirements to fit the package.

   b. **Transfer of records to computer files.** Assuming records are at present held manually the steps involved are as follows:-

   i. A thorough examination of all the manual documents to ensure a high standard of documentation which was possibly not a critical factor previously.

   ii. Data necessary to form the master file is taken from batches of documents and entered at a keyboard of key-to-diskette system say. (Alternatively the data could be manually transcribed onto OMR documents).

   Static data such as 'name', 'clock no' would be entered during early stages. The entry of data which by its nature is subject to change (e.g. 'total pay to date') would be left until the latest possible moment.

   iii. Batch details are listed on the printer and a visual check made of listings against documents (where this is possible).

   iv. Diskettes are used as input data to the computer and master files are created by the 'File Creation Program'.

   v. A printed copy of the newly created file is examine and errors rectified (and re-input as necessary).

   vi. The file is now ready for use in testing procedures prior to operational use.

   The major organisational problem is concerned with the length of time taken for the successful completion of the whole transfer process.

   It is important to ensure that once a record has begun the transfer process, all subsequent changes to the date contained in that record are carried through to the computer file.

   Overall control would be exercised by batching documents, possibly by department; and control/hash totals calculated for checking at the various stages. (e.g. numbers of documents; hash totals of employee clock numbers etc).

A timetable for all these operations would be drawn up and progress monitored. The systems analyst would have the responsibility for this task.

Because of the high work-load involved it may be necessary to use a Bureau for the data preparation stage.

Authors' comments

1. *Payroll packages, being application orientated, have a wide range of potential users. There are many such packages available, some of which will have been designed for use with a particular range of computers.*

2. *Difficulties arise because each company's requirements differ in terms of significant details; this is particularly so where there is an inter-relationship of applications as in this question ie. between payroll and labour cost analysis.*

3. *It may well be necessary to modify the user's information requirements to suit the package, especially if the package is one designed by a manufacturer.*

4. *However some Software Houses design packages on the modular principle and thus are able to accommodate the user's requirements, if not too outrageous.*

5.   a.   Systems Analysis Part Introduction 3.
    b.   Any from 18.3 – 18.10

6.   (18.56)

7.   (19.16 – 19.26)

8.   Chapters 18 – 21 (summary needed).

Chapter 21

1. One of the difficulties in selecting the computer best suited to a company's needs is how to evaluate what each manufacturer has to offer. What a company must attempt to do is to match its objectives against the capabilities of the computer system offered by the manufacturers. The following criteria are suggested but it must be remembered that each user will place a different emphasise on the individual criterion.

    a.   Cost.

    b.   Delivery time.

    c.   Support:

        i.   personnel supplied by manufacturers to aid user.

        ii. education of user's staff.

    d.   Software supplied with system – cost and ease of implementation.

    e.   Reliability – the manufacturer to supply performance data.

    f.   Modularity – the ability to add to system later.

    g.   Conversion – The ease with which conversion from existing system could be accomplished.

    h.   Experience – the manufacturer's experience with systems of the type that company is installing.

2. The contents of a Systems Specification are *included* in a feasibility report, to the level of detail required by management to make a decision between alternative ways of satisfying the objectives (e.g. use of bureau *v* own computer). The feasibility *report* , apart from containing and introduction, current situation statement, etc. would also, therefore, include details of *alternatives*.

3. The review of a computer system must not be regarded as a once only task and ideally should be carried out periodically. The main question to be asked is 'have the objectives been achieved'? This assumes that these were clearly defined in the first place. Thus, if the objective was 'to reduce stock levels by 10' or 'to produce invoices one day earlier', the reviewer must judge the effectiveness of the new system against the achievement of these objectives. Some of the detailed areas which would occupy the attention of the reviewer are:-

    a.   Costs – are these in line with budgeted costs?

    b. Staff – with regard to retraining, redeployment and morale. Are staff happy with the new system?

    c. Are any pats of the 'old' system which should have been dispensed with still in use?

    d. Standards of input and output.

    e. Feedback from the company's customers.

4.   a. 21.1 – 21.38 a – b.

       b. 21.14 – 21.37.

Chapter 22

1.   (22.23) Pseudocode.

Chapter 23

1.   a.   i. Flowchart (showing the clerical procedure for working out discount entitlement).

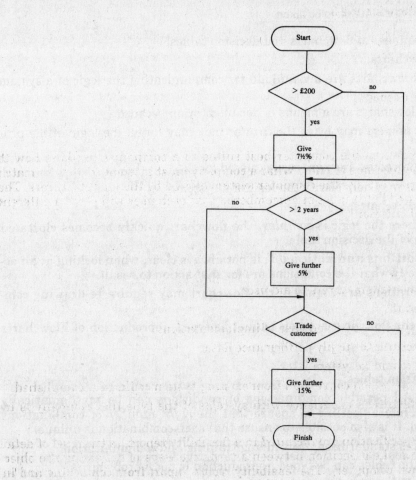

a. ii. Limited entry decision table.

CONDITIONS	1	2	3	4	5	6	7	8
> £200	Y	Y	Y	Y	N	N	N	N
Customer for over 2 yrs	Y	Y	N	N	Y	Y	N	N
Trade customer	Y	N	Y	N	Y	N	Y	N
ACTIONS								
Nil								x
5%						x		
7%				x				
12 2%		x						
15%							x	
20%					x			
22%			x					
27%	x							

Key:-

Y = Yes
N = No
x = Action to be taken.

b. Advantages and disadvantages of flowcharts and decision tables.

Advantages of using flowcharts:

a. **Communication**. Flowcharts are a visual aid for communicating the logic of a system to all concerned.

b. **Documentation**. Flowcharts are a means of documentation because:-

   i. Analysts/Programmers may leave the firm or they may forget the logic of the program.

   ii. Changes to the procedure are more easily catered for.

c. **Analysis**. Flowcharts may help clarify the logic of a system.

Disadvantages of using flowcharts:

a. **Complex logic**. Where the logic is *complex,* the flowchart quickly becomes cluttered and lacks the clarity of the decision table.

b. **Link between conditions and actions.** It is not always clear, when looking at an action to be taken, exactly what the conditions are for that action to result.

c. **Alterations**. If alterations are required, the flowchart may require re-drawing completely.

d. **Reproduction**. As the flowchart symbols cannot be typed, reproduction of Flowcharts is often a problem.

e. Also see 22.19.

Advantages of using decision tables:

a. **Condition rules.** All possible combinations of conditions can be mathematically worked out. It is therefore possible to ensure that the *right number* of combinations have been considered. It is also possible to ensure that each combination is unique.

b. **Format.** The format is standardised, thus aiding training and communication.

c. **Reproduction.** As the tables can be typed, reproduction is not a problem.

d. **Link between conditions and actions.** It is simple to see the conditions applying to particular actions – consequently the *testing* of the logic is simplified.

Disadvantages of using decision tables:

a. **Total sequence.** The total sequence is not clearly shown, ie. no *overall* picture is given as with flowcharts.

b. **Logic.** Where the logic of a system is *simple* , flowcharts nearly always serve the purpose better.

2. a.

CONDITIONS	RULES							
	1	2	3	4	5	6	7	8
Acceptable Academic Qualifications	Y	Y	Y	Y	N	N	N	N
Completed Training Course	Y	Y	N	N	Y	Y	N	N
Recommended by head	Y	N	Y	N	Y	B N	Y	N
ACTIONS								
Grade 'A'								
Grade 'A' Under Review								
Grade 'B' Provisional								
Grade 'B'								

  b. (See to 1(a.)).

Chapter 24

1.
```
BEGIN
    IF   Order > 200  THEN
         Give 7.5% discount
    ENDIF
    IF   Period of ordering > 2   THEN
         Give 5% discount
    ENDIF
    IF   Trade customer THEN
         Give 15% discount
    ENDIF
END
```

2. The types of validation checks that would be applied depend upon the actual details of the order. It is assumed that the following are entered customer number, quantities ordered, catalogue numbers, size codes, colour codes (with first and second choices where appropriate) cash paid, type of order (cash, credit), date of order.

    Invalid characters. All fields would be examined for invalid characters, e.g. the customer number field would be checked to make sure that all characters were numeric.

    Range check. A check would be made to ensure that numbers came within specific ranges, e.g. that the catalogue numbers were between say, 20000 and 60000.

    Reasonableness check. A check would be made on order quantities, to ensure that abnormal amounts have not been punched in error, e.g. 10 pairs of the same shoes.

    Completeness check. A check would be made to ensure that all the fields that *must* have an entry *do* in fact have an entry, e.g. that an entry *has* been made in the 'cash paid' field but not necessarily in a 'second choice' field.

    Control totals. Control totals of quantities ordered and/or number of items in a batch would be compared with an accumulation during the validation run.

    Order quantity availability. A check would be made on the availability of stock or second choice where applicable.

    Credit control. A check would be made on credit requirements, e.g. that a satisfactory deposit has been received relative to the size of order.

    Check digit verification. Check digit calculations would be made on the account number and catalogue numbers.

3. (24.33 – 24.42)

4. a. A series of repeated program instructions.

    b. A point in a program where alternative actions are selected according to the result of testing a condition (as in the start of an IF-THEN...Fig. 16.8).

    c. A series of program statements forming a part of a program and used to perform a specific task.

    d. A point in a program where the sequence of instructions is always changed to continue at another point.

    e. A data value to be taken literally e.g. 'N'.

Chapter 25

1. Amend figure 25.7 and convert into flowchart form. The amendments are quite small ie. you need only change the procedure 'Process-the-transaction'.

Chapter 26

1. a.

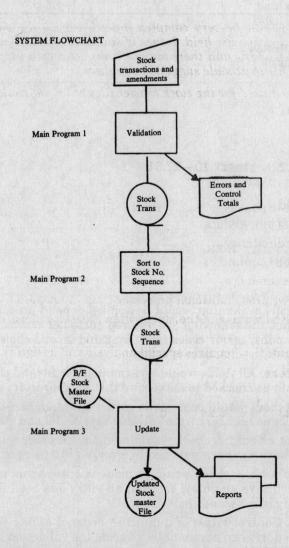

SYSTEM FLOWCHART

Main Program 1 — Stock transactions and amendments → Validation → Errors and Control Totals / Stock Trans

Main Program 2 — Sort to Stock No. Sequence → Stock Trans

Main Program 3 — B/F Stock Master File → Update → Updated Stock master File / Reports

b. i. **Receipts.** Details of goods received, via goods received notes, for increasing the stock level, and reducing 'on order' level.

      Allocations. Details of goods earmarked for a particular purpose (but not yet issued), to decrease 'free stock'.

      Orders. Details of goods on order, via purchase orders, for increasing 'on order' level.

      Master file amendments. Changes to the 'standing' data on a stock file e.g. new stock item; change in maximum/minimum stock level.

  ii. **Re-order list** suggested items needing to be re-ordered, in the light of lead time/current 'free stock' level. Probably provided on a weekly basis to cover a weeks worth of re-order work.

      Stock exception report. Items going outside limits e.g. maximum/minimum stock levels. Supplied each processing run for immediate action.

      Order progress list. Items on order where 'progress' date reached. Supplied each processing run for immediate action.

Outstanding order value. Value of all orders outstanding to aid cash forecasting. Supplied monthly.

Audit trial. A list of all movements on each stock record, for audit purposes. Supplied monthly.

Authors' comments.

Stock control systems can be very complex indeed, especially where raw material, work in progress and finished stocks are held. Issues of standard product parts may be 'exploded' before passing against the stock file and there may be links between a suggested re-order requirements file and the supplier file to provide suggested suppliers.

Magnetic tape has been used for the stock master files but disks could be used if appropriate.

2. a. 7.5, 16.41 b. (26.3)

Chapter 27

1. a. (27.7, 27.18 – 27.21)   b. (27.10 – 27.31)
2. a. 27.7.
   b. i.   Data is pooled.
      ii. Consistency of stored data.
      iii. Controlled redundancy.
      iv. Access control.
      v.   Program independence.
   c. i.   The DBMS requires additional processor time – slowness.
      ii. The generalised nature of the stored data created an overhead in data storage and retrieval.
      iii. The implementation requires special analysis and design skills.
      iv. As in 15.3.
3. (27.7, 27.59)
4. a. 27.23   b. 27.23   c. 26.24   d. 27.44   e. 27.62   f. 27.43   g. 27.35

Chapter 28

1. (28.4)
2. (28.22)

Chapter 29

1. (29.3 – 29.13, 29.14 – 29.24)

2. a.

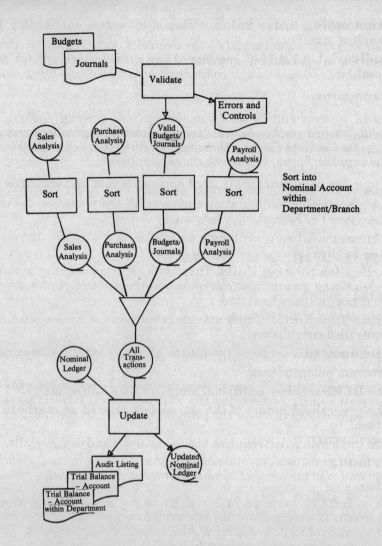

b i. **Sales.** Debtors control totals and sales/cost of sales information. Probably provided automatically from the sales ledger system.

Purchases. Creditors control totals and purchase analysis information. Probably provided automatically from the purchase ledger system.

Payroll. Department and/or job payroll figures. Probably provided automatically from the payroll system.

Journals. All adjustments to accounts (errors in sales/purchases, prepayments, accruals etc.) and payments/receipts not going through the purchase ledger (e.g. capital items/petty cash). These would probably be input directly.

Budgets. Departmental/sales budgets input either monthly or once annually. Input most probably direct.

ii. **Validations checks.** Checks would be carried out on direct input (the validation checks on those passed over from other systems having been carried out within those systems).

Range. Account numbers and department numbers coming within predetermined range of figures.

Character. Each field would be checked to ensure characters were punched correctly e.g. having a numeric character where required.

Completeness. Each record would be checked for the right number of characters.

Author's comments

Nominal ledger systems vary widely – the degree of automaticity depending upon the degree of computerisation of subsidiary systems. Thus other systems (cash book, petty cash book, sales/purchase ledger) may be self controlling with totals only being journalised into the nominal ledger.

3. (29.37)

4. Configuration is the term used to describe the collection of physical units of machinery (otherwise known as hardware) to be found in a computer installation.

Example:

i. **Processor.** The processor consists of an Arithmetic Logic Unit and Control Unit. When describing a particular configuration the power of the processor, measured in MIPs (Millions of Instructions Per Second) may be stated.

ii. **Main Memory.** When describing a particular configuration, the size of main memory may be stated in Megabytes.

iii. **Magnetic Disk Storage Units.** These provide large capacity backing or auxiliary storage. When describing a particular configuration the number of disk drives and their respective storage capacities may be stated.

iv. **Magnetic Tape Units.** These provide input and output facilities and a means for off-line storage or back-up.

v. **Line Printer.** This provides the means of producing the output reports generated by the system.

vi. **Terminals and workstations.** These provide on-line facilities for data entry, file enquiry etc, the most common type being the VDU terminal. A special case is the **Console.** which provides external control over the processing system by the operator.

Authors' comments

To be strictly correct a configuration should specify the number of units required e.g. 2 printers, 4 disk units and also the amount of main storage eg 8Mb (8 million bytes).

5. a. (14.11) b. (29.34)

6. The term on-line is used to describe the situation when peripheral units (e.g. tape units) are connected to, and under the control of, the central processing unit. Thus data can be read directly into or out of main storage from/to a device which is on-line.

Conversely the term off-line is used to describe the situation when peripheral units are *not* under control of the central processing unit.

The advantage of off-line output working is that the comparatively slow task of printing is done independently of the computer's central processing unit thus leaving it free to carry out more profitable processing of data.

The term off-line is also used in connection with tape reels and exchangeable disk packs kept in the tape library. They are said to be stored off-line.

An airline ticket reservation system is an example of an application using the technique of random access. A centralised computer maintains records of all flights on direct access storage devices. Reservation offices world-wide are linked to it by terminals. On receipt of information from a reservation point the flight record is *immediately* accessed and *updated* to show the current seating availability. This would not be possible without this random access facility.

Chapter 30

1. Before entering into a discussion about the impact of computers in business it is necessary to define the functions of management.

Stated simply the functions of management are to *plan* the use of resources at its disposal, to *motivate* the company's work-people and to *co-ordinate* and *control* the activities necessary to carry out the plans. These functions of management have not changed with the advent of the computer, but the ways in which they are carried out have. To carry out these functions effectively managers need information. Information is the production of the processing of data, the amount and variety of which is increasing year by year.

Computers have the ability to process large amounts of data at high speed and with a high degree of accuracy. They relieve the human of a great deal of routine labour. Information is more reliable, is more up-to-date and as a result the quality of decision making is improved.

The use of computers in business allows a greater use of management by exception techniques. The computer only notifies those variations from plan which require management action. This saves the time of managers and helps to focus attention of matters which require attention.

It should be remembered however that the exercising of powers of judgment, leadership and initiative remains the prerogative of the human.

Information requirements at the highest level of management involve many external factors (government actions, competitors plans etc.) and the scope is wide. Nevertheless the use of computers have made possible better integration of plans and enabled quicker response to changed circumstances. Plans can be more frequently reviewed by the provision of more up-to-date information. The computer is invaluable in using models to test the validity and consequences of particular courses of action.

At the lower levels of management, information requirements are largely internal (dictated from above) and therefore quantifiable. The computer's great storage capacity, speed of processing, aid retrieval of data, and the ability to program for quantifiable factors enables it to have a great impact on the functions of co-ordination and control at this level. For example, the information needed to make a good decision on order acceptability includes up-to-date stock level and credit worthiness details. A computer, using terminals, direct access storage and integrated procedures, can provide this information quickly and accurately.

Managers must be fully aware of the criteria upon which the computer system producing the information, is based. For example, a buyer may be supplied, by the computer, with the details of the three most suitable suppliers for him to decide amongst. This is a very good aid to the controlling function as long as he appreciates that, for example, the stability of the suppliers was not considered by the computer. He is then able to exercise his judgment on the outstanding factors.

All levels of management carry out the functions but with the emphasis placed more on one than another e.g. top management spend more of their time on planning than on motivating, whereas the converse is true of lower levels. The computer does not change the functions, but by providing the quantifiable factors required in exercising those functions, can leave the manager, at whatever level, more time to consider those areas for which the computer is not suited, ie. man management and innovation.

Author's comments.

This question emphasises the need to know a definition of management from which to work(!).

It is very easy, in a question like this, to wander off the main theme or say the same thing, in different ways, over and over again. You must jot down the points under which you are going to write.

2. 'Organisation chart' – Fig. 30.1

    Main duties – 30.3 to 30.32

    To whom ... responsible' – 30.4. Note that the suggestion is that he or she should be responsible to the Managing Director, or to a board member, to ensure that no departmental boundaries prevent desirable integration of systems to take place.

Chapter 31

1. **Assumption:** A medium sized in-house computer has been assumed to be the subject of this answer.

Introduction

Some costs are easy to identify precisely e.g. hardware but others are less easy to measure. A suggested division is:

    Development costs.

    Installation costs.

    Conversion costs.

    Running costs.

Development costs:

a. Initial and feasibility studies – staff and associated overheads.

b. Detailed systems study and design – systems analyst etc.

c. Program writing and testing – programmers and analysts.

d. Selection, training and education of personnel.

e. Software.

f. Support.

g. Manuals etc.

Installation costs:

a. Buildings – new or structural alterations to existing buildings.

b. Computer hardware.

c. Ancillary equipment – data preparation etc.

d. Environmental costs e.g. air conditioning.

Conversion costs:

a. File creation and conversion.

b. Conversion program writing.

c. Changeover.

Running costs:

a. Staff.

b. Maintenance of buildings and equipment.

c. Storage of data.

d. Insurance.

e. Stationery.

f. Power – light etc.

g. Rental charges if appropriate.

Notes:

a. A distinction should be made between 'one-time' and 'running' costs.

b. Recovery of 'one-time' costs will be linked to a period of a number of years.

2.   A proposal to consider the use of computers in solving a company's business problems would have led a company to set up a preliminary study. This study would have determined the application areas and would have enabled computer objectives to be formulated. Before the company commits itself to the adoption of computer methods it will need a great deal of information on which to base its decision.

The **feasibility study** is undertaken to provide the information referred to above. It sets out to investigate the practicability of using computers and to assess the effects on the company both in economic and social terms. At the conclusion of the study, which could occupy months, a report will be prepared containing the study group's recommendations. This will then be considered by the board and a decision taken on whether or not to undertake computer methods.

The contents of the report were described in 30.11.

Author's comments.

1. The amount of time and effort required before the feasibility report can be produced depends upon the nature and complexity of the business activity under study.

2. Although the term 'feasibility study' is the term in general use, it is misleading in that most business activities can be carried out by computers (or by conventional methods). A more appropriate term might be justification study.

3. All possible alternative solutions whether involving the use of computers or not, should be included in the report.

3.   When should a systems study take place?

A systems study will follow a recommendation to proceed further with investigation into the use of an alternative system to achieve company objectives. It has been assumed that the alternative system involves the use of a computer.

This recommendation could have come as a result of a preliminary study.

Steps involved in a systems study

The systems study will be developed from all information gathered in the preliminary study previously carried out, but will require a considerable amount of further enquiry in order to reveal possible alternatives, etc. Steps and work involved in such a study are as follows:-

a. **Outline planning.** Make all administrative arrangements. The project leader should be in possession of authority to approach appropriate departments. Study must be publicised and supported by top management.

b. **Definition of task.** There must be precise identification areas to be studied. Objectives must be clearly stated and expected duration of project will be indicated. Although study must not be too protracted, any attempt to work to a tight schedule will almost certainly fail.

c. **Investigation.** This will include getting all the *facts* about the present system, using techniques such as interviewing, examination of records and procedures, and use of questionnaires as appropriate.

Data collected in this way will be recorded and documented using appropriate media, where possible facts should be *verified* .

d. **Analysis and classification.** This involves the sifting of the data gathered and analysing and classifying it into a meaningful form.

In doing this the analyst must be clear about the objectives of system and to any constraints. Controls to be built into the new system must be considered. Any weakness revealed should not be allowed to enter the new system.

e. **Outline design.** An outline design of new system will be drawn up, taking into consideration output requirements in terms of timeliness, accuracy, form etc.

Alternatives, both involving computer and, where appropriate, conventional methods, should be explored for economic justification. Up-to-date comparative costs should be included.

f. **Recommendations.** The results of the study together with recommendations will be presented to the Steering Committee.

If acceptable the report could form the basis of a specification to be forwarded to manufacturers for the purposes of inviting tenders.

Composition of systems study team.

A study covering all the commercial activities of a company would take a considerable amount of time. Such a study undertaken in a motor car manufacturing company for example would entail investigating sales, purchasing of raw materials, stock control etc.

When studying each such system a representative with the detailed technical knowledge of that system would be co-opted in order to ensure that its requirements were made known and understood by the other members of the team. This involvement of the user department is important when the implementation stage is reached.

One team member should have a good knowledge of the information needs of the business and the need for co-ordination. This member would be from the Management Services department.

Someone with a grasp of the technicalities of data processing and a knowledge of computer systems would be needed. This would be a systems analyst. He must have those attributes essential to the maintenance of good relations with his superiors and those people who will be the subject of his investigation. His ability to overcome the natural resistance to change which will be encountered will be vital to the success of the project.

Authors' comments.

1. **When** a computer configuration is decided upon there would follow a more detailed systems study resulting in:-

    a. A detailed systems design. This would entail a fully detailed of the clerical and computer procedures required in the new system.

    b. The writing and coding of the computer programs.

    c. Implementation of the new systems.

2. This is an area which lacks uniformity of terminology. The systems study referred to here is usually called a feasibility study. The study process as a whole consists of:

    a. Preliminary study.

    b. Feasibility study.

    c. Detailed systems study.

    It is a continuous process almost, with each study (or phase) developing from the previous one.

3. It should be understood that a company's approach to the introduction of any new system (especially one involving computers) will depend upon the size of the company, the complexity of its operations, and whether or not it already has well-established procedures.

4. **Time**

    0945   ASSEMBLY – COFFEE.

    1000   Introduction by the Seminar Leader outlining the events. Objective of seminar to be stated, which is to make the board aware of what the proposed system will do and to invite suggested on what additional information is required to suit their needs.

    Questions will be dealt with during the discussion period but if it is considered appropriate board members may put a question during the talks.

    1010   The head of the Computer Planning Committee will relate the background history leading up to the decision to install a computer.

    1025   The computer manufacturer's representative will give general information about the computer and its capabilities particularly in relation to the company's applications.

    1100   The head of Management Services will outline the objectives, the details of the various phases by means of which these objectives will be met, and the time-table to be followed. Emphasis will be placed on their relationship to strategic planning and management control. The need for top management to inject their ideas at this stage will be brought out in order that they may be incorporated into the management information system.

    1200–1400   LUNCH

    1400   A film demonstrating similar applications in other companies, if available, or a film illustrating the use of PERT techniques as applied to the installation of a computer system; the showing of this latter film is designed to make the board aware of the difficulties and problems involved.

    1430   Discussion on the film and any matters arising out of the previous speakers topics. This discussion is to be conducted by the Seminar Leader. (Refreshments will be served during this time).

Remarks

1. A programme will have been prepared in advance and will emphasise the main points to be put over.

2. The atmosphere should be informal.

3. The time-table should be adhered to.

4. It would be desirable at some stage in the discussion session after lunch to bring in the heads of the divisions who are going to be affected by the computer planning and also if not already present the member of the consultancy firm who assisted in any of the studies.

5. The time, place, and the name of the seminar leader, should be noted in the programme.

6. Avoid over-emphasis on technical details about the machine, but concentrate more upon what it can do in relation to the activities of the business.

7. The aim must be to get the directs thoughts turned towards future developments and how best they may be exploited for the benefit of the company.

8. It is recommended that a visit to the manufacturer's premises be arranged in order that the hardware may be viewed.

Assumptions

1. A decision has been taken to install a computer and an order has been placed for a particular system.

2. The Data Processing Manager designate will be present during the seminar, also the person responsible for carrying out the feasibility study.

Authors' comments

1. It cannot be emphasised too strongly that continued top-management involvement in computer planning is vital to its success.

2. Top-management must give its full support to those whose task it is to carry out the plans that they have sanctioned, and to some extent at least, become involved in the implementation of the new systems.

3. The seminar and all other talks, discussions etc. will be designed with these points in mind.

4. It is sometimes helpful in a seminar of this kind to pick a venue away from the company's premises in order to concentrate fully on the matters concerned.

5. a. In a system of business control the management by exception technique is used to isolate those facts which relate to the area in which a decision has to be made. Computer based systems are ideally suited to this task in the following circumstances:-

   i. When large volumes of data, possibly originating at various geographical points, need to be collected and processed in order that relevant information may be extracted.

   ii. When speed of processing is essential to provide management with more timely information in the planning-control feed-back cycle.

   iii. When a high degree of accuracy is required.

   iv. When a greater amount of information is required.

   v. When the capacity for discrimination is required to a high degree.

   An application (reflecting the circumstance at (i) above) is found in stock control where there are many (possibly thousands) stock items and a high stock turnover. The stock records are kept on magnetic storage including, for each type of stock, the balance on hand, reserved stock, re-order quantity, re-order level etc. A demand for stock is compared with the balance on hand, taking into account reserved and ordered stock, and only if the stocks need replenishing will the computer issue a report to management, otherwise the record is updated accordingly.

   Additionally the computer can be programmed to print out reports of stocks with a turnover below a certain percentage.

  b. **Factors to be observed to ensure the system is a viable one.**

   1. **Economy.** Checks should be made to ensure that the objectives are being achieved within the economic limits laid down in the systems study.

   2. **Source data.** The system depends on a high standard of accuracy of source data.

   3. **Program.** The logic of the computer program must be checked to ensure that no exceptions are missed.

   4. **Review.** The system must be constantly reviewed to ensure that exceptions are still being selected using up-to-date criteria.

5. **Communication.** Managers must be fully aware of the criteria upon which the exception system is based and must have confidence and understanding of the methods.

6. **Flexibility.** The system must be capable of responding to changing circumstances indicating the need for new information.

Authors' comments

This was not an easy question. Management by exception is, however, fundamental to management studies in general and is a technique for which the computer is ideally suited.

6. (Chapter 31)

Chapter 32

1. Check digit – 10.70.

   Limit check – 10.70. Note: 'Range check' is also known as a 'limit' check i.e. checking that prescribed limits have not been exceeded e.g. number of hours worked in a week.

   Parity check – 46.20.

   Password – 32.21 .

   Tape mark – 7.24

   Conversational Mode – 14.11

   Batch Mode – Processing by batch (non-conversational mode).

   Turn around document – 10.36

2. 32.1 – 32.21 inclusive. Note that you should use the sub-headings within this chapter as the main headings in your answer.

3. A benchmark test is a test program which is run on a number of computers to compare the processing time to assist in selection of the best system for purchase or use.

   The well known benchmark test is the 'Gibson Mix' which has a fixed proportion of each of the common instruction types such as load/store, test, add and subtract etc. In addition the Analysts and Programmers of a Company may choose to develop their own benchmark programs to assist the assessment of the likely performance of the competing computers in their own company environment.

   The benchmark test may be applied to develop selection criteria in a number of ways. First, as indicated above, to time the performance of two different processors. Secondly to time the corresponding peripherals and thirdly to time the performance of standard software packages such as sort routines and compilers. In addition there may be a requirement to test under multiprogramming conditions or to test performance with a number of terminals operating simultaneously. As well as timing, the benchmarks may be used to test qualitative aspects of software packages.

   Advantages of benchmarks are that they enable a direct comparison to be made even when the two computers are of wildly contrasting concept and architecture.

   Disadvantages include the fact that they only compare the performance on the benchmark which may not be realistic in the live running of the whole range of company systems. It is also difficult, even with a Gibson Mix type, to compare accurately the performance, say, of a byte machine with a word machine, especially if one has a three address assembly code and the other uses one address with, perhaps, indirect addressing instead of index registers and the prices of the two differ by, say, 25%. However, used with caution it does at least provide a basis for comparison.

   ### Authors' comments

   A straightforward question but on a rather specialised topic which may not have been studied by all candidates. Like many questions it invites the student to follow a set structure in the answer.

4. a. i. and ii. 32.13 – 21.   b. i. and ii. (chapter 9)

5. a. 32.21.   b. 32.13 – 32.20 inclusive.

6. 32.14 – 32.16 inclusive.

Appendix 2 Questions without answers

Introduction

This appendix is for use in the classroom.

Questions are of examination standard and have mostly been taken from papers of the ICA, ACA, CIMA, AAT/AAT, IComA and IDPM. The questions are grouped according to the respective Parts of the book.

Introduction to information systems

1.

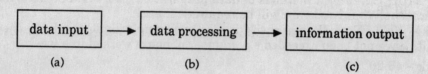

| data input | data processing | information output |
| (a) | (b) | (c) |

The above diagram illustrates, in a simplified way, the three phases of Data Processing irrespective of whether the system is a manual or computerised system.

You are required to:

    i. define for (a) what is meant by data, giving examples, and to state the two sources from which an organisation could obtain data input;

    ii. briefly list the processing carried out under (b);

    iii. for (c) to explain, why Management requires information.

    iv. distinguish between data and information.

2.   a. Define data processing.

    b. Indicate the major data processing stages.

    c. Compare each of these stages in a manual system with similar stages in an electronic system.

Computer storage

1.   a. Compare and contrast the features and uses of magnetic disk storage with optical disk storage.

    b. Name two media which you consider suitable for the off-line archiving of data and explain when you might recommend the use of each.

Computer input and output

1.   When reporting to Management, the line printer is possibly the most used output peripheral.

You are required to give two other methods for providing readable output and to briefly describe, or illustrate, how the output is produced.

                            (AAT)

2.   Describe, with the minimum of technical details, the main features of three devices for obtaining output from a computer and indicate the kinds of application for which the devices you describe are suitable.

                            (ACA)

3.   ABC Limited, a company which markets a range of consumer durables, operates a computer-based inventory control system. Goods are held in three separate warehouses.

Required:

    a. List, and briefly comment on, FOUR items of source data and FOUR printed reports which, as input and output respectively, you would expect to find incorporated in the system.

b. Draft, with a line of sample entries, the form on which warehouse staff record details of goods received from supplies. *(ACA)*

4. a. Briefly describe Optical Character Recognition (OCR) as a method of preparing data for computer input.

    b. Name THREE advantages and THREE disadvantages of this method.

    c. Identify and briefly explain THREE applications for which OCR is suitable. *(ACA)*

    d. The usefulness of a data processing system depends on the accuracy of data submitted to it for processing. Give an account of the methods which can be used to ensure that input data is correct and that corrupt data is identified for correction. *(IDPM)*

    e.

6. a. Describe THREE different methods of data preparation that could be used for a large payroll application. What hardware will be required for each? (15 marks)

    b. How will each method affect the organisation of the D.P. Department that runs the job on a central mainframe? (5 marks)

Computer systems organisation

1. 'Distributed processing is an important option in corporate computer planning. In such an arrangement mini and/or microcomputers working interactively may well replace much of the processing undertaken on mainframes. Distributed processing may well be based on local area networks (LANs) and be implemented using either 'packaged' software or full 'turnkey' operations.'

    a. What are the essential elements of the three main types of computer identified in the above statement? (9 marks)

    b. What is meant by

        i. Distributed processing?

        ii. Local area networks?

        iii. 'Turnkey' implementation? (6 marks)

    c. With reference to the above statement, briefly explain how the growth in distributed systems might change the role of the user manager. (5 marks)

    (Total: 20 marks)

Computer files

1. a. Define the term 'master file' and identify the various elements which may constitute such a file.

    b. Describe how such a file would be updated on magnetic tape. *(IDPM)*

2. Although in the earlier days of computerisation the majority of files were held on magnetic tape nowadays magnetic disks are more common.

    Describe the characteristics of the two storage media given above and discuss some of the problems of storing and accessing records on tapes and on disks. *(CIMA)*

3. a. Define, with a suitable example, the term master file. Your answer should show that you understand the distinction between static (or standing) data and variable (or current) data.

    b. Explain, with the aid of a diagram, how a master file on a magnetic medium is created from existing non-computerised records. *(ACA)*

4. a. Define the term 'Master File' and list the various elements which may constitute such a file in a Stock Control application.

    b. Describe how this file with a dynamic growth pattern would be updated on a disk. *(IDPM)*

Software development

1. In the process of producing a usable program, a number of distinct stages are involved. What are these stages?

   Briefly describe what is involved at each stage. *(AAT)*

2. Programming has become less machine oriented and more problem oriented. Define these terms and explain how changes in programming languages have made this possible. *(CIMA)*

3. Compare and contrast high-level languages as methods of programming data processing applications. Illustrate your answer by reference to programming languages which you have used. *(IDPM)*

4. State the major types of computer software (programs) and describe the purpose and some of the characteristics of each. *(IComA)*

   Write FULL explanatory notes on the following terms:
   a. Macro instruction.
   b. Conditional branch.
   c. Compiler.
   d. Emulator. *(ACA)*

5. Because of ever increasing development costs many companies are using packages for routine applications.
   a. What are application packages?
   b. What are their advantages and disadvantages?
   c. What major factors should be examined when considering the use of a package? *(CIMA)*

6. What methods are used in computer installations, including those using remote terminals, to:
   a. guard against the effects of poor security, and
   b. validate input data and the processing of that data? *(ICA)*

7. 'A modern computer covering both batched operations on conventional peripherals and terminal based demand processing is as much dependent on software as it is on hardware. Ideally it has only minimal dependence on the human being.'

   Discuss the roles of operational software and the human element in the context of this quotation. *(CIMA)*

8. The modern processor has a very small cycle time, but the speed of input and output peripherals is limited. What procedures can be employed to obtain a balance between these marked differences in speed of operation? *(IDPM)*

9. An installed computer application must be 'maintained'.
   i. Explain what is meant by maintenance from the programmer's point of view.
   ii. Describe the procedures involved in maintenance programming.
   iii. Indicate how maintenance programming should be organised within a computer department. *(IDPM)*

10. With the increasing use of microcomputers, one of the most widely used programming languages is BASIC (Beginners Allpurpose Symbolic Instruction Code) which is a relatively simple example of a particular type of programming language.

    You are required to:
    a. state what type of programming language is BASIC and the main features of this type of language; *(6 marks)*
    b. explain why languages of this type were developed and are being increasingly used today; *(6 marks)*

c. state what other levels of programming languages are available and the circumstances in which such languages are used. (8 marks)

(CIMA)

(Total: 20 marks)

File processing

1. a. Describe flowcharting.
    b. List the various stages in compiling a systems flowchart. *(IComA)*

2. An accounts department utilises clerical labour and mechanised facilities (i.e. Accounting Machines) to produce for management monthly departmentalised trading and profit and loss accounts, and a company balance sheet.

    The month end accounting statements are produced on average between fifteen and seventeen working days following the month end to which they relate.

    You are required:

    a. to suggest five advantages that could possibly result from the computerisation of the accounting systems;
    b. to draw a systems flowchart which broadly indicates
        i.   the data inputs (e.g. Purchase data);
        ii. the outputs (e.g. Balance Sheet)

    to be produced by the computer system.

    (*Note:* Only an outline chart is required). *(AAT)*

3. Part of a particular computer program consists of reading the daily sales totals for each of 80 departments of a retail store and printing out the store daily and weekly sales totals.

    The first day's sales in department sequence are in the computer main store commencing at address 000 followed by the next day's sales commencing at address 080 and so on for the six day week. Minus sales can occur.

    You are required to:

    a. prepare a flowchart of a program to print-out daily and weekly store sales totals and
    b. name and describe the techniques you have used to reduce the number of instructions contained in the program. *(ICA)*

4. A Manufacturing Company employing approximately 2,500 uses a computer to deal with payroll accounting. The system is designed to meet the requirements of weekly and monthly paid employees.

    Prior to the main weekly or monthly computer runs an employee master file (held on disk) is updated. There are about 200 transaction records giving details of changes to be made to the master file each week.

    You are required to:

    a. give five reasons for updating the master file;
    b. name three outputs other than weekly and monthly payroll that could be produced from the computerised payroll systems;
    c. draw a systems flowchart for the master file update. *(AAT)*

5. In updating records held sequentially on magnetic tape, transaction record keys are compared with the keys of records on the brought forward master file and, depending on the result of the comparison, different processing paths are followed.

    Required:

    Draw an outline flowchart which shows the matching operations and the processing which normally takes place as a result of them. Your flowchart should provide for the situation when the last records (numbered 99999) of each of the files are read. You are not required to show the logical processes when amendments, deletions and insertions are made to a master file; your chart should deal only with transaction data. *(ACA)*

6. A warehouse operates the following stock control procedures.

A free stock balance (physical stock plus outstanding replenishment orders less unfulfilled orders) is compared with the re-order level and if it is at or below re-order level a replenishment order is placed. If a replenishment order has already been placed, a standard progressing letter is sent.

If the free stock balance is at or below the emergency level, any replenishment order will be subject to the emergency progressing procedures. If no replenishment order is outstanding a rush order will be sent. If the free stock balance is greater than re-order level but below maximum level and a replenishment order is outstanding, the delivery of the replenishment order is delayed for one week.

If the free stock level is at or above maximum level, any replenishment order outstanding is cancelled. If the free stock level goes above the maximum level more than once in any month, all levels and re-order quantities for that item are reviewed.

You are required:

a. to construct a limited entry decision table covering the above procedures;
b. to state the circumstances in which systems analysts would prefer to use decision tables rather than flowcharts.

(CIMA)

7. An alternative term sometimes used for commercial data processing is file processing.
   a. Define file processing.
   b. Describe master and transaction files.
   c. Give the major considerations which govern the choice of the type of hardware storage for a given file. (20 marks)

(CIMA)

Software

1. a. The terms compiler and interpreter are often used in the area of computer software.

   Compare and contrast the operation of a computer program using these two methods.

   (10 marks)

   b. Explain the difference between an assembly language and a high level language, illustrating your answer by referring to a high level language with which you are familiar.(10 marks)

2. What is an operating system? (3 marks)

   Why is it necessary? (3 marks)

   What functions does it perform? (14 marks)

   (Total: 20 marks)

Database systems

1. a. What is the function of a Database Administrator? (8 marks)
   b. Describe briefly any THREE of the following:
      i.   Indexed Sequential Files (4 marks)
      ii. Inverted Files (4 marks)
      iii. Hierarchical Files (4 marks)
      iv. Hashing. (4 marks)

      (Total: 24 marks)

Information systems development

1. Explain how a systems analyst might undertake the task of investigation and analysis of a non-computerised business system. You may assume that management have already approved the feasibility study and authorised ongoing development. *(IDPM)*

2. What are the essential factors a systems analyst should consider when designing financial information systems? *(IComA)*

3. It is not uncommon for system designers involved in the introduction of computer based data processing to encounter resentment and opposition from existing employees.

    For what reasons may employees react in this manner? What steps can the system designer take to reduce this resistance? *(CIMA)*

4. 'Errors in a program are of two main types: errors due to incorrect use of the programming language and errors due to incorrect logic in the solution of the problem.'

    Explain this statement and show fully how errors of both types are detected and amended. *(ACA)*

5. List, and comment on, the principal factors which the systems analyst should take into consideration when designing the output to be produced by a computer-based system. *(ACA)*

6. XYZ Ltd maintains its sales ledger system on a mini-computer. The sales ledger master file is held on magnetic disk. Accounts, which contain the usual standard data, are kept on a brought forward balance basis with the total balance analysed over current month, month 1, month 2, month 3 and month 4 and over. Visual display units are employed for the entry of transaction data and for the retrieval of data for answering enquiries. A variety of printed reports is produced on the line printer.

    Required:
    a. Identify and briefly explain FIVE items of transaction data which would be input to the system.
    b. Draft, with TWO lines of sample entries, the Credit Limit Excess and Aged Balance report which is produced monthly for the Accounts Manager. Your answer should be in the format of a typical computer-produced line-printer report.

7. The auditors have asked that a section of each system specification used by your company should be devoted to the control aspects of the process of data capture through to transfer by the computer on to the magnetic storage media.

    Using, for purposes of illustration, a sales order system, which commences with the completion of sales order forms by sales representatives in the field, prepare the section of the systems specification referred to above. *(CIMA)*

8. Taking a typical sales invoicing system as your subject matter:
    a. illustrate the application of the system design formula: Output data - Input data = File data + Calculated data;
    b. state how you would then determine the contents of the file or files required by the system producing the invoices.

9. a. What are the major tasks to be undertaken in systems analysis and design? (Your answer should be a concise explanation - excessive detail is *NOT* required.)
    b. As a method of systems changeover explain what is meant by parallel running and state its disadvantages. *(AAT)*

10. A firm of chartered accountants has a time recording system on its in-house tape-based computer. The system reports include the following:
    a. Staff report, showing for each employee for the current week and year to date, the chargeable hours, the charge out value of those hours, the non-chargeable hours and value and the percentage of non-chargeable hours to total hours. This is printed in employee sequence, within departments.

b. Fee report, showing for the current week, the amount of each bill in client number sequence, together with the total hours and value written off against each bill and the amount of over/under recovery compared with the scale charge.

c. Work in progress report, showing for each client, the total hours and value of those hours unbilled at the end of each week. This is prepared in client number sequence.

The system includes the following files:

i. Employee charge out rate file.

ii. Employee history file which includes, for each employee, name, chargeable hours and value to date and non-chargeable hours and value to date. Non-chargeable time is time not charged to a client, for example, holidays, study leave and courses.

The input consists of time sheets and draft bill forms which show the information to complete the fee report.

You are required to prepare computer run flowcharts for both types of input and for the printing of the staff report, the fee report and the work in progress report.   *(ICA)*

11. Seymour Spectacles Limited is the sole United Kingdom distributor of a French manufacturer's spectacle frames and its objective is to provide an ex-stock delivery service to its optician customers. This service is seldom achieved and it now aims to carry sufficient stock of each variation of frame to cover the estimated sales of the ensuing eight weeks.

A weekly order is placed on the French manufacturer for delivery in four weeks' time.

The sales manager has been instructed to prepare the necessary estimates of future weekly customer orders for each stock line.

The company has an in-house disk based computer and it is proposed that a weekly computer report should be produced suitable for the purpose of stock ordering.

You are required to:

a. express the elements of information which are required to calculate the number of units of each stock line to be ordered each week, in the form of an order formula,

b. draft a form of 'weekly stock order requirement report' containing these elements, and

c. prepare a flowchart illustrating only the computer run required to produce the report and specify, in supplementary notes, the input into each of the files accessed in the run.   *(ICA)*

12. A manufacturer wishes to maintain a computer based file of all customers' orders outstanding.

A typical order from a customer comprises the following information:

	Maximum number of characters
Customer's name	30
Date of order	9
Delivery date requested	9
Customer's order number	10
Product group	9
Size code	9
Description	30
Quantity	3

(Product group, Size code, Description, Quantity appear as 6 ×)

Each week the master file of outstanding orders will be updated by:

		Approximate number per week
i.	Addition of new works	200
ii.	Deletion of despatches including partial despatches	220
iii.	Order amendments including cancellations	50

400

The outstanding orders master file will contain approximately 1,000 outstanding orders.

You are required to specify a complete data processing system which will provide the following facilities:

1. weekly updating of master file;
2. weekly report of all outstanding orders in order number within customer number within product group sequence;
3. weekly report showing total value of new orders for each product group;
4. weekly report of despatches for week showing total value per customer for each product group;
5. monthly report showing the total value of outstanding orders per size within delivery date.

At a minimum your specification should include:

   a. an outline of the computer configuration required, listing the main items of equipment;
   b. a systems flowchart containing or supported by brief narrative;
   c. details of the file(s) you intend to maintain;
   d. details of the minimum inputs necessary.

Any facts or figures not given above, which you feel are necessary in designing your system, may be included in your answer but must be clearly specified. *(CIMA)*

13. A company is to introduce a computer based production control system. As part of the overall system the weekly production activities are to be planned as follows:

   a. The production controller determines quantities for each assembly to be manufactured for the following week. This is termed the 'assembly build programme'. *(CIMA)*

   b. For each assembly on the programme (approximately 300 per week) the assembly number and quantity are entered to magnetic tape on a key/tape system.

   c. The data processing procedure is as follows:

      i. Input data are read and validated and an error report is produced.

      ii. Input data are checked for the feasibility of ABP, to determine components required for each assembly and to access/update component stock to produce the following two reports:

         1. made-in components in short supply report, showing components needed for ABP, in component number sequence.

         2. bought-out components report, in component number sequence.

   d. Updated component stocks are processed to produce two reports:

      i. made-in component manufacturing programme, showing economic batch quantity for each component that has less stock than minimum stock level;

      ii. similarly, a bought-out components purchasing programme.

   e Check made-in component manufacturing programming data for feasibility, to determine the raw material requirements and availability of raw material for each component to update raw material stock file and to produce the following reports:

      i. made-in components with raw materials shortage report, in component number sequence;

      ii. raw materials in short supply report, in raw material code sequence.

   f. Process updated raw material stocks and produce stock report for items having less stock than minimum stock level.

It may be assumed that the main files have already been determined as follows:

Assembly master file on disk pack A

Indexed sequential form in assembly number sequence containing the breakdown of components per assembly for 3,000 assemblies.

Component master file on disk pack B

Indexed sequential form in component number sequence sub-divided into bought-out and made-in component sub-files. There are 6,000 bought-out component records containing details of suppliers, prices and other information. Also there are 12,000 made-in component records containing details of raw materials, production processes, tools required etc.

Component stock file on disk pack C

Indexed sequential form in component number sequence sub-divided into bought-out and made-in component sub-files. The file contains details of current stock balances, re-order levels, batch quantities, stores locations etc.

Raw material stock file on disk pack C

Indexed sequential form in raw material code sequences containing current stock balances, re-order levels, batch quantities, stores locations etc.

The computer configuration consists of a medium size central processor, two magnetic tape units, three exchangeable disk units and a line printer.

You are required to:

a. Design and flowchart a system for processing the information and producing the results specified above. Your answer should contain sufficient narrative to explain adequately the system you have designed.

b. Note that the system flowchart requested in a. above is but one part of the docu- mentation required for a full specification of the system. Describe, briefly, three other items which would be required for the complete recording of the system, but do not fully specify them.

c. An engineering group consists of eleven branch factories located within a 30 mile radius of its head office.

The group already possesses a medium sized computer with both serial and direct access backing storage. This is used for a variety of production control and accounting work. It is proposed to introduce a computer based plant register and maintenance accounting system for all items of works equipment, machine tools, office machinery and vehicles. Each item of plant is identified by a ten digit code of the following format.

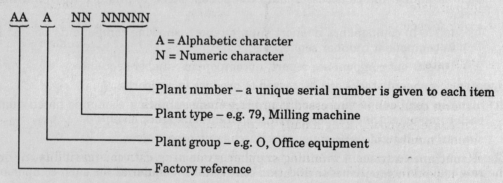

There are some 16,000 plant items in the group which are each serviced under the planned maintenance system approximately once each month. In addition to the planned servicing, approximately 25% of the machines require some intermediate form of attention.

Approximately 10% of the plant items are replaced each year. At a minimum the system must provide for the following reports:

Report 1 (weekly)	Plant maintenance statement showing labour and material costs per item serviced distinguishing between planned and unplanned servicing, in plant number sequence.
Report 2 (monthly)	Machine performance report providing information that will enable management to decide whether it is more economical to replace existing plant items. This report to be in plant number sequence within plant type for each plant group.

Report 3 (monthly)	Cost summary showing (total only) current written down value and past month's maintenance and repair costs per plant type within plant group within factory sequence.
Report 4 (annually)	Plant depreciation report in plant number sequences.

You are required to:

a. produce a systems run flowchart showing how the above four reports could be produced; (Your flowchart should contain sufficient narrative to explain adequately the system proposed. Also, you should describe in particular the contents of report 2).

b. describe briefly the inputs required for the system;

c. describe the contents of the plant register file.

4. Manufacturing Limited has decided to computerise its purchase accounting system. It is expected that extensive expenditure analysis will ultimately be included but initially this aspect of the system will be restricted.

A computer configuration available comprises a medium sized central processor with punched card reader, line printer and two exchangeable disk drive units (each of 30 million characters).

An outline of the new system is as follows:

Source Document

A source document will be created clerically from purchase invoices passed for payment. The contents of this document will be:

source document reference
number

supplier identification code
number

supplier's own reference
number

invoice date
expense code } occurs { minimum ×
amount   average × 1.2
VAT rate   maximum × 5

Output

This source data will be processed to produce these outputs:

i. Purchase daybook, being a daily listing of all prime data input, in source document reference number sequence.

ii. Remittance advices, containing supplier name and address and full details of invoices being paid in supplier identification code number sequence.

iii. Credit transfers, containing payer and payee bank details and amounts, in supplier bank reference number sequence.

iv. Supplier analysis giving total expenditure for this month and this year to date per supplier, in supplier identification code number sequence within supplier category (note: suppliers are categorised according to the type of goods supplied, eg. raw metal, stationery, lubricating oils).

v. Expense code analysis giving total expenditure per each expense code.

It will be noted that i. above will be produced daily, while ii., iii., iv., and v. will be produced at the month end.

Predicted Volumes

Purchase invoices per day	200
Suppliers	2,000
Expense codes	70

Any facts or figures not given may be assumed provided each assumption is clearly stated.

You are required to submit the following:

a. computer system run flowchart(s) with brief narrative for the purchase accounting/expenditure analysis system;

b. a description of the main files required;

c. a suggested lay-out for print-out iv. above, the monthly supplier analysis.

Applications and computer systems

1. Specify and describe hardware and software required for a real time computer application system. *(IDPM)*

2. As systems manager you have been asked to prepare a report on simulation for the board.

    Your report should cover amongst other things:
    i. a full definition of simulation;
    ii. the process by which simulation exercises are developed;
    iii. possible areas where simulation could usefully be employed;
    iv. ways in which the efficiency of a simulation exercise can be judged;
    v. the role of the computer in simulation.

3. An increasing number of organisations are contemplating installing, or have installed, systems involving a database. What factors have led to these developments and what are the characteristics of an efficient database? *(CIMA)*

4. 'The different nature of Batch and Real Time processing requires a completely different approach to the subject of data validation.' Discuss. *(IDPM)*

5. What contribution can the modern microcomputer make to data processing applications? Explain the advantages and disadvantages of this type of equipment for data processing work. *(IDPM)*

6. a. Identify, and briefly explain, FIVE of the characteristics of the minicomputer which distinguish it from the lager main-frame machine.

    b. Define 'distributed data processing' and explain the role played by the minicomputer in a distributed data processing system. *(ACA)*

7. 'Modern hardware developments are causing a movement away from centralised data processing systems to dispersed systems operating at or close to actual business activities.'

    Describe the hardware developments referred to in his quotation.

    What are the advantages and disadvantages of this movement? *(CIMA)*

8. You have been asked to prepare a report for the board of directors explaining the general features of Teletext systems (e.g. Ceefax and Oracle) and Viewdata system (e.g. Prestel). Your report should also include an assessment of the likely commercial uses (if any) of the systems.

    (20 marks)

Information systems management

1. XYZ Limited is about to consider for the first time the use of a computer for data processing work. A small steering committee of senior managers, under the chairmanship of the managing director, has been set up to exercise overall control of this development.

2. What advice would you give the committee to help ensure that computerised systems will be successfully introduced into the company? *(ACA)*

a. What are the characteristics of a business system which signify that the system is potentially suitable for transfer to computer operation?

b. 'A computer may be used for financial modelling.' Explain this statement. (ACA)

3. A production planning and control system is being investigated with a view to computerisation. The systems investigators have been asked to include a financial justification for the new system in their report. What would such a justification include and how might the financial effects of the system be monitored after installation?

4. You are the accountant at XYZ Ltd. Budgetary control is in operation and quarterly accounts are prepared for presentation to management.

Required:

Draft a specimen Budget Performance Report for XYZ's Computer Department. Your form should show clearly the main heads of expenditure with the principal items of expense under each head. *Sample entries are not required.*

5. a. Describe with the aid of a diagram the route which a typical batch processing job would take through the various sections of a computer operations department. (The diagram should start *and* end in the outside user department).

b. Explain the functions of the Data Control staff with respect to the above job.

6. a. Produce an organisation chart for a typical medium sized computer department.

b. Describe four of the jobs that appear on your chart. *(CIMA)*

7. ABC Ltd's computer department contains some 35 members of staff, including the computer manager. Analysts and programmers work together in project teams under team leaders.

Required:

a. Draft what in your opinion would be a typical organisation chart for this computer department. The distribution of staff should be clearly shown.

b. Identify the principal responsibilities of the operations manager in a computer department.

8. Your organisation is about to install a computer system but your auditors have written to you expressing their concern over the proposal as they fear that the audit trail may be lost.

9. Draft a reply to your auditors responding to their concern and, in addition, pointing out ways in which the computer can assist the audit process. *(CIMA)*

a. List and comment on the criteria used in deciding whether or not a particular application is suitable for computer processing, and

b. describe the features of an application for a wholesale stockist which you consider ideally suited to computer processing and state how it meets the listed criteria. *(ICA)*

10. You have been asked to advise a local firm of Solicitors over the operation of their accounting procedures, which are at present done manually. Required:

a. Assuming that your advice is to computerise the operation of its accounting procedures, outline three different options open to the firm. (8 marks)

b. Explain the problem that will be met in file creation and conversion due to the computerisation of the firm's records. (6 marks)

c. Explain three different types of changeover that can be related to the computerisation of the accounting procedures. (6 marks)

(Total: 20 marks)

11. Your DP manager is concerned about security of your company's programs, data and equipment. What measures would you suggest to minimise problems in these areas?

12. File conversion (or file creation) is always a major practical problem when a new computer-based system is being implemented.

Assume that a new computer-based accounting system is to be implemented and source data are at present held in various types of clerical files in several locations.

You are required to describe:

a. the objectives of file conversion; (5 marks)

b. the typical problems that would be encountered in the situation outlined: (8 marks)

c. the way the file conversion process should be planned and controlled. (7 marks)

(Total: 20 marks)

General

1. The advent of the mini-computer represents a threat to both the business of computer bureaux and to the sales of full scale computers.

   Discuss this statement and compare the relative advantages and disadvantages for the smaller business of owning a mini-computer or of using a computer bureaux. (CIMA)

2. a. The introduction of an 'in-house' data processing system incurs costs at different stages.

   You are required to:

   i. suggested four stages under which costs could be grouped;

   ii. for any stage given in i. to briefly describe the costs incurred (eg. clerical costs);

   iii. suggest possible measures of systems performance (eg. cost reduction) which could be used where a 'Sales System' has been computerised.

   iv. What is meant by timesharing? Where timesharing facilities operate, what kind of backing store is required and why? (AAT)

3. Write explanatory notes on the following data processing terms:

   a. Magnetic ledger cards.

   b. Turnaround documents.

   c. Conditional branch.

   d. Application packages. (AAT)

4. In regard to a computerised system, define and describe the main features of each of the following:

   a. utility programs;

   b. serial access;

   c. Kimball tag;

   d. trailer label;

   e. optical scanning, and

   f. parallel running.

5. State

   a. the various types of inputs to and

   b. the various reports produced by

   an efficient information system for the management accounting function in a manufacturing business. (IComA)

6. The master record of a computerised stock control system consists of the following fields:

Field name	Number of characters	Type
Stock Code	4	9
Stock Description	30	A
Bin Number	3	9
Supplier Code	4	9
Balance Data:		
Orders on suppliers	5	9
Bin stock	5	9
Price (Average)	4	9
Stock value	8	9

Note: Type 9 = Numeric; A = Alphanumeric

The three transaction records processed relate to 'Orders Placed on Suppliers'. 'Goods Received from Suppliers' and 'Goods Sold to Customers'.

You are required to design the layout for an input card or cards which would be processed to update the master record.

Assuming the 'Balance Data' for stock item number 5,000 at the commencement of the update run to be:

Orders on Suppliers	10,000 units
Bin Stock	25,000 units
Price	£1.50
Stock value	£37,500

Illustrate the effect on the master record where

a. an order for 2,500 units has been placed on a supplier;

b. a delivery of 7,500 units has been received from a supplier at

c. 5,000 units have been sold to a customer.

7. In regard to a computerised system, define and describe the main features of each of the following:
   a. multi-programming;
   b. magnetic disk;
   c. executive program;
   d. real time;
   e. test pack, and
   f. grandfather-father-son principle.

8. In regard to a computerised system, define and describe the main features of each of the following, indicating its purpose:
   a. buffer;
   b. application package;
   c. assembler program;
   d. optical character reading;
   e. real time processing, and
   f. visual display unit.

9. a. State briefly your understanding of the terms 'data processing' and 'systems design'.
   b. Why do you consider that the Association of Certified Accountants includes these topics for study in its scheme of examinations?

10. a. Control in a data processing department is maintained by setting 'Standards' and the provision of adequate systems documentation.

    i. What are the two types of standards created and what do they seek to ensure?

        (4 marks)

    ii. Why is documentation necessary? Give five reasons.   (10 marks)

    b. One of many services provided by a bureau is 'Timesharing'.

    Explain what is meant by this term and how the user gains access to the computing facilities.   (6 marks)

(Total: 20 marks)

11. A critical stage in the implementation of any new computer-based system is initial file creation.

    You are required to explain:

    a. the objectives and general approach to initial file creation;

    b. the control and security procedures necessary at this stage;

    c. the particular problems involved when the data for file creation emanate from various sources and how these can be overcome.   (20 marks)

12. In the early days of computers a major problem was the high cost of the hardware involved. With the falling real cost of hardware, attention is increasingly being focused on the costs and time involved in developing appropriate software.

    You are required to:

    a. identify the developments which have led to the situation described: (7 marks)

    b. describe possible ways in which a user organisation can minimise the problems and costs involved in software development.   (13 marks)

(Total: 20 marks)

13. Using for illustrative purpose an inventory control system, **you are required to:**

    a. outline the stages in the analysis, design and implementation of an appropriate data processing system; and

    b. explain how management control of the project would be achieved.   (20 marks)

Appendix 3 Omitted details

Details which have been omitted from the text in the interests of clarity.

1. Check digits

Introduction

a.　A check digit is a means of ensuring that a number (eg. a customer account number) maintains its validity.

b.　It is calculated using a modulus. Various moduli are use in practice and each has varying degrees of success at preventing certain types of errors. MODULUS 11 (eleven) is used here.

c.　Check digits are calculated by a computer in the first place and are generally used in conjunction with *fixed* data (ie. customer's number etc). As a result of a test done on Modulus 11 it was discovered that it detected all transcription and transposition errors and 91 of random errors.

Calculating the check digit

a.　Original code number　　　4214

b.　Multiply each *digit* by the *weights*　　　5432

c.　Product =　(4 5) = 20
　　　　　　　(2 4) = 8
　　　　　　　(1 3) = 3
　　　　　　　(4 2) = 8

d.　Sum of products = 39

e.　Divide by modulus (11) = 3 and 6 Remainder.

f.　Subtract *remainder* from modulus (i.e. $11 - 6$) = 5

g.　5 *is the check digit*.

h.　Code number now becomes 42145.

Checking of numbers

When the code number is input to the computer precisely the same calculation can be carried out (using weight of 1 for right-most/or junior digit) and the resultant remainder should be 0. If not then the number is incorrect:-

$42145 = (4\ 5) + (2\ 4) + (1\ 3) + (4\ 2) + (5\ 1) = 44$

Divide by 11; remainder = 0.

Note:

a.　It is best to carry out check digit verification *at the time of data entry*.

b.　Students should have a ready worked example of a check digit in order to impress examiner in an appropriate answer.

c.　An original code giving rise to the check 'digit' 10 is normally discarded.

d.　Check digits are used in many situations. The ISBN number in any book (see the acknowledgements page ii) is just one example.

(Consult your examination regulations to see which symbols you should use in your examination).

2. System flowcharts

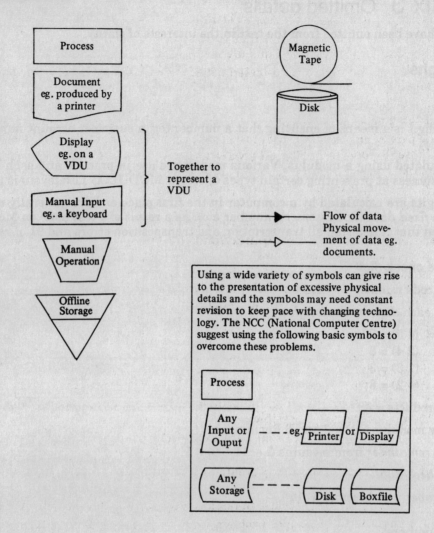

Consult your examination regulations to see which symbols you should use in your examination.
System flowchart symbols

A system flowchart may show what the data processing procedures are, and how the procedures are arranged into sequences, but it will *not* show how the procedures are carried out.

3. Machine language

The details given here supplement those given in Chapter 23.

The example in figure 22.2 was based upon a fictitious 16-bit machine which is described in detail in 'Computer Studies' by C. S. French, published by DP Publications.

The execution of instructions can be understood more fully by reference to this diagram:

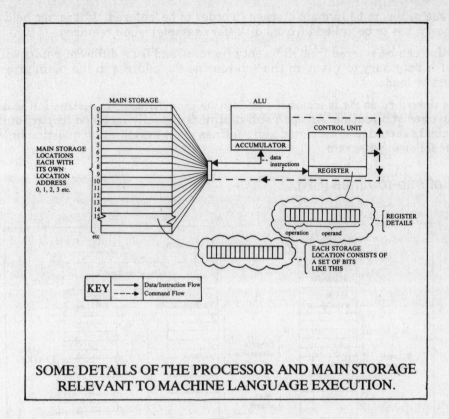

MAIN STORAGE

ALU

CONTROL UNIT

ACCUMULATOR

REGISTER

MAIN STORAGE LOCATIONS EACH WITH ITS OWN LOCATION ADDRESS 0, 1, 2, 3 etc.

data instructions

REGISTER DETAILS

operation   operand

EACH STORAGE LOCATION CONSISTS OF A SET OF BITS LIKE THIS

KEY → Data/Instruction Flow ‑‑‑► Command Flow

SOME DETAILS OF THE PROCESSOR AND MAIN STORAGE RELEVANT TO MACHINE LANGUAGE EXECUTION.

Note

a.   Instructions are fetched from main storage into a register where they can be interpreted by the control unit which then sends the appropriate commands to the hardware.

b.   Data can be 'loaded' into 'accumulators' in the ALU. Once it is in the accumulator, various arithmetic and logic operations may be performed on the data. Results are transferred back into main storage.

Machine language subroutines

Subprograms (18.27) in machine language are normally called 'subroutines'. Further details of subroutines, directly related to machine language, are given here.

A particular processing operation will very often be performed at several *different* points in a program. The particular group of program instructions necessary to carry out the operation *could* be included at *each* of the different points. This is wasteful of storage space especially if the operation involves a *large* number of instructions.

A technique used in these circumstances is *not* to include the instructions in the *main program* but to have them in *another* part of main storage. Such a group of instructions is known as a sub-routine. Examples of sub-routines are PAYE, N.I., etc, calculations.

Control is passed from the main program to the sub-routine (where the particular sequence of instructions is performed) and is then passed back again to the main program. This happens at each point the sub-routine is required.

Definition. A sub-routine, therefore, is said to be a group of instructions designed to carry out a specific task (i.e. a specific operation on data).

It should be noted that:

a.   The sub-routine has to be in main storage in order to be 'entered'. If it is *not* held permanently in store then it has to be 'called in' from disk (for example) when required.

b.   A sub-routine can be entered from different *programs* and from different *points* within the *same* program it is necessary to 'plant' in the sub-routine the address in the main program to which return must be made.

The sub-routine described so far is a *closed* sub-routine. Sometimes the distinction is made between this type and an *open* sub-routine. An open sub-routine is actually included as part of the main program itself. Students should assume *closed* sub-routines in an examination question unless otherwise directed. See the following diagram .

4. Examples of sub-routines (SR)

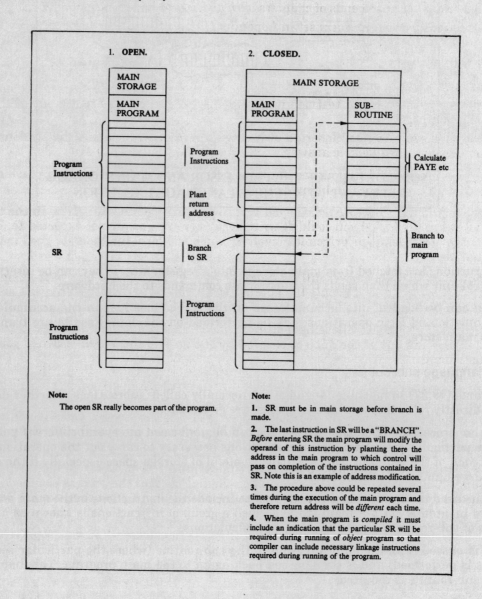

1. OPEN.

MAIN STORAGE

MAIN PROGRAM

Program Instructions

SR

Program Instructions

Program Instructions

Plant return address

Branch to SR

Program Instructions

Note:
The open SR really becomes part of the program.

2. CLOSED.

MAIN STORAGE

MAIN PROGRAM   SUB-ROUTINE

Calculate PAYE etc

Branch to main program

Note:
1.   SR must be in main storage before branch is made.

2.   The last instruction in SR will be a "BRANCH". *Before* entering SR the main program will modify the operand of this instruction by planting there the address in the main program to which control will pass on completion of the instructions contained in SR. Note this is an example of address modification.

3.   The procedure above could be repeated several times during the execution of the main program and therefore return address will be *different* each time.

4.   When the main program is *compiled* it must include an indication that the particular SR will be required during running of *object* program so that compiler can include necessary linkage instructions required during running of the program.

Appendix 4 Study and examination technique

This appendix contains notes on:
- a. Using the questions and answers provided in the manual.
- b. Effective study.
- c. Examination technique.

4.1 Questions and answers

Introduction

1. Two types of question are provided in this manual.
   - a. Questions set at the ends of chapters *with answers* provided in Appendix 1.
   - b. Questions *without answers* set in Appendix 2.

Questions with answers

2. These questions are either
   - a. questions intended to test the understanding of the points arising out of the particular chapter; or
   - b. examination questions inserted at a stage where it is considered the student will be best able to give a reasonable answer.

3. Most answers are given in outline but some examination answers go a little further in order to provide greater guidance and provide students with the basis for study.

4. Where answers are *comprehensive* you couldn't be expected to write them in the time allowed. *Do not worry* if you feel you couldn't write such answers; you are not expected to. But you *must* grasp the *main* points or principles involved which will form the basis for good marks in an examination.

5. Do not worry if your answer differs, there is often more than *one* approach. You must satisfy yourself however, that it is *only* the approach that differs, and that you haven't missed the fundamental principles.

6. **Authors' Comments.** These have been included to give *additional* points or to elaborate on matters arising out of the subject covered by the question to which it is felt you should give some thought.

Using the answers

7. Have a shot at each question yourself *before* consulting the answer, you will achieve nothing if you don't do this. Write your answer out in full or jot down the main points. *Do not* hurry to the answer.

8. Look at the answer. (See para 5 in the case of examination answers). Study the particular area *thoroughly* now making sure of your understanding. *Repeat* the process outlined in para 7 and this para after a suitable interval. You *must* do this to get any benefit at all. Make sure the main points *stick* .

9. Just browsing through the answers will really get you *nowhere*. You *must* test yourself by *writing* down your version of the answer.

Questions without answers

10. The questions are provided in Appendix 2. They are intended for use in conjunction with classroom tuition. The questions, taken from papers of the ICA, ACA, CIMA, IAS, AAT, IComA, IDPM, are grouped according to Parts of the book.

4.2 Effective study

Introduction

1.	These notes are intended for those who are new to studying for examination subjects, although those who are not may also benefit. They have been written in relation to study involving the reading of *text books* , and the apply to *all* subjects. It is often extremely difficult to pick out the important principles from such books. As the **data processing manual** *is* an **instructional** manual your DP studies should be made much easier. Nevertheless careful reading of these notes will be of benefit even in studying the manual.

General

2.	Study means more than *just reading* a piece of literature. It means *close concentrated reading* with a *notebook* at your side. Unless you're one of a *few* people don't kid yourself you can absorb material by *just one* general read through it, you cannot!

3.	Read a small area, *making notes* as you go along. Then ask yourself – what have I just learnt? *Write* down what you think it was all about. Then look again and you may be surprised to find you've missed a *key* point or points – they *must* be down in your notebook and eventually in your head.

Compilation of notebook

4.	A *well compiled* NOTEBOOK is a must. Use block capitals or different colour inks to *headline* the main areas and subdivisions of those areas. Notes made during lectures or private study should *not* go straight into your NOTEBOOK. Take them down on a 'rough' paper and write them in your NOTEBOOK *as soon as possible* after the lecture or study period, thinking about what you are writing. This does not apply to studying the DP manual which itself can be used as your notebook.

Memory aids

5.	**Mnemonics** are very useful – if the sequence of points in the text book *isn't* significant, *change it* it it makes for a better mnemonic.

6.	**Association** of the points with familiar objects which will serve to recall them is also useful.

7.	Some people memorise things by *saying* them over and over *out loud* , others have to *write* them down *time* after *time* .

8.	Many students have *small blank cards* and using one side of each card for each study area, put down the main points. They carry the cards everywhere with them and use every opportunity to study them. As they are small they are easily carried. It is surprising how much of your day can be utilised in this way.

Programme

9.	Map out a programme for yourself; set targets and *achieve* them. One thing is certain, studying is not easy but it is *not* too difficult if you go about it in an orderly purposeful way. Many students fail their examinations through *bad preparation* . Tackle your studies as you would a project at work, *systematically* . Allocate a number of hours each week to each subject. Try fixing *specific times* for each subject, then *keep to them* by refusing to let *anything* keep you from your planned task.

Revision

10.	Revise periodically. The nearer the examination gets, the more you should concentrate on the major headlines in your notebook and less with the supporting details.

4.3 Examination technique

First impressions

1. However well prepared you may be, you are still likely to look at the paper on the day and say to yourself, after a quick look at the questions, 'There's not much *there* I can do'.

2. The atmosphere of the exam room has something to do with this. Try to blot everything from your mind other than the job in hand. *Concentrate* hard. If you feel a bit panicky (most people do – despite the apparent looks of serenity around you) grip the table, take a deep breath, and *get on with it* . Remember things are *never* as bad as they seem!

Time allocation

3. *Allocate* each question *time* appropriate to the number of marks. At the end of the allotted time for a question *go on to the next* – remember, the *first* 5 or 10 marks on the *new* question are more readily picked up than the *last* 1 or 2 on the *previous* question.

4. The *temptation* will be to say 'I'll write just *one* more sentence', but before you know where you are you'll have written *several* more and probably just managed to scrape another mark, whereas the same time spent on the next question could have earned 5 or 6 marks. TIME ALLOCATION IS IMPORTANT.

5. If you *are* running out of time write down the *main headings first,* leaving a few lines between each – at least the examiner will see that you had the overall picture. *Then* go back putting in as much supporting detail as you can.

General approach

6. Read the *instructions* at the top of the paper.

7. **Read the question paper** once through. Make your choice of questions quickly. Pick the easiest (if one appears so) and *get on with it* .

Individual question

8. **Read the question** again carefully. The question will involve a key principle or set of principles. What are they? It is so easy to make the wrong decision at this stage, so read the question, underlining what appear to be the *key words*. This should help you. Irrelevancy has been heavily criticised by examiners.

9. Do not rush into action with your pen *yet* . Jot down on a piece of scrap paper the *main headings* you will use in your answer. All this will take time – about 5 minutes or more, but the *careful thought* and outline answer represents *marks* already earned.

10. If the question is *set out* in a particular sequence, ie:

    a. ....
    b. ....
    c. ....   etc.

    then answer it *in that sequence* or you'll have a *hostile examiner* to cope with.

11. Use the particular terminology *used in the question*, the examiner can then *link the points* in your answer to the relevant parts of the question.

12. **Assumptions** are sometimes required (for example because of the lack of standardisation of terminology in this subject). Having stated your assumptions, make sure that what you write is *consistent* with them. Do ensure, however, that your assumptions *are valid* and are *not* just a device for changing the *meaning* of the question to suit your knowledge!

Layout of answer

13. **Tabulate** where appropriate, using block capitals for your main headings and underline subheadings. Underline *words* or phrases which require emphasis. *Use a ruler.*

14. Leave a line *between* your paragraphs and subparagraphs. This makes for a *good* layout. However, do *not* write on every other line within paragraphs, or on one side of the paper only – examiners are waste conscious!

15. The use of different colour pens, where appropriate, is useful but don't overdo it. In fact one black and one red felt-tip pen would be sufficient (use the felt-tip pens which have a *fine point*).

Charts and diagrams

16. **A descriptive heading or title** must be given to each diagram (using the one in the question if indicated).

17. **Do not** squeeze a diagram into a corner – *spread it out*.

18. **Do not** clutter your diagram up with too much detail – this defeats the object, which should be clarity.

19. Give a *key* to the symbols and the different lines you've used, and again – use a ruler.

End of examination procedure

20. Have a quick look at each answer, checking for grammatical errors and badly formed letters.

21. Ensure each answer sheet has your *number* on it and *don't* leave any lying on the table.

Conlcusion

22. **Good technique** plays a *large* part in examination success; this is a *fact*. *Refuse* to be panicked, keep your head, and with reasonable preparation you *should* make it.

23. Remember – you don't have to score *100%* to pass.

24. A final point; once you're in the examination room *stay there* and make use of every minute at your disposal.

25. **Practise** your technique when answering the questions set in the manual.

Index

Computer Science   *CS French*

COMPUTER SCIENCE
4th Edition

"The Complete Course Text"

C.S. French
dpp

ISBN: **1 873981 19 8** • Date: **1992** • Edition: **4th**
Extent: **640 pp** • Size: **275 x 215 mm**

Courses on which this book is known to be used

A Level Computing; BTEC National and HNC/D Computer Studies; City & Guilds; BCS; AS Level Computer Science; BSc Applied Science.

On reading lists of ICM, IDPM, BCS and ACP

This book provides a simplified approach to the understanding of Computer Science.

Notes on the Fourth Edition

This edition contains changes in content and layout which are aimed not just at covering the material on the latest syllabuses but at assisting the reader's study for the latest examinations. Parts targeted at contemporary computer applications and applications packages have been introduced. This reflects a significant shift in emphasis in examinations over recent years. Graphical User Interfaces (GUIs), development methodologies, desktop computers, applications packages and databases have been given more emphasis to reflect the examination requirements of developing and using computer systems. Obsolete material has been removed.

Contents:

Foundation Topics • Applications I: Document Processing • Storage • Input and Output • Applications II: GUIs and Multimedia • Computer Systems Organisation I • Programming I • File and File Processing • Applications III: Spreadsheets • Logic and Formal Notations • Computer Arithmetic • Computer Systems Organisation II • Software • Applications IV: Applications Areas • Programming II • Databases and 4GLs • Applications V: Information Storage and Retrieval • Systems Development • Applications VI: Business Industrial Computing • Computers in Contexts • Revision Test Questions.

Review Comments:

'I think the presentation is superb and content perfect for my course work.' 'Good basic book – recommended by all academic staff in the department.' 'Still excellent value, and provides both good basis for teaching and private study.' 'Up-to-date information with clear graphical figures.' – Lecturers

⬥ **Free Lecturers' Disk** ⬥

Also available as ELBS edition in member countries at local currency equivalent price of £3.00

Convert to C and C++

BJ Holmes

ISBN: **1 873981 20 1** • Date: **1992** • Edition: **1st**
Extent: **320 pp** • Size: **245 x 190 mm**

Courses on which this book is known to be used
BTEC National and Higher National
Computing; A Level Computing; BA Computing; MSc Computing and Info Systems; C & G 726

This book provides a complete course text book for students who already understand the fundamentals of programming in a high-level language, and are required to extend their knowledge of programming to include C and C++. The advantages of covering both languages in one text are:

❏ the major strengths and weaknesses of both languages can be compared and contrasted;

❏ since ANSI C is a subset of C++, the reader is encouraged, through the order of presentation, to learn about C before embarking on C++;

❏ the transition from ANSI C to C++ is taken in three easy stages, covering enhancements to procedural programming, techniques for data abstraction, and object-oriented programming;

❏ the reader who can already program in an older, non ANSI, version of C can use the text as a refresher course in ANSI C, and quickly progress to learning C++;

❏ those who want a quick guide to C++ can turn to part two, knowing that revision material on ANSI C is available in part one, should it be needed.

The emphasis throughout the book is on the use of carefully chosen examples that highlight the features of the language being studied enabling students to convert to C and C++ in as short a time as possible. Explanation about the language follows from, and is put into context with, the example programs. A section of programming questions to test and reinforce students' understanding can be found at the end of each chapter.

Contents:

Part one – Convert to C
The Organisation of a C Program • Data Types and Input/Output • Control Statements • Arrays • Files • Further Topics.

Par two – Convert to C++
The Transition • Data Abstractions • Object-oriented Programming.

Appendices Answers.

Review Comments:

'Excellent book. Wide range of the language covered, well presented and at a very reasonable price.' 'Excellent progression for students from Pascal.' 'Excellent price, good coverage, straightforward and readable.' 'Covering just the right ground and taking the right pace. Price and presentation good.' 'Appropriate levels of coverage for those who already know the language and are converting.' – Lecturers

---

♠ Free Lecturers' Disk ♠

Management Information Systems

T Lucey

ISBN: **1 870941 80 2** • Date: **1991** • Edition: **6th**
Extent: **336 pp** • Size: **215 x 135 mm**

Courses on which this book is known to be used
ACCA; HND Yr 1; HNC BIS; Info. Systems Fundamentals; DAS; MSD; DBA; HNC Industrial Studies; NEBSM; CMS; IPM (PMFP); Dip. in Int. Audit; Nat. Cert. in Computer Studies; CIPFA; AAT; HND BIT; HND Computing; BSc Computing; IAM; BSc (Bus. Studies); DMS; BEd Bus. Studies; CIMA; CIML Software Eng. Man.; MSc Computing; ICSA; MBA; IMS.

On reading lists of ACCA, AAT, IComA, ABE, ICM, IAM and BCS

Contents:

Management Information Systems – An Overview • Information, Data and Communications • Systems Concepts – Structure and Elements • Systems concepts – Objectives and Types • Organisations – Principles and Structure • Organisations – Adaptability and Behaviour • Organisations – Configuration, Culture and Information Management Levels and Functions • Motivation and Leadership • Organising and Co–ordinating • Planning • Decision Making • Control – Concepts, Loops and Information • Control in Organisations • Information Technology and MIS • Influences on MIS Design • Answers to End of Chapter Questions.

The book deals with the design and application of management information systems in private and public sector organisations.

For the new edition the text has been substantially updated and revised including assignments, case studies and more detail on information technology.

Review Comments:

'...an excellent work on general management with the emphasis on MIS. I have chosen it in preference to the many management books I have recently reviewed.' 'Good coverage at an excellent price.' 'Still the best book for an introductory organisation and information systems course.' 'Easy to read and understand.' 'Excellent value as a first text on MIS.' 'Much improved edition [6th[for this syllabus [ICSA].' 'I like it for its broad management approach.'
– Lecturers

'The book is highly recommended to students, to accountants and to business managers who want a simple guide to modern systems theory.' **"Management Accounting"**

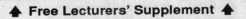

⬥ Free Lecturers' Supplement ⬥

Microprocessors and Microcomputer Technology *T Hanley*

ISBN: **1 85805 030 8** • Date: **August 1993** • Edition: **1st**
Extent: **250 pp (approx)** • Size: **245 x 190 mm**

Courses on which this book is expected to be used

City & Guilds 223, 224, 7261, 2344/5 and other computing and microelectronics courses at a comparable level

---

Contents:

Microcomputers and Microprocessors. Number Systems and computer Arithmetic. Logic Elements. Integrated Circuit (I.C.) Logic Families. Inside the Microprocessor – A First Look. Other Microprocessor Registers. Other Features of Real Microprocessors: The Fetch-Decode-Execute Cycle. Microcomputer Memories. Microprocessor Input/Output. Peripherals & Interfacing. Software and Microcomputer Programming. Mass Storage. Troubleshooting on Digital/Microprocessor Based Systems.

The aim of this book is to provide a straightforward and simplified approach to the understanding of microprocessors and microcomputer technology for students with little or no knowledge of the subject. It fully covers the requirements of the microcomputer/ microprocessor parts of the courses listed above and can be used in conjunction with a course of lectures or on courses with little lecturer contact time. Extensive uses of diagrams, practical illustrative examples throughout, in-text questions and answers and concise, coherent presentation of information ensure complex concepts are more easily understood by students.

The text includes 140 MCQs and answers based on the examinations set for City and Guilds 223, 224, 7261, and 2344/5.

⬆ **Free Lecturers' Supplement** ⬆

Modula-2

BJ Holmes

ISBN: **1 870941 31 4** • Date: **1989** • Edition: **1st**
Extent: **352 pp** • Size: **245 x 190 mm**

Courses on which this book is known to be used

BTEC National and HNC/D Computing; BTEC HNC/D Information Technology; BSc Computer Science; A Level Computing; HNC Software Engineering.

Within this single book there is enough information to provide a foundation for any reader who wishes to develop and implement a wide variety of systems in Modula-2.

Note: With the lecturers' supplement is a free (and copyright free) PC-compatible disk incorporating all the programs in the text – saves keying in! Immediate use for illustrative and development purposes for lecturers and students.

(The programs on the disk need to be compiled using 'JPI Top Speed Modula-2')

Contents:

Computer Environment • Data • Instruction Sequence • Data Types • Selection • Repetition • Procedures • Program Development • Mathematics • Modules • Arrays • Sorting and Searching • Recursion • File Processing • File Maintenance • Pointers • Data Abstraction • Coroutines.

Review Comments:

'Ideal for our BTEC Higher Computer Studies course.' 'Its reasonable price, many examples, large answers section and complete coverage mean we will use it as a course text.'

– Lecturers

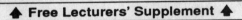

⬆ Free Lecturers' Supplement ⬆

Pascal Programming

BJ Holmes

ISBN: 1 870941 65 9 • Date: **1990** • Edition: **2nd**
Extent: **464 pp** • Size: **245 x 190 mm**

Courses on which this book is known to be used

BCS Part 1; A Level Computing; BSc (Hons) Computer Studies; BTEC National and HNC/D Computer Studies; HNC Software Design; NDI; HEFC Info Tech; C & G 726/223.

On reading list of ICM

Contents:

Computer Environment • Data • Instruction Sequence • Data Types • Selection • Repetition • Procedures • Program Development • Mathematics • Arrays • Sorting and Searching • Recursion • Text Files • Pointers • Dynamic Structures • Record Files • Common Extensions • Turbo Units • Object-oriented Programming (OOP) • Case Studies in OOP.

Pascal Programming can be regarded as a complete text on programming and the use of data structures. The aim of this book is to help the reader acquire and develop the skill of computer programming in a block-structured language and foster an understanding of the related topics of data structures and data processing.

Note: With the lecturers' supplement is a free (and copyright free) PC-compatible disk incorporating all the programs in the text – saves keying in! Immediate use for illustrative and development purposes for lecturers and students.

(The programs on the disk need to be compiled using Borland Turbo Pascal compiler version 5.5 or later.)

Review Comments:

'Excellent – no competition [BTEC ND Computing].' 'Affordable and Turbo Pascal and Syntax diagrams – great!' 'Far better than most books that are twice the price.'

– Lecturers

♠ Free Lecturers' Supplement ♠